T0364897

Volvo 850
Service and Repair Manual

John S. Mead

Models covered

All Volvo 850 models with 1984 cc, 2319 cc and 2435 cc petrol engines

(3260-240-3AG3)

© Haynes Group Limited 2003

A book in the **Haynes Service and Repair Manual Series**

ISBN **978 0 85733 900 3**

British Library Cataloguing in Publication Data
A catalogue record for this book is available from the British Library.

Haynes Group Limited
Haynes North America, Inc

www.haynes.com

The manufacturer's authorised representative in the EU for product safety is:

HaynesPro BV
Stationsstraat 79 F, 3811MH Amersfoort, The Netherlands
gpsr@haynes.co.uk

Contents

LIVING WITH YOUR VOLVO 850

Roadside Repairs

Weekly Checks

MAINTENANCE

Routine Maintenance and Servicing

Contents

REPAIRS & OVERHAUL

Engine and Associated Systems

Transmission

Brakes and Suspension

Body Equipment

Wiring Diagrams

REFERENCE

Index

The Volvo 850 Saloon and Estate models were introduced in 1992 and were a radical departure from the traditional Volvo large vehicle format. The 850 features transverse engine/transmission layout, front-wheel drive and state-of-the-art suspension technology providing excellent handling and driveability for a large car.

The engines used in the 850 range are all fuel-injected, in-line, five-cylinder units of 1984 cc, 2319 cc or 2435 cc displacement. Both normally-aspirated and turbocharged versions are available. The engines feature a comprehensive engine management system with extensive emission control equipment.

Both 5-speed manual and 4-speed computer controlled, automatic transmissions are available throughout the range. The automatic transmission features mode control selection allowing the driver to alter the transmission characteristics to suit economy, sport or winter driving requirements.

Braking is by discs all round, the handbrake acting on drums incorporated in the rear brake discs. Anti-lock braking (ABS) and power-assisted steering is standard on all models.

A wide range of standard and optional equipment is available within the 850 range to suit virtually all tastes. As with all Volvo models, safety features are of paramount importance and the Supplemental Restraint System and Side Impact Protection System offer an exceptional level of driver and passenger protection throughout the vehicle.

Provided that regular servicing is carried out in accordance with the manufacturer's recommendations, the Volvo 850 will provide the enviable reliability for which this marque is famous. The engine compartment is relatively spacious and most of the items requiring frequent attention are easily accessible.

Volvo 850 T-5 Turbo

Volvo 850 SE Estate

The Volvo 850 Team

Haynes manuals are produced by dedicated and enthusiastic people working in close co-operation. The team responsible for the creation of this book included:

Author	**John Mead**
Sub-editors	**Sophie Yar** **Carole Turk**
Editor & Page Make-up	**Steve Churchill**
Workshop manager	**Paul Buckland**
Photo Scans	**John Martin** **Paul Tanswell**
Cover illustration	**Roger Healing**

We hope the book will help you to get the maximum enjoyment from your car. By carrying out routine maintenance as described you will ensure your car's reliability and preserve its resale value.

Your Volvo 850 Manual

The aim of this manual is to help you get the best value from your vehicle. It can do so in several ways. It can help you decide what work must be done (even should you choose to get it done by a garage), provide information on routine maintenance and servicing, and give a logical course of action and diagnosis when random faults occur. However, it is hoped that you will use the manual by tackling the work yourself. On simpler jobs it may even be quicker than booking the car into a garage and going there twice, to leave and collect it. Perhaps most important, a lot of money can be saved by avoiding the costs a garage must charge to cover its labour and overheads.

The manual has drawings and descriptions to show the function of the various components so that their layout can be understood. Then the tasks are described and photographed in a clear step-by-step sequence.

References to the "left" or "right" of the vehicle are in the sense of a person in the driver's seat, facing forwards.

Acknowledgements

Certain illustrations are the copyright of Volvo Car Corporation and are used with their permission. Thanks are also due to Draper Tools Limited, who provided some of the workshop tools, and to all those people at Sparkford who helped in the production of this manual.

We take great pride in the accuracy of information given in this manual, but vehicle manufacturers make alterations and design changes during the production run of a particular vehicle of which they do not inform us. No liability can be accepted by the authors or publishers for loss, damage or injury caused by any errors in, or omissions from the information given.

Working on your car can be dangerous. This page shows just some of the potential risks and hazards, with the aim of creating a safety-conscious attitude.

General hazards

Scalding

• Don't remove the radiator or expansion tank cap while the engine is hot.
• Engine oil, automatic transmission fluid or power steering fluid may also be dangerously hot if the engine has recently been running.

Burning

• Beware of burns from the exhaust system and from any part of the engine. Brake discs and drums can also be extremely hot immediately after use.

Crushing

• When working under or near a raised vehicle, always supplement the jack with axle stands, or use drive-on ramps. *Never venture under a car which is only supported by a jack.*

• Take care if loosening or tightening high-torque nuts when the vehicle is on stands. Initial loosening and final tightening should be done with the wheels on the ground.

Fire

• Fuel is highly flammable; fuel vapour is explosive.
• Don't let fuel spill onto a hot engine.
• Do not smoke or allow naked lights (including pilot lights) anywhere near a vehicle being worked on. Also beware of creating sparks (electrically or by use of tools).
• Fuel vapour is heavier than air, so don't work on the fuel system with the vehicle over an inspection pit.
• Another cause of fire is an electrical overload or short-circuit. Take care when repairing or modifying the vehicle wiring.
• Keep a fire extinguisher handy, of a type suitable for use on fuel and electrical fires.

Electric shock

• Ignition HT voltage can be dangerous, especially to people with heart problems or a pacemaker. Don't work on or near the ignition system with the engine running or the ignition switched on.

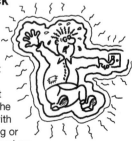

• Mains voltage is also dangerous. Make sure that any mains-operated equipment is correctly earthed. Mains power points should be protected by a residual current device (RCD) circuit breaker.

Fume or gas intoxication

• Exhaust fumes are poisonous; they often contain carbon monoxide, which is rapidly fatal if inhaled. Never run the engine in a confined space such as a garage with the doors shut.

• Fuel vapour is also poisonous, as are the vapours from some cleaning solvents and paint thinners.

Poisonous or irritant substances

• Avoid skin contact with battery acid and with any fuel, fluid or lubricant, especially antifreeze, brake hydraulic fluid and Diesel fuel. Don't syphon them by mouth. If such a substance is swallowed or gets into the eyes, seek medical advice.
• Prolonged contact with used engine oil can cause skin cancer. Wear gloves or use a barrier cream if necessary. Change out of oil-soaked clothes and do not keep oily rags in your pocket.
• Air conditioning refrigerant forms a poisonous gas if exposed to a naked flame (including a cigarette). It can also cause skin burns on contact.

Asbestos

• Asbestos dust can cause cancer if inhaled or swallowed. Asbestos may be found in gaskets and in brake and clutch linings. When dealing with such components it is safest to assume that they contain asbestos.

Special hazards

Hydrofluoric acid

• This extremely corrosive acid is formed when certain types of synthetic rubber, found in some O-rings, oil seals, fuel hoses etc, are exposed to temperatures above 400°C. The rubber changes into a charred or sticky substance containing the acid. *Once formed, the acid remains dangerous for years. If it gets onto the skin, it may be necessary to amputate the limb concerned.*
• When dealing with a vehicle which has suffered a fire, or with components salvaged from such a vehicle, wear protective gloves and discard them after use.

The battery

• Batteries contain sulphuric acid, which attacks clothing, eyes and skin. Take care when topping-up or carrying the battery.
• The hydrogen gas given off by the battery is highly explosive. Never cause a spark or allow a naked light nearby. Be careful when connecting and disconnecting battery chargers or jump leads.

Air bags

• Air bags can cause injury if they go off accidentally. Take care when removing the steering wheel and/or facia. Special storage instructions may apply.

Diesel injection equipment

• Diesel injection pumps supply fuel at very high pressure. Take care when working on the fuel injectors and fuel pipes.

⚠ *Warning: Never expose the hands, face or any other part of the body to injector spray; the fuel can penetrate the skin with potentially fatal results.*

Remember...

DO

• Do use eye protection when using power tools, and when working under the vehicle.

• Do wear gloves or use barrier cream to protect your hands when necessary.

• Do get someone to check periodically that all is well when working alone on the vehicle.

• Do keep loose clothing and long hair well out of the way of moving mechanical parts.

• Do remove rings, wristwatch etc, before working on the vehicle – especially the electrical system.

• Do ensure that any lifting or jacking equipment has a safe working load rating adequate for the job.

DON'T

• Don't attempt to lift a heavy component which may be beyond your capability – get assistance.

• Don't rush to finish a job, or take unverified short cuts.

• Don't use ill-fitting tools which may slip and cause injury.

• Don't leave tools or parts lying around where someone can trip over them. Mop up oil and fuel spills at once.

• Don't allow children or pets to play in or near a vehicle being worked on.

The following pages are intended to help in dealing with common roadside emergencies and breakdowns. You will find more detailed fault finding information at the back of the manual, and repair information in the main chapters.

If your car won't start and the starter motor doesn't turn

☐ If it's a model with automatic transmission, make sure the selector is in 'P' or 'N'.
☐ Open the bonnet and make sure that the battery terminals are clean and tight.
☐ Switch on the headlights and try to start the engine. If the headlights go very dim when you're trying to start, the battery is probably flat. Get out of trouble by jump starting (see next page) using a friend's car.

If your car won't start even though the starter motor turns as normal

☐ Is there fuel in the tank?
☐ Is there moisture on electrical components under the bonnet? Switch off the ignition, then wipe off any obvious dampness with a dry cloth. Spray a water-repellent aerosol product (WD-40 or equivalent) on ignition and fuel system electrical connectors like those shown in the photos. Pay special attention to the ignition coil wiring connector and HT leads. (Note that Diesel engines don't normally suffer from damp.)

A Check that the HT leads are securely connected to the distributor and that the cap is clean and properly fitted

B Check that the HT lead and wiring connections are securely connected to the ignition coil.

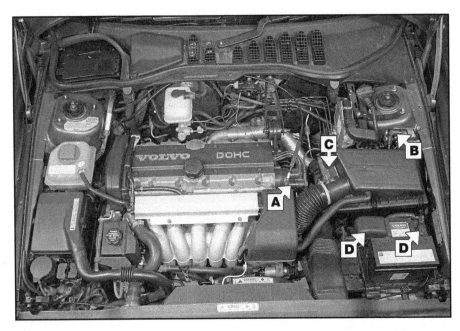

Check that electrical connections are secure (with the ignition switched off) and spray them with a water dispersant spray like WD40 if you suspect a problem due to damp

C Check the mass air flow sensor or inlet air temperature sensor wiring connector for security.

D Check the security and condition of the battery terminals.

Jump starting

HAYNES HINT *Jump starting will get you out of trouble, but you must correct whatever made the battery go flat in the first place. There are three possibilities:*

1 *The battery has been drained by repeated attempts to start, or by leaving the lights on.*

2 *The charging system is not working properly (alternator drivebelt slack or broken, alternator wiring fault or alternator itself faulty).*

3 *The battery itself is at fault (electrolyte low, or battery worn out).*

When jump-starting a car using a booster battery, observe the following precautions:

✔ Before connecting the booster battery, make sure that the ignition is switched off.

✔ Ensure that all electrical equipment (lights, heater, wipers, etc) is switched off.

✔ Take note of any special precautions printed on the battery case.

✔ Make sure that the booster battery is the same voltage as the discharged one in the vehicle.

✔ If the battery is being jump-started from the battery in another vehicle, the two vehicles MUST NOT TOUCH each other.

✔ Make sure that the transmission is in neutral (or PARK, in the case of automatic transmission).

1 Connect one end of the red jump lead to the positive (+) terminal of the flat battery

2 Connect the other end of the red lead to the positive (+) terminal of the booster battery.

3 Connect one end of the black jump lead to the negative (-) terminal of the booster battery

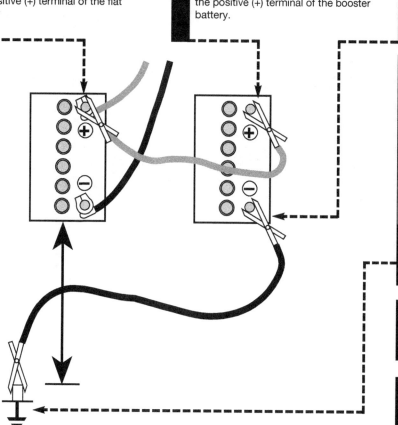

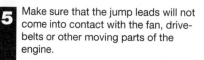

4 Connect the other end of the black jump lead to a bolt or bracket on the engine block, well away from the battery, on the vehicle to be started.

5 Make sure that the jump leads will not come into contact with the fan, drive-belts or other moving parts of the engine.

6 Start the engine using the booster battery and run it at idle speed. Switch on the lights, rear window demister and heater blower motor, then disconnect the jump leads in the reverse order of connection. Turn off the lights etc.

Wheel changing

Some of the details shown here will vary according to model. For instance, the location of the spare wheel and jack is not the same on all cars. However, the basic principles apply to all vehicles.

 Warning: *Do not change a wheel in a situation where you risk being hit by other traffic. On busy roads, try to stop in a lay-by or a gateway. Be wary of passing traffic while changing the wheel – it is easy to become distracted by the job in hand.*

Preparation

☐ When a puncture occurs, stop as soon as it is safe to do so.

☐ Park on firm level ground, if possible, and well out of the way of other traffic.

☐ Use hazard warning lights if necessary.

☐ If you have one, use a warning triangle to alert other drivers of your presence.

☐ Apply the handbrake and engage first or reverse gear (or Park on models with automatic transmission).

☐ Chock the wheel diagonally opposite the one being removed – a couple of large stones will do for this.

☐ If the ground is soft, use a flat piece of wood to spread the load under the jack.

Changing the wheel

1 The spare wheel and tools are stored in the luggage compartment under the carpet (Estate model shown). Release the restraining strap, unscrew the tool and wheel clamp, and lift out the jack and wheel changing tools from the centre of the wheel.

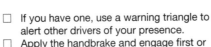

2 With the jack and tools removed, lift the wheel from its well.

3 Remove the wheel trim, either by pulling it straight off (steel wheels) or by prising off the hub cap (alloy wheels). Slacken each wheel bolt by half a turn using the wheel brace in the tool kit.

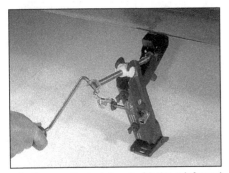

4 Engage the jack head with the reinforced stud located in the middle of the sill on each side of the car (don't jack the vehicle at any other point of the sill). With the base of the jack on firm ground, turn the jack handle clockwise until the wheel is raised clear of the ground. Unscrew the wheel bolts and remove the wheel.

5 Fit the spare wheel, and screw in the bolts. Lightly tighten the bolts with the wheelbrace then lower the vehicle to the ground.

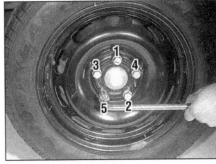

6 Securely tighten the wheel bolts in the sequence shown then refit the wheel trim/hub cap. Stow the punctured wheel and tools back in the luggage compartment and secure them in position. Note that the wheel bolts should be slackened and then retightened to the specified torque at the earliest opportunity.

Finally...

☐ Remove the wheel chocks.

☐ Stow the jack and tools in the correct locations in the car.

☐ Check the tyre pressure on the wheel just fitted. If it is low, or if you don't have a pressure gauge with you, drive slowly to the nearest garage and inflate the tyre to the right pressure.

☐ Have the damaged tyre or wheel repaired as soon as possible.

Identifying leaks

Puddles on the garage floor or drive, or obvious wetness under the bonnet or underneath the car, suggest a leak that needs investigating. It can sometimes be difficult to decide where the leak is coming from, especially if the engine bay is very dirty already. Leaking oil or fluid can also be blown rearwards by the passage of air under the car, giving a false impression of where the problem lies.

 Warning: Most automotive oils and fluids are poisonous. Wash them off skin, and change out of contaminated clothing, without delay.

 HAYNES HiNT The smell of a fluid leaking from the car may provide a clue to what's leaking. Some fluids are distinctively coloured. It may help to clean the car carefully and to park it over some clean paper overnight as an aid to locating the source of the leak.

Remember that some leaks may only occur while the engine is running.

Sump oil

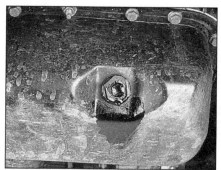

Engine oil may leak from the drain plug...

Oil from filter

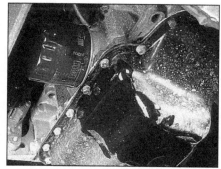

...or from the base of the oil filter.

Gearbox oil

Gearbox oil can leak from the seals at the inboard ends of the driveshafts.

Antifreeze

Leaking antifreeze often leaves a crystalline deposit like this.

Brake fluid

A leak occurring at a wheel is almost certainly brake fluid.

Power steering fluid

Power steering fluid may leak from the pipe connectors on the steering rack.

Towing

When all else fails, you may find yourself having to get a tow home – or of course you may be helping somebody else. Long-distance recovery should only be done by a garage or breakdown service. For shorter distances, DIY towing using another car is easy enough, but observe the following points:

□ Use a proper tow-rope – they are not expensive. The vehicle being towed must display an 'ON TOW' sign in its rear window.
□ Always turn the ignition key to the 'on' position when the vehicle is being towed, so that the steering lock is released, and that the direction indicator and brake lights will work.
□ Only attach the tow-rope to the towing eyes provided.
□ Before being towed, release the handbrake and select neutral on the transmission.
□ Note that greater-than-usual pedal pressure will be required to operate the brakes, since the vacuum servo unit is only operational with the engine running.
□ On models with power steering, greater-than-usual steering effort will also be required.

□ The driver of the car being towed must keep the tow-rope taut at all times to avoid snatching.
□ Make sure that both drivers know the route before setting off.
□ Only drive at moderate speeds and keep the distance towed to a minimum. Drive smoothly and allow plenty of time for slowing down at junctions.
□ On models with automatic transmission, special precautions apply. If in doubt, do not tow, or transmission damage may result.

Introduction

There are some very simple checks which need only take a few minutes to carry out, but which could save you a lot of inconvenience and expense.

These "Weekly checks" require no great skill or special tools, and the small amount of time they take to perform could prove to be very well spent, for example;

☐ Keeping an eye on tyre condition and pressures, will not only help to stop them wearing out prematurely, but could also save your life.

☐ Many breakdowns are caused by electrical problems. Battery-related faults are particularly common, and a quick check on a regular basis will often prevent the majority of these.

☐ If your car develops a brake fluid leak, the first time you might know about it is when your brakes don't work properly. Checking the level regularly will give advance warning of this kind of problem.

☐ If the oil or coolant levels run low, the cost of repairing any engine damage will be far greater than fixing the leak, for example.

Underbonnet check points

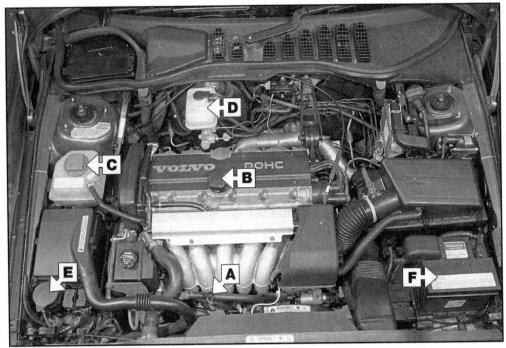

◀ **2.5 litre 10-Valve**

A *Engine oil level dipstick*
B *Engine oil filler cap*
C *Coolant expansion tank*
D *Brake fluid reservoir*
E *Screen washer fluid reservoir*
F *Battery*

Engine oil level

Before you start

✔ Make sure that your car is on level ground.
✔ Check the oil level before the car is driven, or at least 5 minutes after the engine has been switched off.

 HAYNES HINT *If the oil is checked immediately after driving the vehicle, some of the oil will remain in the upper engine components, resulting in an inaccurate reading on the dipstick!*

The correct oil

Modern engines place great demands on their oil. It is very important that the correct oil for your car is used (See "Lubricants, fluids and tyre pressures").

Car Care

● If you have to add oil frequently, you should check whether you have any oil leaks. Place some clean paper under the car overnight, and check for stains in the morning. If there are no leaks, the engine may be burning oil.

● Always maintain the level between the upper and lower dipstick marks (see photo 3). If the level is too low severe engine damage may occur. Oil seal failure may result if the engine is overfilled by adding too much oil.

1 The dipstick top is often brightly coloured for easy identification (see "*Underbonnet check points*" on page 0•10 for exact location). Withdraw the dipstick.

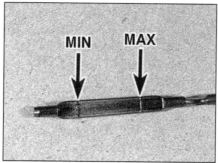

3 Note the oil level on the end of the dipstick, which should be between the upper ("MAX") mark and lower ("MIN") mark. Approximately 1.0 litre of oil will raise the level from the lower mark to the upper mark.

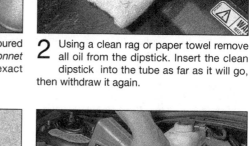

2 Using a clean rag or paper towel remove all oil from the dipstick. Insert the clean dipstick into the tube as far as it will go, then withdraw it again.

4 Oil is added through the filler cap. Unscrew the cap and top-up the level; a funnel may help to reduce spillage. Add the oil slowly, checking the level on the dipstick often. Don't overfill (see "*Car Care*" left).

Coolant level

⚠ *Warning: DO NOT attempt to remove the expansion tank pressure cap when the engine is hot, as there is a very great risk of scalding. Do not leave open containers of coolant about, as it is poisonous.*

Car Care

● With a sealed-type cooling system, adding coolant should not be necessary on a regular basis. If frequent topping-up is required, it is likely there is a leak. Check the radiator, all hoses and joint faces for signs of staining or wetness, and rectify as necessary.

● It is important that antifreeze is used in the cooling system all year round, not just during the winter months. Don't top-up with water alone, as the antifreeze will become too diluted.

1 The coolant level varies with engine temperature. When cold, the coolant level should be between the "MAX" and "MIN" marks. When the engine is hot, the level may rise slightly above the "MAX" mark.

2 If topping up is necessary, **wait until the engine is cold**. Slowly unscrew the expansion tank cap, to release any pressure present in the cooling system, and remove it.

3 Add a mixture of water and antifreeze to the expansion tank until the coolant is at the correct level. Refit the cap and tighten it securely.

Brake and clutch fluid level

Warning:
● Brake fluid can harm your eyes and damage painted surfaces, so use extreme caution when handling and pouring it.
● Do not use fluid that has been standing open for some time, as it absorbs moisture from the air, which can cause a dangerous loss of braking effectiveness.

● Make sure that your car is on level ground.
● The fluid level in the reservoir will drop slightly as the brake pads wear down, but the fluid level must never be allowed to drop below the "MIN" mark.

Safety First!

● If the reservoir requires repeated topping-up this is an indication of a fluid leak somewhere in the system, which should be investigated immediately.

● If a leak is suspected, the car should not be driven until the braking system has been checked. Never take any risks where brakes are concerned.

1 The "MAX" and "MIN" marks are indicated on the side of the reservoir. The fluid level must be kept between the marks at all times.

3 Unscrew the reservoir cap and carefully lift it out of position, taking care not to damage the level sender float. Inspect the reservoir, if the fluid is dirty the hydraulic system should be drained and refilled (see Chapter 1).

2 If topping-up is necessary, first wipe clean the area around the filler cap to prevent dirt entering the hydraulic system.

4 Carefully add fluid, taking care not to spill it onto the surrounding components. Use only the specified fluid; mixing different types can cause damage to the system. After topping-up to the correct level, securely refit the cap and wipe off any spilt fluid.

Power steering fluid level

Before you start:

✔ Park the vehicle on level ground.
✔ Set the steering wheel straight-ahead.
✔ The engine should be turned off.

For the check to be accurate, the steering must not be turned once the engine has been stopped.

Safety First!

● The need for frequent topping-up indicates a leak, which should be investigated immediately.

1 The fluid reservoir is mounted on top of the power steering pump located at the front right-hand side of the engine. Wipe clean the area around the reservoir filler neck and unscrew the filler cap/dipstick from the reservoir.

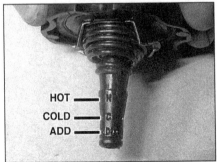

2 Dip the fluid with the reservoir cap/dipstick. When the engine is cold, the fluid level should be between the "ADD" mark and the "COLD" mark; when hot it should be between the "ADD" and "HOT" marks. Top-up when the level is at the "ADD" mark.

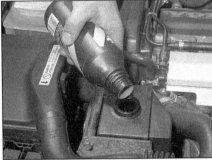

3 When topping-up, use the specified type of fluid and do not overfill the reservoir. When the level is correct, securely refit the cap.

Battery

Caution: *Before carrying out any work on the vehicle battery, read the precautions given in "Safety first" at the start of this manual.*

✔ Make sure that the battery tray is in good condition, and that the clamp is tight. Corrosion on the tray, retaining clamp and the battery itself can be removed with a solution of water and baking soda. Thoroughly rinse all cleaned areas with water. Any metal parts damaged by corrosion should be covered with a zinc-based primer, then painted.

✔ Periodically (approximately every three months), check the charge condition of the battery as described in Chapter 5A.

✔ If the battery is flat, and you need to jump start your vehicle, see ***Roadside Repairs***.

1 The battery is located at the front of the engine compartment on the left-hand side. The exterior of the battery should be inspected periodically for damage such as a cracked case or cover.

2 Check the tightness of battery clamps to ensure good electrical connections. You should not be able to move them. Also check each cable for cracks and frayed conductors.

Battery corrosion can be kept to a minimum by applying a layer of petroleum jelly to the clamps and terminals after they are reconnected.

3 If corrosion (white, fluffy deposits) is evident, remove the cables from the battery terminals, clean them with a small wire brush, then refit them. Automotive stores sell a tool for cleaning the battery post . . .

4 . . . as well as the battery cable clamps

Screen washer fluid level*

*On models so equipped, the screenwasher fluid is also used to clean the headlights and the tailgate rear window.

Screenwash additives not only keep the winscreen clean during foul weather, they also prevent the washer system freezing in cold weather - which is when you are likely to need it most. Don't top up using plain water as the screenwash will become too diluted, and will freeze during cold weather. *On no account use coolant antifreeze in the washer system - this could discolour or damage paintwork.*

1 The washer fluid reservoir filler is located at the front right-hand side of the engine compartment, (the reservoir itself is actually located under the car); release the cap and observe the level in the reservoir by looking down the filler neck.

2 When topping-up the reservoir, a screenwash additive should be added in the quantities recommended on the bottle.

Tyre condition and pressure

It is very important that tyres are in good condition, and at the correct pressure - having a tyre failure at any speed is highly dangerous. Tyre wear is influenced by driving style - harsh braking and acceleration, or fast cornering, will all produce more rapid tyre wear. As a general rule, the front tyres wear out faster than the rears. Interchanging the tyres from front to rear ("rotating" the tyres) may result in more even wear. However, if this is completely effective, you may have the expense of replacing all four tyres at once! Remove any nails or stones embedded in the tread before they penetrate the tyre to cause deflation. If removal of a nail does reveal that the tyre has been punctured, refit the nail so that its point of penetration is marked. Then immediately change the wheel, and have the tyre repaired by a tyre dealer.

Regularly check the tyres for damage in the form of cuts or bulges, especially in the sidewalls. Periodically remove the wheels, and clean any dirt or mud from the inside and outside surfaces. Examine the wheel rims for signs of rusting, corrosion or other damage. Light alloy wheels are easily damaged by "kerbing" whilst parking; steel wheels may also become dented or buckled. A new wheel is very often the only way to overcome severe damage.

New tyres should be balanced when they are fitted, but it may become necessary to re-balance them as they wear, or if the balance weights fitted to the wheel rim should fall off. Unbalanced tyres will wear more quickly, as will the steering and suspension components. Wheel imbalance is normally signified by vibration, particularly at a certain speed (typically around 50 mph). If this vibration is felt only through the steering, then it is likely that just the front wheels need balancing. If, however, the vibration is felt through the whole car, the rear wheels could be out of balance. Wheel balancing should be carried out by a tyre dealer or garage.

1 Tread Depth - visual check

The original tyres have tread wear safety bands (B), which will appear when the tread depth reaches approximately 1.6 mm. The band positions are indicated by a triangular mark on the tyre sidewall (A).

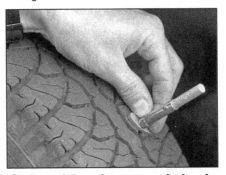

2 Tread Depth - manual check

Alternatively, tread wear can be monitored with a simple, inexpensive device known as a tread depth indicator gauge.

3 Tyre Pressure Check

Check the tyre pressures regularly with the tyres cold. Do not adjust the tyre pressures immediately after the vehicle has been used, or an inaccurate setting will result.

Tyre tread wear patterns

Shoulder Wear

Underinflation (wear on both sides)
Under-inflation will cause overheating of the tyre, because the tyre will flex too much, and the tread will not sit correctly on the road surface. This will cause a loss of grip and excessive wear, not to mention the danger of sudden tyre failure due to heat build-up.
Check and adjust pressures
Incorrect wheel camber (wear on one side)
Repair or renew suspension parts
Hard cornering
Reduce speed!

Centre Wear

Overinflation
Over-inflation will cause rapid wear of the centre part of the tyre tread, coupled with reduced grip, harsher ride, and the danger of shock damage occurring in the tyre casing.
Check and adjust pressures

If you sometimes have to inflate your car's tyres to the higher pressures specified for maximum load or sustained high speed, don't forget to reduce the pressures to normal afterwards.

Uneven Wear

Front tyres may wear unevenly as a result of wheel misalignment. Most tyre dealers and garages can check and adjust the wheel alignment (or "tracking") for a modest charge.
Incorrect camber or castor
Repair or renew suspension parts
Malfunctioning suspension
Repair or renew suspension parts
Unbalanced wheel
Balance tyres
Incorrect toe setting
Adjust front wheel alignment
Note: *The feathered edge of the tread which typifies toe wear is best checked by feel.*

Wiper blades

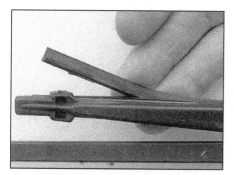

1 Check the condition of the wiper blades; if they are cracked or show any signs of deterioration, or if the glass swept area is smeared, renew them. Wiper blades should be renewed annually.

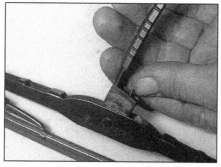

2 To remove a windscreen or tailgate wiper blade, pull the arm fully away from the glass until it locks. Swivel the blade through 90°, press the locking tab with your fingers and slide the blade out of the arm's hooked end.

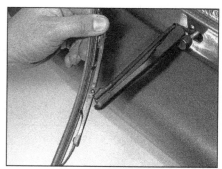

3 Don't forget to check the headlight wiper blades as well. To remove the blade, lift the arm and simply pull the blade out of the arm fitting. Push the blade firmly home to refit.

Bulbs and fuses

✔ Check all external lights and the horn. Refer to the appropriate Sections of Chapter 12 for details if any of the circuits are found to be inoperative.

✔ Visually check all accessible wiring connectors, harnesses and retaining clips for security, and for signs of chafing or damage.

> **HAYNES HINT** *If you need to check your brake lights and indicators unaided, back up to a wall or garage door and operate the lights. The reflected light should show if they are working properly.*

1 If a single indicator light, stop light or headlight has failed it is likely that a bulb has blown and will need to be replaced. Refer to Chapter 12 for details.
If both stop lights have failed, it is possible that the stop light switch above the brake pedal needs adjusting. This operation is described in Chapter 12.

2 If more than one indicator light or headlight has failed it is likely that either a fuse has blown or that there is a fault in the circuit (see Chapter 12). The fuses are located in the electrical control box situated in the engine compartment on the driver's side, just in front of the windscreen.

3 To replace a blown fuse, simply pull it out using the tool provided. Fit a new fuse of the same rating (see Chapter 12). If the fuse blows again, it is important that you find out why - a complete checking procedure is given in Chapter 12.

Lubricants and fluids

Engine	Multigrade engine oil, viscosity SAE 10W/40, or 15W/50, to CCMC G4/G5
Cooling system	Volvo type C coolant
Manual transmission	Volvo synthetic gearbox oil 97308
Automatic transmission	Dexron IIE type automatic transmission fluid
Braking system	Brake and clutch fluid to DOT 4+ (or DOT 4)
Power steering	Dexron type II ATF

Tyre pressures (cold)

	Front	Rear
Non-turbo Saloon models		
Normal use:		
185/65 R15	2.2 bar	2.0 bar
195/60 R15	2.5 bar	2.5 bar
205/55 R15	2.5 bar	2.5 bar
Fully laden or high speed:		
185/65 R15	2.3 bar	2.5 bar
195/60 R15	2.6 bar	2.8 bar
205/55 R15	2.6 bar	2.8 bar
Turbocharged Saloon models		
Normal use		
205/45 R17	2.3 bar	2.1 bar
205/50 R16	2.8 bar	2.6 bar
205/55 R15	2.8 bar	2.6 bar
185/65 R15 (winter tyres)	2.8 bar	2.6 bar
Fully laden or high speed:		
205/45 R17	2.5 bar	2.5 bar
205/50 R16	2.9 bar	2.9 bar
205/55 R15	2.9 bar	2.9 bar
185/65 R15 (winter tyres)	2.9 bar	2.9 bar
T115/70 R15 "Space saver" spare	4.2 bar	4.2 bar
Non-turbo Estate models		
Normal use:		
185/65 R15	2.2 bar	2.1 bar
195/60 R15	2.5 bar	2.5 bar
205/55 R15	2.5 bar	2.5 bar
T115/70 R15 "Space saver" spare	4.2 bar	4.2 bar
Fully laden or high speed:		
185/65 R15	2.4 bar	2.8 bar
195/60 R15	2.6 bar	3.1 bar
205/55 R15	2.6 bar	3.1 bar
T115/70 R15 "Space saver" spare	4.2 bar	4.2 bar
Turbocharged Estate models		
Normal use		
205/45 R17	2.3 bar	2.2 bar
205/50 R16	2.8 bar	2.7 bar
205/55 R15	2.8 bar	2.7 bar
185/65 R15 (winter tyres)	2.8 bar	2.7 bar
T115/70 R15 "Space saver" spare	4.2 bar	4.2 bar
Fully laden or high speed:		
205/45 R17	2.5 bar	2.8 bar
205/50 R16	2.9 bar	3.2 bar
205/55 R15	2.9 bar	3.2 bar
185/65 R15 (winter tyres)	2.9 bar	3.2 bar
T115/70 R15 "Space saver" spare	4.2 bar	4.2 bar

Note: *Refer to the tyre pressure data sticker on the fuel filler flap for the correct tyre pressures for your particular vehicle. Pressures apply only to original-equipment tyres, and may vary if other makes or type is fitted; check with the tyre manufacturer or supplier for correct pressures if necessary.*

Chapter 1
Routine maintenance and servicing

Contents

Degrees of difficulty

Easy, suitable for novice with little experience		**Fairly easy,** suitable for beginner with some experience		**Fairly difficult,** suitable for competent DIY mechanic		**Difficult,** suitable for experienced DIY mechanic		**Very difficult,** suitable for expert DIY or professional	

Servicing Specifications

Lubricants and fluids
Refer to end of *"Weekly checks"*

Capacities

Engine oil
Drain and refill including filter change . . . . 5.3 litres (plus 0.9 litres for turbo oil cooler - if drained)
Cooling system:
   Non-turbo engines . . . . 7.2 litres
   Turbo engines . . . . 7.0 litres
Fuel tank . . . . 73 litres

Cooling system
Specified antifreeze mixture . . . . 50% antifreeze/50% water
Note: *Refer to Chapter 3 for further details.*

Ignition system

Spark plugs:	Type	Electrode gap
Normally-aspirated engines	Bosch FR 7 D+	0.9 mm
Turbocharged engines	Bosch FR 7 DPP 10	0.7 mm

Brakes
Front brake pad minimum lining thickness . . . . 3.0 mm
Rear brake pad minimum lining thickness . . . . 2.0 mm
Handbrake lever travel:
   After adjustment . . . . 3 to 5 clicks
   In service . . . . 11 clicks maximum

Servicing specifications

Tyres

Tyre pressures . . . . See *"Weekly checks"*

Torque wrench settings   **Nm**

Oil sump drain plug 35

Spark plugs 25

Roadwheel bolts 110

Volvo 850 maintenance schedule

The maintenance intervals in this manual are provided with the assumption that you, not the dealer, will be carrying out the work. These are the average maintenance intervals recommended by the manufacturer for vehicles driven daily under normal conditions. Obviously some variation of these intervals may be expected depending on territory of use, and conditions encountered. If you wish to keep your vehicle in peak condition at all times, you may wish to perform some of these procedures more often. We encourage frequent maintenance because it enhances the efficiency, performance and resale value of your vehicle.

If the vehicle is driven in dusty areas, used to tow a trailer, driven frequently at slow speeds (idling in traffic) or on short journeys, more frequent maintenance intervals are recommended.

Every 250 miles (400 km) or weekly

☐ Refer to *"Weekly checks"*.

Every 10 000 miles (16 000 km) or 12 months, whichever comes first

In addition to the items listed above, carry out the following:

☐ Renew the engine oil and filter (Section 3).
☐ Check the condition of the brake pads (Section 4).
☐ Thoroughly inspect the engine for fluid leaks (Section 5).
☐ Check the condition and security of the steering and suspension components (Section 6).
☐ Check the condition of the driveshaft gaiters (Section 7).
☐ Inspect the clutch hydraulic components (Section 8).
☐ Check the manual transmission oil level (Section 9).
☐ Inspect the underbody and the brake hydraulic pipes and hoses (Section 10).
☐ Check the condition of the fuel lines (Section 10).
☐ Check the condition and security of the exhaust system (Section 11).
☐ Check the handbrake adjustment (Section 12).
☐ Check the condition of the seat belts (Section 13).
☐ Lubricate the locks and hinges (Section 14).
☐ Check the headlight beam alignment (Section 15).
☐ Check the condition of the exterior trim and paintwork (Section 16).
☐ Check the automatic transmission selector cable adjustment (Section 17).
☐ Road test (Section 18).
☐ Check the automatic transmission fluid level (Section 19).
☐ Check the operation of the air conditioning system (Section 20).

Every 20 000 miles (32 000 km) or two years, whichever comes first

In addition to the items listed above, carry out the following:

☐ Check the condition of the auxiliary drivebelt and renew if necessary (Section 21).
☐ Renew the coolant (Section 22).
☐ Renew the brake fluid (Section 23).

Every 30 000 miles (48 000 km) or three years, whichever comes first

In addition to the items listed above, carry out the following:

☐ Inspect the distributor cap, rotor arm and HT leads (Section 24).
☐ Renew the spark plugs (Section 25).

Every 40 000 miles (64 000 km) or four years, whichever comes first

In addition to the items listed above, carry out the following:

☐ Renew the air cleaner element (Section 26).

Every 50 000 miles (80 000 km) or five years, whichever comes first

In addition to the items listed above, carry out the following:

☐ Renew the fuel filter (Section 27).
☐ Check the emission control equipment (Section 28).
1992 & 1993 models only (with 21mm wide timing belt);
☐ Renew the timing belt (Section 29).

Every 80 000 miles (129 000 km) or eight years, whichever comes first

In addition to the items listed above, carry out the following:
1994 models onwards (with 23mm wide timing belt);
☐ Renew the timing belt (Section 30).

Underbonnet view of a 2.5 litre, 10-valve non-turbo model

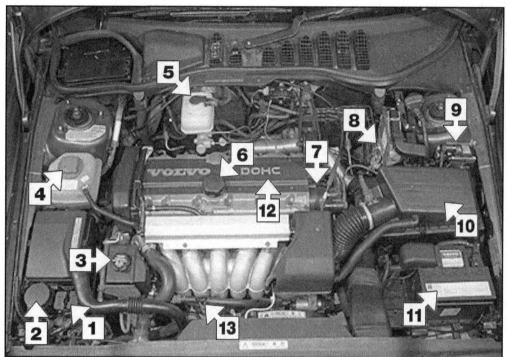

1 Diagnostic unit*
2 Washer reservoir
3 Power steering reservoir
4 Cooling system expansion tank
5 Brake master cylinder reservoir
6 Oil filler cap
7 Distributor
8 ABS modulator and ECU
9 Ignition coil and power stage
10 Air cleaner
11 Battery
12 Spark plug cover
13 Engine oil dipstick

* On models from 1996 the diagnostic unit is located under a cover in front of the gear lever

Front underside view of a 2.5 litre Estate model

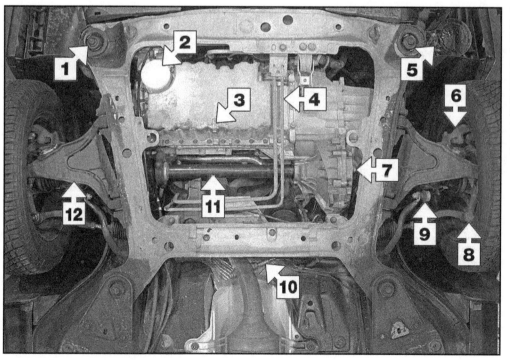

1 Subframe mounting
2 Oil filter
3 Engine oil drain plug
4 Power steering fluid pipes
5 EVAP carbon canister
6 Front brake caliper
7 Manual transmission drain plug
8 Track rod end
9 Anti-roll bar connecting link
10 Heated oxygen sensor
11 Right-hand driveshaft
12 Suspension control arm

Rear underside view of a 2.5 litre Estate model

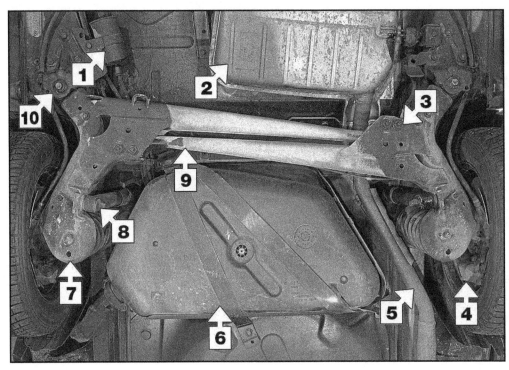

1 Fuel filter
2 Exhaust silencer
3 Suspension trailing arm
4 Rear brake caliper
5 Exhaust rear section
6 Fuel tank
7 Rear spring pan
8 Rear shock absorber
9 Suspension transverse arm
10 Suspension mounting

Maintenance procedures

1 Introduction

This Chapter is designed to help the home mechanic maintain his/her vehicle for safety, economy, long life and peak performance.

This Chapter contains a master maintenance schedule, followed by Sections dealing specifically with each task in the schedule. Visual checks, adjustments, component renewal and other helpful items are included. Refer to the accompanying illustrations of the engine compartment and the underside of the vehicle for the locations of the various components.

Servicing your vehicle in accordance with the mileage/time maintenance schedule and the following Sections will provide a planned maintenance programme, which should result in a long and reliable service life. This is a comprehensive plan, so maintaining some items but not others at the specified service intervals will not produce the same results.

As you service your vehicle, you will discover that many of the procedures can -

and should - be grouped together, because of the particular procedure being performed, or because of the close proximity of two otherwise-unrelated components to one another. For example, if the vehicle is raised for any reason, the exhaust should be inspected at the same time as the suspension and steering components.

The first step of this maintenance programme is to prepare yourself before the actual work begins. Read through all the Sections relevant to the work to be carried out, then make a list and gather together all the parts and tools required. If a problem is encountered, seek advice from a parts specialist or a dealer service department.

2 Intensive maintenance

1 If, from the time the vehicle is new, the routine maintenance schedule is followed closely, and frequent checks are made of fluid levels and high-wear items, as suggested throughout this manual, the engine will be

kept in relatively good running condition, and the need for additional work will be minimised.
2 It is possible that there will be some times when the engine is running poorly due to the lack of regular maintenance. This is even more likely if a used vehicle, which has not received regular and frequent maintenance checks, is purchased. In such cases, additional work may need to be carried out, outside of the regular maintenance intervals.
3 If engine wear is suspected, a compression test (refer to Part A of Chapter 2) will provide valuable information regarding the overall performance of the main internal components. Such a test can be used as a basis to decide on the extent of the work to be carried out. If, for example, a compression test indicates serious internal engine wear, conventional maintenance as described in this Chapter will not greatly improve the performance of the engine, and may prove a waste of time and money, unless extensive overhaul work (Chapter 2B) is carried out first.
4 The following series of operations are those often required to improve the performance of a generally poor-running engine:

Primary operations

a) Clean, inspect and test the battery (See "Weekly checks").
b) Check all the engine-related fluids (See "Weekly checks").
c) Check the condition of the auxiliary drivebelt (Section 21).
d) Inspect the distributor cap, rotor arm and HT leads (Section 24).

e) Renew the spark plugs (Section 25).
f) Check the condition of the air cleaner filter element and renew if necessary (Section 26).
g) Renew the fuel filter (Section 27).
h) Check the condition of all hoses, and check for fluid leaks (Section 5).

5 If the above operations do not prove fully effective, carry out the following operations:

Secondary operations

All the items listed under "Primary operations", plus the following:
a) Check the charging system (Chapter 5A).
b) Check the ignition system (Chapter 5B).
c) Check the fuel system (Chapter 4A and B).
d) Renew the distributor cap and rotor arm (Section 24 and Chapter 5B).
e) Renew the ignition HT leads (Section 24).

Every 10 000 miles (16 000 km) or 12 months

3 Engine oil and filter renewal

1 Frequent oil changes are the best preventive maintenance the home mechanic can give the engine, because ageing oil becomes diluted and contaminated, which leads to premature engine wear.

2 Make sure that you have all the necessary tools before you begin this procedure. You should also have plenty of rags or newspapers handy, for mopping up any spills. The oil should preferably be changed when the engine is still fully warmed-up to normal operating temperature, just after a run; warm oil and sludge will flow out more easily. Take care, however, not to touch the exhaust or any other hot parts of the engine when working under the vehicle. To avoid any possibility of scalding, and to protect yourself

3.3 Unscrew the sump drain plug and allow the oil to drain

from possible skin irritants and other harmful contaminants in used engine oils, it is advisable to wear gloves when carrying out this work. Access to the underside of the vehicle is greatly improved if the vehicle can be lifted on a hoist, driven onto ramps, or supported by axle stands. (see "Jacking and vehicle support"). Whichever method is chosen, make sure that the vehicle remains level, or if it is at an angle, that the drain point is at the lowest point. On earlier vehicles it will be necessary to remove the engine undertray for access to the sump and filter.

3 Position the draining container under the drain plug, and unscrew the plug **(see illustration)**. If possible, try to keep the plug pressed into the sump while unscrewing it by hand the last couple of turns.

> **HAYNES HiNT** As the drain plug releases from the threads, move it away sharply, so the stream of oil issuing from the sump runs into the container, not up your sleeve!

4 Allow the oil to drain into the container, and check the condition of the plug's sealing washer; renew it if worn or damaged.

5 Allow some time for the old oil to drain, noting that it may be necessary to reposition the container as the oil flow slows to a trickle; when the oil has completely drained, wipe clean the drain plug and its threads in the sump and refit the plug, tightening it to the specified torque.

6 The oil filter is located at the base of the sump on the front right-hand side.

7 Reposition the draining container under the oil filter then, using a suitable filter removal tool if necessary, slacken the filter initially, then unscrew it by hand the rest of the way; be prepared for some oil spillage **(see illustrations)**. Empty the oil in the old filter into the container.

8 Using a clean, lint-free rag, wipe clean the cylinder block around the filter mounting. Check the old filter to make sure that the rubber sealing ring hasn't stuck to the engine; if it has, carefully remove it.

9 Apply a light coating of clean engine oil to the sealing ring on the new filter **(see illustration)**. Screw the filter into position on the engine until it seats, then tighten it firmly by hand only - **do not** use any tools.

10 Remove the old oil and all tools from under the vehicle, then lower the vehicle to the ground.

11 Remove the dipstick and the oil filler cap from the engine. Fill the engine with oil, using the correct grade and type of oil (see "Specifications"). Pour in half the specified quantity of oil first, then wait a few minutes for the oil to fall to the sump. Continue adding oil a small quantity at a time, until the level is up to the lower mark on the dipstick. Adding approximately 1.0 litre will raise the level to the upper mark on the dipstick.

12 Start the engine. The oil pressure warning light will take a few seconds to go out while the new filter fills with oil; do not race the engine while the light is on. Run the engine for a few minutes, while checking for leaks around the oil filter seal and the drain plug.

13 Switch off the engine, and wait a few minutes for the oil to settle in the sump once

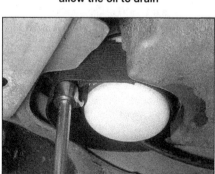

3.7a Slacken the oil filter with a suitable filter removal tool . . .

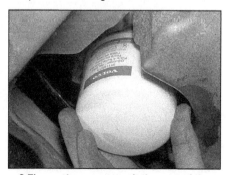

3.7b . . . then unscrew it the rest of the way by hand

3.9 Apply a light coating of clean engine oil to the sealing ring on the new filter

more. With the new oil circulated and the filter now completely full, recheck the level on the dipstick, and add more oil as necessary.

14 Dispose of the used engine oil safely and in accordance with environmental regulations (see *"General repair procedures"*).

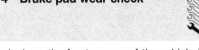

4 Brake pad wear check

1 Jack up the front or rear of the vehicle in turn, and support it on axle stands (see *"Jacking and vehicle support"*).

2 For better access to the brake calipers, remove the roadwheels.

3 Look through the inspection window in the caliper, and check that the thickness of the friction lining material on each of the pads is not less than the recommended minimum thickness given in the *Specifications*. If any one of the brake pads has worn down to, or below, the specified limit, *all four* pads at that end of the car must be renewed as a set (ie all the front pads or all the rear pads).

4 For a comprehensive check, the brake pads should be removed and cleaned. The operation of the brake calipers can then be checked, and the brake discs can be fully examined. Refer to Chapter 9 for details.

5 Underbonnet check for fluid leaks and hose condition

Caution: Renewal of air conditioning hoses must be left to a dealer service department or air conditioning specialist who has the equipment to depressurise the system safely. Never remove air conditioning components or hoses until the system has been depressurised.

General

1 High temperatures in the engine compartment can cause the deterioration of the rubber and plastic hoses used for engine, accessory and emission systems operation. Periodic inspection should be made for cracks, loose clamps, material hardening and leaks.

2 Carefully check the large top and bottom radiator hoses, along with the other smaller-diameter cooling system hoses and metal pipes; do not forget the heater hoses/pipes which run from the engine to the bulkhead. Inspect each hose along its entire length, replacing any that are cracked, swollen or shows signs of deterioration. Cracks may become more apparent if the hose is squeezed.

3 Make sure that all hose connections are tight. If the spring clamps that are used to secure some of the hoses appear to be slackening, they should be renewed to prevent the possibility of leaks.

A leak in the cooling system will usually show up as white- or rust-coloured deposits on the areas adjoining the leak.

4 Some other hoses are secured to their fittings with screw type clips. Where screw type clips are used, check to be sure they haven't slackened, allowing the hose to leak. If clamps or screw type clips aren't used, make sure the hose has not expanded and/or hardened where it slips over the fitting, allowing it to leak.

5 Check all fluid reservoirs, filler caps, drain plugs and fittings etc, looking for any signs of leakage of oil, transmission and/or brake hydraulic fluid, coolant and power steering fluid. If the vehicle is regularly parked in the same place, close inspection of the ground underneath will soon show any leaks; ignore the puddle of water which will be left if the air conditioning system is in use. As soon as a leak is detected, its source must be traced and rectified. Where oil has been leaking for some time, it is usually necessary to use a steam cleaner, pressure washer or similar, to clean away the accumulated dirt, so that the exact source of the leak can be identified.

Vacuum hoses

6 It's quite common for vacuum hoses, especially those in the emissions system, to be numbered or colour-coded, or to be identified by coloured stripes moulded into them. Various systems require hoses with different wall thicknesses, collapse resistance and temperature resistance. When renewing hoses, be sure the new ones are made of the same material.

7 Often the only effective way to check a hose is to remove it completely from the vehicle. If more than one hose is removed, be sure to label the hoses and fittings to ensure correct installation.

8 When checking vacuum hoses, be sure to include any plastic T-fittings in the check. Inspect the fittings for cracks, and check the hose where it fits over the fitting for distortion, which could cause leakage.

9 A small piece of vacuum hose can be used as a stethoscope to detect vacuum leaks. Hold one end of the hose to your ear, and probe around vacuum hoses and fittings, listening for the "hissing" sound characteristic of a vacuum leak.

Warning: When probing with the vacuum hose stethoscope, be very careful not to come into contact with moving engine components such as the auxiliary drivebelt, radiator electric cooling fan, etc.

Fuel hoses

Warning: Before carrying out the following operation, refer to the precautions given in "Safety first!" at the beginning of this manual, and follow them implicitly. Petrol is a highly dangerous and volatile liquid, and the precautions necessary when handling it cannot be overstressed.

10 Check all fuel hoses for deterioration and chafing. Check especially for cracks in areas where the hose bends, and also just before fittings, such as where a hose attaches to the fuel filter.

11 High-quality fuel line, usually identified by the word "Fluoroelastomer" printed on the hose, should be used for fuel line renewal. Never, under any circumstances, use unreinforced vacuum line, clear plastic tubing or water hose for fuel lines.

12 Spring-type clamps are commonly used on fuel lines. These clamps often lose their tension over a period of time, and can be "sprung" during removal. Replace all spring-type clamps with screw clips whenever a hose is replaced.

Metal lines

13 Sections of metal piping are often used for fuel line between the fuel filter and the engine. Check carefully to be sure the piping has not been bent or crimped, and that cracks have not started in the line.

14 If a section of metal fuel line must be renewed, only seamless steel piping should be used, since copper and aluminium piping don't have the strength necessary to withstand normal engine vibration.

15 Check the metal brake lines where they enter the master cylinder and ABS hydraulic unit for cracks in the lines or loose fittings. Any sign of brake fluid leakage calls for an immediate and thorough inspection of the brake system.

6 Steering and suspension check

Front suspension and steering check

1 Apply the handbrake then jack up the front of the vehicle and support it on axle stands (see *"Jacking and vehicle support"*).

2 Visually inspect the balljoint dust covers and the steering gear gaiters for splits, chafing or deterioration. Any wear of these components will cause loss of lubricant, together with dirt and water entry, resulting in rapid deterioration of the balljoints or steering gear.

6.5 Check for wear in the wheel bearing by grasping the wheel and trying to rock it

7.1 Inspect the condition of the CV joint gaiters (arrowed)

3 Check the power steering fluid hoses for chafing or deterioration, and the pipe and hose unions for fluid leaks. Also check for signs of fluid leakage under pressure from the steering gear rubber gaiters, which would indicate failed fluid seals within the steering gear.

4 Check for signs of fluid leakage around the suspension strut body, or from the rubber boot around the piston rod (where fitted). Should any fluid be noticed, the shock absorber is defective internally, and renewal is necessary.

5 Grasp the roadwheel at the 12 o'clock and 6 o'clock positions, and try to rock it (see illustration). Very slight free play may be felt, but if the movement is appreciable, further investigation is necessary to determine the source. Continue rocking the wheel while an assistant depresses the footbrake. If the movement is now eliminated or significantly reduced, it is likely that the wheel bearings are at fault. If the free play is still evident with the footbrake depressed, then there is wear in the suspension joints or mountings.

6 Now grasp the wheel at the 9 o'clock and 3 o'clock positions, and try to rock it as before. Any movement felt now may again be caused by wear in the wheel bearings or the steering track rod end balljoints. If the outer track rod end is worn, the visual movement will be obvious. If the inner joint is suspect, it can be felt by placing a hand over the rack-and-pinion rubber gaiter, and gripping the track rod. If the wheel is now rocked, movement will be felt at the inner joint if wear has taken place.

7 Using a large screwdriver or flat bar, check for wear in the suspension mounting bushes by levering between the relevant suspension component and its attachment point. Some movement is to be expected as the mountings are made of rubber, but excessive wear should be obvious. Also check the condition of any visible rubber bushes, looking for splits, cracks or contamination of the rubber.

8 With the vehicle standing on its wheels, have an assistant turn the steering wheel back-and-forth, about an eighth of a turn each way. There should be very little, if any, lost movement between the steering wheel and roadwheels. If this is not the case, closely observe the joints and mountings previously described, but in addition, check the steering column universal joints for wear, and also check the rack-and-pinion steering gear itself.

9 The efficiency of the shock absorber may be checked by bouncing the car at each front corner. Generally speaking, the body will return to its normal position and stop after being depressed. If it rises and returns on a rebound, the shock absorber is probably suspect. Examine also the shock absorber upper and lower mountings for any signs of wear or fluid leakage.

Rear suspension check

10 Chock the front wheels, then raise the rear of the vehicle and support it on axle stands. (see "Jacking and vehicle support").

11 Check the rear hub bearings for wear, using the method described for the front hub bearings (paragraph 5).

12 Using a large screwdriver or flat bar, check for wear in the suspension mounting bushes by levering between the relevant suspension component and its attachment point. Some movement is to be expected as the mountings are made of rubber, but excessive wear should be obvious. Check the condition of the shock absorbers as described previously.

7 Driveshaft gaiter check

1 With the vehicle raised and securely supported on axle stands (see "Jacking and vehicle support"), turn the steering onto full lock, then slowly rotate the roadwheel.

Inspect the condition of the outer constant velocity (CV) joint rubber gaiters, squeezing the gaiters to open out the folds (see illustration). Check for signs of cracking, splits or deterioration of the rubber, which may allow the grease to escape, and lead to water and grit entry into the joint. Also check the security and condition of the retaining clips. Repeat these checks on the inner CV joints. If any damage or deterioration is found, the gaiters should be renewed as described in Chapter 8.

2 At the same time, check the general condition of the CV joints themselves by first holding the driveshaft and attempting to rotate the wheel. Repeat this check by holding the inner joint and attempting to rotate the driveshaft. Any appreciable movement indicates wear in the joints, wear in the driveshaft splines, or a loose driveshaft retaining nut.

8 Clutch hydraulic check

1 Check that the clutch pedal moves smoothly and easily through its full travel, and that the clutch itself functions correctly, with no trace of slip or drag.

2 Remove the soundproofing panel under the facia for access to the clutch pedal and apply a few drops of light oil to the pedal pivot. Refit the panel.

3 From within the engine compartment check the condition of the fluid lines and hoses. Now have a look under the car at the clutch slave cylinder. Check for signs of fluid leaks around the rubber boot and check the security of the linkage. Apply a few drops of oil to the pushrod clevis pin and linkage.

9.1 Manual transmission filler/level plug (arrowed)

9 Manual transmission oil level check

1 The manual transmission does not have a dipstick. To check the oil level, raise the vehicle and support it securely on axle stands, making sure that the vehicle is level (see *"Jacking and vehicle support"*). On the left-hand side of the transmission casing you will see the filler/level plug and drain plug **(see illustration)**. Wipe all around the filler/level plug (the upper one of the two) with a clean rag then unscrew and remove it. If the lubricant level is correct, the oil should be up to the lower edge of the hole.
2 If the transmission needs more lubricant (if the oil level is not up to the hole), use a syringe, or a plastic bottle and tube, to add more. Stop filling the transmission when the lubricant begins to run out of the hole. Make sure that you use the correct type of lubricant.
3 Refit the filler/level plug, and tighten it securely. Drive the vehicle a short distance, then check for leaks.
4 A need for regular topping-up can only be due to a leak, which should be found and rectified without delay.

10 Underbody and fuel/brake line check

1 With the vehicle raised and supported on axle stands (see *"Jacking and vehicle support"*), or over an inspection pit, thoroughly inspect the underbody and wheel arches for signs of damage and corrosion. In particular, examine the bottom of the side sills, and any concealed areas where mud can collect. Where corrosion and rust is evident, press and tap firmly on the panel with a screwdriver, and check for any serious corrosion which would necessitate repairs. If the panel is not seriously corroded, clean away the rust, and apply a new coating of underseal. Refer to Chapter 11 for more details of body repairs.
2 At the same time, inspect the treated lower body panels for stone damage and general condition.

3 Inspect all of the fuel and brake lines on the underbody for damage, rust, corrosion and leakage. Also make sure that they are correctly supported in their clips. Where applicable, check the PVC coating on the lines for damage.
4 Inspect the flexible brake hoses in the vicinity of the calipers, where they are subjected to most movement. Bend them between the fingers (but do not actually bend them double, or the casing may be damaged) and check that this does not reveal previously-hidden cracks, cuts or splits.

11 Exhaust system check

1 With the engine cold (at least three hours after the vehicle has been driven), check the complete exhaust system, from its starting point at the engine to the end of the tailpipe. Ideally, this should be done on a hoist, where unrestricted access is available; if a hoist is not available, raise and support the vehicle on axle stands (see *"Jacking and vehicle support"*).
2 Check the pipes and connections for evidence of leaks, severe corrosion, or damage. Make sure that all brackets and rubber mountings are in good condition, and tight; if any of the mountings are to be renewed, ensure that the replacements are of the correct type. Leakage at any of the joints or in other parts of the system will usually show up as a black sooty stain in the vicinity of the leak.
3 At the same time, inspect the underside of the body for holes, corrosion, open seams, etc. which may allow exhaust gases to enter the passenger compartment. Seal all body openings with silicone or body putty.
4 Rattles and other noises can often be traced to the exhaust system, especially the rubber mountings. Try to move the system, silencer(s) and catalytic converter. If any components can touch the body or suspension parts, secure the exhaust system with new mountings.

12 Handbrake check and adjustment

In service, the handbrake should be fully applied within approximately 11 clicks of the handbrake lever ratchet. Adjustment will be necessary periodically to compensate for lining wear and cable stretch. Refer to Chapter 9 for the full adjustment procedure.

13 Seat belt check

1 Check the seat belts for satisfactory operation and condition. Inspect the webbing for fraying and cuts. Check that they retract smoothly and without binding into their reels.
2 Check the seat belt mountings, ensuring that all the bolts are securely tightened.

14 Door, boot, tailgate and bonnet check and lubrication

1 Check that the doors, bonnet and tailgate/boot lid close securely. Check that the bonnet safety catch operates correctly. Check the operation of the door check straps.
2 Lubricate the hinges, door check straps, the striker plates and the bonnet catch sparingly with a little oil or grease.
3 If any of the doors, bonnet or tailgate/boot lid do not close effectively or appear not to be flush with the surrounding panels, carry out the relevant adjustment procedures contained in Chapter 11.

15 Headlight beam alignment check

Accurate adjustment of the headlight beam is only possible using optical beam-setting equipment, and this work should therefore be carried out by a Volvo dealer or service station with the necessary facilities.

Basic adjustments can be carried out in an emergency, and further details are given in Chapter 12.

16 Bodywork, paint and exterior trim check

1 The best time to carry out this check is after the car has been washed so that any surface blemish or scratch will be clearly evident and not hidden by a film of dirt.
2 Starting at one front corner, check the paintwork all around the car, looking for minor scratches or more serious dents. Check all the trim and make sure that it is securely attached over its entire length.
3 Check the security of all door locks, door mirrors, badges, bumpers, radiator grille and wheel trim. Anything found loose, or in need of further attention should be done with reference to the relevant Chapters of this manual.
4 Rectify any problems noticed with the paintwork or body panels as described in Chapter 11.

17 Automatic transmission selector cable adjustment check

1 With the engine switched off, check that the selector lever moves freely between the N and D positions but will not move to any other position without depressing the lever locking button.

2 Firmly apply the handbrake and check that the engine will not start with the selector in the P or N positions. Now start the engine and slowly move the lever to the D position. Check that the transmission is felt to engage as D is selected. Return the lever to the N position and check that the transmission is in neutral. Finally check that with the engine switched off and the lever in the P position the transmission is locked. Release the handbrake and attempt to move the car to verify this.

3 If the transmission does not respond as described, adjust the selector cable as described in Chapter 7B.

18 Road test

Check the operation and performance of the braking system

1 Make sure that the vehicle does not pull to one side when braking, and that the wheels do not lock when braking hard.

2 Check that there is no vibration through the steering when braking.

3 Check that the handbrake operates correctly, without excessive movement of the lever, and that it holds the vehicle stationary on a slope.

4 With the engine switched off, test the operation of the brake servo unit as follows. Depress the footbrake four or five times to exhaust the vacuum, then start the engine. As the engine starts, there should be a noticeable "give" in the brake pedal as vacuum builds up. Allow the engine to run for at least two minutes, and then switch it off. If the brake pedal is now depressed again, it should be possible to detect a hiss from the servo as the pedal is depressed. After about four or five applications, no further hissing should be heard, and the pedal should feel considerably harder.

Steering and suspension

5 Check for any abnormalities in the steering, suspension, handling or road "feel".

6 Drive the vehicle, and check that there are no unusual vibrations or noises.

7 Check that the steering feels positive, with no excessive sloppiness or roughness, and check for any suspension noises when cornering and driving over bumps.

Drivetrain

8 Check the performance of the engine, transmission and driveline.

9 Check that the engine starts correctly, both when cold and hot.

10 Listen for any unusual noises from the engine and transmission.

11 Make sure that the engine runs smoothly when idling, and that there is no hesitation when accelerating.

12 On manual transmission models, check that all gears can be engaged smoothly without noise, and that the gear lever action is not abnormally vague or "notchy".

13 On automatic transmission models, make sure that the drive seems smooth without jerks or engine speed "flare-ups". Check that all the gear positions can be selected with the vehicle at rest.

Clutch

14 Check that the clutch pedal moves smoothly and easily through its full travel, and that the clutch itself functions correctly, with no trace of slip or drag. If the movement is uneven or stiff in places, check the system components with reference to Chapter 6.

Instruments and electrical equipment

15 Check the operation of all instruments and electrical equipment.

16 Make sure that all instruments read correctly, and switch on all electrical equipment in turn, to check that it functions properly.

19 Automatic transmission fluid level check

1 The level of the automatic transmission fluid should be carefully maintained. Low fluid level can lead to slipping or loss of drive, while overfilling can cause foaming, loss of fluid and transmission damage.

2 Ideally, the transmission fluid level should be checked when the transmission is hot (at its normal operating temperature). If the vehicle has just been driven for about 30 minutes, the fluid temperature will be around 80° C, and the transmission is hot.

3 Park the vehicle on level ground, apply the handbrake, and start the engine. While the engine is idling, depress the brake pedal and move the selector lever through all gear positions then returning to the "P" position.

4 Wait two minutes then, with the engine still idling, remove the dipstick from its tube which is located at the front of the engine **(see illustration)**. Note the condition and colour of the fluid on the dipstick.

5 Wipe the fluid from the dipstick with a clean rag, and re-insert it into the filler tube until the cap seats.

6 Pull the dipstick out again, and note the fluid level. The level should be between the "MIN" and "MAX" marks, on the side of the dipstick marked "HOT". If the level is on the "MIN" mark, stop the engine, and add the specified automatic transmission fluid through the dipstick tube, using a clean funnel if necessary. It is important not to introduce dirt into the transmission when topping-up.

7 Add the fluid a little at a time, and keep checking the level as previously described until it is correct. The difference between the "MIN" and "MAX" marks on the dipstick is approximately 0.5 litre.

8 If the vehicle has not been driven and the engine and transmission are cold, carry out the procedures in paragraphs 3 to 7, but use the side of the dipstick marked "COLD".

9 The need for regular topping-up of the transmission fluid indicates a leak, which should be found and rectified without delay.

10 The condition of the fluid should also be checked along with the level. If the fluid at the end of the dipstick is black or a dark reddish-brown colour, or if it has a burned smell, the fluid should be changed. If you are in doubt about the condition of the fluid, purchase some new fluid, and compare the two for colour and smell. Refer to Chapter 7B for further information.

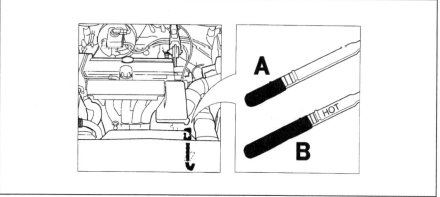

19.4 Automatic transmission fluid dipstick location and markings

20 Air conditioning system check

Warning: The air conditioning system is under high pressure. Do not loosen any fittings or remove any components until after the system has been discharged. Air conditioning refrigerant must be properly discharged into an approved type of container, at a dealer service department or an automotive air conditioning repair facility capable of handling the refrigerant safely. Always wear eye protection when disconnecting air conditioning system fittings.

1 The following maintenance checks should be performed on a regular basis, to ensure that the system continues to operate at peak efficiency:

a) *Check the auxiliary drivebelt. If it's worn or deteriorated, renew it (see Section 21).*

b) *Check the system hoses. Look for cracks, bubbles, hard spots and deterioration.*

Inspect the hoses and all fittings for oil bubbles and seepage. If there's any evidence of wear, damage or leaks, renew the hose(s).

c) *Inspect the condenser fins for leaves, insects and other debris. Use a "fin comb" or compressed air to clean the condenser.*

Warning: Wear eye protection when using compressed air!

d) *Check that the drain tube from the front of the evaporator is clear - note that it is normal to have clear fluid (water) dripping from this while the system is in operation, to the extent that quite a large puddle can be left under the vehicle when it is parked.*

2 It's a good idea to operate the system for about 30 minutes at least once a month, particularly during the winter. Long term non-use can cause hardening, and subsequent failure, of the seals.

3 Because of the complexity of the air conditioning system and the special equipment necessary to service it, in-depth repairs are not included in this manual, apart from those procedures covered in Chapter 3.

4 The most common cause of poor cooling is simply a low system refrigerant charge. If a noticeable drop in cool air output occurs, the following quick check will help you determine if the refrigerant level is low.

5 Warm the engine up to normal operating temperature.

6 Place the air conditioning temperature selector at the coldest setting, and put the blower at the highest setting. Open the doors - to make sure the air conditioning system doesn't cycle off as soon as it cools the passenger compartment.

7 With the compressor engaged - the clutch will make an audible click, and the centre of the clutch will rotate - feel the inlet and outlet pipes at the compressor. One side should be cold, and one hot. If there's no perceptible difference between the two pipes, there's something wrong with the compressor or the system. It might be a low charge - it might be something else. Take the vehicle to a dealer service department or an automotive air conditioning specialist.

Every 20 000 miles (32 000 km) or two years

21 Auxiliary drivebelt check and renewal

1 The auxiliary drivebelt transmits power from the crankshaft pulley to the alternator, steering pump and air conditioning compressor (as applicable).

Check

2 With the engine switched off, open and support the bonnet, then locate the accessory drivebelt at the crankshaft pulley end of the engine.

Warning: Be very careful, and wear protective gloves to minimise the risk of burning your hands on hot components, if the engine has recently been running.

3 Using an inspection light or a small electric torch, and rotating the engine when necessary with a spanner applied to the crankshaft pulley nut, check the whole length of the drivebelt for cracks, separation of the rubber, and torn or worn ribs. Also check for fraying and glazing, which gives the drivebelt a shiny appearance. Both sides of the drivebelt should be inspected, which means you will have to twist the drivebelt to check the underside. Use your fingers to feel the drivebelt where you can't see it. If you are in any doubt as to the condition of the drivebelt, renew it. As there is minimal working clearance, it may be beneficial to jack up and support the front of the car on axle stands. Then, with the roadwheel removed the inner wheel arch panel can be folded back to give access to the crankshaft pulley.

Renewal

4 The correct drivebelt tension is continually maintained by an automatic adjuster and tensioner assembly. This device is bolted to the front of the engine and incorporates a spring-loaded idler pulley.

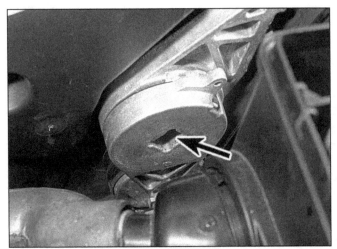

21.5 Square hole in auxiliary drivebelt tensioner bracket arm (arrowed)

21.6 Using the home-made tool (metal strip) to release the tensioner

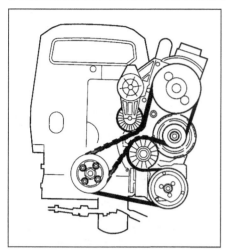

21.8 Auxiliary drivebelt arrangement over the various pulleys

Dotted line shows belt run on cars without air conditioning

5 To release the tensioner idler pulley to allow removal of the belt, observe the tensioner bracket arm which will have either a three eighths inch, or three quarter inch square hole in its centre **(see illustration)**. This is to allow the square end of a standard socket set extension bar to be inserted into the hole to move the bracket against the tension of the spring. In practice, there is so little clearance between the engine and side of the inner wing that it's virtually impossible to insert the socket bar. However, there is an alternative solution!

6 Obtain a strip of metal wide enough to fit diagonally across the square slot. Cut the metal strip so it just protrudes beyond the hole. You can now turn the strip of metal (and hence the tensioner bracket arm) with an adjustable spanner or a pair of grips **(see illustration)**.

7 Turn the tensioner bracket arm to release

the belt tension, then slip the belt off all the pulleys. Release the tensioner and remove the belt.

8 Turn the tensioner as necessary, and fit the new belt over the pulleys as shown, ensuring that it is properly seated **(see illustration)**. Release the tensioner which will now automatically take up the adjustment.

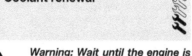

22 Coolant renewal

⚠️ **Warning: Wait until the engine is cold before starting this procedure. Do not allow antifreeze to come into contact with your skin, or with painted surfaces of the vehicle. Rinse off spills immediately with plenty of water. Never leave antifreeze lying around in an open container, or in a puddle in the driveway or on the garage floor. Children and pets are attracted by its sweet smell, but antifreeze can be fatal if ingested.**
Note: *If Volvo type C coolant, in the specified ratio, has been continuously maintained in the system, then coolant renewal will not normally be necessary. However, to be absolutely sure about the integrity of the antifreeze and anti-corrosion properties of the coolant, periodic renewal is to be recommended.*

Coolant draining

1 To drain the system, first remove the expansion tank filler cap (see *"Weekly checks"*). Move the heater temperature control to the hot position.

2 If the additional working clearance is required, raise the front of the vehicle and support it securely on axle stands (see *"Jacking and vehicle support"*).

3 Remove the undertray under the radiator and, where fitted, the engine undertray, then place a large drain tray underneath the radiator. Open the drain tap at the bottom left-

hand corner of the radiator and allow the coolant to drain into the tray **(see illustration)**.

4 When the radiator has drained, move the tray to the rear right-hand side of the engine and unscrew the cylinder block drain tap **(see illustration)**. Allow the cylinder block to drain.

System flushing

5 With time, the cooling system may gradually lose its efficiency, as the radiator core becomes choked with rust, scale deposits from the water, and other sediment. This is especially likely if an inferior grade of antifreeze has been used that has not been regularly renewed. To minimise this, as well as using only the specified type of antifreeze and clean soft water, the system should be flushed as follows whenever any part of it is disturbed, and/or when the coolant is renewed.

6 With the coolant drained, close the drain taps and refill the system with fresh water. Refit the expansion tank filler cap, start the engine and warm it up to normal operating temperature, then stop it and (after allowing it to cool down completely) drain the system again. Repeat as necessary until only clean water can be seen to emerge, then refill finally with the specified coolant mixture.

7 If only clean, soft water and good-quality antifreeze has been used, and the coolant has been renewed at the specified intervals, the above procedure will be sufficient to keep the system clean for a considerable length of time. If, however, the system has been neglected, a more thorough operation will be required, as follows.

8 First drain the coolant, then disconnect the radiator top and bottom hoses. Insert a garden hose into the top hose, and allow water to circulate through the radiator until it runs clean from the bottom outlet.

9 To flush the engine, remove the thermostat (see Chapter 3), insert the garden hose into the thermostat housing, and allow water to circulate until it runs clear from the bottom

22.3 Radiator drain tap location (arrowed)

22.4 Cylinder block drain tap location (arrowed)

hose. If, after a reasonable period, the water still does not run clear, the radiator should be flushed with a good proprietary cleaning agent.

10 In severe cases of contamination, reverse-flushing of the radiator may be necessary. To do this, remove the radiator (see Chapter 3), invert it, and insert the garden hose into the bottom outlet. Continue flushing until clear water runs from the top hose outlet. A similar procedure can be used to flush the heater matrix.

11 The use of chemical cleaners should be necessary only as a last resort. Normally, regular renewal of the coolant will prevent excessive contamination of the system.

Coolant filling

12 With the cooling system drained and flushed, ensure that all disturbed components or hose unions are correctly fitted, and that the two drain taps are securely tightened. Refit the engine undertrays removed for access. If it was raised, lower the vehicle to the ground.

13 Prepare a sufficient quantity of the specified coolant mixture (see "Specifications"); allow for a surplus, so as to have a reserve supply for topping-up.

14 Slowly fill the system through the expansion tank; since the tank is the highest point in the system, all the air in the system should be displaced into the tank by the rising liquid. Slow pouring reduces the possibility of air being trapped and forming air-locks. It helps also, if the large radiator hoses are gently squeezed during the filling procedure.

15 Continue filling until the coolant level reaches the expansion tank "MAX" level line, then refit the expansion tank cap.

16 Start the engine and run it at idle speed, until it has warmed-up to normal operating temperature. If the level in the expansion tank drops significantly, top-up to the "MAX" level line, to minimise the amount of air circulating in the system.

17 Stop the engine, allow it to cool down *completely* (overnight, if possible), then remove the expansion tank filler cap and top-up the tank to the "MAX" level line. Refit the filler cap, tightening it securely, and wash off any spilt coolant from the engine compartment and bodywork.

18 After refilling, always check carefully all components of the system (but especially any unions disturbed during draining and flushing) for signs of coolant leaks. Fresh antifreeze has a searching action, which will rapidly expose any weak points in the system.

Note: *If, after draining and refilling the system, symptoms of overheating are found which did not occur previously, then the fault is almost certainly due to trapped air at some point in the system, causing an air-lock and restricting the flow of coolant; usually, the air is trapped because the system was refilled too quickly. In* *some cases, air-locks can be released by tapping or squeezing the various hoses. If the problem persists, stop the engine and allow it to cool down completely, before unscrewing the expansion tank filler cap or disconnecting hoses to bleed out the trapped air.*

23 Brake fluid renewal

 Warning: Brake hydraulic fluid can harm your eyes and damage painted surfaces, so use extreme caution when handling and pouring it. Do not use fluid that has been standing open for some time as it absorbs moisture from the air. Excess moisture can cause a dangerous loss of braking effectiveness.

The procedure is similar to that for the bleeding of the hydraulic system as described in Chapter 9, except that the brake fluid reservoir should be emptied by siphoning, and allowance should be made for the old fluid to be removed from the circuit when bleeding a section of the circuit.

 Old hydraulic fluid is invariably much darker in colour than the new, making it easy to distinguish between the two.

Every 30 000 miles (48 000 km) or three years

24 Distributor cap, rotor arm and HT lead check

 Warning: Voltages produced by an electronic ignition system are considerably higher than those produced by conventional ignition systems. Extreme care must be taken when working on the system if the ignition is switched on. Persons with surgically-implanted cardiac pacemaker devices should keep well clear of the ignition circuits, components and test equipment.

1 The spark plug (HT) leads should be inspected one at a time, to prevent mixing up the firing order, which is essential for proper engine operation. Gain access to the leads and disconnect them as described for the spark plug check and renewal.

2 Check inside the boot for corrosion, which will look like a white crusty powder. Clean this off as much as possible; if it is excessive, or if cleaning leaves the metal connector too badly corroded to be fit for further use, the lead must be renewed. Push the lead and boot back onto the end of the spark plug. The boot should fit tightly onto the end of the plug - if it doesn't, remove the lead and use pliers carefully to crimp the metal connector inside the boot until the fit is snug.

3 Using a clean rag, wipe the entire length of the lead to remove built-up dirt and grease. Once the lead is clean, check for burns, cracks and other damage. Do not bend the lead sharply, because the conductor might break.

4 Inspect the remaining spark plug (HT) leads, ensuring that each is securely fastened at the distributor cap and spark plug when the check is complete. If any sign of arcing, severe connector corrosion, burns, cracks or other damage is noticed, obtain new spark plug (HT) leads, renewing them as a set.

 If new spark plug leads are to be fitted, remove the leads one at a time and fit each new lead in exactly the same position as the old one.

5 Refer to Chapter 5B and remove the distributor cap then thoroughly clean it inside and out with a dry lint-free rag.

6 Examine the HT lead segments inside the cap. If they appear badly burned or pitted, renew the cap. Also check the carbon brush in the centre of the cap, ensuring that it is free to move and stands proud of its holder. Make sure that there are no sign of cracks or black "tracking" lines running down the inside of the cap, which will also mean renewal if evident.

7 Inspect the rotor arm checking it for security and also for signs of deterioration as described above.

8 Refit the cap as described in Chapter 5B on completion.

25 Spark plug renewal

1 It is vital for the correct running, full performance and proper economy of the engine that the spark plugs perform with maximum efficiency. The most important factor in ensuring this, is that the plugs fitted are appropriate for the engine (a suitable type is specified at the beginning of this Chapter). If this type is used and the engine is in good condition, the spark plugs should not need attention between scheduled renewal intervals. Spark plug cleaning is rarely necessary, and should not be attempted unless specialised equipment is available, as damage can easily be caused to the firing ends.

25.3 Remove the spark plug cover

25.5 Pull off the HT leads by gripping the rubber boot, not the lead itself

2 Spark plug removal and refitting requires a spark plug socket, with an extension which can be turned by a ratchet handle or similar. This socket is lined with a rubber sleeve, to protect the porcelain insulator of the spark plug, and to hold the plug while you insert it into the spark plug hole. You will also need a wire-type feeler blade, to check and adjust the spark plug electrode gap, and a torque wrench to tighten the new plugs to the specified torque.

3 To remove the spark plugs, open the bonnet, undo the screws and remove the spark plug cover in the centre of the cylinder head **(see illustration)**. Note the location of the spark plug HT lead grommet inside the cover and how it is fitted. Note also how the HT leads are routed and secured by clips along the top of the cylinder head. To prevent the possibility of mixing up HT leads, it is a good idea to try to work on one spark plug at a time.

4 If the marks on the original-equipment HT leads cannot be seen, mark the leads 1 to 5, to correspond to the cylinder the lead serves.

5 Pull the leads from the plugs by gripping the rubber boot, not the lead, otherwise the lead connection may be fractured **(see illustration)**.

6 Unscrew the spark plugs, ensuring that the socket is kept in alignment with each plug - if the socket is forcibly moved to either side, the porcelain top of the plug may be broken off **(see illustration)**. If any undue difficulty is encountered when unscrewing any of the spark plugs, carefully check the cylinder head threads and sealing surfaces for signs of wear, excessive corrosion or damage; if any of these conditions is found, seek the advice of a dealer as to the best method of repair.

7 As each plug is removed, examine it as follows - this will give a good indication of the condition of the engine. If the insulator nose of the spark plug is clean and white, with no deposits, this is indicative of a weak mixture.

8 If the tip and insulator nose are covered with hard black-looking deposits, then this is indicative that the mixture is too rich. Should the plug be black and oily, then it is likely that the engine is fairly worn, as well as the mixture being too rich.

9 If the insulator nose is covered with light tan to greyish-brown deposits, then the mixture is correct, and it is likely that the engine is in good condition.

10 The spark plug electrode gap is of considerable importance as, if it is too large or too small, the size of the spark and its efficiency will be seriously impaired. The gap should be set to the value given in the *Specifications*.

11 To set the electrode gap, measure the gap with a feeler blade or adjusting tool, and then bend open, or closed, the outer plug electrode until the correct gap is achieved **(see illustration)**. The centre electrode should never be bent, as this may crack the insulation and cause plug failure, if nothing worse. If the outer electrode is not exactly over the centre electrode, bend it gently to align them.

25.6 Unscrew the spark plugs using a spark plug socket

25.11 Adjusting a spark plug electrode gap

12 Before fitting the spark plugs, check that the threaded connector sleeves at the top of the plugs are tight, and that the plug exterior surfaces and threads are clean.

13 On installing the spark plugs, first check that the cylinder head thread and sealing surface are as clean as possible; use a clean rag wrapped around a paintbrush to wipe clean the sealing surface. Ensure that the spark plug threads are clean and dry then screw them in by hand where possible. Take extra care to enter the plug threads correctly.

14 When each spark plug is started correctly on its threads, screw it down until it just seats lightly, then tighten it to the specified torque wrench setting.

15 Reconnect the HT leads in their correct order, using a twisting motion on the boot until it is firmly seated. Finally, refit the spark plug cover.

HAYNES HiNT

It's often difficult to insert spark plugs into their holes without cross-threading them. To avoid this possibility, fit a short piece of rubber hose over the end of the spark plug. The flexible hose acts as a universal joint, to help align the plug with the plug hole. Should the plug begin to crossthread, the hose will slip on the spark plug, preventing thread damage.

Every 40 000 miles (64 000 km) or four years

26.2 Release the HT lead from the clips at the rear of the air cleaner cover

26 Air cleaner element renewal

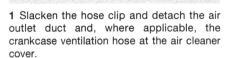

1 Slacken the hose clip and detach the air outlet duct and, where applicable, the crankcase ventilation hose at the air cleaner cover.

2 Disconnect the mass air flow sensor or inlet air temperature sensor wiring connector at the rear of the air inlet on the air cleaner cover. Release the HT lead leading to the ignition coil from the clips at the rear of the cover **(see illustration)**.

3 Release the clips which secure the air cleaner cover to the housing **(see illustration)**.

4 Lift off the cover, and remove the air cleaner element **(see illustration)**.

5 Wipe clean inside the housing and cover with a cloth. Be careful not to sweep debris into the air inlet.

6 Fit the new element, making sure it is the right way up. Press the seal on the rim of the element into the groove on the housing.

7 Refit the cover and secure it with the clips.

8 When applicable, reconnect the sensor wiring connector and secure the HT lead with its clips.

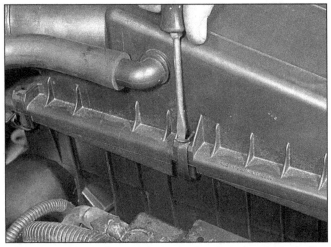

26.3 Release the clips which secure the air cleaner cover to the housing

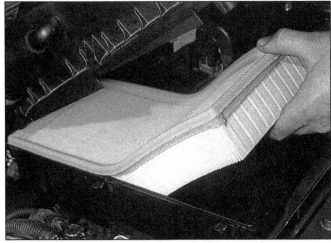

26.4 Lift off the cover, and remove the air cleaner element

Every 50 000 miles (80 000 km) or five years

27 Fuel filter renewal

27.1 Fuel filter location, hose couplings and mounting strap

⚠ *Warning: Before carrying out the following operation, refer to the precautions given in "Safety first!" at the beginning of this manual, and follow them implicitly. Petrol is a highly dangerous and volatile liquid, and the precautions necessary when handling it cannot be overstressed.*

1 The fuel filter is located under the rear of the car, just forward of the fuel tank **(see illustration)**.

2 Disconnect the battery negative lead.

3 Raise the rear of the vehicle on ramps or drive it over a pit (see *"Jacking and vehicle support"*).

4 Thoroughly clean the area around the fuel pipe couplings at each end of the filter, then cover both with absorbent rags.

5 Disconnect the quick-release couplings using a 17 mm spanner to push back the coupling sleeves. Be prepared for an initial release of fuel under pressure as the couplings are released. Plug the couplings after disconnection to prevent further loss of fuel.

6 Undo the filter mounting strap retaining bolt and remove the filter.

7 Fit the new filter, making sure it is the same way round as the old one. Observe the arrow on the new filter showing the direction of fuel flow.

8 Secure the filter with the mounting strap then push the fuel pipe couplings back on the filter outlets.

9 Reconnect the battery. Run the engine and check that there are no leaks.

⚠ *Warning: Dispose of the old filter safely; it will be highly flammable and may explode if thrown on a fire.*

28 Emission control equipment check

Of the emission control systems that may be fitted, only the crankcase ventilation system and the evaporative emission control systems requires regular checking, and even then, the components of this system require minimal attention. Details of these checks will be found in Chapter 4B.

Should it be felt that the other systems are not functioning correctly, the advice of a dealer should be sought.

29 Timing belt renewal - 1992/93 models with 21mm wide belt

Refer to Chapter 2A.

Every 80 000 miles (129 000 km)

30 Timing belt renewal - 1994-on models with 23mm wide belt

Refer to Chapter 2A.

Notes

Chapter 2 Part A:
Engine in-car repair procedures

Contents

Degrees of difficulty

| Easy, suitable for novice with little experience | | Fairly easy, suitable for beginner with some experience | | Fairly difficult, suitable for competent DIY mechanic | | Difficult, suitable for experienced DIY mechanic | | Very difficult, suitable for expert DIY or professional | |

Specifications

General

Identification:
B5202 S	1984 cc, 10-valve, normally-aspirated
B5204 S	1984 cc, 20-valve, normally-aspirated
B5204 T	1984 cc, 20-valve, turbocharged
B5234 S	2319 cc, 20-valve, normally-aspirated
B5234 T/T5	2319 cc, 20-valve, turbocharged
B5252 S	2435 cc, 10-valve, normally-aspirated
B5254 S	2435 cc, 20-valve, normally-aspirated

Bore:
All engines except B5252 S and B5254 S	81.0 mm
B5252 S and B5254 S engines	83.0 mm

Stroke:
B5202 S, B5204 S, B5204 T engines	77.0 mm
B5234 S, B5234 T/ T5, B5252 S, B5254 S engines	90.0 mm

Compression ratio:
B5202 S	10.0 : 1
B5204 S	10.3 : 1
B5204 T	8.4 : 1
B5234 S	10.5 : 1
B5234 T/T5	8.5 : 1
B5252 S	10.0 : 1
B5254 S	10.5 : 1

Compression pressure:
Normally-aspirated engines	13 to 15 bars
Turbocharged engines	11 to 13 bars
Variation between cylinders	2 bars maximum
Firing order	1-2-4-5-3 (No 1 at timing belt end of engine)
Direction of crankshaft rotation	Clockwise (viewed from front of engine)

Camshaft

Identification letter (stamped on end):

B5202 S	HAI (Inlet)	HFE (Exhaust)
B5204 S	PGI (Inlet)	PGE (Exhaust)
B5204 T	PHI (Inlet)	PHE (Exhaust)
B5234 S	PGI (Inlet)	PGE (Exhaust)
B5234 T/T5	PHI (Inlet)	PHE (Exhaust)
B5252 S	HEI (Inlet)	HEE (Exhaust)
B5254 S:		
With LH3.2-Jetronic fuel injection system	PGI (Inlet)	PGE (Exhaust)
With Motronic 4.3 engine management system	PLI (Inlet)	PFE (Exhaust)

Maximum lift (inlet and exhaust):

B5202 S	9.60 mm
B5204 S	8.45 mm
B5204 T	7.95 mm
B5234 S	8.45 mm
B5234 T/T5	7.95 mm
B5252 S	9.60 mm
B5254 S	8.45 mm
Camshaft endfloat	0.05 to 0.20 mm

Tappets (cam followers)

Diameter:

10-valve engines	34.959 to 35.025 mm
20-valve engines	31.959 to 32.025 mm
Height	25.500 to 26.500 mm

Lubrication system

Oil pressure (warm engine @ 4000 rpm)	3.5 bars
Oil pump type	Gear, driven from crankshaft
Maximum pump gear to housing clearance	0.35 mm
Pressure relief valve spring free height	82.13 mm

Torque wrench settings*

	Nm
Timing belt tensioner bolts	25
Timing belt tensioner pulley	40
Timing belt idler pulley	25
Camshaft sprocket bolts	20
Cylinder head upper section to lower section	17
Cylinder head lower section to block:**	
Stage 1	20
Stage 2	60
Stage 3	Tighten through a further 130°
Crankshaft pulley to sprocket bolts:	
Stage 1	25
Stage 2	Tighten through a further 30°
Crankshaft sprocket centre nut	180
Oil pump to cylinder block	10
Flywheel/driveplate**	
Stage 1	45
Stage 2	Tighten through a further 50°
Upper engine steady bar to engine bracket:	
Early models (M8 bolt):**	
Stage 1	18
Stage 2	Tighten through a further 120°
Later models (M10 bolt):**	
Stage 1	35
Stage 2	Tighten through a further 90°
Upper engine steady bar to bulkhead bracket:	
Stage 1	35
Stage 2	Tighten through a further 60°
Upper engine steady bar bracket to engine:	
Upper nut	25
Lower bolts:**	
Stage 1	45
Stage 2	Tighten through a further 90°
Lower engine steady bar bracket to transmission:**	
Stage 1	35
Stage 2	Tighten through a further 40°

Lower engine steady bar bracket to subframe:
   Early models (M8 bolt)   30
   Later models (M12 bolt):**
      Stage 1   65
      Stage 2 . . . .   Tighten through a further 60°
Lower engine steady bar bushes to brackets:**
   Stage 1   35
   Stage 2 . . . .   Tighten through a further 90°
Front/rear engine mounting nuts/bolts   50
Right-hand engine mounting to subframe:**
   Stage 1   65
   Stage 2 . . . .   Tighten through a further 60°
Right-hand engine mounting bracket to engine:
   10 mm bolts:**
      Stage 1   35
      Stage 2 . . . .   Tighten through a further 60°
   8 mm bolt:**
      Stage 1   20
      Stage 2 . . . .   Tighten through a further 60°
Right-hand engine mounting to engine bracket:**
   Stage 1   35
   Stage 2 . . . .   Tighten through a further 90°
Rear engine mounting bracket to transmission   50
Front engine mounting bracket to transmission   25
Roadwheel bolts   110

Oiled threads unless otherwise stated
New nuts/bolts must always be used

1   General information

How to use this Chapter

This Part of Chapter 2 describes those repair procedures that can reasonably be carried out on the engine while it remains in the car. If the engine has been removed from the car and is being dismantled as described in Part B, any preliminary dismantling procedures can be ignored.

Note that, while it may be possible physically to overhaul items such as the piston/connecting rod assemblies while the engine is in the car, such tasks are not normally carried out as separate operations. Usually, several additional procedures (not to mention the cleaning of components and oilways) have to be carried out. For this reason, all such tasks are classed as major overhaul procedures, and are described in Part B of this Chapter.

Part B describes the removal of the engine/transmission from the vehicle, and the full overhaul procedures that can then be carried out.

Engine description

The five-cylinder engine is of the double overhead camshaft type incorporating two or four valves per cylinder according to type. The cylinders are in line and the engine is mounted transversely on a subframe in the engine bay. The B5202 and 5204 engines are all of 2.0 litre capacity, the B5234 is of 2.3 litre capacity, while the B5252 and B5254 engines are 2.5 litre units.

The entire engine is constructed of aluminium and consists of five sections. The cylinder head comprises an upper and lower section, with the cylinder block, intermediate section and sump forming the other three. The upper and lower sections of the cylinder head are mated along the centre line of the camshafts, while the cylinder block and intermediate section are mated along the crankshaft centre line. A conventional cylinder head gasket is used between the cylinder head and block, with liquid gaskets being used in the joints between the other main sections.

The cylinder block incorporates five cast iron dry cylinder liners which are cast into the block and cannot be replaced. Cast iron reinforcements are also used in the intermediate section as strengthening agents in the main bearing areas.

Drive to the camshaft is by a toothed timing belt and sprockets and incorporating an automatic tensioning mechanism. The timing belt also drives the coolant pump. All accessories are driven from the crankshaft pulley by a single multi-ribbed auxiliary drivebelt.

The cylinder head is of the crossflow type, the inlet ports being at the front of the engine and the exhaust ports at the rear. The upper section of the cylinder head functions as a combined valve cover and camshaft cover, the camshafts run in six plain bearings integral to the two cylinder head sections. Valve actuation is by maintenance free hydraulic tappets acted upon directly by the camshaft lobes. The 2.0 and 2.5 litre engines are available in ten or twenty valve configuration while the 2.3 litre engines are all twenty valve units.

The crankshaft runs in six shell type main bearings; the connecting rod big-end bearings are also of the shell type. Crankshaft endfloat is taken by thrustwashers which are an integral part of the No 5 main bearing shells.

The lubrication system is of the full-flow, pressure-feed type. Oil is drawn from the sump by a gear type pump, driven from the front of the crankshaft. Oil under pressure passes through a filter before being fed to the various shaft bearings and to the valve gear. On turbo models, an external oil cooler is fitted which is incorporated in the radiator side tank. Turbo models also have an oil feed and return for the turbocharger bearings.

Repair operations possible with the engine in the car

The following work can be carried out with the engine in the car:

a) *Compression pressure - testing*
b) *Timing belt - removal and refitting.*
c) *Camshaft oil seals - renewal.*
d) *Camshafts and tappets - removal and refitting.*
e) *Cylinder head - removal and refitting.*
f) *Cylinder head and pistons - decarbonising.*
g) *Crankshaft oil seals - renewal.*
h) *Oil pump - removal and refitting.*
i) *Flywheel/driveplate - removal and refitting.*
j) *Engine mountings - removal and refitting.*

2 Compression test - description and interpretation

1 When engine performance is down, or if misfiring occurs which cannot be attributed to the ignition or fuel systems, a compression test can provide diagnostic clues as to the engine's condition. If the test is performed regularly, it can give warning of trouble before any other symptoms become apparent.

2 The engine must be fully warmed-up to normal operating temperature, the battery must be fully charged, and all the spark plugs must be removed (Chapter 1). The aid of an assistant will also be required.

3 Disable the ignition system by disconnecting the RPM sensor wiring at the connector located just below and to the rear of the distributor. Also disconnect the wiring connectors to each fuel injector to prevent fuel from damaging the catalytic converter.

4 Fit a compression tester to the No 1 cylinder spark plug hole - the type of tester which screws into the plug thread is to be preferred.

5 Have the assistant hold the throttle wide open, and crank the engine on the starter motor; after one or two revolutions, the compression pressure should build up to a maximum figure, and then stabilise. Record the highest reading obtained.

6 Repeat the test on the remaining cylinders, recording the pressure in each.

7 All cylinders should produce very similar pressures; a difference of more than 2 bars between any two cylinders indicates a fault. Note that the compression should build up quickly in a healthy engine; low compression on the first stroke, followed by gradually-increasing pressure on successive strokes, indicates worn piston rings. A low compression reading on the first stroke, which does not build up during successive strokes, indicates leaking valves or a blown head

gasket (a cracked head could also be the cause). Deposits on the undersides of the valve heads can also cause low compression.

8 If the pressure in any cylinder is low, carry out the following test to isolate the cause. Introduce a teaspoonful of clean oil into that cylinder through its spark plug hole, and repeat the test.

9 If the addition of oil temporarily improves the compression pressure, this indicates that bore or piston wear is responsible for the pressure loss. No improvement suggests that leaking or burnt valves, or a blown head gasket, may be to blame.

10 A low reading from two adjacent cylinders is almost certainly due to the head gasket having blown between them; the presence of coolant in the engine oil will confirm this.

11 If one cylinder is about 20 percent lower than the others and the engine has a slightly rough idle, a worn camshaft lobe could be the cause.

12 If the compression reading is unusually high, the combustion chambers are probably coated with carbon deposits. If this is the case, the cylinder head should be removed and decarbonised.

13 On completion of the test, refit the spark plugs and reconnect the ignition system and fuel injectors.

3 Timing belt - removal and refitting

Removal

1 Disconnect the battery negative lead.

2 Remove the auxiliary drivebelt as described in Chapter 1.

3 Lift the cooling system expansion tank out of its mounting bracket and place it to one side.

4 Where applicable, release the turbocharger inlet ducting then undo the screws and

3.6 Removing the timing belt cover

remove the spark plug cover from the centre of the cylinder head.

5 Undo the bolts securing the two fuel pipe clamps to the top of the engine and remove the clamps.

6 Undo the bolt and remove the timing belt front cover **(see illustration)**.

7 Jack up the front of the car and support it on axle stands (see *"Jacking and vehicle support"*). Remove the right-hand front roadwheel.

8 Release the fasteners securing the inner wheel arch liner, and fold back the liner for access to the crankshaft pulley **(see illustration)**.

9 Undo the bolts and remove the timing belt guard plate from behind the crankshaft pulley **(see illustration)**.

10 Using a socket on the crankshaft pulley centre nut, rotate the crankshaft clockwise (viewed from the right-hand side of the car) until the timing marks on the camshaft sprocket rims align with the notches on the timing belt rear cover. In this position, the timing mark on the crankshaft sprocket should also be aligned with the cast projection on the oil pump housing **(see illustrations)**. These marks are not at all easy to see - the camshaft sprocket marks being hardly more than faint scratches on the edges of the sprockets. Similarly, the mark on the

3.8 Release the fasteners and fold back the wheel arch liner

3.9 Remove the timing belt guard plate

3.10a Timing marks on camshaft sprockets (A) aligned with the notches (B) on the belt rear cover

3.10b Timing mark on crankshaft sprocket (A) aligned with projection on oil pump housing

crankshaft sprocket is in reality a barely discernible indentation at the root of a sprocket tooth, which can be just about seen from above. It will probably take two or three attempts until you are sure that the marks are correctly aligned.

11 Undo the timing belt tensioner upper retaining bolt and slacken the lower one **(see illustration)**. Move the tensioner assembly anti-clockwise to free it from the tensioner pulley.

12 Remove the previously slackened tensioner lower bolt and remove the tensioner. On some models there is a plastic horseshoe shaped spacer collar fitted to the top of the tensioner. Collect this collar (if fitted) which will fall out at this stage **(see illustration)**.

13 Undo the bolts and lift off the timing belt rear cover.

14 Mark the running direction of the belt if it is to be re-used, then slip it off the sprockets tensioner and idler pulleys and remove it. Clearance is very limited at the crankshaft sprocket and a certain amount of manipulation is necessary. Do not rotate the crankshaft or camshafts with the belt removed.

15 Spin the tensioner and idler pulleys and check for roughness or shake; renew if necessary. Check that the tensioner pulley arm is free to move up and down under the action of the tensioner. If the arm is at all stiff, remove the unit, clean it thoroughly, then lubricate sparingly and refit.

16 Check the timing belt carefully for any signs of uneven wear, splitting, or oil contamination. Pay particular attention to the roots of the teeth. Renew the belt if there is the slightest doubt about its condition. If the engine is undergoing an overhaul, and has covered more than 36 000 miles (60 000 km) with the existing belt fitted, renew the belt as a matter of course, regardless of its apparent condition. The cost of a new belt is nothing when compared to the cost of repairs, should the belt break in service. If signs of oil contamination are found, trace the source of the oil leak, and rectify it. Wash down the engine timing belt area and all related components, to remove all traces of oil.

17 Renew the tensioner assembly if there are signs of oil leaks, if there is no resistance to compression of the plunger, or if the plunger cannot be compressed.

Refitting and tensioning

18 Prior to refitting the timing belt, it is necessary to compress and lock the tensioner plunger ready for installation. To do this, mount the assembly in a vice with protected jaws, with the jaws in contact with the tensioner body and the plunger. Tighten the vice until resistance is felt, then tighten it very slowly a little further. Pause for a few seconds and tighten slowly a little further again. Continue this procedure until the hole in the tensioner body and corresponding hole in the plunger are aligned. It will probably take about five minutes to do this; don't rush it or the internal seals will be damaged by trying to

3.11 Timing belt tensioner retaining bolts (arrowed)

3.12 Where fitted, remove the tensioner spacer collar

3.18 Lock the compressed tensioner using a 2.0 mm diameter twist drill

force oil between the internal chambers too quickly. When the two holes are finally aligned, insert a 2.0 mm diameter rod (a twist drill is ideal) through all the holes to lock the assembly **(see illustration)**.

19 Refit the locked tensioner to the engine and secure with the two bolts tightened to the specified torque.

20 Before refitting the timing belt, make sure that the sprockets are in the correct positions (paragraph 10). It will be necessary to temporarily refit the timing belt rear cover to do this. Slip the belt over the crankshaft sprocket, keep it taught and feed it over the idler pulley, front camshaft sprocket, rear camshaft sprocket, coolant pump sprocket and finally over the tensioner pulley. Observe the correct running direction if the old belt is being re-used.

21 Recheck the alignment of the sprocket marks, then release the belt tensioner by pulling out the locking pin with pliers. Check that the tensioner plunger moves out to tension the belt.

22 Refit the timing belt rear cover and secure with the two bolts, noting that the fuel pipe clip bracket is fitted under the rear bolt head.

23 Turn the crankshaft clockwise through two complete revolutions then check that all the timing marks can be realigned.

24 When all is correct, refit the horseshoe shaped spacer collar (where fitted) to the top of the tensioner.

25 Refit the timing belt guard plate behind the crankshaft pulley.

26 Fold back the wheel arch liner and secure with the fasteners.

27 Refit the roadwheel and lower the car to the ground. Tighten the wheel bolts in a diagonal sequence to the specified torque.

28 Refit the timing belt front cover and the two fuel pipe clamps.

29 Refit the spark plug cover and cooling system expansion tank.

30 Refit the auxiliary drivebelt as described in Chapter 1, then reconnect the battery.

4 Camshaft front oil seals - renewal

Note: For this procedure the Volvo camshaft locking tool 999 5452 will be required to prevent the camshafts from rotating while the sprockets are removed. Details for fabricating a home-made alternative are given in the text. Do not attempt to carry out the work without locking the camshafts or the valve timing will be irretrievably lost.

1 Remove the timing belt as described in Section 3.

2 If both camshaft sprockets are to be removed, suitably mark them, inlet and exhaust for identification when refitting. The inlet sprocket is nearest the front of the car.

3 Undo the three bolts and remove the appropriate sprocket for access to the failed seal. Restrain the sprockets with a suitable tool through the holes in their faces **(see Tool Tip)**.

4 Withdraw the appropriate sprocket from the camshaft **(see illustration)**.

5 Carefully extract the seal by prising it out

To make a camshaft sprocket holding tool, obtain two lengths of steel strip about 6 mm thick by 30 mm wide or similar, one 600 mm long, the other 200 mm long (all dimensions approximate). Bolt the two strips together to form a forked end, leaving the bolt slack so that the shorter strip can pivot freely. At the end of each 'prong' of the fork, bend the strips through 90° about 50 mm from their ends to act as the fulcrums; these will engage with the holes in the sprockets. It may be necessary to grind or cut off their sides slightly to allow them to fit the sprocket holes.

with a small screwdriver or hooked tool. Do not damage the shaft sealing face.

6 Clean the seal seat. Examine the shaft sealing face for wear or damage which could cause premature failure of the new seal.

7 Lubricate the new oil seal. Fit the seal over the shaft, lips inwards, and tap it home with a large socket or piece of tube until its outer face is flush with the housing **(see illustration)**.

8 Refer to Chapter 4A and remove the air cleaner assembly and inlet ducts as necessary for clear access to the rear end of both camshafts.

4.4 Removing the inlet camshaft sprocket

4.7 Fit the oil seal over the shaft, lips inwards

4.9 Remove the steady bar from the engine bracket

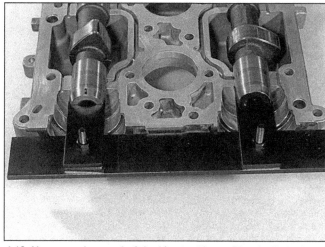

4.18 Home-made camshaft locking tool in position (cylinder head upper section shown removed for clarity)

9 Undo the nut and remove the bolt securing the upper engine steady bar to the bracket on the engine **(see illustration)**. Note that a new nut and bolt will be required for refitting.

10 Undo the nut securing the other end of the engine steady bar to the bulkhead bracket. Swing the steady bar to one side. Note that a new nut and bolt will be required for refitting.

11 Undo the upper nut and two lower bolts securing the steady bar bracket to the side of the engine. Note the location of the wiring connector support plates and move them to one side. Release all the cable-ties and switch wiring connectors as necessary to allow the bracket to be removed, then prise the bracket off its locating dowels on the engine. It will be tight on the dowels and a certain amount of levering will be necessary.

12 Disconnect the camshaft position sensor wiring at the connector located below the distributor cap.

13 Undo the two screws and remove the sensor housing from the cylinder head at the rear of the exhaust camshaft. Undo the bolt and remove the sensor rotor plate from the end of the exhaust camshaft.

14 Undo the three screws and lift off the distributor cap and HT leads.

15 Remove the flash shield then undo the three screws and remove the rotor arm. Undo the bolt and remove the rotor arm mounting plate.

16 Observe the position of the slots in the rear of the camshafts. Before the sprockets can be refitted, the camshafts must be positioned so that these slots are parallel to the join between the upper and lower cylinder head sections, and then locked in that position. Note also that the slots are very slightly offset from the centreline; one slightly above and one slightly below.

17 To lock the camshafts in the correct position for refitting, obtain Volvo tool 999 5452 or fabricate a home-made alternative **(see Tool Tip)**.

18 Check that the crankshaft sprocket timing marks are still aligned, then attach the Volvo tool or the home-made alternative to the rear of the cylinder head. It may be necessary to rotate the camshafts very slightly to bring their slots exactly to the horizontal position to allow the tool to fit **(see illustration)**.

19 Refit the camshaft sprocket(s), with the timing marks aligned and secure with two of the retaining bolts for each. If only one sprocket has been removed, slacken the three bolts on the other sprocket and remove one of them. Tighten the bolts so that they just touch

TOOL TiP

To make a camshaft locking tool, obtain a length of angle iron and cut it to length so that it will fit across the rear of the cylinder head. Mark and drill two holes so that it can be bolted to a distributor cap and camshaft position sensor bolt hole. Obtain a length of steel strip of suitable thickness to fit snugly in the slots in the camshafts. Cut the strip into two lengths and drill accordingly so that both strips can be bolted to the angle iron. Using spacer washers, nuts and bolts, position and secure the strips to the angle iron so that the camshafts can be locked with their slots horizontal. Pack out the strips with spacers to cater for the offset of the slots.

the sprockets, but allow the sprockets to turn within the limits of their elongated bolt holes. Position the sprockets so that the bolts are centred in their holes.

20 Carry out the operations described in Section 3, paragraphs 18 to 20.

21 Release the timing belt tensioner by pulling out the locking pin with pliers. Check that the tensioner plunger moves out to tension the belt.

22 Depress the belt hard, or strike it with a plastic mallet between the sprockets.

23 Refit the remaining bolt to each sprocket and tighten the bolts to the specified torque.

24 Remove the locking tool from the rear of the camshafts.

25 Refit the timing belt rear cover and secure with the two bolts, noting that the fuel pipe clip bracket is fitted under the rear bolt head.

26 Turn the crankshaft clockwise through two complete revolutions then check that all the timing marks can be realigned.

27 Continue with the timing belt refitting procedure as described in Section 3, paragraph 24 onwards. Do not reconnect the battery at this stage.

28 Refit the mounting plate, flash shield, rotor arm, distributor cap and HT leads.

29 Refit the camshaft position sensor rotor plate and housing.

30 Refit the engine steady bar bracket to the side of the engine and secure with the nut and two bolts tightened to the specified torque. Reconnect the wiring disturbed on removal and secure with cable-ties or the relevant clips.

31 Attach the engine steady bar to the brackets using new nuts and bolts. Tighten the steady bar mountings to the specified torque.

32 Refit the air cleaner assembly and air ducts.

33 Check that everything has been refitted correctly then reconnect the battery.

5 Camshaft rear oil seals - renewal

1 Disconnect the battery negative lead.
2 Refer to Chapter 4A and remove the air cleaner assembly and inlet ducts as necessary for clear access to the rear end of both camshafts.
3 Disconnect the camshaft position sensor wiring at the connector located below the distributor cap.
4 Undo the two screws and remove the sensor housing from the cylinder head at the rear of the exhaust camshaft. Undo the bolt and remove the sensor rotor plate from the end of the exhaust camshaft.
5 Undo the three screws and lift off the distributor cap and HT leads.
6 Remove the flash shield then undo the three screws and remove the rotor arm. Undo the bolt and remove the rotor arm mounting plate.
7 Carefully extract the seal by prising it out with a small screwdriver or hooked tool. Do not damage the shaft sealing face.
8 Clean the seal seat. Examine the shaft sealing face for wear or damage which could cause premature failure of the new seal.
9 Lubricate the new oil seal. Fit the seal over the shaft, lips inwards, and tap it home with a large socket or piece of tube until its outer face is flush with the housing.
10 Refit the camshaft position sensor, rotor arm mounting plate, flash shield, rotor arm, distributor cap and HT leads using a reversal of removal.
11 Refit the air cleaner and ducts, then reconnect the battery.

6 Camshafts and tappets - removal, inspection and refitting

Note: *For this procedure, Volvo tools 999 5452, 999 5453 and 999 5454 will be required to lock the camshafts in position in the cylinder head upper section during refitting, and to pull the upper section into place. Details for fabricating home-made alternatives are given in the text. Do not attempt to carry out the work without these tools. A tube of liquid gasket and a short haired application roller (available from Volvo dealers) will also be required.*

Removal

1 Disconnect the battery negative lead.
2 Drain the cooling system as described in Chapter 1.
3 Remove the timing belt as described in Section 3.

4 Suitably mark the camshaft sprockets, inlet and exhaust, for identification when refitting. The inlet sprocket is nearest the front of the car.
5 Undo the three bolts and remove the sprockets from the camshafts. Restrain the sprockets with a suitable tool through the holes in their faces. Refer to Section 4 for details of fabricating a suitable sprocket restraining tool.
6 Carry out the operations described in Section 4, paragraphs 8 to 15.
7 In a progressive diagonal sequence, working inwards, slacken then remove all the bolts securing the cylinder head upper section. Note the location of the earth leads on the rear bolts.
8 Using a soft faced mallet, gently tap, or alternatively prise, the cylinder head upper section upwards off the lower section. Note that parting lugs are provided to allow the upper section to be struck or prised against without damage. Do not insert a screwdriver or similar tool into the joint between the two sections as a means of separation. In practice the upper section will be quite tight as it is located on numerous dowels; patience is necessary.
9 Once the upper section is free, carefully lift it off. The camshafts will rise up under the pressure of the valve springs - be careful they don't tip and jam in the upper section.
10 Withdraw the sealing O-rings from the top of the spark plug recesses in the lower section. Obtain new O-rings for reassembly
11 Suitably mark the camshafts, inlet and exhaust and lift them out complete with front and rear oil seals. Be careful of the lobes, which may have sharp edges.
12 Remove the oil seals from the camshafts, noting their fitted positions. Obtain new seals for reassembly.
13 Have ready a suitable box divided into ten or twenty segments, as applicable, or some containers or other means of storing and identifying the hydraulic tappets after removal. The box or containers must be oil tight and deep enough to allow the tappets to be almost totally submerged in oil. Mark the segments in the box or the containers with the cylinder number for each tappet, together with identification for inlet and exhaust. On twenty valve engines further identify each inlet and exhaust tappet as to whether it is the front or rear of the two.
14 Lift out the tappets, using a suction cup or magnet if necessary. Keep them identified for position and place them upright in their respective positions in the box or containers **(see illustration)**. Once all the tappets have been removed, add clean engine oil to the box or container so that the oil hole in the tappet side is submerged.

Inspection

15 Inspect the cam lobes and the camshaft bearing journals for scoring or other visible evidence of wear. Once the surface hardening of the lobes has been penetrated, wear will progress rapidly.
16 No specific bearing journal diameters or running clearances are specified by Volvo for the camshafts or journals. However, if there is a visual deterioration, then component renewal will be necessary.
17 Inspect the tappets for scuffing, cracking or other damage; measure their diameter in several places with a micrometer. Renew the tappets if they are damaged or worn.

Preparation for refitting

18 Thoroughly clean the sealer from the mating surfaces of the upper and lower cylinder head sections. Use a suitable liquid gasket dissolving agent together with a soft putty knife; do not use a metal scraper or the faces will be damaged. As there is no conventional gasket used, the condition of the faces is of the utmost importance.
19 Clean off any oil, dirt or grease from both components and dry with a clean lint free cloth. Ensure that all the oilways are completely clean.
20 For reassembly, the camshafts are installed in the upper section and retained in place, in the correct position using special tools. This assembly is then fitted to the lower section, clamped in place against the pressure of the valve springs with more special tools, and finally bolted down. If possible, obtain the Volvo special tools mentioned in the note at the beginning of this section and use them in accordance with the instructions provided. Alternatively, fabricate a set of home-made tools as follows.
21 To position and secure the camshafts at the rear, make up the tool described in the Tool Tip in Section 4.
22 To secure the camshafts at the front, make up a strap as shown **(see Tool Tip)**.

6.14 Remove the tappets and place them in a segmented container

TOOL TiP

To retain the camshafts in the cylinder head upper section at the front when refitting, make a retaining strap out of welding rod, bent to shape, which will locate under the camshaft projections at the front and can be secured to the upper section with two bolts.

23 Finally it will be necessary to make up a tool which will allow the upper section to be clamped down against the pressure of the valve springs **(see Tool Tip)**.

TOOL TiP

To pull the cylinder head upper section down against valve spring pressure, obtain two old spark plugs and carefully break away all the porcelain so that only the lower threaded portion remains. Drill out the centre of the spark plugs as necessary, then fit a long bolt or threaded rod to each, and secure tightly with nuts. The bolts or rods must be long enough to project up from the spark plug wells to above the level of the assembled cylinder head. Drill a hole in the centre of two 6 mm thick strips of steel which are long enough to fit across the cylinder head upper section. Fit the strips then fit a nut and locknut to each bolt or rod.

Refitting

24 Commence refitting by liberally oiling the tappet bores and the camshaft bearings in the cylinder head lower section with clean engine oil.
25 Insert the tappets into their original bores unless they have been renewed. Fill new tappets with oil through the oil hole in their side before fitting.

6.28 Apply the liquid gasket solution using a short haired roller

26 Ensure that the mating faces of both cylinder head sections are clean and free of any oil or grease.
27 Check that the crankshaft timing marks are still aligned.
28 Using the short haired roller, apply an even coating of Volvo liquid gasket solution to the mating face of the cylinder head upper section only **(see illustration)**. Ensure that the whole surface is covered, but take care to keep the solution out of the oilways; a thin coating is sufficient for a good seal.
29 Lubricate the camshaft journals in the upper section sparingly with oil, taking care not to allow the oil to spill over onto the liquid gasket.
30 Lay the camshafts in their correct locations in the upper section, remembering that the inlet camshaft must be at the front of the engine.
31 Turn the camshafts so that their slots are parallel to the upper section join, noting that the slots in each camshaft are offset with regards to the centreline **(see illustration)**. When viewing the upper section the right way up, ie as it would be when fitted, the slot on the inlet camshaft is offset above the centreline and the exhaust camshaft slot is offset below the centreline. Verify this by looking at the other end of the camshafts. Again, with the upper section the right way up, there should be two sprocket bolt holes above the centreline on the inlet camshaft, and two bolt holes below the centreline on the exhaust camshaft.
32 With the camshafts correctly positioned,

6.33 Place new sealing O-rings into the recesses around each spark plug well

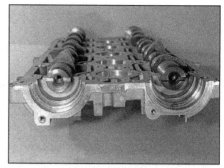

6.31 Position the camshafts so that their slots are parallel to the upper section join

lock them at the rear by fitting the rear locking and holding tool. It should not be possible to rotate the camshafts at all with the tool in place. Now secure the camshafts at the front using the holding tool or the home-made alternative.
33 Place new sealing O-rings into the recesses around each spark plug well in the lower section **(see illustration)**.
34 Lift up the assembled upper section, with camshafts, and lay it in place on the lower section.
35 Insert the pull-down tools into Nos 1 and 5 spark plug holes and tighten securely. If using the home-made tool, make sure that the bolt or threaded rod is a secure fit in the spark plug or you will not be able to remove the tool later.
36 Lay the pull-down tool top plates, or the home-made steel strips, over the bolts or threaded rods and secure with the nuts **(see illustration)**. Slowly and carefully tighten the nuts, a little at a time, so that the tools pull the upper section down onto the lower section. Remember there will be considerable resistance from the valve springs. Make sure that the upper section stays level or the locating dowels will jam.
37 Refit the upper section retaining bolts and tighten them in a progressive diagonal sequence, working outwards, to the specified torque. Don't forget the earth lead on the rear bolt.
38 With the upper section secure, remove the pull-down tool and the camshaft front end holding tool. Leave the rear locking tool in place.

6.36 Home-made pull-down tool in position

7.9 Cylinder head bolt slackening sequence (tightening sequence is the reverse)

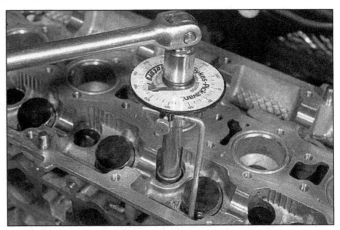

7.17 Tighten the cylinder head bolts to stage 3 using an angle-tightening gauge

39 Lubricate the lips of four new oil seals. Fit each seal the correct way round over the camshaft, and tap it home with a large socket or piece of tube until its outer face is flush with the housing.

40 Refit the camshaft sprockets, aligning the timing marks, and two of the retaining bolts for each. Tighten the bolts so that they just touch the sprockets, but allow the sprockets to turn within the limits of their elongated bolt holes. Position the sprockets so that the bolts are centred in their holes.

41 For the remainder of refitting, refer to Section 4 and carry out the operations from paragraph 20 onwards.

42 Refill the cooling system as described in Chapter 1 on completion.

7 Cylinder head - removal and refitting

Removal

1 Disconnect the battery negative lead.

2 Remove the radiator cooling fan as described in Chapter 3.

3 Remove the inlet and exhaust manifolds as described in Chapters 4A and 4B respectively.

4 Remove the camshafts and tappets as described in Section 6.

5 Undo the bolt securing the timing belt inner cover to the cylinder head.

6 Undo the bolt and remove the earth lead at the rear of the cylinder head.

7 Slacken the clips and remove the radiator top hose from the thermostat housing and radiator. Remove the expansion tank hose from the thermostat housing.

8 Undo the two bolts securing the coolant pipe flange to the rear of the cylinder head.

9 Slacken the cylinder head bolts, half a turn at a time to begin with, in the order shown

(see illustration). Remove the bolts. Note that new bolts will be required for refitting.

10 Lift off the cylinder head and set it down on wooden blocks to avoid damage to protruding valves. Recover the old head gasket.

11 If the cylinder head is to be dismantled for overhaul, refer to Part B of this Chapter.

Preparation for refitting

12 The mating faces of the cylinder head and cylinder block must be perfectly clean before refitting the head. Use a soft putty knife to remove all traces of gasket and carbon; also clean the piston crowns. Take particular care during the cleaning operations, as aluminium alloy is easily damaged. Also, make sure that the carbon is not allowed to enter the oil and water passages - this is particularly important for the lubrication system, as carbon could block the oil supply to the engine's components. Using adhesive tape and paper, seal the water, oil and bolt holes in the cylinder block. To prevent carbon entering the gap between the pistons and bores, smear a little grease in the gap. After cleaning each piston, use a small brush to remove all traces of grease and carbon from the gap, then wipe away the remainder with a clean rag. Clean all the pistons in the same way.

13 Check the mating surfaces of the cylinder block and the cylinder head for nicks, deep scratches and other damage. If slight, they may be removed carefully with a file, but if excessive, machining may be the only alternative to renewal.

14 If warpage of the cylinder head gasket surface is suspected, use a straight-edge to check it for distortion. Refer to Part B of this Chapter if necessary.

Refitting

15 Commence refitting by placing a new head gasket on the cylinder block. Make sure it is the right way up; it should be marked TOP.

16 Lower the head into position then oil the threads of the new cylinder head bolts. Fit the bolts and tighten them to the specified Stage 1 torque, in the reverse sequence to that shown (see illustration 7.9).

17 In the same sequence tighten the bolts to the Stage 2 torque, then, again in the same sequence, tighten the bolts through the angle specified for Stage 3 using an angle-tightening gauge (see illustration).

18 Using a new gasket, refit the coolant pipe flange to the rear of the cylinder head and secure with the two bolts.

19 Refit the radiator top hose to the thermostat housing and radiator.

20 Refit the timing belt cover retaining bolt and the bolt securing the rear earth lead.

21 Refit the camshaft and tappets as described in Section 6, paragraph 25 onwards, but do not reconnect the battery at this stage.

22 Refit the inlet and exhaust manifolds as described in Chapters 4A and 4B respectively.

23 Refit the radiator cooling fan as described in Chapter 3.

8 Crankshaft oil seals - renewal

Front seal

1 Remove the timing belt as described in Section 3.

2 The crankshaft sprocket must be held stationary while its centre retaining nut is slackened. If the Volvo holding tool 999 5433 cannot be obtained, it will be necessary to fabricate a home-made alternative. This will be essentially the same as the camshaft sprocket holding tool described in Section 4, but instead of bending the prongs of the forks through 90º, leave them straight and drill a suitable hole in each. The four bolts securing

the crankshaft pulley to the sprocket are then removed allowing the tool to be bolted to the pulley using two of the bolts. Hold the tool securely and undo the sprocket centre retaining nut using a socket and bar. Remove the tool and lift the pulley off the sprocket.

3 With the pulley removed, insert two of the retaining bolts and draw the sprocket off the crankshaft using a two-legged puller. Engage the puller legs with the protruding bolts at the rear **(see illustration)**.

4 With the sprocket removed, carefully prise out the old oil seal. Do not damage the oil pump housing or the surface of the crankshaft. Alternatively, punch or drill two small holes opposite each other in the oil seal. Screw a self-tapping screw into each, and pull on the screws with pliers to extract the seal.

5 Clean the oil seal location and the crankshaft. Inspect the crankshaft for a wear groove or ridge left by the old seal.

6 Lubricate the housing, the crankshaft and the new seal. Fit the seal, lips inwards, and use a piece of tube (or the old seal, inverted) to tap it into place until flush.

7 Refit the crankshaft sprocket and pulley using a reverse of the removal procedure.

8 Refit the timing belt as described in Section 3.

Rear seal

9 Remove the flywheel or driveplate as described in Section 10.

10 Remove the old seal and fit the new one as described previously in paragraphs 4 to 6.

11 Refit the flywheel or driveplate as described in Section 10.

9   Oil pump - removal, inspection and refitting

Removal

1 Carry out the operations described in Section 8, paragraphs 1 to 3.

2 Undo the four bolts securing the oil pump to the front of the cylinder block.

3 Carefully withdraw the pump assembly by levering behind the upper and lower parting lugs using a screwdriver **(see illustration)**. Remove the pump and recover the gasket.

4 Thoroughly clean the pump and cylinder block mating faces and remove all traces of old gasket.

Inspection

5 Remove the two screws which hold the two halves of the pump together.

6 Remove the gear cover from the pump body. Be prepared for the ejection of the pressure relief valve spring.

7 Remove the relief valve spring and plunger and the pump gears.

8 Remove the crankshaft front oil seal by carefully levering it out of the cover. Obtain a new seal for refitting.

9 Clean all components thoroughly, then inspect the gears, body and gear cover for signs of wear or damage.

10 Measure the free height of the pressure relief valve spring, and compare the dimension with that given in the *Specifications*. Renew it if it is weak or distorted. Also inspect the plunger for scoring or other damage.

11 Refit the gears to the pump body, with the markings on the large gear uppermost. Using feeler blades, check the clearance between the large gear and the pump body. If the clearance is outside the specified limit, renew the pump.

12 If the clearance is satisfactory, liberally lubricate the gears. Lubricate and fit the relief valve plunger and spring.

13 Fit a new O-ring seal to the pump body then fit the cover and secure with the two screws.

Refitting

14 Using a new gasket, fit the pump to the block. Use the pump retaining bolts as guides and draw the pump into place with the crankshaft pulley nut and spacers. With the pump seated, tighten the retaining bolts diagonally to the specified torque.

15 Lubricate the cover, crankshaft and the new oil seal. Fit the seal, lips inwards, and use a piece of tube (or the old seal, inverted) to tap it into place until flush.

16 Refit the crankshaft sprocket and pulley using a reverse of the removal procedure.

17 Refit the timing belt as described in Section 3.

10   Flywheel/driveplate - removal, inspection and refitting

Note: *New flywheel/driveplate retaining bolts will be required for refitting.*

Removal

Flywheel (models with manual transmission)

1 Remove the transmission as described in Chapter 7A.

2 Remove the clutch assembly as described in Chapter 6.

3 Make alignment marks so that the flywheel can be refitted in the same position relative to the crankshaft.

4 Unbolt the flywheel and remove it. Prevent crankshaft rotation by inserting a large screwdriver in the ring gear teeth and in contact with an adjacent dowel in the engine/transmission mating face.

Driveplate (models with automatic transmission)

5 Remove the automatic transmission as described in Chapter 7B.

6 Make alignment marks so that the driveplate can be refitted in the same position relative to the crankshaft.

7 Unbolt the driveplate and remove it, preventing crankshaft rotation as described previously.

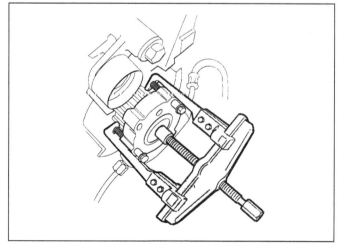

8.3 Using a puller to draw off the crankshaft sprocket

9.3 Parting lugs (arrowed) for oil pump removal

Inspection

8 On manual transmission models, If the flywheel's clutch mating surface is deeply scored, cracked or otherwise damaged, the flywheel must be renewed. However, it may be possible to have it surface-ground; seek the advice of a Volvo dealer or engine reconditioning specialist. If the ring gear is badly worn or has missing teeth, flywheel renewal will also be necessary.

9 On models equipped with automatic transmission, check the torque converter driveplate carefully for signs of distortion. Look for any hairline cracks around the bolt holes or radiating outwards from the centre, and inspect the ring gear teeth for signs of wear or chipping. If any signs of wear or damage are found, the driveplate must be renewed.

Refitting

Flywheel (models with manual transmission)

10 Clean the mating surfaces of the flywheel and crankshaft. Remove any remaining locking compound from the threads of the crankshaft holes, using the correct-size tap, if available.

> **HAYNES HiNT** If a suitable tap is not available, cut two slots into the threads of one of the old flywheel bolts and use the bolt to remove the locking compound from the threads.

11 Continue refitting by reversing the removal operations. Apply thread locking compound to the new flywheel retaining bolts (if not already pre-coated) and tighten them to the specified torque.

12 Refit the clutch as described in Chapter 6, and the transmission as described in Chapter 7A.

Driveplate (models with automatic transmission)

13 Proceed as described above for manual transmission models but ignoring any references to clutch. Refit the transmission as described in Chapter 7B.

11 Engine mountings - removal and refitting

Removal

1 All the individual engine mountings can be renewed with the engine/transmission installed.

2 Disconnect the battery negative lead.

3 Ascertain which components are likely to impede removal and remove, or move aside as necessary, with reference to the relevant Chapters of this manual.

4 Attach a suitable lifting equipment to the engine or position a jack, with protective wooden block under the sump or transmission as necessary.

5 With the engine supported, remove the nuts or bolts from the mounting to be removed **(see illustration)**.

6 Take the weight off the mounting, raise the engine/transmission as necessary for clearance, and remove the mounting. Note any locating pegs or directional arrows as an aid to refitting. Take care not to raise the engine/transmission by more than 30 mm otherwise the inner left-hand constant velocity joint will be damaged.

Refitting

7 Refit by reversing the removal operations, tightening all fastenings to the specified torque.

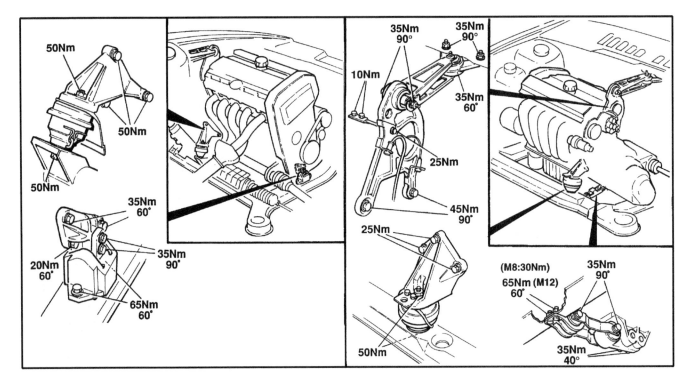

11.5 Engine/transmission mounting details (refer to *Specifications* for latest torque settings)

Chapter 2 Part B:
Engine removal and overhaul procedures

Contents

Degrees of difficulty

Easy, suitable for novice with little experience		**Fairly easy,** suitable for beginner with some experience		**Fairly difficult,** suitable for competent DIY mechanic		**Difficult,** suitable for experienced DIY mechanic		**Very difficult,** suitable for expert DIY or professional	

Specifications

Cylinder head

Warp limit - maximum acceptable for use:
    Lengthways . . . . 0.50 mm
    Across . . . . 0.20 mm
Height:
    10-valve engines . . . . 132.1 ± 0.05 mm
    20-valve engines . . . . 129.0 ± 0.05
Maximum height reduction after machining . . . . 0.30 mm

Inlet valves

Head diameter:
    10-valve engines . . . . 40.0 ± 0.15 mm
    20-valve engines . . . . 31.0 ± 0.15 mm
Stem diameter . . . . 6.955 to 6.970 mm
Length:
    10-valve engines . . . . 98.1 + 0.3 mm
    20-valve engines . . . . 104.05 ± 0.18 mm
Valve seat angle . . . . 44° 30'

Exhaust valves

Head diameter:
    10-valve engines . . . . 35.0 ± 0.15 mm
    20-valve engines . . . . 27.0 ± 0.15 mm
Stem diameter:
    Non-turbo engines . . . . 6.955 to 6.970 mm
    Turbo engines . . . . 6.810 to 6.960 mm
Length:
    10-valve engines . . . . 97.1 ± 0.3 mm
    20-valve engines . . . . 103.30 ± 0.18 mm
Valve seat angle . . . . 44° 30'

Valve seat inserts

Diameter (standard):
    Inlet:
        10-valve engines .... 43.11 mm
        20-valve engines .... 32.61 mm
    Exhaust:
        10-valve engines .... 38.11 mm
        20-valve engines .... 28.61 mm
Oversizes available .... + 0.50 mm
Fit in cylinder head .... Interference
Valve seat angle .... 45° 00'

Valve guides

Valve stem-to-guide clearance:
    New .... 0.03 to 0.06 mm
    Wear limit .... 0.15 mm
Fitted height above cylinder head .... 13.0 ± 0.2 mm
Fit in head .... Interference
External oversizes available .... 2 (marked by grooves)

Valve springs

Diameter:
    10-valve engines .... 30.8 ± 0.2 mm
    20-valve engines .... 27.9 ± 0.2 mm
Free length
    10-valve engines .... 43.2 mm
    20-valve engines .... 42.4 mm

Cylinder bores

Diameter - 2.0 and 2.3 litre engines:
    Classification:
        C .... 81.00 to 81.01 mm
        D .... 81.01 to 81.02 mm
        E .... 81.02 to 81.03 mm
        G .... 81.04 to 81.05 mm
        OS1 (first oversize) .... 81.20 to 81.21 mm
        OS2 (second oversize) .... 81.40 to 81.41 mm
    Wear limit .... 0.10 mm
Diameter - 2.5 litre engines:
    Classification:
        C .... 83.00 to 83.01 mm
        D .... 83.01 to 83.02 mm
        E .... 83.02 to 83.03 mm
        G .... 83.04 to 83.05 mm
        OS1 (first oversize) .... 83.20 to 83.21 mm
        OS2 (second oversize) .... 83.40 to 83.41 mm
    Wear limit .... 0.10 mm

Pistons

Height:
    2.0 litre, 10-valve engines .... 65.8 mm
    2.0 litre, 20-valve engines .... 66.4 mm
    All other engines .... 59.9 mm
Diameter - 2.0 and 2.3 litre engines:
    Classification:
        C .... 80.98 to 80.99 mm
        D .... 80.99 to 81.00 mm
        E .... 81.00 to 81.01 mm
        G .... 81.017 to 81.032 mm
        OS1 (first oversize) .... 81.177 to 81.192 mm
        OS2 (second oversize) .... 81.377 to 81.392 mm
Diameter - 2.5 litre engines:
    Classification:
        C .... 82.98 to 82.99 mm
        D .... 82.99 to 83.00 mm
        E .... 83.00 to 83.01 mm
        G .... 83.017 to 83.032 mm
        OS1 (first oversize) .... 83.177 to 83.192 mm
        OS2 (second oversize) .... 83.377 to 83.392 mm

Piston-to-bore clearance	0.01 to 0.03 mm
Weight variation in same engine	10 g max

Piston rings

Clearance in groove:	
Top compression	0.050 to 0.085 mm
Second compression	0.030 to 0.065 mm
Oil control	0.020 to 0.055 mm
End gap (measured in cylinder):	
Compression rings	0.20 to 0.40 mm
Oil control	0.25 to 0.50 mm Gudgeon pins
Diameter, standard	23.00 mm
Fit in connecting rod	Light thumb pressure
Fit in piston	Firm thumb pressure

Crankshaft

Run-out	0.032 mm max
Endfloat	0.19 mm max
Main bearing journal diameter:	
Standard	64.987 to 65.000 mm
Undersize	64.750 mm
Main bearing running clearance	N/A
Main bearing journal out-of-round	0.004 mm max
Main bearing journal taper	0.004 mm max
Big-end bearing journal diameter:	
Standard	49.984 to 50.000 mm
Undersize	49.750 mm
Big-end bearing running clearance	N/A
Big-end bearing out-of-round	0.004 mm max
Big-end rod bearing taper	0.004 mm max

Torque wrench settings

	Nm
Intermediate section to cylinder block:*	
Stage 1 (M10 bolts only)	20
Stage 2 (M10 bolts only)	45
Stage 3 (M8 bolts only)	24
Stage 4 (M7 bolts only)	17
Stage 5 (M10 bolts only)	Tighten through a further 90°
Big-end bearing cap bolts:**	
Stage 1	20
Stage 2	Tighten through a further 90°
Sump bolts	17
Oil pick-up pipe bolt	17

*M10 bolts should be renewed if their length exceeds 118 mm.
New nuts/bolts must **always be used.
Refer to Chapter 2, Part A for additional engine torque wrench settings.

1 General information

Included in this part of Chapter 2 are details of removing the engine/transmission from the car and general overhaul procedures for the cylinder head, cylinder block and all other engine internal components.

The information ranges from advice concerning preparation for an overhaul and the purchase of replacement parts, to detailed step-by-step procedures covering removal, inspection, renovation and refitting of engine internal components.

After Section 6, all instructions are based on the assumption that the engine has been removed from the car. For information concerning engine in-car repair, as well as removal and installation of those external components necessary for full overhaul, refer to Part A of this Chapter and to Section 4. Ignore any preliminary dismantling operations described in Part A that are no longer relevant once the engine has been removed from the car.

2 Engine/transmission removal - preparation and precautions

If you have decided that an engine must be removed for overhaul or major repair work, several preliminary steps should be taken.

Locating a suitable place to work is extremely important. Adequate work space, along with storage space for the car, will be needed. If a workshop or garage is not available, at the very least, a flat, level, clean work surface is required.

If possible, clear some shelving close to the work area and use it to store the engine components and ancillaries as they are removed and dismantled. In this manner the components stand a better chance of staying clean and undamaged during the overhaul. Laying out components in groups together with their fixing bolts, screws etc will save time and avoid confusion when the engine is refitted.

Clean the engine compartment and engine/transmission before beginning the removal procedure; this will help visibility and help to keep tools clean.

The help of an assistant should be available; there are certain instances when one person cannot safely perform all of the operations required to remove the engine from the vehicle. Safety is of primary importance, considering the potential hazards involved in this kind of operation. A second person should always be in attendance to offer help in an emergency. If this is the first time you have removed an engine, advice and aid from someone more experienced would also be beneficial.

Plan the operation ahead of time. Before starting work, obtain (or arrange for the hire of) all of the tools and equipment you will need. Access to the following items will allow the task of removing and refitting the engine/transmission to be completed safely and with relative ease: an engine hoist - rated in excess of the combined weight of the engine/transmission, a heavy-duty trolley jack, complete sets of spanners and sockets as described at the rear this manual, wooden blocks, and plenty of rags and cleaning solvent for mopping up spilled oil, coolant and fuel. A selection of different sized plastic storage bins will also prove useful for keeping dismantled components grouped together. If any of the equipment must be hired, make sure that you arrange for it in advance, and perform all of the operations possible without it beforehand; this may save you time and money.

Plan on the vehicle being out of use for quite a while, especially if you intend to carry out an engine overhaul. Read through the whole of this Section and work out a strategy based on your own experience and the tools, time and workspace available to you. Some of the overhaul processes may have to be carried out by a Volvo dealer or an engineering works - these establishments often have busy schedules, so it would be prudent to consult them before removing or dismantling the engine, to get an idea of the amount of time required to carry out the work.

When removing the engine from the vehicle, be methodical about the disconnection of external components. Labelling cables and hoses as they removed will greatly assist the refitting process.

Always be extremely careful when lifting the engine/transmission assembly from the engine bay. Serious injury can result from careless actions. If help is required, it is better to wait until it is available rather than risk personal injury and/or damage to components by continuing alone. By planning ahead and taking your time, a job of this nature, although major, can be accomplished successfully and without incident.

On all models covered by this manual, the engine and transmission are removed as a complete assembly, upwards and out of the engine bay. The engine and transmission are then separated with the assembly on the bench.

3 Engine and transmission - removal, separation and refitting

Removal

All models

1 Open the bonnet and raise it to its fully extended (vertical) position.
2 Disconnect the battery negative lead.
3 Refer to Chapter 5A and remove the battery and battery tray.
4 Refer to Chapter 4A and carry out the following:
a) Remove the air cleaner assembly and all air ducting including turbocharger inlet (where applicable).
b) Disconnect the accelerator cable from the throttle drum and support bracket.
5 Refer to Chapter 1 and carry out the following:
a) Drain the cooling system.
b) If the engine is going to be dismantled, drain the engine oil.
c) Remove the auxiliary drivebelt.
6 If the car is fitted with cruise control, disconnect the wiring and vacuum hose to the vacuum motor.
7 Undo the nuts and remove the bolts securing the upper engine steady bar to the bracket on the engine and on the bulkhead. Note that new nuts and bolts will be required for refitting.
8 Undo the earth lead retaining bolt on the bulkhead, adjacent to the steady bar bulkhead bracket.

Right-hand drive models

9 Remove the pedal position switch on the front of the brake vacuum servo unit.
10 Release all the brake pipes leading to the master cylinder from their retaining clips on the bulkhead.
11 Remove the brake master cylinder from the servo unit as described in Chapter 9, but without disconnecting any of the hydraulic pipes or hoses. Lay the cylinder on rags on the scuttle panel. Take great care not to bend any of the rigid brake pipes.

All models

12 Press together the sides of the quick-release couplings and disconnect the two heater hoses at the bulkhead.
13 Disconnect the brake servo vacuum hose at the inlet manifold.
14 Disconnect the heated oxygen sensor wiring at the two connectors at the rear of the engine.
15 Undo the rear engine mounting upper retaining nut.

Manual transmission models

16 Extract the circlip securing the selector inner cable ends to the transmission selector levers. Withdraw the washers and slide the cable ends off the levers.

17 Extract the retaining clips and release the selector outer cables from the transmission brackets.
18 Disconnect the wiring connector at the reversing light switch.
19 Extract the circlip and withdraw the clutch slave cylinder from the bellhousing. Lift off the air cleaner mounting bracket and position the slave cylinder and bracket to one side.
20 Disconnect the earth lead from the front of the transmission and the wiring harness retaining clip(s).

Automatic transmission models

21 Extract the locking clip and washer securing the selector inner cable to the transmission selector lever.
22 Undo the two nuts and remove the washers (where fitted) securing the selector outer cable bracket to the transmission. Lift the bracket off the mounting studs and release the inner cable end from the selector lever.
23 Disconnect the main wiring harness connector on top of the transmission casing.
24 Remove the cable clamps securing the wiring harness and earth lead.
25 On early models disconnect the transmission vacuum hose from its clip. On later models, detach the cable conduit from the transmission and release the oxygen sensor connector from the transmission bracket.
26 Disconnect the transmission oil cooler inlet hose from the upper quick release connector on the side of the radiator. Disconnect the oil cooler return hose at the transmission union. Cover or seal the disconnected hoses and unions.

All models

27 Remove the radiator cooling fan as described in Chapter 3.
28 On cars equipped with air conditioning, from under the inlet manifold undo the two long bolts securing the air conditioning compressor to the mounting bracket. Leave the compressor in place until the engine is ready to be lifted out.
29 On turbo models, disconnect the oil cooler hoses at the engine oil cooler.
30 Undo the front engine mounting upper retaining nut.
31 Undo the bolts and remove the inlet manifold support bracket. Undo the starter motor support bracket bolts and the wiring conduit bracket bolts. Remove the dipstick.
32 Disconnect the radiator upper and lower hoses at the radiator, thermostat housing and coolant pipe, and remove the hoses.
33 Disconnect the expansion tank hose at the thermostat housing.
34 Undo the steering pump guard plate upper mounting bolt and remove the spacer sleeve, then slacken the guard plate lower mounting nut. Undo the five pump mounting bolts; three are accessible through the holes in the pump pulley and two are at the rear of the pump. Leave the pump in place until the engine is ready to be lifted out.

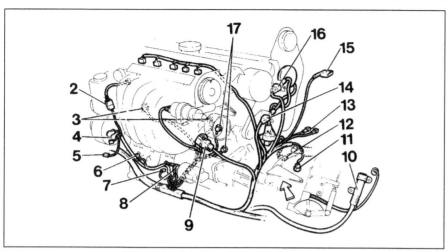

3.51 Wiring harness disconnection points

2 Coolant temperature sensor
3 Knock sensors
4 Alternator
5 Air conditioning compressor
6 Radiator cooling fan
7 Starter motor
8 Oil pressure sensor
9 Throttle position sensor

10 Automatic transmission main loom
    connector
11 Reversing light switch
13 Oxygen sensor
14 Camshaft position sensor
15 Mass air flow/intake air temperature sensor
16 RPM sensor
17 Earth points

35 If not already done, jack up the front of the car and support it on axle stands (see *"Jacking and vehicle support"*). Remove the front roadwheels.

36 Remove the ABS wheel sensors from the steering knuckles and release the sensor wiring from the suspension strut brackets.

37 Undo the bolt securing the brake hose and ABS wiring bracket to each inner wheel arch.

38 Working on one side at a time, undo the nut and remove the clamp bolt securing the suspension control arm balljoint to each steering knuckle. Push down on the suspension arm using a stout bar if necessary, to release the balljoint shank from the knuckle. If the balljoint is tight, spread the slot in the steering knuckle with a chisel or large screwdriver. Take care not to damage the balljoint dust cover during and after disconnection.

39 On the left-hand side, free the driveshaft inner CV joint from the transmission by levering between the edge of the joint and the transmission casing with a large screwdriver or similar tool. Take care not to damage the transmission oil seal or the inner CV joint gaiter. Swivel the suspension strut and steering knuckle assembly outwards and withdraw the driveshaft CV joint from the transmission. Rest the driveshaft on the subframe.

40 On the right-hand side, undo the two bolts and remove the cap from the intermediate shaft support bearing on the rear of the engine. Swivel the suspension strut and steering knuckle assembly outwards and pull the intermediate shaft out of the transmission.

Rest the shaft on the steering fluid pipes under the engine.

41 Disconnect the vacuum hoses leading from the engine to the EVAP carbon canister under the left-hand wheel arch.

42 Disconnect the exhaust front pipe at the manifold flange joint or turbocharger.

43 Disconnect the vehicle speed sensor wiring at the connector.

44 Undo the two bolts securing the lower engine steady bar bracket to the transmission.

45 On right-hand drive models, undo the two steering gear crash guard bolts at the rear of the subframe and the nut securing the crash guard base to the subframe.

46 Undo the two bolts securing the right-hand engine mounting to the engine bracket.

47 Undo the bolts securing the two fuel pipe clamps to the engine and remove the clamps.

48 Disconnect the wiring plug from each fuel injector. If difficulty is experienced, pull off the fuel rail cover over the injectors for greater access.

49 Disconnect the vacuum hose from the pressure regulator on the underside of the fuel rail.

50 Undo the two bolts securing the fuel rail to the inlet manifold. Pull the rail upwards to release the injectors from the manifold, and carefully lay the rail, complete with injectors, on the expansion tank.

51 Disconnect all relevant wiring connectors and harness clips still connected, from the engine **(see illustration)**.

52 Attach suitable lifting gear to the engine by fabricating brackets and bolting them to either end of the engine. The engine will need to be angled upwards slightly at the timing

belt end for adequate clearance. Ensure that the lifting gear is substantial, and securely attached to the engine.

53 Lift off the air conditioning compressor (where applicable) and place it on the subframe. Do not disconnect the refrigerant hoses.

54 Lift off the steering pump and place it to one side.

55 Check that no wires, hoses etc have been overlooked. Raise the engine/transmission and manipulate it to clear all adjacent components. Take great care not to damage the radiator as the engine is being manoeuvred; remove the engine mounting brackets from the transmission if this will provide more clearance. When sufficient height exists, lift it over the front panel, clear of the engine bay and lower it to the ground.

Separation

56 With the engine/transmission removed, support the assembly on suitable blocks of wood, on a workbench (or failing that, on a clean area of the workshop floor).

57 Remove the starter motor.

Manual transmission models

58 Remove the bolts securing the transmission to the engine.

59 With the aid of an assistant, draw the transmission off the engine. Once it is clear of the dowels, do not allow it to hang on the input shaft.

Automatic transmission models

60 Rotate the crankshaft, using a socket on the pulley nut, until one of the torque converter-to-driveplate retaining bolts becomes accessible through the opening on the rear facing side of the engine. Working through the opening, undo the bolt. Rotate the crankshaft as necessary and remove the remaining bolts in the same way. Note that new bolts will be required for refitting.

61 Remove the bolts securing the transmission to the engine.

62 With the aid of an assistant, draw the transmission squarely off the engine dowels making sure that the torque converter remains in position on the transmission. Use the access hole in the transmission housing to hold the converter in place.

Refitting

Manual transmission models

63 Make sure that the clutch is correctly centred and that the clutch release components are fitted to the bellhousing. Do not apply any grease to the transmission input shaft, the guide sleeve, or the release bearing itself as these components have a friction reducing coating which does not require lubrication.

64 Manoeuvre the transmission squarely into position and engage it with the engine dowels. Refit the bolts securing the transmission to the engine and tighten them to the specified torque. Refit the starter motor.

Automatic transmission models

65 Before refitting the transmission, flush out the oil cooler with fresh transmission fluid. To do this, attach a hose to the upper union, pour ATF through the hose and collect it in a container positioned beneath the return hose.

66 Clean the contact surfaces on the torque converter and driveplate, and the transmission and engine mating faces. Lightly lubricate the torque converter guide projection and the engine/transmission locating dowels with grease.

67 Check that the torque converter is fully seated by measuring the distance from the edge of the transmission housing face to the retaining bolt tabs on the converter. The dimension should be approximately 14 mm.

68 Manoeuvre the transmission squarely into position and engage it with the engine dowels. Refit the bolts securing the transmission to the engine and tighten lightly first in a diagonal sequence, then again to the specified torque.

69 Attach the torque converter to the driveplate using new bolts. Rotate the crankshaft for access to the bolts as was done for removal, then rotate the torque converter by means of the access hole in the transmission housing. Fit and tighten all the bolts hand tight first then tighten again to the specified torque.

All models

70 The remainder of refitting is essentially a reversal of removal, noting the following points:
 a) Tighten all fastenings to the specified torque and, where applicable, torque angle. Refer to the relevant Chapters of this manual for torque wrench settings not directly related to the engine.
 b) When refitting the fuel rail and injectors, check that the injector O-rings and manifold seals are in good condition and renew them if necessary; smear them with petroleum jelly or silicone grease as an assembly lubricant.
 c) When refitting the left-hand driveshaft, ensure that the inner CV joint is pushed fully into the transmission so that the retaining circlip locks into place in the differential gear.
 d) Ensure that the ABS sensor, and sensor location in the steering knuckle, are perfectly clean before refitting.
 e) When reconnecting the manual transmission selector cables, note that the outermost cable (marked with yellow paint) attaches to the vertical selector lever on the end of the transmission (also marked yellow).
 f) On automatic transmission models, reconnect and adjust the selector cable as described in Chapter 7B.
 g) Refit the brake master cylinder and associated components on the servo unit as described in Chapter 9.
 h) Refit the air cleaner assembly and reconnect the accelerator cable as described in Chapter 4A.
 i) Refit the auxiliary drivebelt, then refill the engine with coolant and oil as described in Chapter 1.
 j) Refill the transmission with lubricant if necessary as described in Chapter 1, 7A or 7B as applicable.
 k) Refer to Section 16 before starting the engine.

4 Engine overhaul - preliminary information

It is much easier to dismantle and work on the engine if it is mounted on a portable engine stand. These stands can often be hired from a tool hire shop. Before the engine is mounted on a stand, the flywheel/driveplate should be removed so that the stand bolts can be tightened into the end of the cylinder block/crankcase.

If a stand is not available, it is possible to dismantle the engine with it suitably supported on a sturdy, workbench or on the floor. Be careful not to tip or drop the engine when working without a stand.

If you intend to obtain a reconditioned engine, all ancillaries must be removed first, to be transferred to the replacement engine (just as they will if you are doing a complete engine overhaul yourself). These components include the following.
 a) Engine mountings and brackets (Chapter 2A).
 b) Alternator including accessories mounting bracket (Chapter 5A).
 c) Starter motor (Chapter 5A).
 d) The ignition system and HT components including all sensors, distributor cap and rotor arm, HT leads and spark plugs (Chapters 1 and 5B).
 e) Exhaust manifold, with turbocharger if fitted (Chapter 4B).
 f) Inlet manifold with fuel injection components (Chapter 4A).
 g) All electrical switches, actuators and sensors and the engine wiring harness (Chapters 4A, 4B and 5B).
 h) Coolant pump, thermostat, hoses, and distribution pipe (Chapter 3).
 i) Clutch components - manual transmission models (Chapter 6).
 j) Flywheel/driveplate (Chapter 2A).
 k) Oil filter (Chapter 1).
 l) Dipstick, tube and bracket.
Note: When removing the external components from the engine, pay close attention to details that may be helpful or important during refitting. Note the fitting positions of gaskets, seals, washers, bolts and other small items.

If you are obtaining a "short" engine (cylinder block/crankcase, crankshaft, pistons and connecting rods all assembled), then the cylinder head, timing belt (together with tensioner, tensioner and idler pulleys and covers) and auxiliary drivebelt tensioner will have to be removed also.

If a complete overhaul is planned, the engine can be dismantled in the order given below.
 a) Inlet and exhaust manifolds and turbocharger (where applicable).
 b) Timing belt, sprockets, tensioner, pulleys and covers.
 c) Cylinder head.
 d) Oil pump.
 e) Flywheel/driveplate.
 f) Sump.
 g) Oil pick-up pipe.
 h) Intermediate section.
 i) Pistons/connecting rods.
 j) Crankshaft.

5 Cylinder head - dismantling, cleaning, inspection and reassembly

Note: New and reconditioned cylinder heads are available from the manufacturer and from engine overhaul specialists. Specialist tools are required for the dismantling and inspection procedures, and new components may not be readily available. it may, therefore, be more practical and economical for the home mechanic to purchase a reconditioned head rather than dismantle, inspect and recondition the original head.

Dismantling

1 Remove the cylinder head as described in Part A of this Chapter.

2 If still in place, remove the camshafts and tappets as described in Part A of this Chapter.

3 According to components still fitted, remove the thermostat housing (Chapter 3), the spark plugs (Chapter 1) and any other unions, pipes, sensors or brackets as necessary.

4 Tap each valve stem smartly, using a light hammer and drift, to free the spring and associated items.

5 Fit a deep reach type valve spring compressor to each valve in turn and compress each spring until the collets are exposed **(see illustration)**. Lift out the collets; a small screwdriver, a magnet or a pair of tweezers may be useful. Carefully release the spring compressor and remove it.

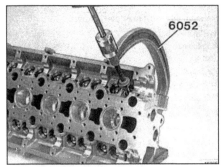

5.5 Compressing the valve springs with a valve spring compressor tool

5.9 Keep groups of components together in labelled bags or boxes

6 Remove the valve spring upper seat and the valve spring. Pull the valve out of its guide.

7 Pull off the valve stem oil seal with a pair of long-nosed pliers. It may be necessary to use a tool such as a pair of electrician's wire strippers, the "legs" of which will engage under the seal, if the seal is tight.

8 Recover the valve spring lower seat. If there is much carbon build-up round the outside of the valve guide, this will have to be scraped off before the seat can be removed.

9 It is essential that each valve is stored together with its collets, spring and seats. The valves should also be kept in their correct sequence, unless they are so badly worn or burnt that they are to be renewed. If they are going to be kept and used again, place each valve assembly in a labelled polythene bag or similar container **(see illustration)**.

10 Continue removing all the remaining valves in the same way.

Cleaning

11 Thoroughly clean all traces of old gasket material and sealing compound from the cylinder head upper and lower mating surfaces. Use a suitable liquid gasket dissolving agent together with a soft putty knife; do not use a metal scraper or the faces will be damaged.

12 Remove the carbon from the combustion chambers and ports, then clean all traces of oil and other deposits from the cylinder head, paying particular attention to the bearing journals, tappet bores, valve guides and oilways.

13 Wash the head thoroughly with paraffin or a suitable solvent. Take plenty of time and do a thorough job. Be sure to clean all oil holes and galleries very thoroughly, dry the head completely and coat all machined surfaces with light oil.

14 Scrape off any heavy carbon deposits that may have formed on the valves, then use a power-operated wire brush to remove deposits from the valve heads and stems.

Inspection

Note: *Be sure to perform all the following inspection procedures before concluding that the services of an engineering works are required. Make a list of all items that require attention.*

Cylinder head

15 Inspect the head very carefully for cracks, evidence of coolant leakage, and other damage. If cracks are found, a new cylinder head should be obtained.

16 Use a straight edge and feeler blade to check that the cylinder head gasket surface is not distorted. If it is, it may be possible to re-surface it; consult your dealer or engine overhaul specialist **(see illustration)**.

17 Examine the valve seats in each of the combustion chambers. If they are severely pitted, cracked or burned, then they will need to be renewed or re-cut by an engine overhaul specialist. If they are only slightly pitted, this can be removed by grinding-in the valve heads and seats with fine valve-grinding compound, as described below.

18 If the valve guides appear worn, indicated by a side-to-side motion of the valve, new

guides must be fitted. Verify this by mounting a dial gauge on the cylinder head and check the side-to-side rock with the valve lifted clear of its seat **(see illustration)**. Compare the results with the figures given in the *Specifications*. If outside the permitted tolerance, measure the diameter of the existing valve stems (see below) and the bore of the guides, renew the valves or guides as necessary. The renewal of valve guides should be carried out by an engine overhaul specialist.

19 If the valve seats are to be re-cut, this must be done *only after* the guides have been renewed.

20 The threaded holes in the cylinder head must be clean to ensure accurate torque readings when tightening fixings during reassembly. Carefully run the correct size tap (which can be determined from the size of the relevant bolt which fits in the hole) into each of the holes to remove rust, corrosion, thread sealant or other contamination, and to restore damaged threads. If possible, use compressed air to clear the holes of debris produced by this operation. Do not forget to clean the threads of all bolts and nuts as well.

21 Any threads which cannot be restored in this way can often be reclaimed by the use of thread inserts. If any threaded holes are damaged, consult your dealer or engine overhaul specialist and have them install any thread inserts where necessary.

Valves

22 Examine the head of each valve for pitting, burning, cracks and general wear, and check the valve stem for scoring and wear ridges. Rotate the valve, and check for any obvious indication that it is bent. Look for pits and excessive wear on the tip of each valve stem. Renew any valve that shows any such signs of wear or damage.

5.16 Measuring the distortion of the cylinder head gasket surface

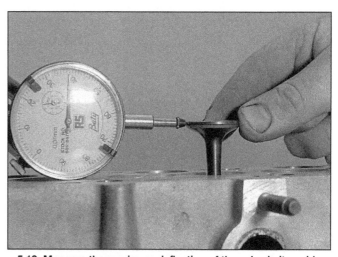

5.18 Measure the maximum deflection of the valve in its guide using a dial gauge

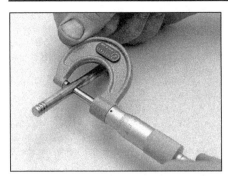

5.23 Measure the valve stem diameter with a micrometer

23 If the valve appears satisfactory at this stage, measure the valve stem diameter at several points, using a micrometer **(see illustration)**. Any significant difference in the readings obtained indicates wear of the valve stem. Should any of these conditions be apparent, the valve(s) must be renewed.

24 If the valves are in satisfactory condition, they should be ground (lapped) into their respective seats, to ensure a smooth gas-tight seal. If the seat is only lightly pitted, or if it has been re-cut, fine grinding compound *only* should be used to produce the required finish. Coarse valve-grinding compound should *not* be used unless a seat is badly burned or deeply pitted; if this is the case, the cylinder head and valves should be inspected by an expert, to decide whether seat re-cutting, or even the renewal of the valve or seat insert, is required.

25 Valve grinding is carried out as follows. Place the cylinder head upside-down on a bench, with a block of wood at each end to give clearance for the valve stems.

26 Smear a trace of (the appropriate grade) valve-grinding compound on the seat face, and press a suction grinding tool onto the valve head. With a semi-rotary action, grind the valve head to its seat, lifting the valve occasionally to redistribute the grinding compound. A light spring placed under the valve head will greatly ease this operation.

27 If coarse grinding compound is being used, work only until a dull, matt even surface is produced on both the valve seat and the valve, then wipe off the used compound, and repeat the process with fine compound. When a smooth unbroken ring of light grey matt finish is produced on both the valve and seat, the grinding operation is complete. *Do not* grind in the valves any further than absolutely necessary, or the seat will be prematurely sunk into the cylinder head.

28 When all the valves have been ground-in, carefully wash off *all* traces of grinding compound, using paraffin or a suitable solvent, before reassembly of the cylinder head.

Valve components

29 Examine the valve springs for signs of damage and discoloration, and also measure their free length by comparing each of the existing springs with a new component.

30 Stand each spring on a flat surface, and check it for squareness. If any of the springs are damaged, distorted, or have lost their tension, obtain a complete set of new springs. It is normal to fit new springs as a matter of course if a major overhaul is being carried out.

31 Renew the valve stem oil seals regardless of their apparent condition.

Reassembly

32 Oil the stem of one valve and insert it into its guide then fit the spring lower seat.

33 The new valve stem oil seals should be supplied with a plastic fitting sleeve to protect the seal when it is fitted over the valve. If not, wrap a thin piece of polythene around the valve stem allowing it to extend about 10 mm above the end of the valve stem.

34 With the fitting sleeve, or polythene in place around the valve, fit the valve stem oil seal, pushing it onto the valve guide as far as it will go with a suitable socket or piece of tube. Once the seal is seated, remove the protective sleeve or polythene.

35 Fit the valve spring and upper seat. Compress the spring and fit the two collets in the recesses in the valve stem. Carefully release the compressor.

Use a little dab of grease to hold the collets in position on the valve stem while the spring compressor is released.

36 Cover the valve stem with a cloth and tap it smartly with a light hammer to verify that the collets are properly seated.

37 Repeat these procedures on all the other valves.

38 Refit the remainder of the disturbed components then refit the cylinder head as described in Part A of this Chapter.

6 Sump and intermediate section - removal

1 If not already done, drain the engine oil then remove the oil filter, referring to Chapter 1 if necessary.

2 Remove the oil pump as described in Part A of this Chapter.

3 If the pistons and connecting rods are to be removed later, position all the pistons approximately half way down their bores.

4 Undo the bolts securing the sump to the intermediate section, noting the different bolt lengths and their locations.

5 Carefully tap the sump free using a rubber or hide mallet. Recover the O-ring seals.

6 Undo the mounting bracket bolt and remove the oil pick-up pipe **(see illustration)**. Recover the O-ring seal on the end of the pipe.

7 Undo all the M7 and M8 bolts securing the intermediate section to the cylinder block in the reverse order to that shown **(see illustration)**. With all those bolts removed, undo the M10 bolts in the same sequence.

6.6 Undo the mounting bracket bolt and remove the oil pick-up pipe

6.7 Intermediate section bolt tightening sequence. Slacken bolts in reverse order in matched pairs across the block

7.3 Mark the big-end caps and connecting rods with their cylinder numbers

7.10 Removing piston rings with the help of feeler blades

8 Carefully tap the intermediate section free using a rubber or hide mallet. Lift off the intermediate section complete with crankshaft lower main bearing shells. If any of the shells have stayed on the crankshaft, transfer them to their correct locations in the intermediate section.

9 Remove the crankshaft rear oil seal.

7 Pistons and connecting rods - removal and inspection

Removal

1 Remove the cylinder head, oil pump and flywheel/driveplate as described in Part A of this Chapter. Remove the sump and intermediate section as described in Section 6.

2 Feel inside the tops of the bores for a pronounced wear ridge. Some authorities recommend that such a ridge be removed (with a scraper or ridge reamer) before attempting to remove the pistons. However, a ridge big enough to damage the pistons and/or piston rings will almost certainly mean that a rebore and new pistons/rings are needed anyway.

3 Check that there are identification numbers or marks on each connecting rod and cap; paint or punch suitable marks if necessary, so that each rod can be refitted in the same position and the same way round **(see illustration)**.

4 Remove the two connecting rod bolts. Tap the cap with a soft-faced hammer to free it. Remove the cap and lower bearing shell. Note that new bolts will be needed for reassembly.

5 Push the connecting rod and piston up and out of the bore. Recover the other half bearing shell if it is loose.

6 Refit the cap to the connecting rod, the correct way round, so that they do not get mixed up.

7 Check to see if there is an arrow on the top of the piston which should be pointing toward the timing belt end of the engine. If no arrow can be seen, make a suitable direction mark yourself.

8 Without rotating the crankshaft, repeat the operations on the remaining connecting rods and pistons.

Inspection

9 Before the inspection process can be carried out, the piston/connecting rod assemblies must be cleaned, and the original piston rings removed from the pistons

10 Carefully expand the old rings and remove them from the top of the pistons. The use of two or three old feeler blades will be helpful in preventing the rings dropping into empty grooves **(see illustration)**. Be careful not to scratch the pistons with the ends of the ring. The rings are brittle and will snap if they are spread too far. They are also very sharp - protect your hands and fingers.

11 Scrape all traces of carbon from the top of the piston. A hand-held wire brush (or a piece of fine emery cloth) can be used, once the majority of the deposits have been scraped away.

12 Remove the carbon from the ring grooves in the piston, using an old ring. Break the ring in half to do this (be careful not to cut your fingers - piston rings are sharp). Be careful to remove only the carbon deposits - do not remove any metal, and do not nick or scratch the sides of the ring grooves.

13 Once the deposits have been removed, clean the piston/rod assemblies with paraffin or a suitable solvent, and dry thoroughly. Make sure the oil return holes in the ring grooves, are clear.

14 If the pistons and cylinder bores are not damaged or worn excessively, and if the cylinder block does not need to be rebored (where applicable), the original pistons can be refitted. Normal piston wear appears as even vertical wear on the piston thrust surfaces,

and slight looseness of the top ring in its groove. New piston rings should always be used when the engine is reassembled.

15 Carefully inspect each piston for cracks around the skirt, around the gudgeon pin holes, and at the ring "lands" (between the ring grooves).

16 Look for scoring and scuffing on the piston skirt, holes in the piston crown, and burned areas at the edge of the crown. If the skirt is scored or scuffed, the engine may have been suffering from overheating and/or abnormal combustion, which caused excessively-high operating temperatures. The cooling and lubrication systems should be checked thoroughly. Scorch marks on the sides of the piston show that blow-by has occurred. A hole in the piston crown or burned areas at the edge of the piston crown, indicates that abnormal combustion (pre-ignition, knocking, or detonation) has been occurring. If any of the above problems exist, the causes must be investigated and corrected, or the damage will occur again. The causes may include inlet air leaks, incorrect fuel/air mixture or an emission control system fault.

17 Corrosion of the piston, in the form of pitting, indicates that coolant has been leaking into the combustion chamber and/or the crankcase. Again, the cause must be corrected, or the problem may persist in the rebuilt engine.

18 Examine each connecting rod carefully for signs of damage, such as cracks around the big-end and small end bearings. Check that the rod is not bent or distorted. Damage is highly unlikely, unless the engine has been seized or badly overheated. Detailed checking of the connecting rod assembly can only be carried out by an engine overhaul specialist with the necessary equipment.

19 The gudgeon pins are of the floating type, secured in position by two circlips. Where necessary, the pistons and connecting rods can be separated as follows.

7.20 **Push the gudgeon pin out of the piston and connecting rod**

7.21a **Measure the piston diameters using a micrometer**

20 Remove one of the circlips which secure the gudgeon pin. Push the gudgeon pin out of the piston and connecting rod **(see illustration)**.

21 Using a micrometer, measure the diameter of all five pistons at a point 10 mm from the bottom of the skirt, at right angles to the gudgeon pin axis **(see illustration)**. Compare the measurements obtained, with those listed in the *Specifications*. Note that four standard size grades are available - the grade letter is stamped on the piston crown and on the cylinder block **(see illustration)**. If new pistons are to be obtained, they must be of the same grade marking as the cylinder bore to which they will be fitted.

22 If the diameter of any of the pistons is out of the tolerance band listed for its particular grade, then all five pistons must be renewed. Note that if the cylinder block was re-bored during a previous overhaul, oversize pistons may have been fitted. Record the measurements and use them to check the piston-to-bore clearance when the cylinder bores are measured later in this Chapter.

23 Hold a new piston ring in the appropriate groove and measure the ring-to-groove clearance using a feeler blade **(see illustration)**. Note that the rings are of different sizes, so use the correct ring for the groove. Compare the measurements with those listed in the *Specifications*; if the clearances are outside the tolerance range, then the pistons must be renewed.

24 Check the fit of the gudgeon pin in the connecting rod bush and in the piston. If there is perceptible play, a new bush or an oversize gudgeon pin must be fitted. Consult a Volvo dealer or engine reconditioning specialist.

25 Examine all components and obtain any new parts required. If new pistons are purchased, they will be supplied complete with gudgeon pins and circlips. Circlips can also be purchased separately.

26 Oil the gudgeon pin. Reassemble the connecting rod and piston, making sure the rod is the right way round, and secure the gudgeon pin with the circlip. Position the circlip so that its opening is facing downward.

27 Repeat these operations for the remaining pistons.

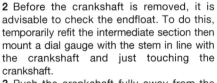

8 Crumbshaft - removal and inspection

Removal

Note: *If no work is to be done on the pistons and connecting rods, then removal of the cylinder head and pistons will not be necessary. Instead, the pistons need only be pushed far enough up the bores so that they are positioned clear of the crankpins.*

1 With reference to Part A of this Chapter, and earlier Sections of this part as applicable, carry out the following:

a) *Remove the oil pump.*
b) *Remove the sump and intermediate section.*
c) *Remove the clutch components and flywheel/driveplate.*
d) *Remove the pistons and connecting rods (refer to the Note above).*

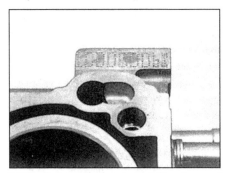

7.21b **Piston/cylinder grade letter stamped on the cylinder block**

2 Before the crankshaft is removed, it is advisable to check the endfloat. To do this, temporarily refit the intermediate section then mount a dial gauge with the stem in line with the crankshaft and just touching the crankshaft.

3 Push the crankshaft fully away from the gauge, and zero it. Next, lever the crankshaft towards the gauge as far as possible, and check the reading obtained. The distance that the crankshaft moved is its endfloat; if it is greater than specified, check the crankshaft thrust surfaces for wear. If no wear is evident, new thrustwashers (which are integral with the main bearing shells) should correct the endfloat.

4 Remove the intermediate section again, then lift out the crankshaft. Do not drop it, it is heavy.

5 Remove the upper half main bearing shells from their seats in the crankcase by pressing the end of the shell furthest from the locating tab. Keep all the shells in order.

Inspection

6 Clean the crankshaft using paraffin or a suitable solvent, and dry it, preferably with compressed air if available. Be sure to clean the oil holes with a pipe cleaner or similar probe to ensure that they are not obstructed.

7.23 **Measure the ring-to-groove clearance using a feeler blade**

8.11 Use a micrometer to measure the crankshaft journal diameters

 Warning: Wear eye protection when using compressed air!

7 Check the main and big-end bearing journals for uneven wear, scoring, pitting and cracking.
8 Big-end bearing wear is accompanied by distinct metallic knocking when the engine is running (particularly noticeable when the engine is pulling from low speed) and some loss of oil pressure.
9 Main bearing wear is accompanied by severe engine vibration and rumble - getting progressively worse as engine speed increases - and again by loss of oil pressure.
10 Check the bearing journal for roughness by running a finger lightly over the bearing surface. Any roughness (which will be accompanied by obvious bearing wear) indicates that the crankshaft requires regrinding (where possible) or renewal.
11 Using a micrometer, measure the diameter of the main and big-end journals, and compare the results with the *Specifications* **(see illustration)**. By measuring the diameter at a number of points around each journal's circumference, you will be able to determine whether or not the journal is out-of-round. Take the measurement at each end of the journal, near the webs, to determine if the journal is tapered. Compare the results obtained with those given in the *Specifications*. If the crankshaft journals are outside the tolerance range specified, a new crankshaft will be needed as only graded, standard size bearing shells are available from the manufacturer. However, seek the advice of an engine overhaul specialist first, as to whether regrinding may be possible and whether graded bearing shells can be supplied to match.
12 Check the oil seal contact surfaces at each end of the crankshaft for wear and damage. If either seal has worn a deep groove in the surface of the crankshaft, consult an engine overhaul specialist; repair may be possible, otherwise a new crankshaft will be required.
13 Refer to Section 10 for details of main and big-end bearing selection.

9 Cylinder block/crankcase - cleaning and inspection

Cleaning

1 Prior to cleaning, remove all external components and senders, and any gallery plugs or caps that may be fitted.
2 If any of the castings are extremely dirty, all should be steam-cleaned.
3 After the castings are returned from steam-cleaning, clean all oil holes and oil galleries one more time. Flush all internal passages with warm water until the water runs clear. If you have access to compressed air, use it to speed the drying process, and to blow out all the oil holes and galleries.

 Warning: Wear eye protection when using compressed air!

4 If the castings are not very dirty, you can do an adequate cleaning job with hot soapy water (as hot as you can stand!) and a stiff brush. Take plenty of time, and do a thorough job. Regardless of the cleaning method used, be sure to clean all oil holes and galleries very thoroughly, and to dry all components completely. Apply clean engine oil to the cylinder bores to prevent rusting.
5 The threaded holes in the cylinder block must be clean to ensure accurate torque readings when tightening fixings during reassembly. Carefully run the correct size tap (which can be determined from the size of the relevant bolt which fits in the hole) into each of the holes to remove rust, corrosion, thread sealant or other contamination, and to restore damaged threads. If possible, use compressed air to clear the holes of debris produced by this operation. Do not forget to clean the threads of all bolts and nuts as well.
6 Any threads which cannot be restored in this way can often be reclaimed by the use of thread inserts. If any threaded holes are damaged, consult your dealer or engine overhaul specialist and have them install any thread inserts where necessary.
7 If the engine is not going to be reassembled right away, cover it with a large plastic bag to keep it clean; protect the machined surfaces as described above, to prevent rusting.

Inspection

8 Visually check the castings for cracks and corrosion. Look for stripped threads in the threaded holes. If there has been any history of internal coolant leakage, it may be worthwhile having an engine overhaul specialist check the cylinder block/crankcase for cracks with special equipment. If defects are found, have them repaired, if possible, or renew the assembly.
9 Check the condition of the cylinder head mating face and the intermediate section mating surfaces. Check the surfaces for any

possible distortion using the straight-edge and feeler blade method described earlier for cylinder head inspection. If distortion is slight, consult an engine overhaul specialist as to the best course of action.
10 Check each cylinder bore for scuffing and scoring. Check for signs of a wear ridge at the top of the cylinder, indicating that the bore is excessively worn.
11 If the necessary measuring equipment is available, measure the diameter of each cylinder at the top (just under the ridge area), centre and bottom of the cylinder bore, parallel to the crankshaft axis using a cylinder bore gauge. Next, measure the bore diameter at the same three locations across the crankshaft axis. Note the measurements obtained. Have this work carried out by an engine overhaul specialist if you do not have access to the measuring equipment needed.
12 To obtain the piston-to-bore clearance, measure the piston diameter as described earlier in this Chapter, and subtract the piston diameter from the largest bore measurement.
13 Repeat these procedures for the remaining pistons and cylinder bores.
14 Compare the results with the *Specifications* at the beginning of this Chapter; if any measurement is beyond the dimensions specified for that grade, or if any bore measurement is significantly different from the others (indicating that the bore is tapered or oval), the piston or bore is excessively-worn. Note that each cylinder is identified by a classification marking (C, D, E, or G) stamped into the rear of the cylinder block. There are four classifications (or grades) for standard diameter cylinder bores and two oversize classifications (stamped OS1 and OS2).
15 If any of the cylinder bores are badly scuffed or scored, or if they are excessively-worn, out-of-round or tapered, the usual course of action would be to have the cylinder block/crankcase rebored, and to fit new, oversized, pistons on reassembly. Consult a dealer or engine reconditioning specialist for advice.
16 If the bores are in reasonably good condition and not excessively-worn, then it may only be necessary to renew the piston rings.
17 If this is the case, the bores should be honed, to allow the new rings to bed in correctly and provide the best possible seal. Honing is an operation that will be carried out for you by an engine reconditioning specialist.
18 After all machining operations are completed, the entire block/crankcase must be washed very thoroughly with warm soapy water to remove all traces of abrasive grit produced during the machining operations. When the cylinder block/crankcase is completely clean, rinse it thoroughly and dry it, then lightly oil all exposed machined surfaces, to prevent rusting.
19 The final step is to measure the length of the M10 bolts used to secure the intermediate

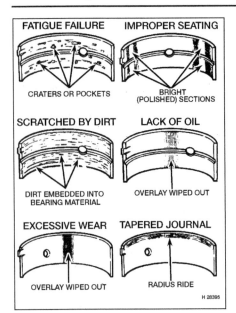

10.2 Typical bearing failures

Classification markings on block

Crankshaft classification		A small diameter		B medium diameter		C large diameter	
		block	int. sect.	block	int. sect.	block	int. sect.
A small		yellow medium	yellow medium	yellow medium	blue thick	blue thick	blue thick
B medium		red thin	yellow medium	yellow medium	yellow medium	yellow medium	blue thick
C large		red thin	red thin	red thin	yellow medium	yellow medium	yellow medium

10.11 Main bearing shell selection table

section to the cylinder block. If the length of any is greater than 118 mm, they should be renewed. It is a wise precaution to renew these bolts anyway considering the significance of their location. As with all bolts that are tightened through a torque angle, they are prone to stretch, often up to the extent of their elastic limit. It is virtually impossible to judge the strain that this imposes on a particular bolt, and if any are in any way flawed, breakage when retightening, or failure in service could be the result.

10 Main and big-end bearings - inspection and selection

Inspection

1 Even though the main and big-end bearing shells should be renewed during the engine overhaul, the old shells should be retained for close examination, as they may reveal valuable information about the condition of the engine.

2 Bearing failure occurs because of lack of lubrication, the presence of dirt or other foreign particles, overloading the engine, and corrosion **(see illustration)**. Regardless of the cause of bearing failure, the cause must be corrected (where applicable) before the engine is reassembled, to prevent it from happening again.

3 When examining the bearing shells, remove them from the cylinder block/crankcase and main bearing caps, and from the connecting rods and the big-end bearing caps, then lay them out on a clean surface in the same general position as their location in the engine. This will enable you to match any bearing problems with the corresponding

crankshaft journal. *Do not* touch any of the shell's bearing surface with your fingers while checking it, or the delicate surface may be scratched.

4 Dirt or other foreign matter gets into the engine in a variety of ways. It may be left in the engine during assembly, or it may pass through filters or the crankcase ventilation system. It may get into the oil, and from there into the bearings. Metal chips from machining operations and normal engine wear are often present. Abrasives are sometimes left in engine components after reconditioning, especially when parts are not thoroughly cleaned using the proper cleaning methods. Whatever the source, these foreign objects often end up embedded in the soft bearing material, and are easily recognised. Large particles will not embed in the material, and will score or gouge the shell and journal. The best prevention for this cause of bearing failure is to clean all parts thoroughly, and to keep everything spotlessly-clean during engine assembly. Frequent and regular engine oil and filter changes are also recommended.

5 Lack of lubrication (or lubrication breakdown) has a number of inter-related causes. Excessive heat (which thins the oil), overloading (which squeezes the oil from the bearing face) and oil leakage (from excessive bearing clearances, worn oil pump or high engine speeds) all contribute to lubrication breakdown. Blocked oil passages, which usually are the result of misaligned oil holes in a bearing shell, will also starve a bearing of oil, and destroy it. When lack of lubrication is the cause of bearing failure, the bearing material is wiped or extruded from the shell's steel backing. Temperatures may increase to the point where the steel backing turns blue from overheating.

6 Driving habits can have a definite effect on bearing life. Full-throttle, low-speed operation (labouring the engine) puts very high loads on bearings, which tends to squeeze out the oil film. These loads cause the shells to flex,

which produces fine cracks in the bearing face (fatigue failure). Eventually, the bearing material will loosen in pieces, and tear away from the steel backing.

7 Short-distance driving leads to corrosion of bearings, because insufficient engine heat is produced to drive off condensed water and corrosive gases. These products collect in the engine oil, forming acid and sludge. As the oil is carried to the engine bearings, the acid attacks and corrodes the bearing material.

8 Incorrect shell refitting during engine assembly will lead to bearing failure as well. Tight-fitting shells leave insufficient bearing running clearance, and will result in oil starvation. Dirt or foreign particles trapped behind a bearing shell result in high spots on the bearing, which lead to failure.

9 *Do not* touch any shell's bearing surface with your fingers during reassembly; there is a risk of scratching the delicate surface, or of depositing particles of dirt on it.

Selection - main and big-end bearings

10 To ensure that the main bearing running clearance will be correct, there are three different grades of bearing shell. The grades are indicated by a colour coding (red, yellow or blue) marked on each bearing shell, which denotes the shell's thickness.

11 New main bearing shells for each journal can be selected using the reference letters (A, B and C) which are stamped on the cylinder block and on the crankshaft, in accordance with the table shown **(see illustration)**.

12 From the table, it can be seen that if the marking on the cylinder block for a particular journal was B, and the corresponding marking on the crankshaft was C, then a red bearing shell would be fitted to the cylinder block, and a yellow shell would be fitted into the intermediate section.

13 Check all the markings and select the main bearing shells necessary for all journals.

14 Big-end bearing shells are not graded and are supplied in one size only to match the dimensions of the respective journal. As the manufacturer's do not specify an actual running clearance dimension for the big-end bearings, the only safe course of action is to fit new shells whenever an overhaul is being undertaken. Assuming that the relevant crankshaft journals are all within tolerance, the running clearances will then be correct.

11 Engine overhaul - reassembly sequence

1 Before reassembly begins ensure that all new parts have been obtained and that all necessary tools are available. Read through the entire procedure to familiarise yourself with the work involved, and to ensure that all items necessary for reassembly of the engine are at hand. In addition to all normal tools and materials, thread locking compound will be needed in most areas during engine reassembly. A tube of Volvo liquid gasket solution together with a short-haired application roller will also be needed to assemble the main engine sections.
2 In order to save time and avoid problems, engine reassembly can be carried out in the following order:
a) *Crankshaft.*
b) *Pistons/connecting rods.*
c) *Sump.*
d) *Oil pump.*
e) *Flywheel/driveplate.*
f) *Cylinder head.*
g) *Camshaft and tappets.*
h) *Timing belt, tensioner, sprockets and idler pulleys.*
i) *Engine external components.*
3 At this stage, all engine components should be absolutely clean and dry, with all faults repaired. The components should be laid out (or in individual containers) on a completely clean work surface.

12 Crankshaft - refitting

1 Crankshaft refitting is the first stage of engine reassembly following overhaul. It is assumed at this point that the cylinder block/crankcase and crankshaft have been cleaned, inspected and repaired or reconditioned as necessary. Position the cylinder block on a clean level worksurface, with the crankcase facing upwards.
2 If they're still in place, remove the old bearing shells from the block and the intermediate section.
3 Wipe clean the main bearing shell seats in the crankcase and clean the backs of the bearing shells. Insert the previously selected upper shells into their correct position in the

crankcase. Press the shells home so that the tangs engage in the recesses provided.
4 Liberally lubricate the bearing shells in the crankcase with clean engine oil.
5 Wipe clean the crankshaft journals, then lower the crankshaft into position. Make sure that the shells are not displaced.
6 Inject oil into the crankshaft oilways then wipe any traces of excess oil from the crankshaft and intermediate section mating faces.
7 Using the short haired application roller, apply an even coating of Volvo liquid gasket solution to the cylinder block mating face of the intermediate section. Ensure that the whole surface is covered, but note that a thin coating is sufficient for a good seal.
8 Wipe clean the main bearing shell seats in the intermediate section and clean the backs of the bearing shells. Insert the previously selected lower shells into their correct position in the intermediate section. Press the shells home so that the tangs engage in the recesses provided.
9 Lightly lubricate the bearing shells in the intermediate section, but take care to keep the oil away from the liquid gasket solution.
10 Lay the intermediate section on the crankshaft and cylinder block, and insert the retaining bolts. Tighten the bolts in the five stages listed in the *Specifications*, to the specified torque and torque angle, in the sequence shown **(see illustration 6.7)**.
11 Rotate the crankshaft. Slight resistance is to be expected with new components, but there must be no tight spots or binding.
12 It is a good idea at this stage, to once again check the crankshaft endfloat as described in Section 8. If the thrust surfaces of the crankshaft have been checked and new bearing shells have been fitted, then the endfloat should be within specification.
13 Lubricate the rear oil seal location, the crankshaft, and a new oil seal. Fit the seal, lips inwards, and use a piece of tube (or the old seal, inverted) to tap it into place until flush.

13 Pistons and piston rings - assembly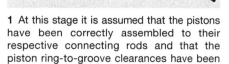

1 At this stage it is assumed that the pistons have been correctly assembled to their respective connecting rods and that the piston ring-to-groove clearances have been checked. If not, refer to the end of Section 7.
2 Before the rings can be fitted to the pistons, the end gaps must be checked with the rings inserted into the cylinder bores.
3 Lay out the piston assemblies and the new ring sets so the components are kept together in their groups, during and after end gap checking. Position the cylinder block on the work surface, on its side, allowing access to the top and bottom of the bores.
4 Take the No 1 piston top ring and insert it into the top of the first cylinder. Push it down the

bore using the top of the piston; this will ensure that the ring remains square with the cylinder walls. Position the ring near the bottom of the cylinder bore, at the lower limit of ring travel. Note that the top and second compression rings are different. The second ring is easily identified by the step on its lower surface.
5 Measure the ring gap using feeler blades.
6 Repeat the procedure with the ring at the top of the cylinder bore, at the upper limit of its travel and compare the measurements with the figures given in the *Specifications*.
7 If new rings are being fitted it is unlikely that the end gaps will be too small. If a measurement is found to be undersize, it must be corrected or there is the risk that the ring ends may contact each other during engine operation, possibly resulting in engine damage. Ideally, new piston rings providing the correct end gap should be fitted, however, as a last resort the end gaps can be increased by filing the ring ends very carefully with a fine file. Mount the ring in a vice equipped with soft jaws, slip the ring over the file with the ends contacting the file face, and slowly move the ring to remove material from the ends. Take care as piston rings are sharp and are easily broken.
8 It is equally unlikely that the end gap will be too large. If the gaps are too large, check that you have the correct rings for your engine and for the cylinder bore size.
9 Repeat the checking procedure for each ring in the first cylinder, and then for the rings in the remaining cylinders. Remember to keep rings, pistons and cylinders matched up.
10 Once the ring end gaps have been checked and if necessary corrected, the rings can be fitted to the pistons.
11 Fit the piston rings using the same technique as for removal. Fit the bottom scraper ring first, and work up. Observe the text markings on one side of the top and bottom rings; this must face upwards when the rings are fitted **(see illustration)**. The

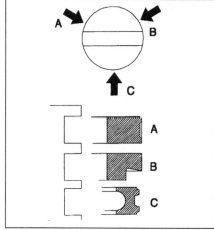

13.11 Piston ring identification and end gap positioning

Position the ring gaps (arrowed) for each ring accordingly middle ring is bevelled and the bevel must face downwards when installed. Do not expand the compression rings too far or they will break. **Note:** *Always follow any instructions supplied with the new piston ring sets - different manufacturers may specify different procedures. Do not mix up the top and second compression rings, as they have different cross-sections.*

12 When all the rings are in position arrange the ring gaps 120° apart as shown.

14 Pistons and connecting rod assemblies - refitting

1 Before refitting the piston/connecting rod assemblies, the cylinder bores must be perfectly clean, the top edge of each cylinder must be chamfered, and the crankshaft and intermediate section must be in place.

2 Remove the big-end bearing cap from No 1 cylinder connecting rod (refer to the marks noted or made on removal). Remove the original bearing shells, and wipe the bearing recesses of the connecting rod and cap with a clean, lint-free cloth. They must be kept spotlessly-clean. Ensure that new big-end bearing cap retaining bolts are available.

4 Clean the back of the new upper bearing shell, fit it to No 1 connecting rod, then fit the other shell of the bearing to the big-end bearing cap. Make sure the tab on each shell fits into the notch in the rod or cap recess.

5 Position the piston ring gaps in their correct positions around the piston, lubricate the piston and rings with clean engine oil, and attach a piston ring compressor to the piston. Leave the skirt protruding slightly, to guide the piston into the cylinder bore. The rings must be compressed until they're flush with the piston.

6 Rotate the crankshaft until No 1 big-end journal is at BDC (Bottom Dead Centre), and apply a coat of engine oil to the cylinder walls.

7 Arrange the No 1 piston/connecting rod assembly so that the arrow on the piston crown points to the timing belt end of the engine. Gently insert the assembly into the No 1 cylinder bore, and rest the bottom edge of the ring compressor on the engine block.

8 Tap the top edge of the ring compressor to make sure it's contacting the block around its entire circumference.

9 Gently tap on the top of the piston with the end of a wooden hammer handle while guiding the connecting rod big-end onto the crankpin. The piston rings may try to pop out of the ring compressor just before entering the cylinder bore, so keep some pressure on the ring compressor. Work slowly, and if any

resistance is felt as the piston enters the cylinder, stop immediately. Find out what is binding, and fix it before proceeding. *Do not*, for any reason, force the piston into the cylinder - you might break a ring and/or the piston.

10 Make sure the bearing surfaces are perfectly clean, then apply a uniform layer of clean engine oil, to both of them. You may have to push the piston back up the cylinder bore slightly to expose the bearing surface of the shell in the connecting rod.

11 Slide the connecting rod back into place on the big-end journal, refit the big-end bearing cap. Lubricate the bolt threads, fit the bolts and tighten them in two stages to the specified torque.

12 Repeat the entire procedure for the remaining piston/connecting rod assemblies.

13 The important points to remember are:
a) *Keep the backs of the bearing shells and the recesses of the connecting rods and caps perfectly clean when assembling them.*
b) *Make sure you have the correct piston/rod assembly for each cylinder.*
c) *The arrow on the piston crown must face the camshaft drivebelt end of the engine.*
d) *Lubricate the cylinder bores with clean engine oil.*
e) *Lubricate the bearing surfaces before fitting the big-end bearing caps.*

14 After all the piston/connecting rod assemblies have been properly installed, rotate the crankshaft a number of times by hand, to check for any obvious binding.

15 Sump - refitting

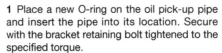

1 Place a new O-ring on the oil pick-up pipe and insert the pipe into its location. Secure with the bracket retaining bolt tightened to the specified torque.

2 Wipe off any oil smears from the sump and intermediate section joint faces, then locate new O-rings in the recesses in the intermediate section.

3 Using the short haired application roller, apply an even coating of Volvo liquid gasket solution to the sump mating face. Ensure that the whole surface is covered, but note that a thin coating is sufficient for a good seal.

4 Place the sump in position and insert four of the retaining bolts tightened finger tight only.

5 Using a straight edge, ensure that the rear edges of the sump and cylinder block are flush, then tighten the four bolts to just hold the sump in position.

6 Refit the remaining bolts and tighten all progressively, working towards the centre, to the specified torque.

16 Engine - initial start-up after overhaul and reassembly

1 Refit the remainder of the engine components in the order listed in Section 11, with reference to the relevant Sections of this part of Chapter 2, and Part A. Refit the engine and transmission to the vehicle as described in Section 3 of this Part. Double-check the engine oil and coolant levels and make a final check that everything has been reconnected. Make sure that there are no tools or rags left in the engine compartment.

2 Remove the spark plugs and disable the ignition system by disconnecting the camshaft position sensor wiring at the connector. Disconnect the fuel injector wiring connectors to prevent fuel being injected into the cylinders.

3 Turn the engine over on the starter motor until the oil pressure warning light goes out. If the light fails to extinguish after several seconds of cranking, check the engine oil level and oil filter security. Assuming these are correct, check the security of the oil pressure sensor wiring - do not progress any further until you are sure that oil is being pumped around the engine at sufficient pressure.

4 Refit the spark plugs and HT leads, and reconnect the camshaft position sensor and fuel injector wiring connectors.

5 Start the engine, noting that this also may take a little longer than usual, due to the fuel system components being empty.

6 While the engine is idling, check for fuel, coolant and oil leaks. Don't be alarmed if there are some odd smells and smoke from parts getting hot and burning off oil deposits. Note also that it may initially be a little noisy until the hydraulic tappets fill with oil.

7 Keep the engine idling until hot water is felt circulating through the top hose, check that it idles reasonably smoothly and at the usual speed, then switch it off.

8 After a few minutes, recheck the oil and coolant levels, and top-up as necessary (see Chapter 1).

9 If new components such as pistons, rings or crankshaft bearings have been fitted, the engine must be run-in for the first 500 miles (800 km). Do not operate the engine at full-throttle, or allow it to labour in any gear during this period. It is recommended that the oil and filter be changed at the end of this period.

Chapter 3
Cooling, heating and air conditioning systems

Contents

Degrees of difficulty

Easy, suitable for novice with little experience		Fairly easy, suitable for beginner with some experience		Fairly difficult, suitable for competent DIY mechanic		Difficult, suitable for experienced DIY mechanic		Very difficult, suitable for expert DIY or professional	

Specifications

General

System type	Water-based coolant, pump-assisted circulation, thermostatically controlled

Thermostat

Opening commences:	
Type 1 thermostat	87°C
Type 2 thermostat	90°C
Fully open at:	
Type 1 thermostat	102°C
Type 2 thermostat	105°C

Torque wrench settings

	Nm
Radiator mounting bolts	30
Coolant pump bolts	20

1 General information and precautions

General information

The cooling system is of pressurised semi-sealed type with the inclusion of an expansion tank to accept coolant displaced from the system when hot and to return it when the system cools.

Water-based coolant is circulated around the cylinder block and head by the coolant pump which is driven by the engine timing belt. As the coolant circulates around the engine it absorbs heat as it flows then, when hot, it travels out into the radiator to pass across the matrix. As the coolant flows across the radiator matrix, air flow created by the forward motion of the vehicle cools it, and it returns to the cylinder block. Air flow through the radiator matrix is assisted by a two-speed electric fan, which is controlled by the engine management system ECU.

A thermostat is fitted to control coolant flow through the radiator. When the engine is cold, the thermostat valve remains closed so that the coolant flow which occurs at normal operating temperatures through the radiator matrix is interrupted.

As the coolant warms up, the thermostat valve starts to open and allows the coolant flow through the radiator to resume.

The engine temperature will always be maintained at a constant level (according to the thermostat rating) whatever the ambient air temperature.

On turbo models, bypass connections are fitted to allow cold coolant flow to cool the turbocharger.

The vehicle interior heater operates by means of coolant from the engine cooling system. Coolant flow through the heater matrix is constant; temperature control being achieved by blending cool air from outside the vehicle with the warm air from the heater matrix, in the desired ratio.

The climate control (air conditioning) systems are described in detail in Section 9.

Precautions

 Warning: Do not attempt to remove the expansion tank filler cap, or to disturb any part of the cooling system, while it or the engine is hot, as there is a very great risk of scalding. If the expansion tank filler cap must be removed before the engine and radiator have fully cooled down (even though this is not recommended) the pressure in the cooling system must first be released. Cover the cap with a thick layer of cloth, to avoid scalding, and slowly unscrew the filler cap until a hissing sound can be heard. When the hissing has stopped, showing that pressure is released, slowly unscrew the filler cap further until it can be removed; if more hissing sounds are heard, wait until they have stopped before unscrewing the cap completely. At all times, keep well away from the filler opening.

 Warning: Do not allow antifreeze to come in contact with your skin, or with the painted surfaces of the vehicle. Rinse off spills immediately with plenty of water. Never leave antifreeze lying around in an open container, or in a puddle in the driveway or on the garage floor. Children and pets are attracted by its sweet smell, but antifreeze is fatal if ingested.

 Warning: Refer to Section 9 for precautions to be observed when working on vehicles equipped with air conditioning.

2 Cooling system hoses - disconnection and renewal

Note: *Refer to the warnings given in Section 1 of this Chapter before proceeding. Hoses should only be disconnected once the engine has cooled sufficiently to avoid scalding.*

1 If the checks described in Chapter 1 reveal a faulty hose, it must be renewed as follows.
2 First drain the cooling system (see Chapter 1); if the antifreeze is not due for renewal, the drained coolant may be re-used, if it is collected in a clean container.

3 To disconnect any hose, use a pair of pliers to release the spring clamps (or a screwdriver to slacken screw-type clamps), then move them along the hose clear of the union. Carefully work the hose off its stubs. The hoses can be removed with relative ease when new - on an older vehicle, they may have stuck.
4 If a hose proves to be difficult to remove, try to release it by rotating it on its unions before attempting to work it off. Gently prise the end of the hose with a blunt instrument (such as a flat-bladed screwdriver), but do not apply too much force, and take care not to damage the pipe stubs or hoses. Note in particular that the radiator hose unions are fragile; do not use excessive force when attempting to remove the hoses.

 HAYNES HiNT *If all else fails, cut the hose with a sharp knife, then slit it so that it can be peeled off in two pieces. Although this may prove expensive if the hose is otherwise undamaged, it is preferable to buying a new radiator.*

5 When refitting a hose, first slide the clamps onto the hose, then engage the hose with its unions. Work the hose into position, then check that the hose is settled correctly and is properly routed. Slide each clip along the hose until it is behind the union flared end, before tightening it securely.

 HAYNES HiNT *If the hose is stiff, use a little soapy water as a lubricant, or soften the hose by soaking it in hot water. Do not use oil or grease, which may attack the rubber.*

6 Refill the system with coolant (Chapter 1).
7 Check carefully for leaks as soon as possible after disturbing any part of the cooling system.

3 Antifreeze - general information

Note: *Refer to the warnings given in Section 1 of this Chapter before proceeding.*

1 The cooling system should be filled with Volvo type C coolant (antifreeze) in a ratio of 50/50 with pure water. At this strength, the coolant will protect against freezing down to 35°C. Antifreeze also provides protection against corrosion, and increases the coolant boiling point. As the engine is of all aluminium construction, the corrosion protection properties of the antifreeze are critical. Only Volvo antifreeze should be used in the system and should never be mixed with different antifreeze types.
2 The cooling system should be maintained according to the schedule described in Chapter 1. If antifreeze is used that is not to Volvo's specification, old or contaminated coolant mixtures are likely to cause damage, and encourage the formation of corrosion and scale in the system.
3 Before adding antifreeze, check all hoses and hose connections, because antifreeze tends to leak through very small openings. Engines don't normally consume coolant, so if the level goes down, find the cause and correct it.
4 The specified mixture is 50% antifreeze and 50% clean soft water (by volume). Mix the required quantity in a clean container and then fill the system as described in Chapter 1, and *"Weekly checks"*. Save any surplus mixture for topping-up.

4 Radiator cooling fan - removal and refitting

Removal

1 Disconnect the battery negative lead.
2 Detach the air cleaner inlet duct and the ECU module box air duct from each side of the fan shroud **(see illustration)**.
3 On cars equipped with exhaust gas recirculation, disconnect the two hoses at the EGR controller noting their locations.
4 Undo the two bolts each side securing the fan shroud and relay carrier to the front body panel **(see illustration)**.
5 Lift up the relay carrier and disconnect the fan wiring connectors **(see illustration)**. Lay the carrier to one side, clear of the fan shroud.

4.2 Removing the air cleaner intake duct from the fan shroud

4.4 Fan shroud and relay carrier left-hand retaining bolts (arrowed)

4.5 Lift up the relay carrier and disconnect the fan wiring connectors

4.7 Lift the fan shroud up and out to remove

4.9 Ensure the lower locating pegs engage with the bottom of the radiator when refitting

cooler pipe unions from the radiator right-hand side tank. Plug or cap the lines to keep dirt out.
8 On turbo models, detach the intercooler air ducts as necessary for radiator removal.
9 Support the radiator, undo the lower mounting bolt on each side and lift the radiator out of the engine compartment.

Refitting

10 Refit by reversing the removal operations. With reference to Chapter 1, refill the cooling system on completion, and where applicable top-up the automatic transmission fluid and engine oil.

6 On turbo models, detach the intercooler air duct above the fan shroud.
7 Lift the shroud upwards to release the two lower locating pegs and remove the shroud and fan from the car **(see illustration)**.
8 Undo the four bolts and remove the motor and fan guard assembly from the shroud. This is the limit of dismantling as the motor, fan and guard are not available as separate components.

Refitting

9 Refitting is the reversal of removal. Ensure that the lower locating pegs engage with the bottom of the radiator as the shroud is refitted **(see illustration)**.

5.3a Undo the retaining bolt each side (arrowed) . . .

5 Radiator - removal and refitting

HAYNES HINT *If leakage is the reason for wanting to remove the radiator, bear in mind that minor leaks can often be cured using a radiator sealant with the radiator in situ.*

Removal

1 Drain the cooling system (see Chapter 1).
2 Remove the radiator cooling fan as described in Section 4.
3 Undo the retaining bolt each side, release the clips and remove the splash guard under the radiator **(see illustrations)**.
4 Disconnect the top and bottom hoses, from the radiator.
5 On cars equipped with air conditioning, undo the condenser upper mounting bolt on each side. Secure the condenser to the upper body panel with string or wire to retain it in position, then undo the two lower bolts **(see illustration)**.
6 On automatic transmission models, disconnect the fluid cooler lines from the radiator left-hand side tank. Be prepared for fluid spillage. Plug or cap the lines to keep dirt out.
7 Where fitted, disconnect the engine oil

6 Coolant temperature sensor - testing, removal and refitting

Testing

1 The coolant temperature sensor is located in the thermostat housing and is used by both the engine management system and the instrument panel temperature gauge to supply an engine temperature source signal.
2 In the event of a fault in the sensor or a loss of signal due to poor electrical connections a fault code will be logged in the engine management system ECU which can be read out via the diagnostic unit in the engine compartment. Refer to Chapter 4A, or Chapter 5B, for further information on fault code read out.
3 Should a fault code be logged, a careful check should be made of the sensor wiring and the wiring connector. Apart from testing by substitution with a new unit, further checks require the use of Volvo test equipment and should be entrusted to a dealer.

Removal

4 Partially drain the cooling system (see Chapter 1) to below the level of the sensor unit. Slacken the clip and disconnect the radiator top hose at the thermostat housing.
5 Disconnect the wiring at the adjacent connector then unscrew the sensor from its location in the thermostat housing **(see illustration)**.

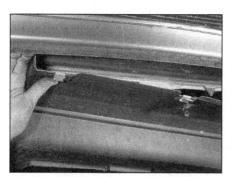

5.3b . . . release the front clips and remove the splash guard under the radiator

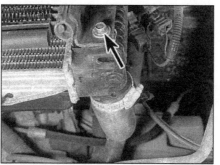

5.5 Left-hand air conditioning condenser lower mounting bolt (arrowed)

6.5 The coolant temperature sensor wiring connector is located above the alternator

7.3 Three of the seven coolant pump retaining bolts (arrowed)

8.3a Lift off the thermostat housing . . .

Refitting

6 Screw in the new sensor unit, using a smear of sealant on the threads. Reconnect the wiring connector and radiator hose.
7 Top-up the coolant level as described in *"Weekly checks"*.

7   Coolant pump - removal and refitting

Note: *Refer to the warnings given in Section 1 of this Chapter before proceeding.*

Removal

1 Disconnect the battery negative lead.
2 Refer to Chapter 2A and remove the timing belt.
3 Undo the seven bolts and remove the coolant pump from its locating dowels **(see illustration)**. Access is very limited and patience is needed. Recover the gasket after removing the pump.
4 Thoroughly clean all traces of old gasket from the pump and cylinder block mating faces.

Refitting

5 Using a new gasket, locate the pump in position.

8.3b . . . and remove the thermostat

6 Apply hydraulic sealing compound (available from Volvo dealers) to the threads of the retaining bolts and refit the bolts. Tighten the bolts progressively and in a diagonal sequence to the specified torque.
7 Refit the timing belt as described in Chapter 2A.

8   Thermostat - removal, testing and refitting

Note: *Refer to the warnings given in Section 1 of this Chapter before proceeding.*

Removal

1 Partially drain the cooling system (see Chapter 1) to below the level of the thermostat housing.
2 Release the radiator top hose and expansion tank hose from the thermostat housing then undo the two housing retaining bolts.
3 Lift off the housing and remove the thermostat and sealing ring **(see illustrations)**.

Testing

4 Check the temperature marking stamped on the thermostat which will be either 87°C or 90°.
5 Using a thermometer and container of water, heat the water until the temperature corresponds with the temperature marking stamped on the thermostat.
6 Suspend the (closed) thermostat on a length of string in the water and check that maximum opening occurs within two minutes.
7 Remove the thermostat and allow it to cool down; check that it closes fully.
8 If the thermostat does not open and close as described, or if it sticks in either position, it must be renewed.

Refitting

9 Fit a new sealing ring to the thermostat.
10 Refit the thermostat and housing and secure with the two bolts.
11 Reconnect the top hose and expansion tank hose, then refill the cooling system as described in Chapter 1 and *"Weekly checks"*.

9   Heating, ventilation and air conditioning systems - general information and precautions

Manual climate control system

1 On models equipped with a manual climate control system, the heater may be fitted alone, or in conjunction with a manually controlled air conditioning unit. The same housings and heater components are used in both cases
2 The heater is of the fresh air type. Air enters through a grille in front of the windscreen. On its way to the various vents a variable proportion of the air passes through the heater matrix, where it is warmed by engine coolant flowing through the matrix.
3 Distribution of air to the vents, and through or around the matrix, is controlled by flaps (dampers). These are operated by cables (except for the air recirculation damper, which is operated by an electric motor).
4 A four-speed electric fan is fitted to boost the airflow through the heater.
5 Where manual climate control including air conditioning is fitted, the system works In conjunction with the heater to enable any reasonable air temperature to be achieved inside the car. It also reduces the humidity of the incoming air, aiding demisting even when cooling is not required.
6 The refrigeration side of the air conditioning system functions in a similar way to a domestic refrigerator. A compressor, belt-driven from the crankshaft pulley, draws

refrigerant in its gaseous phase from an evaporator. The compound refrigerant passes through a condenser where it loses heat and enters its liquid phase. After dehydration the refrigerant returns to the evaporator where it absorbs heat from air passing over the evaporator fins. The refrigerant becomes a gas again and the cycle is repeated.

7 Various subsidiary controls and sensors protect the system against excessive temperature and pressures. Additionally, engine idle speed is increased when the system is in use to compensate for the additional load imposed by the compressor.

Electronic climate control system

8 On models with electronic climate control, the temperature inside the car can be automatically maintained at the level selected by the operator, irrespective of outside temperature. The computer controlled system operates the heater, air conditioner and fan functions as necessary to achieve this. The refrigeration side of the system is the same as for models with manual climate control; the fully automatic electronic control operates as follows.

9 An electronic control unit (ECU) receives signal inputs from sensors that detect the air duct temperatures on the driver's and passenger's side, interior temperature on the driver's and passenger's side, and outside temperature. A solar sensor is used to detect the presence of sunlight. Signals are also received from the dampers (air flaps) on their position at any given time. Information on engine temperature, whether or not the engine is running, and if so, the vehicle road speed, are also sent to the ECU from the engine management system. When the automatic function is engaged, the ECU can establish the optimum settings needed, based on the sensor signals, for the selected temperature and air distribution. These settings can then be maintained irrespective of driving conditions and weather.

10 Distribution of air to the various vents, and the blending of hot or cold air to achieve the selected temperature is controlled by dampers (flaps). These are operated by electric motors which are in turn controlled by the ECU. A variable speed fan which can be manually or automatically controlled is used to boost airflow through the system.

11 The ECU, which is located behind the control panel, incorporates a built-in fault diagnosis facility. A fault is signalled to the driver by the flashing of the two warning lights on the control panel for approximately 20 seconds every time the engine is started.

12 Should a fault occur, the ECU stores a series of signals (or fault codes) for subsequent read-out via the diagnostic unit located in the engine compartment.

Precautions

13 When an air conditioning system is fitted, it is necessary to observe special precautions whenever dealing with any part of the system, or its associated components. If for any reason the system must be discharged, entrust this task to your Volvo dealer or a refrigeration engineer.

 Warning: The refrigeration circuit contains R143a liquid refrigerant, and it is therefore dangerous to disconnect any part of the system without specialised knowledge and equipment.

14 The refrigerant is potentially dangerous, and should only be handled by qualified persons. If it is splashed onto the skin, it can cause frostbite. It is not itself poisonous, but in the presence of a naked flame (including a cigarette) it forms a poisonous gas. Uncontrolled discharging of the refrigerant is dangerous, and potentially damaging to the environment.

15 In view of the above points, removal and refitting of any air conditioning system components, except for the sensors and other peripheral items covered in this Chapter, must be left to a specialist.

---

10 Manual climate control system components - removal and refitting

Note: On cars equipped with manual climate control including air conditioning, the contents of this Section are limited to those operations which can be carried out without discharging the refrigerant. Renewal of the auxiliary (compressor) drivebelt is described in Chapter 1, but all other operations except those described below must be entrusted to a Volvo dealer or air conditioning specialist. If necessary, the compressor can be unbolted and moved aside, without disconnecting the refrigerant unions, after removing the drivebelt.

Control panel

Removal

1 Carefully pull off the three rotary control knobs from the front of the panel.

2 Undo the two screws now exposed behind the temperature control knobs, then withdraw the control panel front plate **(see illustration)**.

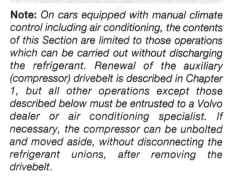

10.2 Manual climate control panel front plate retaining screws (arrowed)

3 Remove the fan control switch and recirculation control switch from the panel then undo the four screws and slide the panel out of its aperture.

4 Disconnect the wiring connector after undoing the two screws and removing the panel rear cover.

5 Note the location of the control cables as an aid to refitting. Release the retaining clips securing the outer cables, and detach the inner cables from the control lever pegs.

6 Remove the control panel from the car.

Refitting

7 Refit by reversing the removal operations. When reconnecting the cables, position the two temperature control cables so that the outer cable is flush with the retaining clip. Position the ventilation control and floor/defrost cables so that the outer cable protrudes through the retaining clip by 17.0 mm.

8 On completion, adjust the cables at the heater unit as described in the following sub-section.

Control cables

Removal

9 Undo the screws and remove the trim/sound proofing panels from under the facia on the left and right-hand sides.

10 Remove the heating/ventilation control panel as described previously.

11 Note the location of the control cables at the heater unit as an aid to refitting. Release the retaining clips securing the outer cables and detach the inner cables from the control lever pegs **(see illustration)**.

12 Remove the cables from the car.

Refitting and adjustment

13 Refit the cables to the heating/ventilation control panel then refit the panel as described in the previous sub-section.

14 Turn the temperature control knobs on the control panel to the "O" position. Connect the left-hand temperature control inner cable to the control lever peg on the heater unit. Move the control lever downwards to shut the damper, then secure the outer cable with the retaining clip. Reconnect and adjust the right-hand cable in the same way.

15 Set the function selector knob on the control panel to "defrost" (12 o'clock position). Connect the ventilation control and floor/defrost inner cables to the control lever pegs on the heater unit. Move the control levers forward, toward the front of the car, as far as they will go, then secure the outer cables with the retaining clips.

16 Check the operation of the controls and cables then refit the trim/sound proofing panels under the facia.

Heater fan motor

Removal

17 Undo the screws and remove the trim/sound proofing panel from under the facia on the passenger's side.

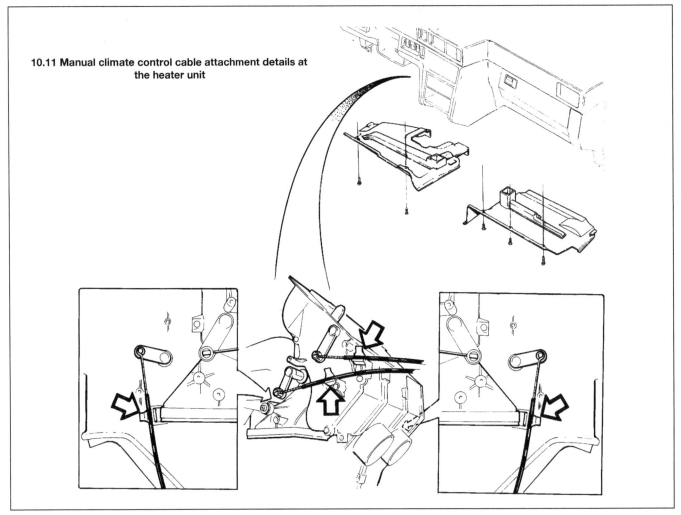

10.11 Manual climate control cable attachment details at the heater unit

18 Undo the four screws securing the glovebox compartment and the four screws securing the glovebox lid hinges. Remove the glovebox and lid from the facia.

19 Working through the glovebox aperture, disconnect the fan motor wiring connector.

20 Remove the cable duct from the fan motor and the two wiring connectors from their support brackets.

21 Undo the four screws and remove the fan motor from the heater unit **(see illustration).**

Refitting

22 Refit by reversing the removal operations.

Heater matrix

Removal

Note: *Refer to the warnings given in Section 1 of this Chapter before proceeding.*

23 Disconnect the battery negative lead.

24 Depressurise the cooling system by removing the expansion tank cap. Take precautions against scalding if the coolant is hot.

25 From within the engine compartment, clamp the coolant hoses which lead to the heater matrix stubs on the bulkhead.

26 Undo the screws and remove the trim/sound proofing panels from under the facia on the left- and right-hand sides.

27 Undo the screws and remove the carpet support plates on each side of the heater unit. Bend back the carpet to allow the support plates to be withdrawn.

28 Remove the amplifier (if fitted) and amplifier bracket.

29 Remove the drain hose from the front of the unit.

30 Undo the two screws each side securing the matrix housing to the heater unit **(see illustration).**

31 Place absorbent rags and/or paper beneath the heater pipe attachment at the rear of the matrix.

32 Undo the screw securing the heater pipe flange to the rear of the matrix. Be prepared for coolant spillage.

33 Pull the bottom of the housing rearwards to disengage the heater pipes. Manoeuvre the housing to free it from the heater unit then, once free, move it sideways and out from under the facia.

34 With the housing removed, undo the four screws and withdraw the matrix from the housing.

Refitting

35 Refit by reversing the removal operations. Use new O-rings on the heater pipes and top-up the cooling system as described in *"Weekly checks"* on completion.

Recirculation damper motor

Removal

36 Undo the four screws securing the glovebox compartment and the four screws securing the glovebox lid hinges. Remove the glovebox and lid from the facia.

37 Working through the glovebox aperture, disconnect the damper motor wiring connector.

38 Undo the two screws and remove the damper motor from the side of the heater fan motor housing.

Refitting

39 Refit by reversing the removal operations.

Heater fan motor resistor

Removal

40 Undo the four screws securing the glovebox compartment and the four screws

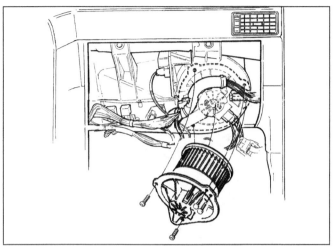

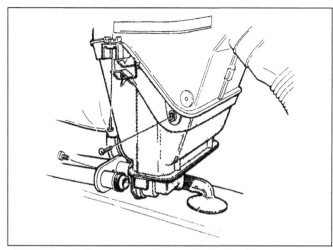

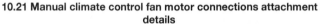

10.21 Manual climate control fan motor connections attachment details

10.30 Manual climate control heater matrix housing components and attachments

securing the glovebox lid hinges. Remove the glovebox and lid from the facia.

41 Working through the glovebox aperture, disconnect the wiring connector, undo the screws and remove the resistor from alongside the heater fan motor housing.

Refitting

42 Refit by reversing the removal operations.

Panel vents

Removal

43 Tip the vent downwards and pull it out of its location, or carefully lever out sideways using a screwdriver.

Refitting

44 Push the vent firmly into place to refit.

---

11 Electronic climate control system components -
removal and refitting

Note: *The contents of this Section is limited to those operations which can be carried out without discharging the refrigerant. Renewal of the auxiliary (compressor) drivebelt is described in Chapter 1, but all other operations except those described below must be entrusted to a Volvo dealer or air conditioning specialist. If necessary, the compressor can be unbolted and moved aside, without disconnecting the refrigerant unions, after removing the drivebelt.*

Many of the components used in the heating/ventilation side of the system are also used on cars equipped with manual climate control. Refer to Section 10 for procedures relating to the heater fan motor, heater matrix, and panel vents.

Control panel and ECU

Removal

1 Remove the radio as described in Chapter 12.

2 Reach up through the radio aperture and depress the locking button on the underside of the unit.

3 Push out one rear corner of the unit to free it from its location and remove it from the facia aperture.

4 Disconnect the three wiring connectors and remove the unit from the car.
Refitting

5 Refit by reversing the removal operations. Refit the radio with reference to Chapter 12.

Outside temperature sensor

Removal

6 Remove the windscreen wiper arms as described in Chapter 12.

7 Undo the five screws securing the windscreen wiper well cover to the scuttle at the front. Disconnect the two drain hoses and lift off the well cover.

8 Locate the outside temperature sensor on the side of the interior air inlet duct on the driver's side **(see illustration)**.

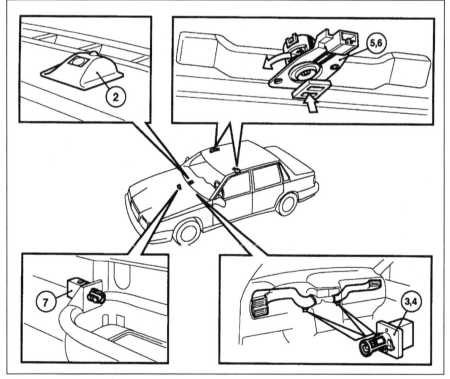

11.8 Electronic climate control sensor location details

2	Solar sensor	5,6	Interior temperature sensors
3,4	Air duct temperature sensors	7	Outside temperature sensor

9 Carefully prise the sensor out of its mounting bracket, depress the catches and disconnect the wiring connector.

Refitting

10 Refit by reversing the removal operations. Refit the wiper arms with reference to Chapter 12.

Interior temperature sensor

Removal

11 The temperature sensor for the car interior is located behind the grab handle over the front door on either the driver's or passenger's side. It can be identified by the presence of a small inlet hole in the trim cover behind the relevant handle.

12 Lift up the grab handle end covers using a small screwdriver inserted into the top of the cover.

13 Undo the two retaining screws and carefully prise the handle off using a screwdriver.

14 Carefully release the B-pillar trim panel at the top then pull off the roof sill panel between the A and B-pillars.

15 Disconnect the wiring connector, undo the two screws and remove the sensor.

Refitting

16 Refit by reversing the removal operations.

Air duct temperature sensor

Removal

17 Remove the control panel and ECU as described earlier in this Section.

18 Undo the screws and remove the trim/sound proofing panels from under the facia on the left and right-hand sides.

19 Undo the four screws securing the glovebox compartment and the four screws securing the glovebox lid hinges. Remove the glovebox and lid from the facia.

20 Disconnect the wiring connector from the temperature sensor located in the air duct.

21 Release the cable-tie and pull the sensor downward to remove it from the air duct.

Refitting

22 Refit by reversing the removal operations.

Damper motors

Removal

23 Five damper motors are fitted; three on the passenger's side and two on the driver's side **(see illustration)**. Removal and refitting procedures are essentially the same for all five, although access limitations will vary between left-hand and right-hand drive models.

24 Undo the screws and remove the trim/sound proofing panels from under the facia on the left and right-hand sides.

25 Undo the four screws securing the glovebox compartment and the four screws securing the glovebox lid hinges. Remove the glovebox and lid from the facia.

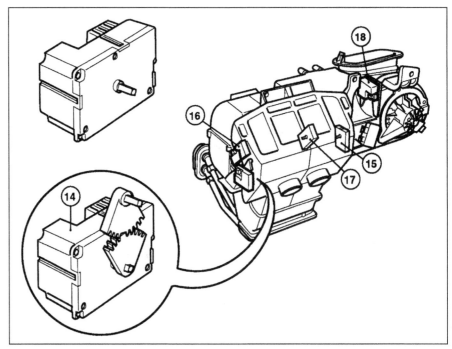

11.23 Electronic climate control damper motor details

14	Ventilation damper motor	17	Passenger's side temperature
15	Floor/defrost damper motor		damper motor
16	Driver's side temperature damper	18	Recirculation damper motor
	motor		

26 Locate the relevant damper motor then disconnect the wiring connector by depressing the catches on the side and pulling off.

27 Undo the three screws and remove the motor from the damper shaft. Note that the ventilation damper motors are fitted with a geared segment on their output shaft which engages with a matching geared segment on the damper shaft.

Refitting

28 Refit by reversing the removal operations. If a new damper motor has been fitted it will be necessary for the ECU to "learn" the limit stop positions of the new motor by running it in a self-adjustment mode as follows.

Automatic self-adjustment

Note: *The following procedure is only necessary when a new damper motor has been fitted.*

29 Move the fan speed control switch on the control panel to one of the manually active settings (ie any position except "O" or "AUT").

30 Turn the function selector knob to the "AUT" position.

31 Locate the diagnostic unit which is situated in the front right-hand side of the engine compartment, alongside the windscreen washer reservoir filler. The diagnostic unit consists of two modules mounted side by side, with a plastic cover over each. Lift off the covers and note that the two modules are marked A and B, each having six numbered sockets on their top face.

32 Switch on the ignition and press the test button on top of module A four times, for about one second each time, then release it and wait for the LED to flash. When the LED starts flashing the ECU is ready to receive a control code.

33 Enter the control code 9-9-9 by pressing the test button nine times quickly in succession. Wait for the LED to light then press the button nine times again, wait for the LED once more then press the button a further nine times. You must enter each digit (each series of nine presses of the button) within four seconds, otherwise the ECU will not accept the digit.

34 Wait for about ten seconds to let the fan motor start then switch off the ignition and switch it on again; the "AC" and "REC" lights on the control panel should flash.

35 Drive the car at a speed over 20 mph for a few minutes to let the ECU "learn" the new values. Stop the car but leave the ignition switched on for two minutes to allow the ECU to store the new values now learned.

36 Check whether the self-adjustment procedure has been successful as follows.

37 Unclip the flylead from the holder on the side of the diagnostic unit and insert it into socket 1 of module B.

38 With the ignition switched on, press the test button on top of module A once, for about one second, then release it and wait for the LED to flash. Copy down the three-digit code which will be displayed as a series of blinks of the red LED. with a slight pause between each digit.

39 If code 1-1-1 is obtained, this indicates that the self-adjustment procedure has been completed successfully. If code 5-1-1 appears this indicates that the self-adjustment procedure has not been successfully completed and it should be carried out again. If a code other than 1-1-1 or 5-1-1 appears, this indicates that there is a fault in the system, refer to Section 12 if this is the case.
40 On completion, switch off the ignition, locate the flylead in its holder and refit the unit covers.

Air conditioning relay and power stage

Removal

41 Undo the screws and remove the trim/sound proofing panels from under the facia on the left and right-hand sides.
42 Undo the four screws securing the glovebox compartment and the four screws securing the glovebox lid hinges. Remove the glovebox and lid from the facia.
43 The relay can now be removed by pulling it up and out of the holder base.
44 Disconnect the power stage wiring connector by depressing the catches on the side and pulling off.
45 Undo the retaining screw and remove the power stage.

Refitting

46 Refit by reversing the removal operations.

Solar sensor

Removal

47 The solar sensor is combined with the anti-theft alarm system diode and is located on top of the facia cover.
48 Carefully prise up the sensor using a screwdriver inserted under its base at the side.
49 Disconnect the wiring connector and remove the sensor.

Refitting

50 Refit by reversing the removal operations.

12 Electronic climate control system - fault diagnosis

General information

1 The electronic climate control system (together with many of the other systems on the Volvo 850) incorporates an on-board diagnostic system to facilitate fault finding and system testing. The diagnostic system is a feature of the electronic climate control electronic control unit (ECU) which continually monitors the system components and their operation. Should a fault occur, the ECU stores a series of signals (or fault codes) for subsequent read-out via the diagnostic unit located in the engine compartment.
2 If a fault occurs, indicated by the flashing of the "REC" and "AC OFF" warning lights on the control panel, the on-board diagnostics can be

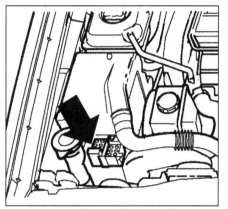

12.4 Diagnostic unit location (arrowed) adjacent to washer reservoir

used to initially pinpoint any problem areas without the use of special test equipment. Once this has been done, however, further tests may often be necessary to determine the exact nature of the fault; ie, whether a component itself has failed, or whether it is a wiring or other inter-related problem.

Fault code read-out

Note: *On models from 1996 the diagnostic unit is located under a cover in front of the gear lever and has a 16-pin socket for connection to a fault code reader.*

3 In the event of a fault suspected in the system, or indicated by the illumination of the warning lights, the first step is to check whether a fault code has been logged and if so, to interpret the meaning of the code.
4 Locate the diagnostic unit which is situated in the front right-hand side of the engine compartment, alongside the windscreen washer reservoir filler **(see illustration)**. The diagnostic unit consists of two modules mounted side by side, with a plastic cover over each. Lift off the covers and note that the two modules are marked A and B, each having six numbered sockets on their top face.
5 With the ignition switched off, unclip the flylead from the holder on the side of the unit and insert it into socket 1 of module B **(see illustration)**.
6 Have a paper and pen ready to copy down the fault codes as they are displayed. The three-digit codes will be displayed as a series of blinks of the red LED (located on the top face of module A, next to the test button) with a slight pause between each digit.
7 With the flylead inserted, switch on the ignition. Press the test button on top of module A once, for about one second, then release it and wait for the LED to flash. As the LED flashes, copy down the fault code. Now press the button again and copy down the next fault code, if there is one. Continue until the first fault code is displayed again indicating that all the stored codes have been accessed, then switch off the ignition.
8 If code 1-1-1 is obtained, this indicates that

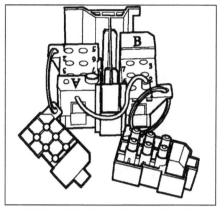

12.5 Insert the flylead into socket 1 of diagnostic module B to access the electronic climate control fault codes

there are no fault codes stored in the ECU and the system is operating correctly.
9 Given in the accompanying table (shown overleaf) are the possible electronic climate control fault codes and their meaning.
10 Once all the fault codes have been recorded they should be deleted from the ECU. Note that the fault codes cannot be deleted until all of them have been displayed at least once, and the first one is displayed again. With the flylead still inserted in position 1 of module B, switch on the ignition, press the test button and hold it down for approximately five seconds. Release the test button and after three seconds the LED will light. When the LED lights, press and hold the test button down for a further five seconds then release it - the LED will go out. Switch off the ignition and check that all the fault codes have been deleted by switching the ignition on again and pressing the test button for one second - code 1-1-1 should appear. If a code other than 1-1-1 appears, record the code then repeat the deleting procedure. When all the codes have been deleted, switch off the ignition, locate the flylead in its holder and refit the unit covers.
11 Once the location of a fault has been established from the fault code read-out, investigations can be concentrated in that area. In many instances, the fault may be nothing more serious than a corroded, trapped or loose wiring connection, or a loose, dirty, or badly fitted component. Remember that if the fault has appeared only a short time after any part of the vehicle has been serviced or overhauled, the first place to check is where that work was carried out, however unrelated it may appear, to ensure that no carelessly-refitted components are causing the problem.
12 If the fault cannot be easily cured in this way, further detailed checking of the system components will require the use of Volvo test equipment. Therefore the only alternatives possible at this time are the substitution of a suspect component with a known good unit, or entrusting further work to a Volvo dealer. If a substitute unit can be obtained (or borrowed), removal and refitting procedures are given in the previous Section of this Chapter.

Electronic climate control system - fault diagnosis

Fault code	Meaning
1-1-1	No fault detected
1-2-1	Outside temperature sensor shorted to earth
1-2-2	Outside temperature sensor open circuit or shorted to 12 volts
1-2-3	Driver's side interior temperature sensor shorted to earth
1-2-4	Driver's side interior temperature sensor open circuit or shorted to 12 volts
1-2-5	Passenger's side interior temperature sensor shorted to earth
1-2-6	Passenger's side interior temperature sensor open circuit or shorted to 12 volts
1-3-1	Driver's side air duct temperature sensor shorted to earth
1-3-2	Driver's side air duct temperature sensor open circuit or shorted to 12 volts
1-3-3	Passenger's side air duct temperature sensor shorted to earth
1-3-4	Passenger's side air duct temperature sensor open circuit or shorted to 12 volts
1-3-5	No signal from engine coolant temperature sensor
1-4-1	Faulty signal from driver's side temperature selector switch
1-4-3	Faulty signal from passenger's side temperature selector switch
1-4-5	Faulty signal from function selector switch
1-5-1	Signal from fan speed sensor missing or too high
1-5-2	Signal from fan speed sensor shorted to earth
2-1-1	Driver's side damper motor position sensor open circuit or shorted to 12 volts
2-1-2	Driver's side damper motor position sensor shorted to earth
2-2-1	Passenger's side damper motor position sensor open circuit or shorted to 12 volts
2-2-2	Passenger's side damper motor position sensor shorted to earth
2-3-1	Ventilation damper motor position sensor open circuit or shorted to 12 volts
2-3-2	Ventilation damper motor position sensor shorted to earth
2-3-3	Floor/defrost damper motor position sensor open circuit or shorted to 12 volts
2-3-4	Floor/defrost damper motor position sensor shorted to earth
2-3-5	Recirculation damper motor position sensor open circuit or shorted to 12 volts
2-3-6	Recirculation damper motor position sensor shorted to earth
3-1-1	Driver's side damper motor shorted to earth or 12 volts
3-1-2	Passenger's side damper motor shorted to earth or 12 volts
3-1-3	Ventilation damper motor shorted to earth or 12 volts
3-1-4	Floor/defrost damper motor shorted to earth or 12 volts
3-1-5	Recirculation damper motor shorted to earth or 12 volts
3-2-1	Driver's side damper motor active too long
3-2-2	Passenger's side damper motor active too long
3-2-3	Ventilation damper motor active too long
3-2-4	Floor/defrost side damper motor active too long
3-2-5	Recirculation damper motor active too long
4-1-1	Blower fan seized or drawing excessive current
4-1-2	Driver's side interior temperature sensor inlet fan shorted to earth
4-1-3	No control voltage at driver's side interior temperature sensor inlet fan
4-1-4	Driver's side interior temperature sensor inlet fan seized
4-1-5	Passenger's side interior temperature sensor inlet fan shorted to earth
4-1-6	No control voltage at passenger's side interior temperature sensor inlet fan
4-1-7	Passenger's side interior temperature sensor inlet fan seized
4-1-8	No control signal to blower fan power stage
4-1-9	Faulty diagnostic signal from blower fan power stage
4-2-0	ECU fault in program memory
5-1-1	Damper motor limit position self-adjustment not carried out

Chapter 4 Part A:
Fuel system

Contents

Degrees of difficulty

Easy, suitable for novice with little experience		**Fairly easy,** suitable for beginner with some experience		**Fairly difficult,** suitable for competent DIY mechanic		**Difficult,** suitable for experienced DIY mechanic		**Very difficult,** suitable for expert DIY or professional	

Specifications

System type
B5204 S, and B5234 S	LH3.2-Jetronic fuel injection system
B5202 S, and B5252 S engines	Fenix 5.2 engine management system
B5204 T, and B5234 T engines	Motronic 4.3 engine management system
B5254 S engines	LH3.2-Jetronic fuel injection system, or Motronic 4.3 engine management system (according to market territory)

Fuel system data
Idle speed*:	
Pre-1994 models	800 rpm
1994 models onward	850 rpm
Idle mixture CO content*	0.6 ± 0.4%
Fuel pump delivery rate	1.45 to 2.41 litres/minute (at 12 volts)
Regulated fuel pressure	3.03 bars

Non-adjustable - controlled by ECU

Recommended fuel
Octane rating:	
Recommended	95 RON unleaded*
Minimum	91 RON unleaded

98 RON unleaded fuel is recommended for B 5234 T5 engines

Torque wrench settings

	Nm
Inlet manifold bolts	20
Fuel rail to inlet manifold:	
Stage 1	10
Stage 2	Tighten through a further 75°
Fuel pump plastic retaining nut	40
Fuel gauge sender unit plastic retaining nut	30

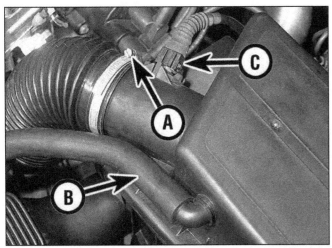
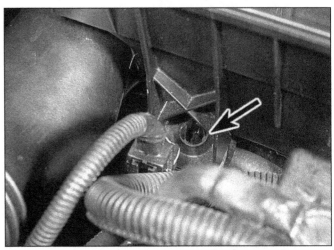

2.1 Disconnect the air duct (A), ventilation hose (B), and wiring connector (C) at the air cleaner cover

2.7a Disengage the air cleaner housing lower retainer (arrowed) . . .

1 General information and precautions

General information

The fuel system consists of a centrally-mounted fuel tank, an electric fuel pump, a fuel filter and a fully electronic fuel injection system. Further details of the fuel injection systems will be found in Section 8.

Twenty valve, non turbo engines are equipped with a variable venturi inlet system whereby the inlet manifold incorporates two separate inlet tracts, each of different length and diameter, for each cylinder. The shorter tracts can be opened or closed by means of vacuum operated flap valves under the control of the ignition system ECU. At low engine speeds, both inlet tracts are opened to allow a rapid increase in airflow when the throttle is opened. At the mid-range speed, the flap valves are closed and airflow is through the longer tracts only. These are tuned for this speed range to cause the inlet air to resonate with the movement of the engine pistons and valves. These "pulses" coincide with inlet valve opening, providing a greater inlet charge than that of a conventional system. At high engine speeds both tracts are once again opened to provide maximum torque in this range.

Depending on engine type, models for some market territories are also equipped with an exhaust gas recirculation (EGR) system and secondary air injection system, as part of an emissions control package. Further details of these systems will be found in Part B of this Chapter.

Precautions

Warning: Petrol is extremely flammable - great care must be taken when working on any part of the fuel system. Do not smoke

or allow any naked flames or uncovered light bulbs near the work area. Note that gas powered domestic appliances with pilot flames, such as heaters, boilers and tumble dryers, also present a fire hazard - bear this in mind if you are working in an area where such appliances are present. Always keep a suitable fire extinguisher close to the work area and familiarise yourself with its operation before starting work. Wear eye protection when working on fuel systems and wash off any fuel spilt on bare skin immediately with soap and water. Note that fuel vapour is just as dangerous as liquid fuel; a vessel that has just been emptied of liquid fuel will still contain vapour and can be potentially explosive. Petrol is a highly dangerous and volatile liquid, and the precautions necessary when handling it cannot be overstressed.

Many of the operations described in this Chapter involve the disconnection of fuel lines, which may cause an amount of fuel spillage. Before commencing work, refer to the above Warning and the information in "Safety first" at the beginning of this manual.

When working with fuel system components, pay particular attention to cleanliness - dirt entering the fuel system may cause blockages which will lead to poor running.

2 Air cleaner assembly and air ducts - removal and refitting

Removal

Air cleaner assembly

1 Slacken the hose clip and detach the air outlet duct and, where applicable, the crankcase ventilation hose at the air cleaner cover **(see illustration)**.

2 Disconnect the wiring connector from the mass air flow sensor or inlet air temperature sensor in the cover outlet.

3 Release the HT lead to the ignition coil from the clips at the rear of the cover.

4 Spring back the retaining clips, lift off the cover and remove the air cleaner element.

5 Detach the cold air inlet duct from the air inlet adjacent to the radiator.

6 Detach the warm air inlet duct or turbocharger inlet duct, as applicable, from the air cleaner housing. On turbo models, detach the turbo control valve from the air cleaner housing (where fitted).

7 Lift the housing upwards at the engine side to release the lower retainers, then move it sideways to disengage the side locating peg **(see illustrations)**. Remove the housing from the car.

2.7b . . . lift the housing up at the engine side . . .

2.7c . . . and move it sideways to release the side peg . . .

Air ducts

8 All ducting is retained either by simple snap fit connectors or by hose clips. The routing of the ducts varies between normally-aspirated and turbo models, but in all cases removal is straight forward and self-explanatory. To gain access to the lower ducts it will be necessary to remove the air cleaner assembly as previously described.

Refitting

9 In all cases, refit by reversing the removal operations.

---

3 Intake air pre-heating system - testing

1 An inlet air pre-heating system is incorporated in the air cleaner housing on non-turbo models for certain markets. The system utilises a flap valve arrangement controlled by a wax capsule to blend cold air from the inlet adjacent to the radiator, with warm air from the exhaust manifold heat shield. The capsule responds to ambient temperature to move the flap valve accordingly.

2 To gain access to the unit, remove the air cleaner assembly as described in Section 2.

4.1 Remove the cover over the accelerator cable drum and linkage

3.3a Remove the intake body from the air cleaner housing . . .

3 Remove the inlet body from the air cleaner housing by depressing the two tabs and pulling the body free **(see illustrations)**.

4 Check the condition of the spindle bearings, capsule and spring, then test the operation of the capsule as follows.

5 Cool the unit by placing it in a refrigerator for a few minutes. Check that at a temperature of approximately 5°C or less, the flap valve has moved to shut off the cold air inlet.

6 As the unit warms in response to room temperature, check that at approximately 10°C the flap valve is in the mid-position, and that at 15°C or higher, the flap has moved to shut off the warm air inlet.

7 If the unit does not function as described, it should be renewed.

8 On completion, reassemble the inlet body, then refit the air cleaner assembly as described in Section 2.

---

4 Accelerator cable - removal, refitting and adjustment

Removal

1 Undo the screw and remove the cover over the accelerator cable drum and linkage **(see illustration)**.

3.3b . . . for access to the pre-heating wax capsule

2 Release the outer cable retaining clip from the cable adjuster and unhook the inner cable from the drum **(see illustrations)**.

3 Undo the screws and remove the trim/sound proofing panel from under the facia on the driver's side. Pull the cable inner through the end of the pedal and slide the split bush off the end of the cable.

4 On manual transmission models, release the cable grommet from the bulkhead and pull the cable into the engine compartment. Note the routing of the cable, release it from any clips or ties, and remove it.

5 On automatic transmission models, disconnect the wiring connector from the kickdown switch attached to the cable at the bulkhead entry. Release the kickdown switch from the bulkhead by depressing the switch lugs with a screwdriver, whilst at the same time pushing the cable through. Note the routing of the cable, release it from any clips or ties, and remove it.

Refitting

6 Refit by reversing the removal operations, ensuring that on automatic transmission models the kickdown switch lugs fully engage in the bulkhead, and that the switch wiring connector is upright. Adjust the cable as follows before re-connecting it at the throttle housing end.

4.2a Release the outer cable retaining clip . . .

4.2b . . . then unhook the inner cable from the drum

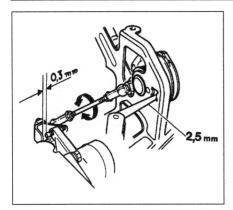

4.9 Throttle linkage adjustment details

5.4 Remove the access cover over the sender unit

5.6 Unscrew the sender unit plastic retaining nut using a wide opening pair of grips

Adjustment (early models)

7 Locate the link rod which joins the cable drum to the linkage on the throttle housing. If the two plastic balljoints on the link are both secured by locknuts, proceed as follows. If only one is secured by a locknut, proceed as from paragraph 14.

8 Slacken both the link balljoint locknuts.

9 Insert a 2.5 mm feeler blade between the drum and the idle stop on the drum bracket **(see illustration)**.

10 Turn the link rod as necessary until the throttle lever is clear of the adjusting screw on the throttle housing by 0.3 mm. Do not alter the position of the adjusting screw.

11 Hold the link rod and tighten the two locknuts.

12 Remove the feeler blade and allow the cable drum to rest against the idle stop. Check that a 0.5 mm feeler blade will not fit between the throttle lever and the adjusting screw, but a 1.0 mm feeler blade will. Repeat the adjustment procedure if necessary.

13 Reconnect the inner cable to the drum and secure the outer cable with the retaining clip. Adjust the cable at the adjuster so that it is taut, but does not prevent the drum from closing onto the idle stop. Depress the accelerator pedal to the floor and check that the drum reaches the full-load stop.

Adjustment (later models)

14 Check that the cable drum is seated against the idle stop on the drum bracket and that the throttle lever on the throttle housing is contacting the adjusting screw. If this is not the case, slacken the link rod balljoint locknut so that the link rod will slide easily within the balljoint. Position the drum and throttle lever as just described, then tighten the locknut.

15 Reconnect the inner cable to the drum and secure the outer cable with the retaining clip. Adjust the cable at the adjuster so that it is taut, but does not prevent the drum from closing onto the idle stop. Depress the accelerator pedal to the floor and check that the drum reaches the full-load stop.

5 Fuel gauge sender unit - removal and refitting

Note: *Observe the precautions in Section 1 before working on any component in the fuel system.*

Removal

1 Disconnect the battery negative lead.

2 On Saloon models, fold down the rear seat backrest and release the front edge of the boot carpet. Remove the support panel under the carpet. Undo the backrest catch, release the fasteners and remove the boot side trim panel

3 On Estate models, undo the retaining screws from the luggage compartment front floor panel. Pull the panel to the rear to release the front mountings and remove the panel.

4 Undo the nuts and remove the access covers over the fuel pump and sender unit. The sender unit is beneath the cover nearest the front of the car **(see illustration)**.

5 Trace the wiring for the sender unit, which runs across the top of the fuel tank to the fuel pump, then out to the group of connectors adjacent to the shock absorber upper mounting. Disconnect the relevant connector, release any cable-ties, then feed the wiring back and through the sender unit aperture in the floor.

6 Unscrew the sender unit plastic retaining nut using a wide opening pair of grips **(see illustration)**. Certain types of oil filter removal tools are an ideal alternative.

7 Withdraw the sender unit from the fuel tank and recover the seal. Refit the plastic nut to the tank while the sender unit is removed to prevent the pipe stub swelling.

Refitting

8 Refitting is a reversal of removal, bearing in mind the following points:
   a) *Use a new seal smeared with petroleum jelly.*
   b) *Position the sender unit so that the wiring is toward the centre of the car.*
   c) *Route the wiring over the top of the fuel tank and out through the fuel pump aperture. Reconnect and secure with cable-ties where applicable.*

6 Fuel pump - removal and refitting

Note: *Observe the precautions in Section 1 before working on any component in the fuel system.*

Removal

1 Carry out the operations described in Section 5, paragraphs 1 to 3.

2 Undo the nuts and remove the access cover over the fuel pump (the rearmost cover of the two).

3 Trace the wiring for the pump, which runs across to the group of connectors adjacent to the shock absorber upper mounting. Disconnect the relevant connector and release any cable-ties.

4 Identify the fuel hose connections on top of the pump as an aid to refitting. The delivery hose should be marked with a yellow band with a corresponding yellow mark on top of the pump flange **(see illustration)**. Make your own marks if none are visible.

5 Place absorbent rags around the fuel hose connections then disconnect the quick-release couplings using a forked tool. Insert the tool under the edge of the outer sleeve of each coupling, and lever upwards without squeezing the sleeve. Be prepared for an initial release of fuel under pressure as the couplings are released.

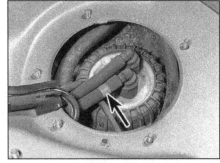

6.4 The fuel delivery hose at the pump connection should be marked with a yellow band (arrowed)

6 Unscrew the pump plastic retaining nut using a wide opening pair of grips. Certain types of oil filter removal tools are an ideal alternative.

7 Withdraw the pump from the tank and recover the seal. Refit the plastic nut to the tank while the pump is removed to prevent the pipe stub swelling.

Refitting

8 Lubricate a new seal sparingly with petroleum jelly and ensure it is correctly seated.

9 Refit the pump with the wiring connection towards the right-hand side of the car. Refit the plastic nut and tighten securely.

10 Lubricate the fuel hose coupling O-rings with petroleum jelly, position them squarely over the pump outlets and push down on the outer sleeves to lock. Ensure that the hoses are fitted to their correct outlets as noted during removal.

11 The remainder of refitting is a reversal of removal.

7 Fuel tank - removal and refitting

Note: *Observe the precautions in Section 1 before working on any component in the fuel system.*

Removal

1 Before the tank can be removed, it must be drained of as much fuel as possible. To avoid the dangers and complications of fuel handling and storage, it is advisable to carry out this operation with the tank almost empty. Any fuel remaining can be drained as follows.

2 Disconnect the battery negative lead.

3 Using a hand pump or syphon inserted through the filler neck, remove any remaining fuel from the bottom of the tank. Alternatively, chock the front wheels then jack up the rear of the vehicle and support it on axle stands (see *"Jacking and vehicle support"*). Place a suitable large capacity container under the fuel filter. Clean the fuel inlet quick-release coupling on the filter, place rags around the coupling, then disconnect it. Be prepared for an initial release of fuel under pressure as the coupling is released. Hold the disconnected fuel line over the container and allow the fuel to drain. Store the fuel in a suitable sealed container.

4 Carry out the operations described in Section 5, paragraphs 1 to 5, and Section 6, paragraphs 3 to 5.

5 Remove the circlip securing the filler neck to the body and release the filler neck and seals from their locations.

6 Position a trolley jack under the centre of the tank. Insert a protective wooden pad between the jack head and tank base, then raise the jack to just take the weight of the tank.

7 Undo the tank retaining straps and carefully lower the jack and tank slightly. When sufficient clearance exists, disconnect the vent hoses leading to the front of the car. The hoses between the tank and filler tube can be left in place.

8 Lower the jack and tank, and remove the tank from under the car.

9 If the tank is contaminated with sediment or water, remove the gauge sender unit and the fuel pump as described previously, and disconnect the ventilation hoses and filler tube. Swill the tank out with clean fuel. The tank is moulded from a synthetic material and if damaged, it should be renewed. However, in certain cases it may be possible to have small leaks or minor damage repaired. Seek the advice of a dealer or suitable specialist concerning tank repair.

10 If a new tank is to be fitted, transfer all the components from the old tank to the new. Always renew the filler tube seal and the seals and plastic nuts securing the fuel pump and gauge sender unit. Once used, they may not seat and seal properly on a new tank.

Refitting

11 Refitting is a reversal of removal bearing in mind the following points:

a) *Locate the tank in position and tighten the rear strap mountings. Push the tank forward and centre the fuel gauge sender unit and fuel pump plastic nuts with respect to their access holes in the floor. Now tighten the front strap mountings.*

b) *Lubricate the filler neck seals and ensure that they are properly located. Make sure that the drain tube is on the inside of the inner seal.*

c) *On completion, refill the tank with fuel and check exhaustively for signs of leakage before driving the car on the road.*

8 Fuel injection systems - general information

Bosch LH3.2-Jetronic system

The Bosch LH3.2-Jetronic system is fitted to the non-turbocharged 20-valve engines, except for some versions of the B5254 S engine which utilise the Motronic 4.3 system described later in this Section.

LH3.2-Jetronic is a microprocessor-controlled fuel injection system, designed to meet stringent emission control legislation whilst still providing excellent engine performance and fuel economy. This is achieved by continuously monitoring the engine using various sensors, whose data is input to the system's electronic control unit (ECU). Based on this information, the ECU program and memory then determine the exact amount of fuel necessary, which is injected directly into the inlet manifold, for all actual and anticipated driving conditions.

The LH3.2-Jetronic ECU, interacts with the EZ-29K ignition system ECU, to provide a total engine management package. In addition, it also controls various aspects of the emissions control systems described in Part B of this Chapter.

The main components of the fuel side of the system and their individual operation is as follows.

Electronic control unit

The ECU is a microprocessor, which controls the entire operation of the fuel system. Contained in the unit memory is a program which controls the fuel supply to the injectors, and their opening duration. The program enters sub-routines to alter these parameters, according to inputs from the other components of the system. In addition to this, the engine idle speed is also controlled by the ECU, which uses an idle air control valve to open or close an air passage as required. The ECU also incorporates a self-diagnostic facility in which the entire fuel system is continuously monitored for correct operation. Any detected faults are logged as fault codes which can be displayed by activating the on-board diagnostic unit. In the event of a fault in the system due to loss of a signal from one of the sensors, the ECU reverts to an emergency ("limp-home") program. This will allow the car to be driven, although engine operation and performance will be limited.

Fuel injectors

Each fuel injector consists of a solenoid-operated needle valve, which opens under commands from the ECU. Fuel from the fuel rail is then delivered through the injector nozzle into the inlet manifold.

Coolant temperature sensor

This resistive device is screwed into the thermostat housing, where its element is in direct contact with the engine coolant. Changes in coolant temperature are detected by the ECU as a change in sensor resistance. Signals from the coolant temperature sensor are also used by the ignition system ECU and by the temperature gauge in the instrument panel.

Mass air flow sensor

The MAF sensor measures the mass of air drawn into the engine. The sensor is of the "hot-film" type containing four different resistive elements and related circuitry. The unit is located in the air cleaner inlet and uses the inlet air to alter the resistance of the elements. By comparing the changing resistance values with a calibration resistance, the ECU can establish the inlet air temperature, and from its cooling effect, the inlet air volume.

Throttle position sensor

The throttle position sensor is a potentiometer attached to the throttle shaft in the throttle housing. The unit sends a linear signal to both the fuel and ignition system ECUs proportional to throttle opening.

Idle air control valve

The idle air control valve contains a small electric motor that open or shuts a bypass air passage inside the valve. The valve only operates when the throttle is closed, and in response to signals from the ECU, maintains the engine idle speed at a constant value irrespective of any additional load from the various accessories.

Fuel pump

The electric fuel pump is located in the fuel tank, and totally submerged in the fuel. The unit is a two stage device consisting of an electric motor which drives an impeller pump to draw in fuel, and a gear pump to discharge it under pressure. The fuel is then supplied to the fuel rail on the inlet manifold via an in-line fuel filter.

Fuel pressure regulator

The regulator is a vacuum-operated mechanical device, which ensures that the pressure differential between fuel in the fuel rail and fuel in the inlet manifold is maintained at a constant value. As manifold depression increases, the regulated fuel pressure is reduced in direct proportion. When fuel pressure in the fuel rail exceeds the regulator setting, the regulator opens to allow fuel to return via the return line to the tank.

System relay

The main system relay is energised by the fuel system ECU and provides power for the fuel pump. The relay remains energised only as long as the ECU receives an RPM signal from the ignition system ECU. In the event of that signal being lost (ie, in the event of an accident) the relay will de-energise and the fuel pump will stop.

Motronic 4.3 system

The Motronic 4.3 system is fitted to the turbocharged 20-valve engines, and some versions of the B5254 S engine. The components and their operation are very similar to the LH3.2-Jetronic, except that a single ECU is used to control both the fuel and ignition sides of the system. Regulation of the turbocharger boost pressure by means of the turbo regulator valve is also controlled by the Motronic ECU.

Fenix 5.2 system

The Fenix 5.2 system is used on the 10-valve non-turbocharged engines covered by this manual. The components and their operation are very similar to the LH3.2-Jetronic system apart from the method of calculating the volume of air entering the engine and other minor differences which are described below. Also, as with Motronic 4.3, a single ECU is used to control both the fuel and ignition sides of the system.

Manifold absolute pressure sensor

Instead of the mass air flow sensor used in the other systems, the Fenix system utilises a MAP sensor and inlet air temperature sensor to calculate the volume of air being drawn into the engine. The MAP sensor is connected to the inlet manifold via a hose and uses a piezo-electrical crystal to convert manifold pressure to an electrical signal to be transmitted to the ECU.

Intake air temperature sensor

This resistive device is located in the air inlet ducting, where its element is in direct contact with the air entering the engine. Changes in air temperature are detected by the ECU as a change in sensor resistance. From the signals received from the inlet air temperature sensor and pressure sensor, the ECU can calculate the volume of air inducted into the engine.

9 Fuel injection system - testing

General information

1 As the fuel injection and ignition systems must be treated as one integrated engine management package, first carry out all the checks described in Chapter 5B, Section 2, then proceed as follows, according to the system being worked on:

LH3.2-Jetronic system
a) Carry out all the checks described in Chapter 5B, Section 3.
b) Proceed as described in this Section.

Motronic 4.3 and Fenix 5.2 systems
a) Carry out all the checks described in Chapter 5B, Section 3, paragraphs 1 to 20.
b) Proceed as described in this Section.

Fault code read-out

Note: On models from 1996 the diagnostic unit is located under a cover in front of the gear lever and has a 16-pin socket for connection to a fault code reader.

2 Firstly, locate the diagnostic unit which is situated in the front right-hand side of the engine compartment, alongside the windscreen washer reservoir filler **(see illustration)**. The diagnostic unit consists of two modules mounted side by side, with a plastic cover over each. Lift off the covers and note that the two modules are marked A and B, each having six numbered sockets on their top face.

3 With the ignition switched off, unclip the flylead from the holder on the side of the unit and insert it into socket (2) of module (A) **(see illustration)**.

4 Have a paper and pen ready to copy down the fault codes as they are displayed. The three-digit codes will appear as a series of blinks of the red LED (located on the top face of the unit next to the test button) with a slight pause between each digit.

9.2 Diagnostic unit location (arrowed) in the engine compartment

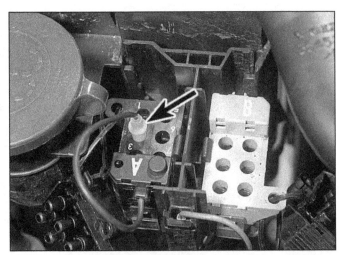

9.3 Insert the flylead into socket (2) of module (A) to access the fuel system fault codes

5 With the flylead inserted, switch on the ignition. Press the test button on top of module A once, for about one second, then release it and wait for the LED to flash. As the LED flashes, copy down the fault code. Now press the button again and copy down the next fault code, if there is one. Continue until the first fault code is displayed again, indicating that all the stored codes have been accessed, then switch off the ignition.

6 Given in the accompanying tables are the possible fuel, or combined fuel/ignition fault codes for the three systems, and their meaning. A description of the separate ignition system fault codes for the LH3.2-Jetronic system is given in Chapter 5B

7 If code 1-1-1 is obtained, this indicates that there are no fault codes stored in the ECU. and the system is operating correctly. In this case, Switch off the ignition, locate the flylead in its holder and refit the unit covers.

Fenix 5.2 system

Fault Code	Meaning
1-1-1	No fault detected
1-1-2	ECU fault
1-1-3	Short term fuel mixture too weak
1-1-5	Faulty signal to No 1 cylinder injector
1-2-1	MAP sensor signal absent or faulty
1-2-2	Intake air temperature sensor signal absent or faulty
1-2-3	Coolant temperature sensor signal absent or faulty
1-2-5	Faulty signal to No 2 cylinder injector
1-3-2	Battery voltage too low or too high
1-3-5	Faulty signal to No 3 cylinder injector
1-4-3	Front knock sensor signal absent or faulty
1-4-4	Load signal absent or faulty
1-4-5	Faulty signal to No 4 cylinder injector
1-5-2*	Air pump valve signal absent or faulty
1-5-4*	Leak in EGR system
1-5-5	Faulty signal to No 5 cylinder injector
2-1-2	Heated oxygen sensor signal absent or faulty
2-1-4	Engine RPM sensor signal absent
2-2-1	Long term fuel mixture too weak in part-load stage
2-2-2	Main relay signal absent or faulty
2-2-3	Idle air control valve signal absent or faulty
2-2-5	Air conditioning pressure sensor signal absent or faulty
2-3-1	Long term fuel mixture too rich in part-load stage
2-3-2	Long term fuel mixture too weak at idle
2-3-3	Long term idle air trim outside control range
2-3-5*	EGR controller signal absent or faulty
2-4-1*	EGR system flow fault
2-4-3	Throttle position sensor signal outside voltage range
2-4-4	Knock control at limit
3-1-1	Vehicle speed sensor (speedometer) signal absent
3-1-3*	EVAP valve signal absent or faulty
3-1-4	Camshaft position sensor signal absent or faulty
3-2-3	Malfunction indicator lamp signal faulty
3-2-5	ECU memory loss
3-3-5	Request for malfunction indicator lamp from automatic transmission ECU
3-4-2	Air conditioning system relay control signal faulty
3-4-3	Fuel pump relay control signal faulty
4-1-1	Throttle position sensor signal outside voltage range
4-1-3*	EGR temperature sensor signal absent or faulty
4-3-2	High temperature in ECU module box
4-3-3	Rear knock sensor signal absent or faulty
4-3-5	Heated oxygen sensor response slow
4-4-2*	Air pump relay signal absent or faulty
5-1-1	Long term fuel mixture too rich at idle
5-1-2	Short term fuel mixture too rich
5-1-3	Excessively high temperature in ECU module box
5-1-4	Engine cooling fan faulty at half speed
5-1-5	Engine cooling fan faulty at full speed
5-2-1	Oxygen sensor heating faulty
5-2-3	Signal to ECU module box cooling fan shorted to 12 volts
5-2-4	Transmission torque control signal faulty
5-3-5	Turbo regulator valve fault

Only applicable to engines with certain emission control equipment (see Chapter 4B).

Motronic 4.3 system

Fault Code	Meaning
1-1-2	ECU fault
1-1-5	Faulty signal to No 1 cylinder injector
1-2-1	MAF sensor signal absent or faulty
1-2-3	Coolant temperature sensor signal absent or faulty
1-2-5	Faulty signal to No 2 cylinder injector
1-3-1	Engine RPM sensor signal absent or faulty
1-3-2	Battery voltage too low or too high
1-3-5	Faulty signal to No 3 cylinder injector
1-4-3	Front knock sensor signal absent or faulty
1-4-4	Load signal absent or faulty
1-4-5	Faulty signal to No 4 cylinder injector
1-5-2*	Air pump valve signal absent or faulty
1-5-4*	Leak in EGR system
1-5-5	Faulty signal to No 5 cylinder injector
2-1-2	Heated oxygen sensor signal absent or faulty
2-1-4	Engine RPM sensor signal absent intermittently
2-2-3	Idle air control valve opening signal absent or faulty
2-2-5	Air conditioning pressure sensor signal absent or faulty
2-3-1	Long term fuel mixture too weak or too rich in part load stage
2-3-2	Long term fuel mixture too weak or too rich at idle
2-3-3	Long term idle air trim outside control range
2-3-5*	EGR controller signal absent or faulty
2-4-1*	EGR system flow fault
2-4-3	Throttle position sensor signal outside voltage range
2-4-4	Knock control at limit
2-4-5	Idle air control valve closing signal absent or faulty
3-1-1	Vehicle speed sensor (speedometer) signal absent
3-1-3*	EVAP valve signal absent or faulty
3-1-4	Camshaft position sensor signal absent or faulty
3-1-5*	EVAP system fault
3-2-3	Malfunction indicator lamp signal faulty
3-2-5	ECU memory loss
3-3-5	Request for malfunction indicator lamp from automatic transmission ECU
3-4-2	Air conditioning system relay control signal faulty
3-4-3	Fuel pump relay control signal faulty
4-1-1	Throttle position sensor signal outside voltage range
4-1-3*	EGR temperature sensor signal absent or faulty
4-1-4	Turbo boost pressure too high
4-1-6	Turbo boost pressure reduced by automatic transmission ECU
4-3-2	High temperature in ECU module box
4-3-3	Rear knock sensor signal absent or faulty
4-3-5	Heated oxygen sensor response slow
4-4-2*	Air pump relay signal absent or faulty
5-1-1	Long term fuel mixture too rich at idle
5-1-2	Short term fuel mixture too rich
5-1-3	Excessively high temperature in ECU module box
5-1-4	Engine cooling fan faulty at half speed
5-1-5	Engine cooling fan faulty at full speed
5-2-1	Oxygen sensor heating faulty
5-2-3	Signal to ECU module box cooling fan shorted to 12 volts
5-2-4	Transmission torque control signal faulty
5-3-5	Turbo regulator valve fault
5-4-1*	EVAP valve fault

Only applicable to engines with certain emission control equipment (see Chapter 4B).

LH3.2-Jetronic system

Fault Code	Meaning
1-1-1	No fault detected
1-1-2	ECU fault
1-1-3	Short term fuel mixture too weak
1-2-1	MAF sensor signal absent or faulty
1-2-3	Coolant temperature sensor signal absent or faulty
1-3-1	Engine RPM signal from ignition system absent or faulty
1-3-2	Battery voltage too low or too high
2-1-2	Heated oxygen sensor signal absent or faulty
2-2-1	Long term fuel mixture too weak in part-load stage
2-2-3	Idle air control valve signal absent or faulty
2-3-1	Long term fuel mixture too rich in part-load stage
2-3-2	Long term fuel mixture too weak at idle
3-1-1	Vehicle speed sensor (speedometer) signal absent
4-1-1	Throttle position sensor signal absent
5-1-1	Long term fuel mixture too rich at idle
5-1-2	Short term fuel mixture too rich

8 Once all the fault codes have been recorded they should be deleted. Note that the fault codes cannot be deleted until all of them have been displayed at least once, and the first one is displayed again. With the flylead still inserted in socket 2 of module A, switch on the ignition, press the test button and hold it down for approximately five seconds. Release the test button and after three seconds the LED will light. When the LED lights, press and hold the test button down for a further five seconds then release it - the LED will go out. Switch off the ignition and check that all the fault codes have been deleted by switching the ignition on again and pressing the test button for one second - code 1-1-1 should appear. If a code other than 1-1-1 appears, record the code then repeat the deleting procedure. When all the codes have been deleted, switch off the ignition, locate the flylead in its holder and refit the unit covers.

9 Once the location of a fault has been established from the fault code read-out, investigations can be concentrated in that area. Go through the checks carried out previously in case anything was missed the first time. Further detailed checking of the system components will require the use of Volvo test equipment. Therefore, the only alternatives possible at this time are the substitution of a suspect component with a known good unit, or entrusting further work to a Volvo dealer. If a substitute unit can be obtained (or borrowed), removal and refitting procedures are given in the following Sections of this Chapter.

10 Fuel injection system components - removal and refitting

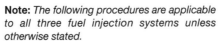

Note: *The following procedures are applicable to all three fuel injection systems unless otherwise stated.*
Note: *Refer to the precautions in Section 1 before working on any component in the fuel system.*

Mass air flow sensor (LH3.2-Jetronic and Motronic 4.3)

Removal

1 Disconnect the battery negative lead.

2 Slacken the hose clip and detach the air outlet duct and, where applicable the crankcase ventilation hose at the air cleaner cover.
3 Disconnect the wiring connector from the sensor in the cover outlet.
4 Release the HT lead to the ignition coil from the clips at the rear of the cover.
5 Spring back the retaining clips and lift off the air cleaner cover.
6 Undo the two screws and remove the sensor from the air cleaner cover.

Refitting

7 Refit by reversing the removal operations.

Intake air temperature sensor (Fenix 5.2)

Removal

8 Carry out the operations described in paragraphs 1 to 5.
9 Carefully prise the sensor out of its rubber retaining grommet in the air cleaner cover outlet **(see illustration)**.

Refitting

10 Refit by reversing the removal operations.

Manifold absolute pressure sensor (Fenix 5.2)

Removal

11 Disconnect the battery negative lead.
12 Detach the air cleaner inlet duct and cowl from the side of the radiator fan shroud.
13 Undo the bolts each side securing the relay carrier to the front body panel above the fan shroud.
14 Lift up the relay carrier and disconnect the vacuum hose and wiring connector from the manifold absolute pressure sensor **(see illustration)**.
15 Detach the pressure sensor and remove it from the centre of the relay carrier.

Refitting

16 Refit by reversing the removal operations.

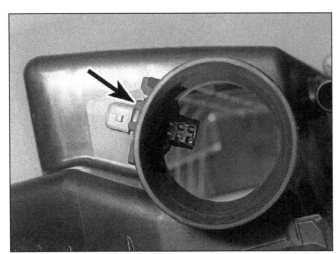

10.9 Prise the intake air temperature sensor out of its rubber retaining grommet (arrowed)

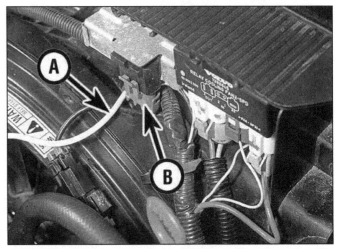

10.14 Disconnect the vacuum hose (A) and wiring connector (B) from the manifold absolute pressure sensor

10.18 Disconnect the fuel feed and return pipes (arrowed) at the hose unions behind the engine

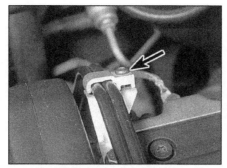

10.19 Remove the fuel pipe clamps (arrowed) from the engine

10.20 Disconnect the wiring plug from each injector

Fuel rail and injectors

Removal

17 Disconnect the battery negative lead.
18 Disconnect the fuel feed and return pipes at the hose unions behind the engine **(see illustration)**. Access is difficult from above, but is slightly better from below. Place absorbent rags around the unions and be prepared for an initial release of fuel under pressure as the unions are slackened.
19 Undo the bolts securing the two fuel pipe clamps to the engine and remove the clamps **(see illustration)**.
20 Where applicable, release the turbocharger inlet ducting then disconnect the wiring plug from each injector **(see illustration)**. If difficulty is experienced, pull off the fuel rail cover over the injectors for greater access.

21 Disconnect the vacuum hose from the pressure regulator on the underside of the fuel rail **(see illustration)**.
22 Undo the two bolts securing the fuel rail to the inlet manifold. Pull the rail upwards to release the injectors from the manifold, and remove the rail complete with injectors and fuel pressure regulator **(see illustrations)**.
23 Individual injectors may now be removed from the rail by simply pulling them out **(see illustration)**.

Refitting

24 Refit by reversing the removal operations. Check that the injector O-rings and manifold seals are in good condition and renew them if necessary; smear them with petroleum jelly or silicone grease as an assembly lubricant **(see illustration)**. Tighten the fuel rail retaining

bolts to the specified torque setting, first using a torque wrench, then through the specified angle using an angle tightening gauge.

Fuel pressure regulator

Removal

25 Disconnect the battery negative lead.
26 Remove the fuel rail and injectors as described previously, but leave the injectors in place in the fuel rail.
27 Undo the two bolts and remove the fuel pressure regulator from the fuel rail **(see illustration)**.

Refitting

28 Refit the regulator to the fuel rail then refit the fuel rail and injectors as described previously.

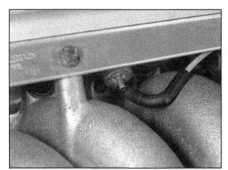

10.21 Disconnect the vacuum hose from the pressure regulator

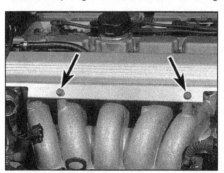

10.22a Undo the two fuel rail retaining bolts (arrowed) . . .

10.22b . . . and remove the fuel rail with injectors

10.23 Remove the injectors by pulling them out of the fuel rail

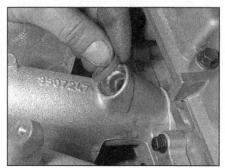

10.24 Renew the injector seals in the manifold when refitting

10.27 Undo the two bolts and remove the fuel pressure regulator

10.29 Disconnecting the isle air control valve wiring connector

10.36 Throttle housing retaining bolts (arrowed)

Idle air control valve

Removal

29 Disconnect the wiring connector from the end of the valve **(see illustration)**.
30 Release the hose clips and carefully pull the air hoses off the valve stubs.
31 Undo the mounting bracket retaining bolt and withdraw the valve from the inlet manifold.

10.42 Lift off the module box lid

Refitting

32 Refit by reversing the removal operations, using new hoses and clips if necessary.

Throttle housing

Removal

33 Disconnect the throttle position sensor wiring connector.
34 Disconnect the idle air control valve hose, the vacuum hoses and the air inlet duct from the housing.
35 Disconnect the throttle linkage balljoint from the throttle valve operating lever.
36 Remove the bolts which secure the housing and withdraw it from the manifold **(see illustration)**. Recover the gasket.

Refitting

37 Refit by reversing the removal operations, using a new gasket, and hose clips if necessary.

Throttle position sensor

Removal

38 Disconnect the sensor wiring connector.

39 Remove the two bolts which secure the sensor and withdraw it from the throttle housing.

Refitting

40 Refit by reversing the removal operations.

Coolant temperature sensor

41 Refer to Chapter 3, Section 6.

Electronic control unit

Note: *The fuel/ignition ECU and, where applicable, the automatic transmission ECU and EZ-129K ignition ECU, are all located in the ECU module box which is situated at the front right-hand side of the engine compartment in front of the cooling system expansion tank.*

Removal

42 Ensure that the ignition is switched off then release the two catches on the side of the module box lid. Lift off the lid and place it to one side **(see illustration)**.
43 Pull the locking lever on top of the ECU forward, and withdraw the ECU from its location **(see illustrations)**. The fuel system ECU is located in slot two, in the centre of the module box.

10.43a Pull the locking lever forward . . .

10.43b . . . and withdraw the ECU

12.16 Removing the inlet manifold

12.20 Use the lower bolts to retain the gasket when refitting the manifold

Refitting

44 Locate the ECU in the module box engaging it with the connector in the base.
45 Push the locking lever down and refit the module box lid.

11 Cruise control - general information

When fitted, the cruise control allows the vehicle to maintain a steady speed selected by the driver, regardless of gradients or prevailing winds.

The main components of the system are a control unit, a control switch, a vacuum servo and a vacuum pump. Brake and (when applicable) clutch pedal switches protect the engine against excessive speeds or loads should a pedal be depressed whilst the system is in use.

In operation, the driver accelerates to the desired speed and then brings the system into use by means of the switch. The control unit then monitors vehicle speed (from the speedometer pulses) and opens or closes the throttle by means of the servo to maintain the set speed. If the switch is moved to "OFF", or the brake or clutch pedal is depressed, the servo immediately closes the throttle. The set speed is stored in the control unit memory and the system can be reactivated by moving the switch to "RESUME", provided that vehicle speed has not dropped below 25 mph.

The driver can override the cruise control for overtaking simply by depressing the throttle pedal. When the pedal is released, the set speed will be resumed.

The cruise control cannot be engaged at speeds below 25 mph, and should not be used in slippery or congested conditions.

No specific removal, refitting or adjustment procedures were available at the time of writing. Problems should be referred to a Volvo dealer or other specialist.

12 Inlet manifold - removal and refitting

Note: *Observe the precautions in Section 1 before working on any component in the fuel system.*

Removal

1 Disconnect the battery negative lead.
2 Disconnect the air inlet duct from the throttle housing and, where applicable, release the turbocharger inlet ducting
3 Undo the screw and remove the cover over the accelerator cable drum and linkage.
4 Release the outer cable retaining clip from the cable adjuster and unhook the inner cable from the drum.
5 Undo the bolts securing the two fuel pipe clamps to the engine and remove the clamps.
6 Disconnect the wiring plug from each fuel injector. If difficulty is experienced, pull off the fuel rail cover over the injectors for greater access.
7 Disconnect the vacuum hose from the pressure regulator on the underside of the fuel rail.
8 Undo the two bolts securing the fuel rail to the inlet manifold. Pull the rail upwards to release the injectors from the manifold and lay the fuel rail with injectors on the top of the engine. Take care not to damage the injector tips.
9 Disconnect the throttle position sensor wiring connector at the throttle housing.
10 Disconnect the idle air control valve hoses and the control valve wiring connector.
11 Disconnect the brake servo vacuum hose, the EGR hoses (where applicable) and the vacuum hoses at the throttle housing.
12 Disconnect any remaining vacuum hoses which connect to services external to the manifold.
13 Release the wiring harness from the manifold cable clamps.

14 Undo the bolt securing the dipstick tube to the manifold, and the bolt securing the underside of the manifold to the steady bracket.
15 Slacken the lower manifold retaining bolts by about two or three turns, and remove all the upper manifold bolts.
16 Lift the manifold upwards, where applicable feed the crankcase ventilation hose through the ducts, then remove the manifold from the cylinder head **(see illustration)**. Note that the lower bolt holes are slotted allowing the manifold to slide up and off, leaving them in position. If the manifold will not lift up, make sure that the gasket has not stuck to the manifold face; the gasket lower holes are not slotted, and it must remain on the engine to allow manifold removal.
17 With the manifold removed, take out the lower bolts and remove the gasket.
18 If required, the components remaining on the manifold can be removed with reference to earlier Sections of this Chapter.
19 On engines with a variable venturi inlet system, check the condition of the flap valves and spindles ensuring smooth operation. If any problems are noticed in this area, entrust the necessary repair work to a Volvo dealer as special gauges are required to install and set up the flap valve clearances.

Refitting

20 Refit by reversing the removal operations, using a new manifold gasket, and new seals and O-rings for the injectors if necessary. Locate the manifold gasket on the cylinder head and fit the lower manifold bolts a few turns, prior to placing the manifold in position **(see illustration)**. Where applicable, remember to feed the crankcase ventilation hose up between the second and third ducts. Tighten the bolts to the specified torque setting.
21 Refit and adjust the accelerator cable as described in Section 4.

Notes

Chapter 4 Part B:
Exhaust and emission control systems

Contents

Degrees of difficulty

Easy, suitable for novice with little experience	Fairly easy, suitable for beginner with some experience	Fairly difficult, suitable for competent DIY mechanic	Difficult, suitable for experienced DIY mechanic	Very difficult, suitable for expert DIY or professional

Specifications

Torque wrench settings	Nm
Exhaust manifold heat shield bolts	15
Exhaust manifold to cylinder head	25
Exhaust front pipe to turbocharger	30
Turbocharger to manifold	25
Exhaust front pipe to manifold:	
Spring loaded flange joint	10
Flexible lattice flange joint	25
Exhaust ball and socket clamp joint	30
Heated oxygen sensor	45
EGR valve bolts	50
Oil separator bolts	20
Upper engine steady bar to engine bracket:	
Early models (M8 bolt):*	
Stage 1	18
Stage 2	Tighten through a further 120°
Later models (M10 bolt):*	
Stage 1	35
Stage 2	Tighten through a further 90°
Upper engine steady bar to bulkhead bracket:*	
Stage 1	35
Stage 2	Tighten through a further 60°
Steady bar bracket to engine:	
Upper nut	25
Lower bolts:*	
Stage 1	45
Stage 2	Tighten through a further 90°

*New nuts/bolts must **always** be used

1 General information

Exhaust system

The exhaust system comprises the exhaust manifold, a front section incorporating the catalytic converter and front pipe, and a rear section incorporating the intermediate pipe, silencer and tail pipe. The system is supported under the car on rubber mountings.

On B5204 T, and B234 T/T5 engines a water cooled turbocharger is fitted to the exhaust manifold. Further information on the turbocharger is contained in Section 5.

Emission control systems

All models covered by this manual have various features built into the fuel and exhaust systems to help minimise harmful emissions. These features fall broadly into three categories; crankcase emission control, evaporative emission control, and exhaust emission control. The main features of these systems are as follows.

Crankcase emission control

To reduce the emissions of unburned hydrocarbons from the crankcase into the atmosphere, a Positive Crankcase Ventilation (PCV) system is used whereby the engine is sealed and the blow-by gasses and oil vapour are drawn from inside the crankcase, through an oil separator, into the inlet tract to be burned by the engine during normal combustion.

Under conditions of high manifold depression (idling, deceleration) the gasses will be sucked positively out of the crankcase. Under conditions of low manifold depression (acceleration, full-throttle running) the gasses are forced out of the crankcase by the (relatively) higher crankcase pressure; if the engine is worn, the raised crankcase pressure (due to increased blow-by) will cause some of the flow to return under all manifold conditions.

Evaporative emission control

The evaporative emission control (EVAP) system is used to minimise the escape of unburned hydrocarbons into the atmosphere. To do this, the fuel tank filler cap is sealed, and a carbon canister is used to collect and store petrol vapours generated in the tank. When the engine is running, the vapours are cleared from the canister either via a vacuum operated, or by an ECU controlled electrically operated, EVAP valve, into the inlet tract, to be burned by the engine during normal combustion.

To ensure that the engine runs correctly when idling, the valve only opens when the engine is running under load; the valve then opens to allow the stored vapour to pass into the inlet tract.

As a safety measure, and to further reduce

hydrocarbon emissions, a roll-over valve is incorporated into the system which closes when the car tilts sideways by more than 45°. This prevents fuel leakage in the event of an accident.

Exhaust emission control

To minimise the amount of pollutants which escape into the atmosphere, all models are fitted with a catalytic converter in the exhaust system. The system is of the closed-loop type, in which a heated oxygen sensor in the exhaust system provides the fuel injection system ECU with constant feedback on the oxygen content of the exhaust gasses. This enables the ECU to adjust the mixture by altering injector opening time, thus providing the best possible conditions for the converter to operate. The system functions in the following way.

The oxygen sensor has a built-in heating element, activated by the ECU to quickly bring the sensor's tip to an efficient operating temperature. The sensor's tip is sensitive to oxygen, and sends the control module a varying voltage depending on the amount of oxygen in the exhaust gasses; if the inlet air/fuel mixture is too rich, the exhaust gasses are low in oxygen, so the sensor sends a voltage signal proportional to the oxygen detected, the voltage altering as the mixture weakens and the amount of oxygen in the exhaust gasses rises. Peak conversion efficiency of all major pollutants occurs if the inlet air/fuel mixture is maintained at the chemically-correct ratio for complete combustion of petrol - 14.7 parts (by weight) of air to 1 part of fuel (the "stoichiometric" ratio). The sensor output voltage alters in a large step at this point, the ECU using the signal change as a reference point, and correcting the inlet air/fuel mixture accordingly, by altering the fuel injector opening time.

In addition to the catalytic converter, certain models are fitted with an exhaust gas recirculation (EGR) system. This system is designed to recirculate small quantities of exhaust gas into the inlet tract, and therefore into the combustion process. This reduces the level of oxides of nitrogen present in the final exhaust gas which is released into the atmosphere.

The volume of exhaust gas recirculated is controlled by vacuum (supplied from the inlet manifold) via an EGR valve mounted on the inlet manifold. Before reaching the EGR valve, the vacuum from the manifold passes to an EGR controller. The purpose of which is to modify the vacuum supplied to the EGR valve according to engine operating conditions.

The EGR system is controlled by the fuel/ignition ECU, which receives information on engine operating parameters from its various sensors.

A secondary air injection system is fitted to certain models intended for markets with stringent emission control regulations. The

system is designed to inject fresh air into the exhaust passages in the cylinder head during the engine warm-up phase. This creates an afterburn effect to reduce HC and CO emissions upstream of the catalytic converter.

The system comprises an electrically driven air pump, solenoid, non-return valve, shut-off valve and interconnecting pipework.

Under the control of the fuel/ignition ECU the system operates for under two minutes and starts approximately twenty seconds after the car has started to move.

2 Exhaust system - general information and component renewal

General information

1 The exhaust system consists of a front section which comprises a front pipe and catalytic converter and a rear section comprising an intermediate pipe, silencer and tailpipe. The system is suspended from the underbody on rubber mountings, and bolted to the exhaust manifold at the front. A self-aligning ball and socket joint is used to connect the front and rear sections together. The front pipe to manifold connection is by either a spring loaded flange joint, or a flange joint incorporating a flexible lattice type coupling.

2 The exhaust system should be examined for leaks, damage and security at regular intervals (see Chapter 1). To do this, apply the handbrake, and allow the engine to idle in a well-ventilated area. Lie down on each side of the car in turn, and check the full length of the system for leaks, while an assistant temporarily places a wad of cloth over the end of the tailpipe. If a leak is evident, stop the engine and use a proprietary repair kit to seal it. If the leak is excessive, or damage is evident, renew the section. Check the rubber mountings for deterioration, and renew them if necessary.

Removal

Front section

3 Jack up the front, and preferably the rear, of the car and support it on axle stands (see "Jacking and vehicle support").

4 Disconnect the two heated oxygen sensor wiring connectors and release the wiring from any cable-ties.

5 Undo the nuts securing the front pipe flange to the manifold. Recover the tension springs where fitted. On some models access may be improved from above after removing the heat shield over the manifold.

6 Undo the nuts and bolts at the ball and socket joint connecting the front and rear sections, and remove the clamps (see illustration).

7 Where fitted, undo the four bolts and remove the stiffener plate from the underbody.

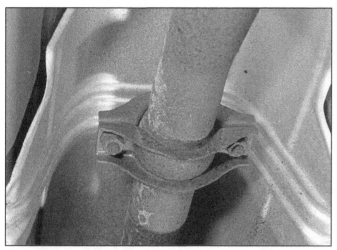

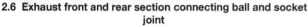

2.6 Exhaust front and rear section connecting ball and socket joint

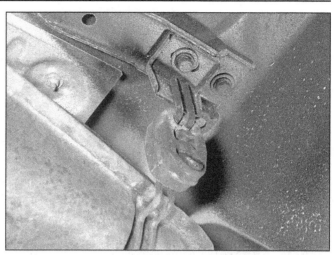

2.11 Exhaust silencer side mounting

8 Separate the front pipe to manifold joint and remove the front section from under the car.

Rear section

9 Jack up the rear, and preferably the front, of the car and support it on axle stands (see *"Jacking and vehicle support"*).
10 Undo the nuts and bolts at the ball and socket joint connecting the front and rear sections, and remove the clamps.
11 Release the tailpipe and silencer from their rubber mountings and slide the rear section forward until the tailpipe is clear of the rear suspension **(see illustration)**. Remove the system from under the car.

Refitting

12 Refitting is a reversal of removal, bearing in mind the following points:
  a) *Use a new sealing ring or flange gasket as applicable on the front pipe to manifold joint.*
  b) *When refitting the front section, loosely attach the front pipe to the manifold and the catalytic converter to the intermediate pipe. Align the system, then tighten the front pipe to manifold nuts first, followed by the intermediate pipe clamp nuts, to the specified torque.*
  c) *Ensure that there is a minimum clearance of 20 mm between the exhaust system and underbody/suspension components.*

3 Catalytic converter - general information and precautions

The catalytic converter is a reliable and simple device, which needs no maintenance in itself, but there are some facts of which an owner should be aware if the converter is to function properly for its full service life.
  a) *DO NOT use leaded petrol in a vehicle equipped with a catalytic converter - the lead will coat the precious metals,*
reducing their converting efficiency, and will eventually destroy the converter.
  b) *Always keep the ignition and fuel systems well-maintained in accordance with the manufacturer's schedule (see Chapter 1).*
  c) *If the engine develops a misfire, do not drive the vehicle at all (or at least as little as possible) until the fault is cured.*
  d) *DO NOT push - or tow-start the vehicle - this will soak the catalytic converter in unburned fuel, causing it to overheat when the engine does start.*
  e) *DO NOT switch off the ignition at high engine speeds, ie do not "blip" the throttle immediately before switching off.*
  f) *DO NOT use fuel or engine oil additives - these may contain substances harmful to the catalytic converter.*
  g) *DO NOT continue to use the vehicle if the engine burns oil to the extent of leaving a visible trail of blue smoke.*
  h) *Remember that the catalytic converter operates at very high temperatures. DO NOT, therefore, park the vehicle in dry undergrowth, over long grass or piles of dead leaves, after a long run.*
  l) *Remember that the catalytic converter is FRAGILE. Do not strike it with tools during servicing work.*
  j) *In some cases, a sulphurous smell (like that of rotten eggs) may be noticed from the exhaust. This is common to many catalytic converter-equipped vehicles. Once the vehicle has covered a few thousand miles, the problem should disappear - in the meantime, try changing the brand of petrol used.*
  k) *The catalytic converter used on a well-maintained and well-driven vehicle should last for between 50 000 and 100 000 miles. If the converter is no longer effective, it must be renewed.*

4 Exhaust manifold - removal and refitting

Removal

Left-hand drive models

1 Disconnect the battery negative lead.
2 On turbo models, remove the turbocharger as described in Section 6.
3 Jack up the front of the car and support it on axle stands (see *"Jacking and vehicle support"*).
4 Undo the nuts securing the exhaust front pipe flange to the manifold. Recover the tension springs where fitted. On some models access may be better from above after removing the heat shield over the manifold.
5 Remove the air cleaner hot air inlet duct from the manifold heat shield.
6 Undo the nuts securing the manifold to the cylinder head.
7 Move the manifold rearwards off the cylinder head studs, then separate the front pipe flange joint. Twist the manifold through 90° to the right, and manipulate it out from the rear of the engine. On cars so equipped, take care not to damage the air conditioning high pressure switch as the manifold is removed.
8 Recover the front pipe flange joint gasket or sealing ring, and the five individual manifold to cylinder head gaskets.

Right-hand drive models

9 Disconnect the battery negative lead.
10 Drain the cooling system as described in Chapter 1.
11 On turbo models, remove the turbocharger as described in Section 6.
12 Refer to Part A of this Chapter and remove the air cleaner assembly and the hot air inlet duct from the manifold heat shield.
13 Undo the nut and remove the bolt securing the upper engine steady bar to the bracket on the engine. Note that a new nut and bolt will be required for refitting.

4.15 Removing the engine steady bar bracket

4.17 Manipulate the exhaust heat shield out from behind the engine

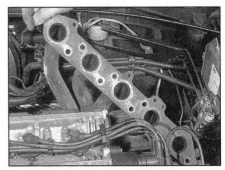

4.22 Exhaust manifold removal

14 Undo the nut securing the other end of the engine steady bar to the bulkhead bracket. Swing the steady bar to one side. Note that a new nut and bolt will be required for refitting.
15 Undo the upper nut and two lower bolts securing the steady bar bracket to the side of the engine. Note the location of the wiring connector support plates and move them to one side. Release all the cable-ties and switch wiring connectors as necessary to allow the bracket to be removed, then prise the bracket off its locating dowels on the engine **(see illustration)**. It will be tight on the dowels and a certain amount of levering will be necessary.
16 Disconnect the two heater hoses at the pipe stubs on the side of the engine.
17 Undo the bolts securing the heat shield to the exhaust manifold and manoeuvre the heat shield out from behind the engine. Note that clearance is **very** limited and the shield will have to be turned and twisted until the right position is found for its removal **(see illustration)**.
18 Jack up the front of the car and support it on axle stands (see *"Jacking and vehicle support"*).
19 Undo the nuts securing the exhaust front pipe flange to the manifold. Recover the tension springs where fitted.
20 Lower the car to the ground.
21 Undo the nuts securing the manifold to the cylinder head.
22 Move the manifold rearwards off the cylinder head studs, then separate the front pipe flange joint. Twist the manifold through 90° to the right and manipulate it out from the rear of the engine **(see illustration)**. Again, clearance is very limited and considerable manoeuvring will be necessary. On cars so equipped, take care not to damage the air conditioning high pressure switch as the manifold is removed.
23 Recover the front pipe flange joint gasket or sealing ring and the five individual manifold to cylinder head gaskets.

Refitting

All models

24 Refitting is a reversal of removal bearing in mind the following points:
 a) *Return any studs that were removed with their nuts back to the cylinder head,*

sealing them with suitable thread sealer.
 b) *Thoroughly clean the manifold and cylinder head mating faces prior to refitting.*
 c) *Use new manifold gaskets and a new sealing ring or flange gasket as applicable on the front pipe to manifold joint.*
 d) *Tighten all nuts and bolts to the specified torque, then further through the specified angle, where applicable. Note that angle-tightened nuts/bolts must always be renewed.*
 e) *On right-hand drive models, refill the cooling system as described in Chapter 1 on completion.*

---

5 Turbocharger - general information and precautions

General information

1 A water-cooled turbocharger is used on all turbo models covered by this manual. The turbocharger increases the efficiency of the engine by raising the pressure in the inlet manifold above atmospheric pressure. Instead of the air/fuel mixture being simply sucked into the cylinders it is actively forced in.
2 Energy for the operation of the turbocharger comes from the exhaust gas. The gas flows through a specially-shaped housing (the turbine housing) and in so doing spins the turbine wheel. The turbine wheel is attached to a shaft, at the other end of which is another vaned wheel known as the compressor wheel. The compressor wheel spins in its own housing and compresses the inducted air on the way to the inlet manifold.
3 After leaving the turbocharger, the compressed air passes through an intercooler, which is an air-to-air heat exchanger mounted with the radiator. Here the air gives up heat which it acquired when being compressed. This temperature reduction improves engine efficiency and reduces the risk of detonation.
4 Boost pressure (the pressure in the inlet manifold) is limited by a wastegate, which diverts the exhaust gas away from the turbine wheel in response to a pressure-sensitive actuator. The actuator is controlled by the turbocharger valve, under signals from the fuel system electronic control unit.

5 The turbo shaft is pressure-lubricated by means of a feed pipe from the engine's main oil gallery. The shaft "floats" on a cushion of oil. A drain pipe returns the oil to the sump.
6 Water cooling keeps the operating temperature of the turbo bearings lower than previously. Water continues to circulate by convection after the engine has stopped, so cooling the turbocharger if it is hot after a long run.

Precautions

7 The turbocharger operates at extremely high speeds and temperatures. Certain precautions must be observed to avoid premature failure of the turbo or injury to the operator.
 a) *Do not operate the turbo with any parts exposed. Foreign objects falling onto the rotating vanes could cause extensive damage and (if ejected) personal injury.*
 b) *Do not race the engine immediately after start-up, especially if it is cold. Give the oil a few seconds to circulate.*
 c) *Always allow the engine to return to idle speed before switching it off - do not blip the throttle and switch off, as this will leave the turbo spinning without lubrication.*
 d) *Allow the engine to idle for several minutes before switching off after a high-speed run.*
 e) *Observe the recommended intervals for oil and filter changing, and use a reputable oil of the specified quality. Neglect of oil changing, or use of inferior oil, can cause carbon formation on the turbo shaft and subsequent failure.*

---

6 Turbocharger - removal and refitting

Removal

1 Disconnect the battery negative lead.
2 Drain the cooling system as described in Chapter 1.
3 Undo the bolts and remove the heat shield over the turbocharger.
4 Disconnect the upper air inlet pipe and rubber hose from the turbocharger inlet.

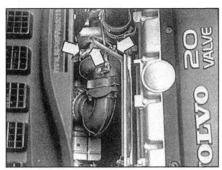

6.6 Turbocharger upper coolant return pipe and oil inlet pipe unions (arrowed)

6.8 Turbocharger pipe clamp bracket bolt, oil return pipe flange, support bracket, and manifold flange bolts (arrowed)

6.15 Disconnect the turbocharger boost pressure hose (red), the bypass valve hose (white) and the pressure regulator hose (yellow)

5 Disconnect the fresh air inlet hose from the side of the turbocharger and remove the second heat shield.
6 Undo the upper coolant return pipe and oil inlet pipe unions and recover the seals (see illustration).
7 Jack up the front of the car and support it on axle stands (see *"Jacking and vehicle support"*).
8 Undo the bolt and remove the clamp bracket securing the oil feed and return pipes (see illustration).
9 Undo the two bolts and separate the oil return pipe flange joint from the base of the turbocharger.
10 Undo the two lower nuts securing the turbocharger to the exhaust manifold and the single lower nut securing the unit to the exhaust front pipe.
11 Undo the bolt securing the support bracket to the turbocharger then lower the car to the ground.
12 Undo the two remaining nuts securing the front pipe to the turbocharger.
13 Undo the coolant inlet pipe union and recover the seals.
14 Undo the turbocharger to manifold upper nuts, then carefully ease the unit off the manifold studs.
15 Lift the unit upwards and disconnect the boost pressure hose (marked red), the bypass valve hose (marked white) and the pressure regulator hose (marked yellow) (see illustration). Note the locations of these hoses on the turbocharger to avoid confusion when refitting.
16 Remove the turbocharger from the car and recover the gaskets.

Refitting

17 Refitting is a reversal of removal bearing in mind the following points:
 a) *Return any studs that were removed with their nuts back to their original locations, sealing them with suitable thread sealer.*
 b) *Thoroughly clean the turbocharger and manifold mating faces prior to refitting.*
 c) *Use a new manifold gasket and new seals on all disturbed unions..*
 d) *Tighten all nuts and bolts to the specified torque.*

 e) *Refill the cooling system as described in Chapter 1 on completion.*

7 Crankcase emission control system - checking and component renewal

Checking

1 The components of this system require no attention other than to check that the hoses are clear and undamaged and to renew the flame trap at regular intervals.

Component renewal

Flame trap (non-turbo models only)

2 Undo the screw and remove the cover over the accelerator cable drum and linkage.
3 Slacken the hose clip and detach the air outlet duct at the air cleaner cover.
4 Bend the hose forward for access to the flame trap which is located in the duct elbow, in front of the throttle housing.
5 Turn the flame trap casing 15 mm to the left to release the bayonet fastening. Withdraw the casing but do not disconnect the ventilation hoses (see illustration).
6 Remove the flame trap from the casing and clean the casing thoroughly. It is advisable to blow through all the hoses with compressed air and to change the engine oil whenever the flame trap is renewed.
7 Fit the new flame trap using a reversal of removal.

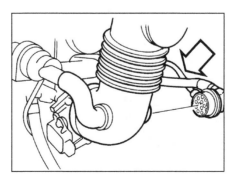

7.5 Removing the flame trap. Do not disconnect the hoses (arrowed)

Oil separator

8 The oil separator is located on the front facing side of the cylinder block, below the inlet manifold (see illustration).
9 Remove the inlet manifold as described in Part A of this Chapter.
10 Disconnect the upper hose at the oil separator and remove the inlet manifold support bracket. On later models remove the clips securing the connecting hoses to the cylinder block connecting sleeves.
11 Undo the two bolts and remove the unit from the engine.
12 On early models, clean the oil trap seal surfaces in the cylinder block and fit new seals to the oil trap stubs. On later models obtain new hose clips as necessary.
13 Refit the oil separator using a reversal of removal. Refit the inlet manifold as described in Part A of this Chapter.

8 Evaporative emission control system - checking and component renewal

Checking

1 Poor idle, stalling and poor driveability can be caused by an inoperative canister vacuum valve, a damaged canister, split or cracked hoses, or hoses connected to the wrong fittings. Check the fuel filler cap for a damaged or deformed gasket.

7.8 Oil separator location at the front of the engine

8.7 EVAP carbon canister retaining strap bolt (arrowed)

2 Fuel loss or fuel odour can be caused by liquid fuel leaking from fuel lines, a cracked or damaged canister, an inoperative canister vacuum valve, and disconnected, misrouted, kinked or damaged vapour or control hoses.

3 Inspect each hose attached to the canister for kinks, leaks and cracks along its entire length. Repair or renew as necessary.

4 Inspect the canister. If it is cracked or damaged, renew it. Look for fuel leaking from the bottom of the canister. If fuel is leaking, renew the canister, and check the hoses and hose routing.

Component renewal

Carbon canister

5 The canister is located under the left-hand wheel arch at the front.

6 Note the location of the vacuum and fuel vent hose connections at the canister and carefully disconnect them.

7 Release the canister retaining strap and remove the unit from its location **(see illustration)**.

8 Refitting is a reversal of removal.

Vacuum (EVAP) valve

9 The EVAP valve is either mounted on the top of the carbon canister (vacuum operated valve) or remotely sighted in the fuel vapour line to the canister (electronically operated valve).

10 The vacuum operated valve is an integral part of the carbon canister and is renewed with that component as a unit.

11 The electronically operated valve can be renewed by tracing back the vapour line from the canister to the valve, disconnecting the hoses and wiring connector and removing the valve from its location.

12 Refitting is a reversal of removal.

9 Exhaust emission control systems - checking and component renewal

Checking

1 Checking of the system as a whole entails a close visual inspection of all hoses, pipes and connections for condition and security. Apart from this, any known or suspected faults should be attended to by a Volvo dealer. At the time of writing, no specific information was available on the secondary air injection system. Detailed checks in the event of a fault in the system, or component renewal should also be entrusted to a dealer.

Component renewal

Heated oxygen sensor

Note: *The sensor is delicate, and will not work if it is dropped or knocked, if its power supply is disrupted, or if any cleaning materials are used on it.*

2 Jack up the front of the car and support it on axle stands (see "*Jacking and vehicle support*").

3 Disconnect the two heated oxygen sensor wiring connectors and release the wiring from any cable-ties.

4 Unscrew the sensor from the exhaust system front pipe and collect the sealing washer (where fitted) **(see illustration)**.

5 On refitting, clean the sealing washer (where fitted) and renew it if it is damaged or worn. Apply a smear of anti-seize compound to the sensor's threads, then refit the sensor, tightening it to the specified torque. Reconnect the wiring and secure with cable-ties where applicable.

Catalytic converter

6 The catalytic converter is part of the

exhaust system front section. Refer to Sections 2 and 3 for renewal procedures and additional information.

EGR controller

7 The EGR controller is mounted on the relay panel above the radiator.

8 Disconnect the two hoses at the EGR controller noting their locations.

9 Undo the outer bolt from the EGR controller mounting bracket.

10 Remove the controller and bracket, disconnect the wiring connector then remove the controller from the bracket.

11 Refitting is a reversal of removal.

EGR valve

12 Disconnect the battery negative lead.

13 Undo the screw and remove the cover over the accelerator cable drum.

14 Detach the air cleaner inlet duct and the ECU module box air duct from each side of the radiator fan shroud.

15 Undo the two bolts each side securing the fan shroud and relay carrier to the front body panel.

16 Lift up the relay carrier and disconnect the fan wiring connectors, EGR controller wiring connector and EGR vacuum hoses. Lay the carrier to one side, clear of the fan shroud.

17 Lift the shroud upwards to release the two lower locating pegs and remove the shroud and fan from the car.

18 Disconnect the air inlet duct at the throttle housing and the crankcase ventilation and carbon canister hoses.

19 Remove the starter motor as described in Chapter 5A.

20 Disconnect the EGR temperature sensor wiring at the connector, and release the connector from its clip

21 Disconnect the EGR pipe from the valve **(see illustration)**,

22 Undo the two bolts, remove the valve and recover the gasket.

23 If required the EGR temperature sensor can be unscrewed from the side of the valve.

24 Refitting is a reversal of removal but use a new gasket and tighten all nuts and bolts to the specified torque.

9.4 Oxygen sensor location in exhaust front pipe

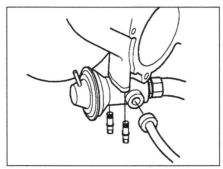

9.21 EGR valve connections and mountings

Chapter 5 Part A:
Starting and charging systems

Contents

Degrees of difficulty

Easy, suitable for novice with little experience	**Fairly easy,** suitable for beginner with some experience	**Fairly difficult,** suitable for competent DIY mechanic	**Difficult,** suitable for experienced DIY mechanic	**Very difficult,** suitable for expert DIY or professional

Specifications

System type . . . . 12-volt, negative earth

Battery
Type . . . . Low maintenance or "maintenance-free" sealed for life
Capacity . . . . 45 to 60 Ah (depending on model)
Charge condition:
  Poor . . . . 12.5 volts
  Normal . . . . 12.6 volts
  Good . . . . 12.7 volts

Alternator
Type . . . . Bosch or Nippon-Denso

Starter motor
Type . . . . Bosch

---

1 General information and precautions

General information

The engine electrical system consists mainly of the charging and starting systems. Because of their engine-related functions, these components are covered separately from the body electrical devices such as the lights, instruments, etc (which are covered in Chapter 12). Information on the ignition system is covered in Part B of this Chapter.

The electrical system is of the 12-volt negative earth type.

The battery is of the low maintenance or "maintenance-free" (sealed for life) type and is charged by the alternator, which is belt-driven from the crankshaft pulley.

The starter motor is of the pre-engaged type incorporating an integral solenoid. On starting, the solenoid moves the drive pinion into engagement with the flywheel ring gear before the starter motor is energised. Once the engine has started, a one-way clutch prevents the motor armature being driven by the engine until the pinion disengages from the flywheel.

Precautions

Further details of the various systems are given in the relevant Sections of this Chapter. While some repair procedures are given, the usual course of action is to renew the component concerned. The owner whose interest extends beyond mere component renewal should obtain a copy of the "Automobile Electrical & Electronic Systems Manual", available from the publishers of this manual.

It is necessary to take extra care when working on the electrical system to avoid damage to semi-conductor devices (diodes and transistors), and to avoid the risk of personal injury. In addition to the precautions given in "Safety first!" at the beginning of this manual, observe the following when working on the system:

Always remove rings, watches, etc before working on the electrical system. Even with the battery disconnected, capacitive discharge could occur if a component's live terminal is earthed through a metal object. This could cause a shock or nasty burn.

Do not reverse the battery connections. Components such as the alternator, electronic control units, or any other components having semi-conductor circuitry could be irreparably damaged.

If the engine is being started using jump leads and a slave battery, connect the batteries *positive-to-positive* and *negative-to-negative* (see "Booster battery (jump) starting"). This also applies when connecting a battery charger.

Never disconnect the battery terminals, the alternator, any electrical wiring or any test instruments when the engine is running.

Do not allow the engine to turn the alternator when the alternator is not connected.

Never "test" for alternator output by "flashing" the output lead to earth.

Never use an ohmmeter of the type incorporating a hand-cranked generator for circuit or continuity testing.

Always ensure that the battery negative lead is disconnected when working on the electrical system.

Before using electric-arc welding equipment on the car, disconnect the battery, alternator and components such as the fuel injection/ignition electronic control unit to protect them from the risk of damage.

The radio/cassette units fitted as standard or optional equipment are equipped with a built-in security code to deter thieves. If the power source to the unit is cut, the anti-theft system will activate. Even if the power source is immediately reconnected, the radio/cassette unit will not function until the correct security code has been entered. Therefore, if you do not know the correct security code for the radio/cassette unit do not disconnect the negative terminal of the battery or remove the radio/cassette unit from the car. Refer to the Owner's Manual, or your Volvo dealer for further information on security codes.

2   Battery - testing and charging

Standard and low maintenance battery - testing

1 If the vehicle covers a small annual mileage, it is worthwhile checking the specific gravity of the electrolyte every three months to determine the state of charge of the battery. Use a hydrometer to make the check and compare the results with the following table.

	Above 25°C	Below 25°C
Fully-charged	1.210 to 1.230	1.270 to 1.290
70% charged	1.170 to 1.190	1.230 to 1.250
Discharged	1.050 to 1.070	1.110 to 1.130

Note that the specific gravity readings assume an electrolyte temperature of 15°C (60°F); for every 10°C (48°F) below 15°C (60°F) subtract 0.007. For every 10°C (48°F) above 15°C (60°F) add 0.007.

2 If the battery condition is suspect, first check the specific gravity of electrolyte in each cell. A variation of 0.040 or more between any cells indicates loss of electrolyte or deterioration of the internal plates.

3 If the specific gravity variation is 0.040 or more, the battery should be renewed. If the cell variation is satisfactory but the battery is discharged, it should be charged as described later in this Section.

Maintenance-free battery - testing

4 In cases where a "sealed for life" maintenance-free battery is fitted, topping-up and testing of the electrolyte in each cell is not possible. The condition of the battery can therefore only be tested using a battery condition indicator or a voltmeter.

5 If testing the battery using a voltmeter, connect the voltmeter across the battery and compare the result with those given in the *Specifications* under "charge condition". The test is only accurate if the battery has not been subjected to any kind of charge for the previous six hours. If this is not the case, switch on the headlights for 30 seconds, then wait four to five minutes before testing the battery after switching off the headlights. All other electrical circuits must be switched off, so check that the doors and tailgate are fully shut when making the test.

6 If the voltage reading is less than 12.2 volts, then the battery is discharged, whilst a reading of 12.2 to 12.4 volts indicates a partially discharged condition.

7 If the battery is to be charged, remove it from the vehicle (Section 3) and charge it as described later in this Section.

Standard and low maintenance battery - charging

Note: *The following is intended as a guide only. Always refer to the manufacturer's recommendations (often printed on a label attached to the battery) before charging a battery.*

8 Charge the battery at a rate of 3.5 to 4 amps and continue to charge the battery at this rate until no further rise in specific gravity is noted over a four hour period.

9 Alternatively, a trickle charger charging at the rate of 1.5 amps can safely be used overnight.

10 Specially rapid "boost" charges which are claimed to restore the power of the battery in 1 to 2 hours are not recommended, as they can cause serious damage to the battery plates through overheating.

11 While charging the battery, note that the temperature of the electrolyte should never exceed 37.8°C (100°F).

Maintenance-free battery - charging

Note: *The following is intended as a guide only. Always refer to the manufacturer's recommendations (often printed on a label attached to the battery) before charging a battery.*

12 This battery type takes considerably longer to fully recharge than the standard type, the time taken being dependent on the extent of discharge, but it can take anything up to three days.

13 A constant voltage type charger is required, to be set, when connected, to 13.9 to 14.9 volts with a charger current below 25 amps. Using this method, the battery should be usable within three hours, giving a voltage reading of 12.5 volts, but this is for a partially discharged battery and, as mentioned, full charging can take considerably longer.

14 If the battery is to be charged from a fully discharged state (condition reading less than 12.2 volts), have it recharged by your Volvo dealer or local automotive electrician, as the charge rate is higher and constant supervision during charging is necessary.

3   Battery - removal and refitting

Note: *Make sure that you have a copy of the radio/cassette unit security code number before disconnecting the battery. Also, ensure that the unit is switched off before battery disconnection to avoid damage to the radio microprocessor circuitry.*

Removal

1 The battery is located at the front left-hand side of the engine compartment.

2 Slacken the clamp bolt and disconnect the clamp from the battery negative (earth) terminal **(see illustration)**.

3 Remove the insulation cover (where fitted) and disconnect the positive terminal lead(s) in the same way **(see illustration)**.

4 Unscrew the bolt and remove the battery retaining clamp bolt. Lift the battery out of the engine compartment.

3.2 Slacken the bolt (arrowed) to disconnect the battery negative terminal clamp

3.3 Lift up the cover for access to the battery positive terminal clamp

Refitting

5 Refitting is a reversal of removal, but smear petroleum jelly on the terminals when reconnecting the leads, and always reconnect the positive lead first, and the negative lead last.

4 Charging system - testing

Note: *Refer to the warnings given in "Safety first!" and in Section 1 of this Chapter before starting work.*

1 If the ignition warning light fails to illuminate when the ignition is switched on, first check the alternator wiring connections for security. If satisfactory, check that the warning light bulb has not blown, and that the bulbholder is secure in its location in the instrument panel. If the light still fails to illuminate, check the continuity of the warning light feed wire from the alternator to the bulbholder. If all is satisfactory, the alternator is at fault and should be renewed or taken to an auto-electrician for testing and repair.

2 If the ignition warning light illuminates when the engine is running, stop the engine and check that the drivebelt is correctly tensioned (see Chapter 1) and that the alternator connections are secure. If all is so far satisfactory, have the alternator checked by an auto-electrician for testing and repair.

3 If the alternator output is suspect even though the warning light functions correctly, the regulated voltage may be checked as follows.

4 Connect a voltmeter across the battery terminals and start the engine.

5 Increase the engine speed until the voltmeter reading remains steady; the reading should be between 13.5 and 14.8 volts.

6 Switch on as many electrical accessories (eg, the headlights, heated rear window and heater blower) as possible, and check that the alternator maintains the regulated voltage between 13.5 and 14.8 volts.

7 If the regulated voltage is not as stated, the fault may be due to worn brushes, weak brush springs, a faulty voltage regulator, a faulty diode, a severed phase winding or worn or damaged slip rings. The alternator should be renewed or taken to an auto-electrician for testing and repair.

5 Alternator - removal and refitting

Removal

1 Disconnect the battery negative lead.
2 Remove the auxiliary drivebelt as described in Chapter 1.
3 Disconnect the wiring multiplugs and the leads from the terminal studs at the rear of the alternator **(see illustration)**.

4 Unscrew and remove the mounting nuts and bolts at the front and rear and lift the alternator from its mounting bracket.

Refitting

5 Refitting is a reversal of removal. Refit the auxiliary drivebelt as described in Chapter 1.

6 Alternator - testing and overhaul

If the alternator is thought to be suspect, it should be removed from the vehicle and taken to an auto-electrician for testing. Most auto-electricians will be able to supply and fit brushes at a reasonable cost. However, check on the cost of repairs before proceeding as it may prove more economical to obtain a new or exchange alternator.

7 Starting system - testing

Note: *Refer to the precautions given in "Safety first!" and in Section 1 of this Chapter before starting work.*

1 If the starter motor fails to operate when the ignition key is turned to the appropriate position, the following possible causes may be to blame.
 a) *The battery is faulty.*
 b) *The electrical connections between the switch, solenoid, battery and starter motor are somewhere failing to pass the necessary current from the battery through the starter to earth.*
 c) *The solenoid is faulty.*
 d) *The starter motor is mechanically or electrically defective.*

2 To check the battery, switch on the headlights. If they dim after a few seconds, this indicates that the battery is discharged - recharge (see Section 2) or renew the battery. If the headlights glow brightly, operate the ignition switch and observe the lights. If they dim, then this indicates that current is reaching the starter motor, therefore the fault must lie in the starter motor. If the lights

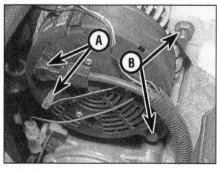

5.3 Alternator wiring connections (A) and rear mounting bolts (B)

continue to glow brightly (and no clicking sound can be heard from the starter motor solenoid), this indicates that there is a fault in the circuit or solenoid - see following paragraphs. If the starter motor turns slowly when operated, but the battery is in good condition, then this indicates that either the starter motor is faulty, or there is considerable resistance somewhere in the circuit.

3 If a fault in the circuit is suspected, disconnect the battery leads (including the earth connection to the body), the starter/solenoid wiring and the engine/transmission earth strap. Thoroughly clean the connections, and reconnect the leads and wiring, then use a voltmeter or test lamp to check that full battery voltage is available at the battery positive lead connection to the solenoid, and that the earth is sound. Smear petroleum jelly around the battery terminals to prevent corrosion - corroded connections are amongst the most frequent causes of electrical system faults.

4 If the battery and all connections are in good condition, check the circuit by disconnecting the wire from the solenoid blade terminal. Connect a voltmeter or test lamp between the wire end and a good earth (such as the battery negative terminal), and check that the wire is live when the ignition switch is turned to the "start" position. If it is, then the circuit is sound - if not the circuit wiring can be checked as described in Chapter 12.

5 The solenoid contacts can be checked by connecting a voltmeter or test lamp between the battery positive feed connection on the starter side of the solenoid, and earth. When the ignition switch is turned to the "start" position, there should be a reading or lighted bulb, as applicable. If there is no reading or lighted bulb, the solenoid is faulty and should be renewed.

6 If the circuit and solenoid are proved sound, the fault must lie in the starter motor. In this event, it may be possible to have the starter motor overhauled by a specialist, but check on the cost of spares before proceeding, as it may prove more economical to obtain a new or exchange motor.

8 Starter motor - removal and refitting

Removal

1 Disconnect the battery negative lead.
2 Disconnect the wiring from the starter motor solenoid **(see illustration)**.
3 Unbolt the starter motor rear support bracket from the engine **(see illustration)**.
4 Undo the bolts securing the starter motor to the transmission bellhousing and manoeuvre the unit from its location **(see illustration)**. Note the position of the locating dowel and ensure it is in place when refitting.

8.2 Wiring connections at the rear of the starter solenoid

8.3 Starter motor rear support bracket retaining bolt (arrowed)

Refitting

5 Refitting is a reversal of removal.

9   Starter motor - testing and overhaul

If the starter motor is thought to be suspect, it should be removed from the vehicle and taken to an auto-electrician for testing. Most auto-electricians will be able to supply and fit brushes at a reasonable cost. However, check on the cost of repairs before proceeding as it may prove more economical to obtain a new or exchange motor.

10   Ignition switch - removal and refitting

Refer to Chapter 12, Section 4.

8.4 Removing the starter motor from the bellhousing. Note the location of the dowel (arrowed)

Chapter 5 Part B:
Ignition system

Contents

Degrees of difficulty

Easy, suitable for novice with little experience	**Fairly easy,** suitable for beginner with some experience	**Fairly difficult,** suitable for competent DIY mechanic	**Difficult,** suitable for experienced DIY mechanic	**Very difficult,** suitable for expert DIY or professional

Specifications

General

System type:

B5204 S, and B5234 S	EZ-129K ignition system with LH3.2 Jetronic fuel system
B5202 S, and B5252 S engines	Fenix 5.2 engine management system
B5204 T, and B5234 T engines	Motronic 4.3 engine management system
B5254 S engines	EZ-129K ignition system with LH3.2 Jetronic fuel system, or Motronic 4.3 engine management system (according to market territory)
Firing order	1-2-4-5-3 (No. 1 cylinder at timing belt end of engine)

Spark plugs

Type	See Chapter 1 *Specifications*

Ignition timing*

B5202 S, B5204 S, B5234 S, and B5252 S engines	10° ± 2° BTDC @ 800 ± 50 rpm
B5204 T and B5234 T engines	6° ± 2° BTDC @ 850 ± 50 rpm
B5254 S engines:	
With EZ-129K ignition system	10° ± 2° BTDC @ 800 ± 50 rpm
With Motronic 4.3 engine management system	5° ± 2° BTDC @ 850 ± 50 rpm

Values given are for checking purposes only, no adjustment is possible

Ignition coil

All engines except pre-1994, B5252 S:	
Primary resistance	0.5 to 1.5Ω
Secondary resistance	8000 to 9000Ω
Pre-1994, B5252 S engines:	
Primary resistance	Not specified
Secondary resistance	6000 to 7000Ω

Torque wrench settings

	Nm
Knock sensors	20

1 General information

The ignition system is responsible for igniting the compressed fuel/air charge in each cylinder in turn at precisely the right moment for the prevailing engine speed and load. This is achieved by using a sophisticated engine management system, which utilises computer technology and electro-magnetic circuitry to achieve the required ignition characteristics. Three systems are used on 850 models covered by this manual, dependant on engine size and type. On the Fenix 5.2 and Motronic 4.3 systems, a single electronic control unit (ECU) is used to control the complete engine management system including both the fuel and ignition functions. On the LH3.2-Jetronic system, two ECU's are used, one for the fuel system and one for the EZ-129 K ignition system. On this system both ECUs work in conjunction with each other to form one inter-related engine management package. The operation of all three systems in terms of ignition control is virtually identical, with only minor differences in component arrangement.

The main components of the ignition side of the system are the ECU, the ignition power stage, the ignition coil, the distributor, the spark plugs and HT leads, and the various sensors that supply information to the ECU on engine operating conditions. The operation of the system is as follows.

A series of holes drilled in the periphery of the engine flywheel, and an RPM sensor whose inductive head runs just above the drilled flywheel periphery, allow the ECU to compute engine speed and crankshaft position. As the crankshaft rotates, the land (or "teeth") between the drilled holes in the flywheel, pass the RPM sensor, which transmits a pulse to the ECU every time a tooth passes it. There is one missing hole in the flywheel periphery, which allows the land (or tooth) at that point to be twice as wide as the others. The ECU recognises the absence of a pulse from the RPM sensor at this point, and uses it to establish the TDC position for No 1 piston. The time interval between pulses, and the location of the missing pulse, allow the ECU to accurately determine the position of the crankshaft and its speed. The camshaft position sensor enhances this information by detecting whether a particular piston is on an inlet or an exhaust cycle.

Information on engine load is supplied to the ECU via the mass air flow sensor (or via the manifold absolute pressure sensor and inlet air temperature sensor on the Fenix 5.2 system). The load being determined by computation based on the quantity of air being drawn into the engine. Further information is sent to the ECU from two knock sensors. These sensors are sensitive to vibration and detect the knocking which

occurs when the engine starts to "pink" (pre-ignite). Sensors monitoring coolant temperature, throttle position, road speed, automatic transmission gear position (where applicable) and air conditioning system operation, provide additional input signals to the ECU on vehicle operating conditions.

From this constantly-changing data, the ECU selects, and if necessary modifies, a particular ignition advance setting from a map of ignition characteristics stored in its memory.

With the firing point established, the ECU sends a signal to the ignition power stage, which is an electronic switch controlling the current to the ignition coil primary windings. On receipt of the signal from the ECU, the power stage interrupts the primary current to the ignition coil, which induces a high-tension voltage in the coil secondary windings. This HT voltage is passed to the distributor cap, and then on to the spark plugs, via the distributor rotor arm and HT leads. The cycle is then repeated many times a second for each cylinder in turn.

In the event of a fault in the system due to loss of a signal from one of the sensors, the ECU reverts to an emergency ("limp-home") program. This will allow the car to be driven, although engine operation and performance will be limited. A warning light on the instrument panel will illuminate if the fault is likely to cause an increase in harmful exhaust emissions.

To facilitate fault diagnosis, the ignition system is provided with an on-board diagnostic facility which displays detected faults in the system as a series of three-digit fault codes on a flashing LED.

In addition to the above operations, many of the ignition system components have a second function in the control and operation of the fuel injection system. Further details will be found in Part A of Chapter 4.

2 Ignition system - testing

Warning: Voltages produced by an electronic ignition system are considerably higher than those produced by conventional ignition systems. Extreme care must be taken when working on the system if the ignition is switched on. Persons with surgically-implanted cardiac pacemaker devices should keep well clear of the ignition circuits, components and test equipment.

General

1 The components of the ignition system are normally very reliable; most faults are far more likely to be due to loose or dirty connections, or to "tracking" of HT voltage due to dirt, dampness or damaged insulation, than to the

failure of any of the system's components. **Always** check all wiring thoroughly before condemning an electrical component, and work methodically to eliminate all other possibilities before deciding that a particular component is faulty.

2 The old practice of checking for a spark by holding the live end of an HT lead a short distance away from the engine is **not** recommended; not only is there a high risk of a powerful electric shock, but the ECU, HT coil, or power stage may be damaged. Similarly, **never** try to "diagnose" misfires by pulling off one HT lead at a time.

3 The following tests should be carried out when an obvious fault such as non-starting or a clearly detectable misfire exists. Some faults, however, are more obscure and are often disguised by the fact that the ECU will adopt an emergency program ("limp-home") mode to maintain as much driveability as possible. Faults of this nature usually appear in the form of excessive fuel consumption, poor idling characteristics, lack of performance, knocking or "pinking" noises from the engine under certain conditions, or a combination of these conditions. Where problems such as this are experienced, the on-board diagnostic facility described in Section 3 should be used to isolate the problem. This facility should also be used if an engine problem is accompanied by illumination of the emission control system fault warning light on the instrument panel.

Engine will not start

4 If the engine either will not turn over at all, or only turns very slowly, check the battery and starter motor. Connect a voltmeter across the battery terminals (meter positive probe to battery positive terminal) then note the voltage reading obtained while turning the engine over on the starter for (no more than) ten seconds. If the reading obtained is less than approximately 9.5 volts, first check the battery, starter motor and charging system as described in Part A of this Chapter.

5 If the engine turns over at normal speed but will not start, check the HT circuit by connecting a timing light (following its manufacturer's instructions) and turning the engine over on the starter motor; if the light flashes, voltage is reaching the spark plugs, so these should be checked first. If the light does not flash, check the HT leads themselves, followed by the distributor cap, carbon brush and rotor arm, using the information given in Chapter 1.

6 If there is a spark, continue with the checks described in Section 3 of this Chapter.

7 If there is still no spark, check the condition of the coil, if possible by substitution with a known good unit, or by checking the primary and secondary resistances. If the fault persists, the problem lies elsewhere; if the fault is now cleared, a new coil is the obvious cure. However, check carefully the condition of the LT connections themselves before doing so, to ensure that the fault is not due to dirty or poorly-fastened connectors.

8 If the coil is in good condition, the fault is probably within the power stage, one of the system sensors, or related components (as applicable). In this case a fault code should be logged in the diagnostic unit which should help to isolate the component concerned (see Section 3).

Engine misfires

9 An irregular misfire suggests either a loose connection or intermittent fault on the primary circuit, or an HT fault on the coil side of the rotor arm.

10 With the ignition switched off, check carefully through the system, ensuring that all connections are clean and securely fastened. If the equipment is available, check the LT circuit as described above.

11 Check that the ignition coil, the distributor cap and the HT leads are clean and dry. Check the leads themselves and the spark plugs (by substitution if necessary), then check the distributor cap, carbon brush and rotor arm as described in Chapter 1.

12 Regular misfiring is almost certainly due to a fault in the distributor cap, HT leads or spark plugs. Use a timing light (paragraph 5 above) to check whether HT voltage is present at all leads.

13 If HT voltage is not present on any particular lead, the fault will be in that lead, or in the distributor cap. If HT is present on all leads, the fault will be in the spark plugs; check and renew them if there is any doubt about their condition.

14 If no HT is present, check the ignition coil; its secondary windings may be breaking down under load.

15 Any further checking of the system components should be carried out by a Volvo dealer.

3 On-board diagnostic system - general information and operation
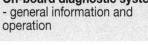

Note: *Both the ignition and fuel systems must ideally be treated as one inter-related engine management system. Although the contents of this section is mainly concerned with the ignition side of the system, many of the components perform dual functions and some of the following procedures of necessity relate to the fuel system.*

General information

1 The fuel and ignition systems on all engines covered by this manual incorporate an on-board diagnostic system to facilitate fault finding and system testing. The diagnostic system works in conjunction with the fuel, and where applicable, the ignition system ECUs to continually monitor the system components. Should a fault occur, the ECU stores a series of signals (or fault codes) for subsequent

read-out via the diagnostic unit located in the engine compartment.

2 If driveability problems have been experienced and engine performance is suspect, the on-board diagnostic system can be used to pinpoint any problem areas without the use of special test equipment. Once this has been done, however, further tests may often be necessary to determine the exact nature of the fault; ie, whether a component itself has failed, or whether it is a wiring or other inter-related problem. Apart from checking visually the wiring and connections, these additional tests will require the use of Volvo test equipment and should be entrusted to a dealer.

Preliminary checks

Note: *When carrying out these checks to trace a fault, remember that if the fault has appeared only a short time after any part of the vehicle has been serviced or overhauled, the first place to check is where that work was carried out, however unrelated it may appear, to ensure that no carelessly-refitted components are causing the problem.*

If you are tracing the cause of a "partial" engine fault, such as lack of performance, in addition to the checks outlined below, check the compression pressures. Check also that the fuel filter and air cleaner element have been renewed at the recommended intervals. Refer to Chapters 1, 2A or 4A for details of these procedures.

3 Open the bonnet and check the condition of the battery connections - remake the connections or renew the leads if a fault is found. Use the same techniques to ensure that all earth points in the engine compartment provide good electrical contact through clean, metal-to-metal joints, and that all are securely fastened.

4 Next work methodically around the engine compartment, checking all visible wiring, and the connections between sections of the wiring loom. What you are looking for at this stage is wiring that is obviously damaged by chafing against sharp edges, or against moving suspension/transmission components and/or the auxiliary drivebelt, by being trapped or crushed between carelessly-refitted components, or melted by being forced into contact with hot engine castings, coolant pipes, etc. In almost all cases, damage of this sort is caused in the first instance by incorrect routing on reassembly after previous work has been carried out (see the note at the beginning of this sub-Section).

5 Obviously wires can break or short together inside the insulation so that no visible evidence betrays the fault, but this usually only occurs where the wiring loom has been incorrectly routed so that it is stretched taut or kinked sharply; either of these conditions should be obvious on even a casual inspection. If this is thought to have happened and the fault proves elusive, the suspect section of wiring should be checked very

carefully during the more detailed checks which follow.

6 Depending on the extent of the problem, damaged wiring may be repaired by rejoining the break or splicing-in a new length of wire, using solder to ensure a good connection, and remaking the insulation with adhesive insulating tape or heat-shrink tubing, as desired. If the damage is extensive, given the implications for the vehicle's future reliability, the best long-term answer may well be to renew that entire section of the loom, however expensive this may appear.

7 When the actual damage has been repaired, ensure that the wiring loom is re-routed correctly, so that it is clear of other components, is not stretched or kinked, and is secured out of harm's way using the plastic clips, guides and ties provided.

8 Check all electrical connectors, ensuring that they are clean, securely fastened, and that each is locked by its plastic tabs or wire clip, as appropriate. If any connector shows external signs of corrosion (accumulations of white or green deposits, or streaks of "rust"), or if any is thought to be dirty, it must be unplugged and cleaned using electrical contact cleaner. If the connector pins are severely corroded, the connector must be renewed; note that this may mean the renewal of that entire section of the loom.

9 If the cleaner completely removes the corrosion to leave the connector in a satisfactory condition, it would be wise to pack the connector with a suitable material which will exclude dirt and moisture, and prevent the corrosion from occurring again; a Volvo dealer may be able to recommend a suitable product.

10 Working methodically around the engine compartment, check carefully that all vacuum hoses and pipes are securely fastened and correctly routed, with no signs of cracks, splits or deterioration to cause air leaks, or of hoses that are trapped, kinked, or bent sharply enough to restrict air flow. Check with particular care at all connections and sharp bends, and renew any damaged or deformed lengths of hose.

11 Working from the fuel tank, via the filter, to the fuel rail (and including the feed and return), check the fuel lines, and renew any that are found to be leaking, trapped or kinked.

12 Check that the accelerator cable is correctly secured and adjusted; renew the cable if there is any doubt about its condition, or if it appears to be stiff or jerky in operation. Refer to Chapter 4A for further information, if required.

13 Unclip the air cleaner cover, and check that the air filter is not clogged or soaked. (A clogged air filter will obstruct the inlet air flow, causing a noticeable effect on engine performance. Renew the filter if necessary; refer to the relevant Sections of Chapter 1 for further information, if required.

14 Start the engine and allow it to idle.

Caution: Working in the engine

3.21 Diagnostic unit location alongside washer reservoir filler

3.22 Insert the flylead into socket (6) of module (A) (arrowed) to access the ignition system fault codes

compartment while the engine is running requires great care if the risk of personal injury is to be avoided; among the dangers are burns from contact with hot components, or contact with moving components such as the radiator cooling fan or the auxiliary drivebelt. Refer to "Safety first!" at the front of this manual before starting, and ensure that your hands, and long hair or loose clothing, are kept well clear of hot or moving components at all times.

15 Working from the air inlet, via the air cleaner assembly and the mass air flow sensor (or inlet air temperature sensor) to the throttle housing and inlet manifold (and including the various vacuum hoses and pipes connected to these), check for air leaks. Usually, these will be revealed by sucking or hissing noises, but minor leaks may be traced by spraying a solution of soapy water on to the suspect joint; if a leak exists, it will be shown by the change in engine note and the accompanying air bubbles (or sucking-in of the liquid, depending on the pressure difference at that point). If a leak is found at any point, tighten the fastening clamp and/or renew the faulty components, as applicable.

16 Similarly, work from the cylinder head, via the manifold to the tailpipe, to check that the exhaust system is free from leaks. The simplest way of doing this, if the vehicle can be raised and supported safely and with complete security while the check is made, is to temporarily block the tailpipe while listening for the sound of escaping exhaust gases; any leak should be evident. If a leak is found at any point, tighten the fastening clamp bolts and/or nuts, renew the gasket, and/or renew the faulty section of the system, as necessary, to seal the leak.

17 It is possible to make a further check of the electrical connections by wiggling each electrical connector of the system in turn as the engine is idling; a faulty connector will be immediately evident from the engine's response as contact is broken and remade. A

faulty connector should be renewed to ensure that the future reliability of the system; note that this may mean the renewal of that entire section of the loom.

18 Switch off the engine. If the fault is not yet identified, the next step is to check the fault code read out at the diagnostic unit as described below.

Fault code read-out

Note: *On models from 1996 the diagnostic unit is located under a cover in front of the gear lever and has a 16-pin socket for connection to a fault code reader.*

19 As noted in the general comments at the beginning of this Section, the preliminary checks outlined above should eliminate the majority of faults from the ignition (or fuel) system. If the fault has not yet been identified, the next step is to check whether a fault code has been logged and if so, to interpret the meaning of the code.

20 As mentioned in Section 1 of this Chapter, the LH3.2-Jetronic engine management system employs a separate ECU to control the EZ-129 K ignition system. On the other two systems used on the 850 range, a single ECU is responsible for control of both the fuel and ignition systems. Therefore, if working on a vehicle equipped with LH3.2/EZ-129 K, the following procedures are applicable. For all other systems, refer to the procedures contained in Chapter 4A, Section 9.

21 Firstly, locate the diagnostic unit which is situated in the front right-hand side of the engine compartment, alongside the windscreen washer reservoir filler **(see illustration)**. The diagnostic unit consists of two modules mounted side by side, with a plastic cover over each. Lift off the covers and note that the two modules are marked A and B, each having six numbered sockets on their top face.

22 With the ignition switched off, unclip the flylead from the holder on the side of the unit and insert it into socket (6) of module (A) **(see illustration)**.

23 Have a paper and pen ready to copy down the fault codes as they are displayed. The three-digit codes will appear as a series of blinks of the red LED (located on the top face of the unit next to the test button) with a slight pause between each digit.

24 With the flylead inserted, switch on the ignition. Press the test button on top of module (A) once, for about one second, then release it and wait for the LED to flash. As the LED flashes, copy down the fault code. Now press the button again and copy down the next fault code, if there is one. Continue until the first fault code is displayed again, indicating that all the stored codes have been accessed, then switch off the ignition.

25 If code 1-1-1 is obtained, this indicates that there are no ignition system fault codes stored in the ECU. In this case refer to Chapter 4A, Section 9 and conduct a fault code read-out for the fuel injection side of the system.

26 Given in the accompanying table are the possible EZ-129 K ignition system fault codes and their meaning. A description of the fuel system fault codes for the LH3.2 system, and the combined fuel/ignition fault codes for the other two systems is given in Chapter 4A, Section 9.

27 Once all the fault codes have been recorded they should be deleted. Note that the fault codes cannot be deleted until all of them have been displayed at least once, and the first one is displayed again. With the flylead inserted in socket (6) of module (A), switch on the ignition, press the test button and hold it down for approximately five seconds. Release the test button and after three seconds the LED will light. When the LED lights, press and hold the test button down for a further five seconds then release it - the LED will go out. Switch off the ignition and check that all the fault codes have been deleted by switching the ignition on again and pressing the test button for one second - code 1-1-1 should appear. If a code other than 1-1-1 appears, record the code then repeat the deleting procedure. When all the

Fault code	Meaning
1-1-1	No fault detected
1-1-2	Fault in ECU
1-2-3	Coolant temperature sensor signal absent or faulty
1-3-1	RPM sensor signal absent
1-4-3	Front knock sensor signal absent or faulty
1-4-4	Load signal from fuel injection system ECU absent
1-5-4*	Leak in EGR system
2-1-4	RPM sensor signal absent intermittently
2-4-1*	EGR system flow faulty
3-1-1	Vehicle speed sensor signal absent or faulty
3-1-4	Camshaft position sensor signal absent
3-2-4	Camshaft position sensor signal absent intermittently
4-1-1	Throttle position sensor signal absent or faulty
4-1-3*	EGR temperature sensor signal absent or faulty
4-3-2	High temperature in ECU module box
4-3-3	Rear knock sensor signal absent or faulty
5-1-3	Excessively high temperature in ECU module box

Only applicable to engines with electronically controlled exhaust gas recirculation system (see Chapter 4B).

codes have been deleted, switch off the ignition, locate the flylead in its holder and refit the unit covers.

28 Once the location of a fault has been established from the fault code read-out, investigations can be concentrated in that area. Go through the checks outlined earlier in this section in case anything was missed the first time. As mentioned previously, further detailed checking of the system components will require the use of Volvo test equipment. Therefore, the only alternatives possible at this time are the substitution of a suspect component with a known good unit, or entrusting further work to a Volvo dealer. If a substitute unit can be obtained (or borrowed), removal and refitting procedures are given in the following Sections of this Chapter.

4 Ignition HT coil - removal and refitting

Removal

1 Disconnect the battery negative lead.
2 Disconnect the HT king lead from the centre of the coil and the wiring connector from the ignition power stage just below the coil.
3 Undo the bolts securing the coil and power stage mounting bracket to the side of the suspension strut tower and remove the assembly from the engine compartment **(see illustration)**. Note that the ignition coil and the power stage are an integrated assembly and the two components cannot be separated.

4 Inspect the coil visually for cracks, leakage of insulating oil or other obvious damage. Renew it if such damage is evident.

Refitting

5 Refit by reversing the removal operations.

5 Ignition system power stage - removal and refitting

The power stage and ignition coil are an integrated assembly and the two components cannot be separated. Removal and refitting procedures are as for the ignition coil described in Section 4.

6 Distributor cap and rotor arm - removal and refitting

Removal

1 Undo the screws and lift off the spark plug HT lead cover from the centre of the cylinder head.
2 Pull the HT leads off the spark plugs and release them from the retaining clips. Mark the leads if necessary to avoid confusion when refitting.
3 Undo the three screws which secure the distributor cap. The screws are captive, so do not attempt to remove them from the cap. Access can be improved, if necessary, by releasing the clips and moving the air cleaner lid to one side.
4 Lift off the distributor cap and HT leads **(see illustration)**.
5 Remove the flash shield then undo the three screws and remove the rotor arm **(see illustrations)**.

4.3 Ignition coil and power stage mounting bracket bolts (arrowed)

6.4 Removing the distributor cap from the rear of the cylinder head

6.5a Remove the flash shield . . .

6.5b . . . then undo the three screws and remove the rotor arm

Refitting

6 Refitting is a reversal of removal. Ensure that the HT leads are secured by their clips and not trapped when the cover is refitted.

7   Ignition system sensors – removal and refitting

RPM sensor

Removal

1 The RPM sensor is located on the top of the transmission bellhousing.

2 Disconnect the RPM sensor wiring at the connector just below the distributor cap.

3 Remove the sensor retaining bolt, withdraw the sensor from its mounting bracket on the bellhousing **(see illustration)**.

Refitting

4 Refit by reversing the removal operations.

Knock sensors

Removal

5 The two knock sensors are located on the front facing side of the cylinder block under the inlet manifold.

6 Refer to Chapter 4A and remove the inlet manifold.

7 Disconnect the wiring connector from the front or rear knock sensor as applicable.

8 Undo the sensor securing bolt and remove the sensor **(see illustration)**.

Refitting

9 Locate the sensor on the cylinder block and refit and tighten the retaining bolt to the specified torque. When tightening the bolt, hold the front sensor (nearest the timing belt) with its connector at the 3 o'clock position, and the rear sensor with its connector at the 5 o'clock position.

10 Refit the inlet manifold as described in Chapter 4A.

Camshaft position sensor

Removal

11 The camshaft position sensor is located on the left-hand rear of the cylinder head and is driven by the exhaust camshaft.

12 Disconnect the sensor wiring at the connector located below the distributor cap **(see illustration)**.

13 Undo the two screws and manipulate the sensor from its location on the cylinder head, behind the engine tie-bar support bracket **(see illustration)**.

Refitting

14 Refit by reversing the removal operations.

Coolant temperature sensor

15 Refer to Chapter 3, Section 6.

Vehicle speed sensor

16 Refer to Chapter 12, Section 8.

7.3 RPM sensor location and retaining bolt (arrowed)

7.8 Rear knock sensor location and retaining bolt (arrowed)

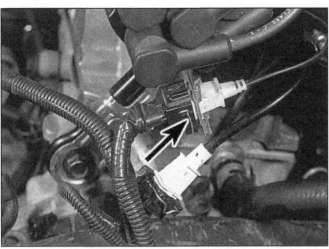

7.12 Camshaft position sensor wiring connector (arrowed)

7.13 Camshaft position sensor retaining screws (arrowed)

Throttle position sensor

17 Refer to Chapter 4A, Section 10.

8 Electronic control unit (ECU) - removal and refitting

Note: *The fuel and ignition ECUs together with the automatic transmission ECU (where applicable), are all located in the ECU module box which is situated at the front right-hand side of the engine compartment in front of the cooling system expansion tank. Note that only the LH3.2-Jetronic/EZ-129 K system have a separate ignition ECU.*

Removal

1 Ensure that the ignition is switched off then release the two catches on the side of the module box lid. Lift off the lid and place it to one side.
2 Pull the locking lever on top of the ECU forward and withdraw the ECU from its location. The ignition system ECU is located in slot one of the module box, nearest to the engine.

Refitting

3 Locate the ECU in the module box engaging it with the connector in the base.
4 Push the locking lever down and refit the module box lid.

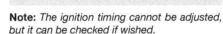

9 Ignition timing - checking

Note: *The ignition timing cannot be adjusted, but it can be checked if wished.*
1 Bring the engine to operating temperature with the air conditioning switched off. With the engine stopped, connect a timing light (stroboscope) as instructed by the manufacturers.
2 Undo the retaining bolt and remove the timing belt outer cover. The ignition timing marks consist of a scale on the timing belt inner cover, above the inlet camshaft sprocket, and a faint line on the inlet camshaft sprocket tooth.
3 Highlight the notch on the sprocket and the desired mark on the timing scale with white

paint or typist's correction fluid. (See *Specifications* for the desired values).
4 Run the engine at idle speed and shine the timing light on the timing scale. The sprocket notch will appear stationary and (if the timing is correct) in alignment with the appropriate mark on the timing scale.
Caution: Take great care not to get electrical leads, clothing, long hair etc, caught in the timing belt or auxiliary drivebelt.
5 Stop the engine, disconnect the timing light and refit the timing belt cover.
6 If the timing is incorrect, there is likely to be a fault in the RPM sensor, the fuel/ignition system ECU or associated wiring. Any faults in these areas are likely to be accompanied by a fault code which will be logged in the ECU for subsequent read-out (see Section 3).

Notes

Chapter 6
Clutch

Contents

Degrees of difficulty

Easy, suitable for novice with little experience	Fairly easy, suitable for beginner with some experience	Fairly difficult, suitable for competent DIY mechanic 	Difficult, suitable for experienced DIY mechanic	Very difficult, suitable for expert DIY or professional

Specifications

General
Clutch type . . . . Single dry plate, diaphragm spring, hydraulic actuation

Driven plate
Diameter:
  All engines except B5234T and B5234T-5 . . . . 228 mm
  B5234T and B5234T-5 engines . . . . 240 mm

Pressure plate
Warp limit . . . . 0.2 mm

Torque wrench settings
	Nm
Pressure plate retaining bolts	25
Master cylinder retaining nuts	25

1 General information

A single dry plate diaphragm spring clutch is fitted to all manual transmission models. The clutch is hydraulically operated via a master and slave cylinder.

The main components of the clutch are the pressure plate, the driven plate (sometimes called the friction plate or disc) and the release bearing. The pressure plate is bolted to the flywheel, with the driven plate sandwiched between them. The centre of the driven plate carries female splines which mate with the splines on the transmission input shaft. The release bearing is attached to the release fork and acts on the diaphragm spring fingers of the pressure plate.

When the engine is running and the clutch pedal is released, the diaphragm spring clamps the pressure plate, driven plate and flywheel firmly together. Drive is transmitted through the friction surfaces of the flywheel and pressure plate to the linings of the driven plate and thus to the transmission input shaft.

When the clutch pedal is depressed, the pedal movement is transmitted hydraulically to the release fork. The fork moves the bearing to press on the diaphragm spring fingers. Spring pressure on the pressure plate is relieved, and the flywheel and pressure plate spin without moving the driven plate. As the pedal is released, spring pressure is restored and the drive is gradually taken up.

The clutch hydraulic system consists of a master cylinder, a slave cylinder and the associated pipes and hoses. The fluid reservoir is shared with the brake master cylinder.

Wear in the driven plate linings is compensated for automatically by the hydraulic system components and no adjustment is necessary.

2 Clutch pedal - removal and refitting

Removal

1 Disconnect the battery negative lead.
2 Remove the trim panel under the facia on the driver's side. On cars equipped with an airbag, remove the kneeguard beneath the steering column.

2.3 Master cylinder pushrod to clutch pedal retaining clip (arrowed)

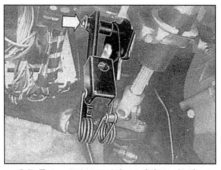

2.5 Extract the pedal retaining circlip (arrowed) and slide the pedal off the shaft

3 Fold back the carpet, then release the clip securing the master cylinder pushrod to the clutch pedal (see illustration).
4 Hold the pedal to prevent it moving upward under spring pressure, then release the pushrod from the pedal. Push the pedal down and disconnect the assistance spring from the pedal.
5 Extract the pedal retaining circlip and slide the pedal off the pivot shaft (see illustration).
6 With the pedal removed, check the condition of the pivot bushes and renew as necessary.

Refitting

7 Refit by reversing the removal operations. Apply grease to the pedal bushes and use a new circlip to secure the pedal if the old one is in any way damaged or distorted.

3   Clutch master cylinder - removal and refitting

Warning: Hydraulic fluid is poisonous; wash off immediately and thoroughly in the case of skin contact, and seek immediate medical advice if any fluid is swallowed or gets into the eyes. Certain

types of hydraulic fluid are inflammable, and may ignite when allowed into contact with hot components; when servicing any hydraulic system, it is safest to assume that the fluid IS inflammable, and to take precautions against the risk of fire as though it is petrol that is being handled. Hydraulic fluid is also an effective paint stripper, and will attack plastics; if any is spilt, it should be washed off immediately, using copious quantities of clean water. Finally, it is hygroscopic (it absorbs moisture from the air) - old fluid may be contaminated and unfit for further use. When topping-up or renewing the fluid, always use the recommended type, and ensure that it comes from a freshly-opened sealed container.
Note: *Master cylinder internal components are not available separately and no repair or overhaul of the cylinder is possible. In the event of a hydraulic system fault, or any sign of visible fluid leakage on or around the master cylinder or clutch pedal, the unit should be renewed.*

Removal

1 Disconnect the battery negative lead.
2 On left-hand drive models, refer to Chapter 4A and remove the air cleaner assembly.
3 Disconnect the fluid supply hose from the

brake master cylinder reservoir (see illustration). Have ready a container and rags to catch the fluid which will spill.
4 Unscrew the hydraulic pipe union from the end of the clutch master cylinder (see illustration). Be prepared for further fluid spillage. Cover the open pipe union with a piece of polythene and a rubber band to keep dirt out. Where a snap-on coupling is used on the pipe union, extract the spring clip and pull out the pipe.
5 Remove the trim panel under the facia on the driver's side. On cars equipped with an airbag, remove the kneeguard beneath the steering column.
6 Fold back the carpet, then release the clip securing the master cylinder pushrod to the clutch pedal.
7 Hold the pedal to prevent it moving upward under spring pressure, then release the pushrod from the pedal. Push the pedal down and disconnect the assistance spring from the pedal.
8 Remove the two nuts and bolts which secure the master cylinder to the bulkhead.
9 Remove the master cylinder from the engine compartment, being careful not to drip fluid onto the paintwork.

Refitting

10 Refit by reversing the removal operations, noting the following points:
a) If a new master cylinder is being fitted, transfer the fluid supply hose from the old cylinder to the new one prior to installation.
b) If the hydraulic pipe union is of the snap-on type, fit a new O-ring to the connector.
c) Tighten the master cylinder retaining nuts to the specified torque.
d) Bleed the clutch hydraulic system on completion (Section 5).

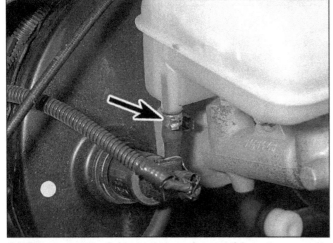

3.3 Disconnect the fluid supply hose (arrowed) from the reservoir

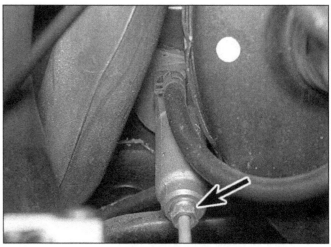

3.4 Unscrew the pipe union (arrowed) from the end of the master cylinder

4.2 Extract the slave cylinder retaining circlip (arrowed)

5.2 Slave cylinder bleed screw and dust cover (arrowed)

4 Clutch slave cylinder - removal and refitting

Note: *Slave cylinder internal components are not available separately and no repair or overhaul of the cylinder is possible. In the event of a hydraulic system fault, or any sign of visible fluid leakage on or around the slave cylinder push rod or rubber gaiter, the unit should be renewed.*

Removal

Note: *Refer to the warning at the beginning of Section 3 before proceeding.*

1 Unscrew the hydraulic pipe union on the end of the slave cylinder and carefully withdraw the pipe. Have ready a container and rags to catch the fluid which will spill. Cover the open pipe union with a piece of polythene and a rubber band to keep dirt out.
2 Extract the slave cylinder retaining circlip and withdraw the unit from the transmission **(see illustration)**.

Refitting

3 Refit by reversing the removal operations. Bleed the clutch hydraulic system on completion (Section 5).

5 Clutch hydraulic system - bleeding

Note: *Refer to the warning at the beginning of Section 3 before proceeding.*

1 Top-up the hydraulic fluid reservoir on the brake master cylinder with fresh clean fluid of the specified type (see *"Weekly checks"*).
2 Remove the dust cover and fit a length of clear hose over the bleed screw on the slave cylinder **(see illustration)**. Place the other end of the hose in a jar containing a small amount of hydraulic fluid.

3 Slacken the bleed screw then have an assistant depress the clutch pedal. Tighten the bleed screw when the pedal is depressed. Have the assistant release the pedal, then slacken the bleed screw again.
4 Repeat the process until clean fluid, free of air bubbles, emerges from the bleed screw. Tighten the screw at the end of a pedal downstroke and remove the hose and jar. Refit the dust cover.
5 Top-up the hydraulic fluid reservoir.
6 Pressure bleeding equipment may be used if preferred - see Chapter 9.

6 Clutch assembly - removal, inspection and refitting

⚠ **Warning: Dust created by clutch wear and deposited on the clutch components may contain asbestos which is a health hazard. DO NOT blow it out with compressed air or inhale any of it. DO NOT use petrol or petroleum-based solvents to clean off the dust. Brake system cleaner or methylated spirit should be used to flush the dust into a suitable receptacle. After the clutch components are wiped clean with rags, dispose of the contaminated rags and cleaner in a sealed, marked container.**

Removal

1 Access to the clutch may be gained in one of two ways. Either the engine/transmission assembly can be removed as described in Chapter 2B, and the transmission then separated from the engine, or the engine may be left in the car and the transmission removed independently as described in Chapter 7A.
2 Having separated the transmission from the engine, undo and remove the clutch cover bolts, working in a diagonal sequence and

slackening the bolts only a few turns at a time. To prevent the flywheel rotating as the bolts are undone, lock the flywheel using a screwdriver engaged with the ring gear teeth and resting against an engine/transmission locating dowel. Alternatively a locking tool can be fabricated from scrap metal.
3 Ease the clutch cover off its locating dowels and be prepared to catch the driven plate which will drop out as the cover is removed. Note which way round the plate is fitted.
4 It is important that no oil or grease is allowed to come into contact with the friction material or the pressure plate and flywheel faces during inspection and refitting.

Inspection

5 With the clutch assembly removed, clean off all traces of asbestos dust using a dry cloth. This is best done outside or in a well ventilated area; asbestos dust is harmful, and must not be inhaled
6 Examine the linings of the driven plate for wear and loose rivets, and the rim for distortion, cracks, broken torsion springs and worn splines. The surface of the friction linings may be highly glazed, but, as long as the friction material pattern can be clearly seen, this is satisfactory. If there is any sign of oil contamination, indicated by a continuous or patchy, shiny black discolouration, the plate must be renewed and the source of the contamination traced and rectified. This will be either a leaking crankshaft oil seal or transmission input shaft oil seal - or both. The driven plate must also be renewed if the lining thickness has worn down to, or just above, the level of the rivet heads.
7 Check the machined faces of the flywheel and pressure plate. If either is grooved, or heavily scored, renewal is necessary. The pressure plate must also be renewed if any cracks are apparent, if the diaphragm spring is damaged or its pressure suspect, or if there is excessive warpage of the pressure plate face **(see illustration)**.

8 With the transmission removed, check the condition of the release bearing, as described in Section 7.

Refitting

9 It is advisable to refit the clutch assembly with clean hands and to wipe down the pressure plate and flywheel faces with a clean dry rag before assembly begins.

10 Place the driven plate in position with its flat side facing the flywheel.

11 Place the clutch cover over the dowels, refit the bolts and tighten them finger tight so that the driven plate is gripped, but can still be moved.

12 The plate must now be centralised so that, when the engine and transmission are mated, the splines of the transmission input shaft will pass through the splines in the centre of the driven plate hub.

13 Centralisation can be carried out quite easily by inserting a round bar or long screwdriver through the hole in the centre of the driven plate so that the end of the bar rests in the hole in the end of the crankshaft.

14 Using this as a fulcrum, moving the bar sideways or up and down will move the clutch driven plate in whichever direction is necessary to achieve centralisation.

15 Centralisation is easily judged by removing the bar and viewing the driven plate hub in relation to the hole in the centre of the crankshaft. When the hole appears exactly in the centre of the driven plate hub, all is correct.

16 An alternative and more accurate method of centralisation is to use a commercially available clutch aligning tool obtainable from most accessory shops **(see illustration)**.

17 Once the clutch is centralised, progressively tighten the cover bolts in a diagonal sequence to the torque setting given in the *Specifications*.

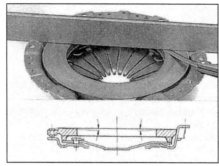

6.7 Check for warpage of the pressure plate using a straight edge and feeler blades

18 The engine and/or transmission can now be refitted by referring to the appropriate Chapters of this manual.

7   Clutch release bearing - removal, inspection and refitting

Removal

1 Access to the clutch release bearing may be gained in one of two ways. Either the engine/transmission assembly can be removed as described in Chapter 2B, and the transmission then separated from the engine, or the engine may be left in the car and the transmission removed independently as described in Chapter 7A.

2 Having separated the transmission from the engine, remove the bearing from the release fork and slide it off the input shaft guide sleeve.

3 Free the release fork dust boot from the bellhousing and withdraw the release fork from the pivot ball-stud.

6.16 Using a clutch aligning tool (arrowed) to centralise the driven plate

Inspection

4 Check the bearing for smoothness of operation and renew it if there is any roughness or harshness as the bearing is spun. It is a good idea to renew the bearing as a matter of course during clutch overhaul, regardless of its apparent condition. Also check the condition of the dust boot and renew it if any signs of deterioration are apparent.

Refitting

5 Refitting the release bearing is a reversal of removal, but lubricate the release fork pivot ball stud sparingly with molybdenum disulphide grease. Do not apply any grease to the transmission input shaft, the guide sleeve, or the release bearing itself as these components have a friction reducing coating which does not require lubrication.

6 With the bearing and release fork in position, secure the release fork to the slave cylinder lug on the bellhousing with a cable-tie or similar, to hold it in place as the transmission is refitted.

Chapter 7 Part A:
Manual transmission

Contents

Degrees of difficulty

Easy, suitable for novice with little experience 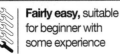	Fairly easy, suitable for beginner with some experience 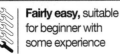	Fairly difficult, suitable for competent DIY mechanic	Difficult, suitable for experienced DIY mechanic 	Very difficult, suitable for expert DIY or professional 

Specifications

General

Transmission type	5 forward gears and one reverse. Synchromesh on all gears
Designation	M56

Ratios

M56L transmission:

1st	3.38 : 1
2nd	1.90 : 1
3rd	1.19 : 1
4th	0.87 : 1
5th	0.70 : 1
Reverse	3.30 : 1

M56H transmission:

1st	3.07 : 1
2nd	1.77 : 1
3rd	1.19 : 1
4th	0.87 : 1
5th	0.70 : 1
Reverse	2.99 : 1
Final drive ratio	3.77:1, 4.00:1 or 4.45:1 according to engine type and year

Lubrication

Lubricant type	Volvo synthetic gearbox oil 97308
Capacity	2.1 litres

Torque wrench settings

	Nm
Gear lever housing bolts	25
Gear lever housing cross plate bolts	25
Release bearing guide sleeve bolts	10
Anti-roll bar clamp bolts	50
Upper engine steady bar to bracket:	
Early models (M8 bolt):*	
Stage 1	18
Stage 2	Tighten through a further 120°
Later models (M10 bolt):*	
Stage 1	35
Stage 2	Tighten through a further 90°
Transmission to engine bolts	50
Lower engine steady bar bracket to transmission:**	
Stage 1	35
Stage 2	Tighten through a further 40°
Engine mounting nuts/bolts	50
Rear engine mounting bracket to transmission	50
Subframe rear mounting brackets to body	50
Subframe front and rear mounting bolts:*	
Stage 1	105
Stage 2	Tighten through a further 120°
Steering gear crash guard bolts	80
Steering gear to subframe nuts*	50
Roadwheel bolts	110

*New nuts/bolts must **always** be used

1 General information

The manual transmission and final drive are housed in an aluminium casing, bolted directly to the left-hand side of the engine. Gear selection is by a remotely sighted lever assembly operating the transmission selector mechanism via cables.

The transmission internal components comprise the input shaft, the upper and lower layshafts, the final drive differential and the selector mechanism. The input shaft contains the fixed 1st, 2nd and 5th gears, the freewheeling 3rd and 4th gearwheels and the 3rd/4th synchro unit. The upper layshaft contains the freewheeling 5th and reverse gearwheels, the 5th/reverse synchro unit and a final drive pinion. The lower layshaft contains the fixed 3rd and 4th gears, the freewheeling 1st, 2nd and reverse intermediate gearwheels, the 1st/2nd synchro unit and a final drive pinion.

Drive from the engine is transmitted to the input shaft by the clutch. The gears on the input shaft are permanently meshed with the gears on the two layshafts but when drive is transmitted, only one gear at a time is actually locked to its shaft, the others are freewheeling. The selection of gears is by sliding synchro units; movement of the gear lever is transmitted to selector forks, which slide the appropriate synchro unit towards the gear to be engaged and lock it to the relevant shaft. In neutral, none of the gears are locked, all are freewheeling.

Reverse gear is obtained by locking the reverse gearwheel to the upper layshaft. Drive is transmitted through the input shaft to the reverse intermediate gearwheel on the lower layshaft then to the reverse gearwheel and final drive pinion on the upper layshaft. Reverse is therefore obtained by transmitting power through all three shafts, instead of only two as in the case of the forward gears. By eliminating the need for a separate reverse idler gear, synchromesh can also be provided on reverse gear.

2 Gear lever housing - removal and refitting

Removal

1 Remove the centre console as described in Chapter 11.

2 Undo the four bolts securing the housing assembly to the floor (see illustration).

3 On later models, undo the two bolts and release the cross plate at the rear of the housing from the side reinforcement members on each side.

4 Lift up the housing and prise off the selector inner cable socket joints from the base of the gear lever, and from the link plate on the side of the housing.

5 Extract the retaining clips securing the selector outer cables to the housing and remove the assembly from the car (see illustration).

Refitting

6 Refit by reversing the removal operations. Tighten the four securing bolts and, where fitted, the cross plate bolts, to the specified torque. Refit the centre console as described in Chapter 11.

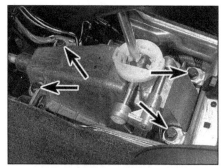

2.2 Gear lever housing retaining bolt locations (arrowed)

2.5 Selector outer cable to housing retaining clip (arrowed)

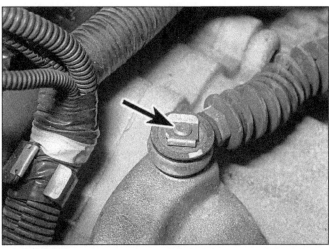

3.3 Selector inner cable to transmission lever retaining clip (arrowed)

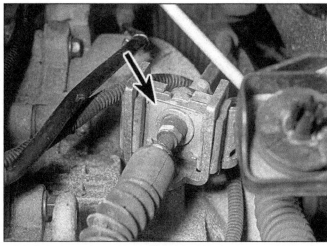

3.4 Selector outer cable to transmission bracket retaining clip (arrowed)

3   Selector cables - removal and refitting

Removal

1 Disconnect the battery negative lead.
2 Refer to Chapter 4A and remove the air cleaner assembly.
3 Extract the circlip securing the inner cable ends to the transmission selector levers **(see illustration)**. Withdraw the washers and slide the cable ends off the levers.
4 Extract the retaining clips and release the outer cables from the transmission brackets **(see illustration)**.
5 Remove the centre console as described in Chapter 11.
6 Undo the screws and remove the trim/sound proofing panel from under the facia on the left-hand side.
7 Undo the screws and remove the carpet support plate under the centre of the facia on the left-hand side. Bend back the carpet to allow the support plate to be withdrawn.
8 Undo the bolts securing the cable entry cover plate to the bulkhead.
9 Pull apart the left-hand air duct under the facia.
10 Remove the gear lever housing as described in Section 2.
11 Note the routing of the cables under the facia, and in the engine compartment, as an aid to refitting. Release any adjacent components as necessary then pull the cables, one at a time, into the passenger compartment and remove them from the car.

Refitting

12 From inside the car, carefully feed the cables through into the engine compartment ensuring that they are routed correctly. Note that the cable which is attached to the gear lever housing left-hand link plate, and the link plate itself, are marked with yellow paint.

13 Reconnect the cables to the gear lever housing and refit the housing as described in Section 2.
14 Reconnect the air duct, then refit the cable entry cover plate, carpet support plate and the trim/sound proofing panel.
15 Refit the centre console as described in Chapter 11.
16 Attach the outer cables to the transmission brackets and the inner cables to the selector levers. Note that the outermost cable (marked with yellow paint) attaches to the vertical selector lever on the end of the transmission (also marked yellow).
17 Secure the outer cables with the retaining clips and the inner cables with the washers and circlips.
18 Refit the air cleaner assembly (Chapter 4A), and reconnect the battery.

4   Oil seals - renewal

Right-hand differential side gear oil seal

1 Jack up the front of the car and support it on axle stands (see *"Jacking and vehicle support"*). Remove the right-hand front roadwheel.
2 Remove the ABS wheel sensor from the steering knuckle and release the sensor wiring from the suspension strut bracket.
3 Undo the bolt securing the brake hose and ABS wiring bracket to the inner wheel arch.
4 On early models, remove the splash guard under the engine.
5 Undo the nut and remove the clamp bolt securing the suspension control arm balljoint to the steering knuckle. Push down on the suspension arm using a stout bar if necessary, to release the balljoint shank from the knuckle. If the balljoint is tight, spread the slot in the steering knuckle with a chisel or

large screwdriver. Take care not to damage the balljoint dust cover during and after disconnection.
6 Undo the two bolts and remove the cap from the intermediate shaft support bearing.
7 Swivel the suspension strut and steering knuckle assembly outwards and pull the intermediate shaft out of the transmission. Move the shaft to one side and rest it on one of the steering gear fluid pipes.
8 Using a large screwdriver or suitable lever, carefully prise the oil seal out of the transmission casing, taking care not to damage the casing **(see illustration)**.
9 Wipe clean the oil seal seating in the transmission casing.
10 Dip the new oil seal in clean oil, then press it a little way into the casing by hand, making sure that it is square to its seating.
11 Using suitable tubing or a large socket, carefully drive the oil seal fully into position until it is flush with the casing edge.
12 Refit the driveshaft using the reverse sequence to removal. Tighten all nuts and bolts to the specified torque with reference to Chapters 8, 9 and 10 as applicable. Ensure that the ABS sensor, and sensor location in the steering knuckle, are perfectly clean before refitting.

4.8 Using a lever to prise out the side gear oil seal

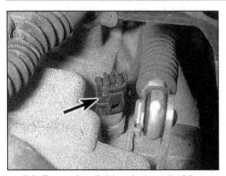

5.2 Reversing light switch and wiring connector (arrowed)

Left-hand differential side gear oil seal

13 Carry out the operations described previously in paragraphs 1 to 5.

14 Swivel the suspension strut and steering knuckle assembly outwards and free the inner CV joint from the transmission by levering between the edge of the joint and the transmission casing with a large screwdriver or similar tool. Pull the joint out of the transmission and rest the driveshaft on the subframe.

15 Carry out the operations described previously in paragraphs 8 to 11.

16 Refit the driveshaft using the reverse sequence to removal. Ensure that the inner CV joint is pushed fully into the transmission so that the retaining circlip locks into place in the differential gear. Tighten all nuts and bolts to the specified torque with reference to Chapters 8, 9 and 10 as applicable. Ensure that the ABS sensor, and sensor location in the steering knuckle, are perfectly clean before refitting.

Input shaft oil seal

17 Remove the transmission as described in Section 6.

18 Remove the clutch release bearing from the release fork and slide it off the input shaft guide sleeve.

19 Free the release fork dust boot from the bellhousing and withdraw the release fork from the pivot ball-stud.

20 Undo the three bolts and remove the guide sleeve from the bellhousing.

21 Lever the old oil seal out of the bellhousing and clean out its seat

22 Lubricate the new seal and fit it to the bellhousing, lips pointing to the gearcase side. Use a socket or suitable tubing to seat it.

23 Refit the release bearing components using a reversal of removal, but lubricate the release fork pivot ball stud sparingly with molybdenum disulphide grease. Do not apply any grease to the transmission input shaft, the guide sleeve, or the release bearing itself as these components have a friction reducing coating which does not require lubrication.

24 With the bearing and release fork in position, secure the release fork to the slave

cylinder lug on the bellhousing with a cable-tie or similar, to hold it in place as the transmission is refitted.

25 Refit the transmission as described in Section 6.

5 Reversing light switch - removal and refitting

Removal

1 The reversing light switch is located on the upper face of the transmission between the two gear selector levers.

2 Clean around the switch, disconnect the wiring connector and unscrew the switch **(see illustration)**.

Refitting

3 Refit by reversing the removal operations.

6 Manual transmission oil - draining and refilling

Note: *Renewal of the transmission oil is not a service requirement and will normally only be necessary if the unit is to be removed for overhaul or replacement.*

Draining

1 Jack up the front of the vehicle and support it securely on axle stands (see *"Jacking and*

vehicle support"). Position a suitable container beneath the transmission.

2 On the left-hand side of the transmission casing you will see the filler/level plug and drain plug **(see illustration)**. Unscrew and remove the drain plug (the lower of the two) and allow the oil to drain into the container.

3 When all the oil has drained, refit the drain plug and tighten it securely.

Refilling

4 Wipe clean the area around the filler/level plug and unscrew the plug from the casing.

5 Fill the transmission through the filler plug orifice with the correct type of oil until the oil begins to run out of the orifice.

6 Refit the filler/level plug, and tighten it securely. Lower the vehicle to the ground, drive it for a short distance, then check for leaks.

7 Dispose of the old oil safely in accordance with environmental regulations.

7 Manual transmission - removal and refitting

Note: *Arrangements must be made to support the engine from above to allow the subframe to be detached on the left-hand side. The best way to support the engine is with a bar resting in the bonnet channels with an adjustable hook appropriately placed. Trolley jacks and the help of an assistant will also be required throughout the procedure.*

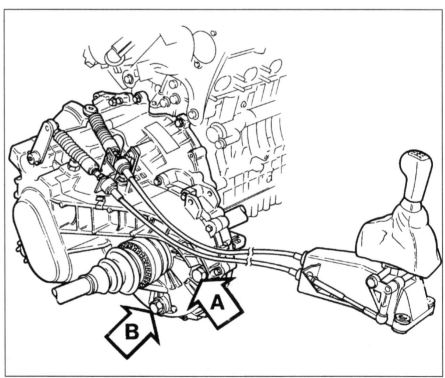

6.2 Transmission filler/level plug (A) and drain plug (B)

7.15 Removing the upper engine steady bar from its bracket

7.24 Lower engine steady bar bracket to transmission bolts (arrowed)

Removal

1 Set the steering wheel and roadwheels in the straight-ahead position. Release the steering column adjuster and push the steering wheel in and upwards as far as it will go. Lock it in this position.

2 Put the gear lever in neutral.

3 Refer to Chapter 5A and remove the battery, then undo the bolts and remove the battery tray.

4 Refer to Chapter 4A and remove the air cleaner assembly and all relevant inlet ducting around the left-hand side of the engine.

5 Extract the circlip securing the selector inner cable ends to the transmission selector levers. Withdraw the washers and slide the cable ends off the levers.

6 Extract the retaining clips and release the selector outer cables from the transmission brackets.

7 Tap out the retaining pin and remove the vertical selector lever on the end of the transmission.

8 Disconnect the wiring connector at the reversing light switch.

9 On turbo models, remove the cover over the throttle housing and disconnect the air inlet pipe to the throttle housing. Move the pipe clear and secure it with a cable-tie. Also disconnect the upper oil cooler hose at the engine oil cooler.

10 Extract the circlip and withdraw the clutch slave cylinder from the bellhousing.

11 Disconnect the earth lead from the front of the transmission and the wiring harness retaining clip(s).

12 Refer to Chapter 5A and remove the starter motor.

13 Lift the coolant expansion tank out of its mounting and allow it to hang free.

14 Where exhaust gas recirculation is fitted, disconnect the hoses at the EGR controller above the radiator.

15 Undo the nut and remove the bolt securing the upper engine steady bar to the

bracket on the engine (see illustration). Note that a new nut and bolt will be required for refitting.

16 Undo the earth lead retaining bolt on the bulkhead, adjacent to the steady bar body bracket.

17 Undo all the transmission-to-engine retaining bolts that are accessible from above.

18 Referring to Chapter 8, remove the left-hand driveshaft completely, but only remove the right-hand driveshaft from the transmission, leaving it connected at the steering knuckle end.

19 Remove the splash guard under the radiator and, on early models, the large splash guard under the engine.

20 Remove the clips and release the pipe running under the front of the subframe.

21 Release the cable-ties and lift the charcoal canister from its location on the left-hand side of the subframe. Support the canister clear of the subframe using a cable-tie.

22 Release the exhaust system from its mounting at the rear of the catalytic converter.

23 Undo the steering gear fluid pipe retaining clip bolts at the front and rear of the subframe.

24 Undo the two bolts securing the lower engine steady bar bracket to the transmission (see illustration).

25 On right-hand drive models, undo the two steering gear crash guard bolts at the rear of the subframe and the nut securing the crash guard base to the subframe.

26 With reference to the note at the beginning of this Section, suitably support the engine from above and adjust the support so that the load is just taken off the engine mountings.

27 Undo the bolt securing the front engine mounting to the subframe.

28 Slacken the bolt securing the rear engine mounting to the steering gear, then undo the five nuts securing the steering gear to the subframe. Note that new nuts will be required for refitting.

29 Position a sturdy trolley jack beneath, and in contact with, the left-hand side of the subframe. Ensure that the engine is securely supported from above.

30 Undo the two bolts each side securing the subframe rear mounting brackets to the body (see illustration).

31 Slacken the two subframe mounting bolts on the right-hand side by approximately 15 mm. Note that new bolts will be required for refitting.

32 Undo the two subframe mounting bolts on the left-hand side. Collect the mounting bracket when the rear bolt is removed. Note that new bolts will be required for refitting.

33 Carefully lower the jack and allow the subframe to drop on the left-hand side by approximately 100 mm. Ensure that the steering gear mounting bolts clear the subframe as it is lowered.

34 On right-hand drive models, undo the bolts securing the anti-roll bar clamps on the left-hand side of the subframe, and slacken the right-hand side clamp bolts until they are only held by a few turns. Secure the left-hand side of the anti-roll bar to the steering gear using a cable-tie.

35 Lower the jack completely and allow the subframe to hang free from the right-hand side mountings.

7.30 Subframe left-hand attachments and steering gear attachment (arrowed)

36 Secure the left-hand side of the steering gear to a convenient place on the underbody using strong wire.

37 Undo the nut and bolt and remove the rear engine mounting from the steering gear and the transmission bracket.

38 Disconnect the vehicle speed sensor wiring connector, and release the oxygen sensor wiring from the rear engine mounting bracket cover. Remove the cover, then remove the mounting bracket from the transmission.

39 Lower the engine/transmission by means of the overhead support, until sufficient clearance exists to enable the transmission to be withdrawn. Take care not to lower the unit too far or the exhaust downpipe will foul the steering gear. Also, make sure that the engine oil dipstick tube clears the radiator fan, and that no hoses or leads are trapped.

40 Securely and safely support the transmission from below on a trolley jack.

41 Undo the remaining bolts securing the transmission to the engine. Withdraw the transmission squarely off the engine dowels taking care not to allow the weight of the transmission to hang on the input shaft.

42 Lower the jack and remove the unit from under the car.

Refitting

43 Secure the clutch release fork to the slave cylinder lug on the bellhousing with a cable-tie or similar, to hold it in place as the transmission is refitted. Do not apply any grease to the transmission input shaft, the guide sleeve, or the release bearing itself as these components have a friction reducing coating which does not require lubrication.

44 Manoeuvre the transmission squarely into position and engage it with the engine dowels. Refit the lower bolts securing the transmission to the engine and tighten them to the specified torque.

45 Raise the engine to its approximate fitted position. Refit the rear engine mounting bracket and cover and secure with the three bolts tightened to the specified torque.

46 Refit the rear engine mounting to the transmission bracket and steering but do not fully tighten the nut and bolt at this stage.

47 Reconnect the vehicle speed sensor wiring connector and secure the oxygen sensor wiring to the mounting bracket cover.

48 On right-hand drive models, raise the subframe to within 100 mm of the body, align the steering gear and crash guard with their subframe locations then refit the anti-roll bar clamps. Tighten all the clamp bolts to the specified torque.

49 On all models raise the subframe to its fitted position ensuring that the steering gear bolts engage in their locations.

50 Fit the new subframe mounting bolts and rear mounting bracket and bolts on the left-hand side. Tighten the subframe bolts to the specified torque using a torque wrench, then further, through the specified angle, using an angle tightening gauge. Tighten the mounting bracket bolts to the specified torque.

51 Support the right-hand side of the subframe on the jack and remove the two previously slackened subframe bolts. Fit the new bolts and the two mounting bracket bolts and tighten them as described in the previous paragraph.

52 Secure the steering gear to the subframe using five new nuts tightened to the specified torque.

53 Refit the front engine mounting bolt then tighten both the front and rear engine mountings to the specified torque.

54 On right-hand drive models, refit the two steering gear crash guard bolts at the rear of the subframe and the nut securing the crash guard base to the subframe. Tighten to the specified torque.

55 Refit the lower engine steady bar bracket to the transmission and tighten the bolts to the specified torque using a torque wrench, then further, through the specified angle, using an angle tightening gauge.

56 Refit the steering gear fluid pipe retaining clip bolts at the front and rear of the subframe and reconnect the exhaust system mounting.

57 Reconnect the charcoal canister and the pipe clips at the front of the subframe.

58 Refit the driveshafts as described in Chapter 8.

59 Refit the splash guard under the radiator and where applicable, under the engine.

60 Refit the starter motor and all the upper transmission to engine bolts. Tighten the bolts to the specified torque.

61 Reconnect the earth lead to the bulkhead.

62 Secure the upper engine steady bar to its bracket using a new nut and bolt tightened to the specified torque using a torque wrench, then further, through the specified angle, using an angle tightening gauge.

63 Where applicable, reconnect the EGR controller hoses.

64 Reconnect the earth lead at the front of the transmission and the wiring harness clips.

65 Refit the clutch slave cylinder and secure with the circlip.

66 Refit the coolant expansion tank, the oil cooler hose and air inlet pipe (where applicable) and the reversing light switch connector.

67 Refit the transmission selector lever and secure with the retaining pin.

68 Reconnect the selector cables, noting that the cable with the yellow marking attaches to the outer selector lever.

69 Refit the battery tray, battery, air cleaner assembly and inlet ducting.

70 Check, and if necessary refill or top-up the transmission oil level.

8 Manual transmission overhaul - general information

Overhauling a manual transmission is a difficult job for the do-it-yourselfer. It involves the dismantling and reassembly of many small parts. Numerous clearances must be precisely measured and, if necessary, changed with selected spacers and circlips. As a result, if transmission problems arise, while the unit can be removed and refitted by a competent do-it-yourselfer, overhaul should be left to a transmission specialist. Rebuilt transmissions may be available - check with your dealer parts department, motor factors, or transmission specialists. At any rate, the time and money involved in an overhaul is almost sure to exceed the cost of a rebuilt unit.

Nevertheless, it's not impossible for an inexperienced mechanic to rebuild a transmission, providing the special tools are available, and the job is done in a deliberate step-by-step manner so nothing is overlooked.

The tools necessary for an overhaul include: internal and external circlip pliers, a bearing puller, a slide hammer, a set of pin punches, a dial test indicator, and possibly a hydraulic press. In addition, a large, sturdy workbench and a vice or transmission stand will be required.

During dismantling of the transmission, make careful notes of how each part comes off, where it fits in relation to other parts, and what holds it in place.

Before taking the transmission apart for repair, it will help if you have some idea what area of the transmission is malfunctioning. Certain problems can be closely tied to specific areas in the transmission, which can make component examination and replacement easier. Refer to the "*Fault finding*" section at the rear of this manual for information regarding possible sources of trouble.

Chapter 7 Part B:
Automatic transmission

Contents

Degrees of difficulty

Easy, suitable for novice with little experience	**Fairly easy,** suitable for beginner with some experience	**Fairly difficult,** suitable for competent DIY mechanic	**Difficult,** suitable for experienced DIY mechanic	**Very difficult,** suitable for expert DIY or professional

Specifications

General
Type .... Computer controlled four-speed with torque converter lock-up on three highest gears
Designation .... AW 50-42

Ratios
1st .... 3.61 : 1
2nd .... 2.06 : 1
3rd .... 1.37 : 1
4th .... 0.98 : 1
Reverse .... 3.95 : 1
Final drive .... 2.54 : 1, 2.74 : 1 or 3.16 : 1 (according to engine type)

Lubrication
Lubricant type .... Dexron IIE type automatic transmission fluid
Capacity:
  Drain and refill .... 7.6 litres
  From dry (including torque converter) ..... 10.1 litres (approximately)

Torque wrench settings   Nm
Transmission drain plug 40
Selector cable bracket to transmission 25
Selector cable entry cover plate 6
Selector housing bolts 25
Selector housing cross plate bolts 25
RPM sensor bolt 5.5
Oil temperature sensor 25
Torque converter to driveplate bolts 35
Anti-roll bar clamp bolts 50
Upper engine steady bar to bracket:
  Early models (M8 bolt):*
    Stage 1 18
    Stage 2 .... Tighten through a further 120°
  Later models (M10 bolt):*
    Stage 1 35
    Stage 2 .... Tighten through a further 90°

Torque wrench settings (continued)

	Nm
Transmission to engine bolts	50
Lower engine steady bar bracket to transmission:	
Early models (M8 bolt):*	
Stage 1	18
Stage 2	Tighten through a further 90°
Later models (M10 bolt):*	
Stage 1	35
Stage 2	Tighten through a further 40°
Engine mounting nuts/bolts	50
Rear engine mounting bracket to transmission	50
Subframe rear mounting brackets to body	50
Subframe front and rear mounting bolts:*	
Stage 1	105
Stage 2	Tighten through a further 120°
Steering gear crash guard bolts	80
Steering gear to subframe nuts*	50
Roadwheel bolts	110

*New nuts/bolts must **always** be used

1 General information

The AW 50-42 is a computer controlled fully automatic four-speed transmission with torque converter lock-up on the highest three gears.

The unit is controlled by an electronic control unit (ECU) which receives signal inputs from various sensors relating to transmission operating conditions. Information on engine parameters are also sent to the ECU from the engine management system. From this data, the ECU can establish the optimum gear shifting speeds and lock-up engagement points according to the driving mode selected.

Drive is taken from the engine to the transmission by a torque converter. This is a type of fluid coupling which under certain conditions has a torque multiplying effect. The torque converter is mechanically locked to the engine, under the control of the ECU, when the transmission is operating in the three highest gears. This eliminates losses due to slip, and improves fuel economy.

The gear selector has six positions: P, R, N, D, 3 and L. The engine can only be started in positions P and N. In position P the transmission is mechanically locked: this position must only be engaged when the vehicle is stationary. In position R reverse is engaged, in N neutral. In position D, gear changing is automatic throughout the range. In positions 3, fourth gear is blocked and automatic gear changing occurs in the other gears. In position L, only first and second gears are available.

The mode selector has three functions; ECON, SPORT and WINTER. In ECON mode the transmission changes up to a higher gear and engages lock-up as early as possible for maximum economy, whilst in SPORT mode

the gear changing points are selected for maximum performance. In WINTER mode the transmission will allow starting from rest in a higher than normal gear to avoid wheelspin in poor road conditions. This mode can also be used to restrict gear changing in D, 3 and L when road conditions dictate the need for more direct control of gear selection.

A "kickdown" facility causes the transmission to shift down a gear (subject to engine speed) when the throttle is fully depressed. This is useful when extra acceleration is required. Kickdown, like the other transmission functions, is controlled by the ECU.

A shift lock facility is also incorporated into the gear selector mechanism on certain models. This security device prevents movement of the selector lever when the engine has been stopped, or when the ignition is switched off with the selector lever in the P position.

In addition to control of the transmission, the ECU incorporates a built-in fault diagnosis facility. A fault is signalled to the driver by the flashing of the warning light on the instrument panel. The ECU then reverts to an emergency ("limp-home") program which ensures that two forward gears and reverse will always be available, but gear changing must be performed manually.

If a fault of this nature does occur, the ECU stores a series of signals (or fault codes) for subsequent read-out via the diagnostic unit located in the engine compartment.

The automatic transmission is a complex unit, but if it is not abused it is reliable and long-lasting. Repair or overhaul operations are beyond the scope of many dealers, let alone the home mechanic; specialist advice should be sought if problems arise which cannot be solved by the procedures given in this Chapter.

2 Automatic transmission fluid - draining and refilling

1 Renewal of the automatic transmission fluid is not a service requirement and will normally only be necessary in the following circumstances:

a) *If the on-board diagnostic system has logged a fault code indicating oil temperature too high (see Section 11).*

b) *If the fluid is discoloured or has a burnt smell resulting from hard and continuous operation of the transmission.*

b) *If the car is continuously used for taxi work or extended periods of trailer towing, the fluid should be changed at the 37 500 mile (75 000 km) service interval.*

2 Raise and securely support the front of the car (see "Jacking and vehicle support").

3 Remove the splash guard under the radiator and, on early models, the large splash guard under the engine.

4 Remove the drain plug located on the right-hand side of the casing, below and just forward of the driveshaft. Allow the contents of the transmission to drain into a suitable draining container. Refit and tighten the drain plug using a new seal if necessary.

Caution: If the vehicle has just been run, the transmission fluid may be very hot

5 Refit the splash guard(s) and lower the car to the ground.

6 Refer to Chapter 5A if necessary and remove the battery and battery tray.

7 Clean the oil cooler return hose union on the transmission, then disconnect the hose at the transmission union. Suitably plug the open union on the transmission.

8 Attach a clear plastic hose to the end of the oil cooler return hose. Lead the hose into the draining container.

9 Temporarily refit the battery tray and battery.

10 Apply the handbrake and move the gear selector lever to the P (Park) position.
11 Add 2.0 litres of fresh automatic transmission fluid of the specified type via the dipstick tube.
12 Start the engine and allow it to idle. Fluid will flow into the draining container. When bubbles appear in the fluid, stop the engine.
13 Add a further 2.0 litres of fresh automatic transmission fluid of the specified type via the dipstick tube.
14 Repeat paragraph 12, then remove the battery and battery tray. Remove the plastic hose and reconnect the oil cooler return hose to the transmission.
15 Refit the battery tray and battery securely.
16 Add a further 2.0 litres of fresh automatic transmission fluid.
17 Start the engine and allow it to idle. Move the gear selector lever through all the gear positions stopping for four to five seconds in each position. Return the selector lever to the P position, wait for two minutes then check the fluid level as described in Chapter 1, using the "COLD" markings on the dipstick. Top-up as necessary.
18 Dispose of the old fluid safely (see "General repair procedures").

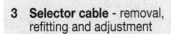

3 Selector cable - removal, refitting and adjustment

Removal

1 Park the car on a level surface then refer to Chapter 4A and remove the air cleaner assembly.
2 Refer to Chapter 5A and remove the battery and battery tray.
3 Working in the engine compartment, extract the locking clip and washer securing the selector inner cable to the transmission selector lever **(see illustration)**.
4 Undo the two nuts and remove the washers (where fitted) securing the selector outer cable bracket to the transmission. Lift the bracket off the mounting studs and release the inner cable end from the selector lever.
5 Remove the centre console as described in Chapter 11.
6 Extract the retaining clip securing the selector inner cable to the gear selector lever.
7 Extract the retaining clip securing the selector outer cable to the gear selector housing.
8 Undo the screws and remove the trim/sound proofing panel from under the facia on the left-hand side.
9 Undo the screws and remove the carpet support plate under the centre of the facia on the left-hand side. Bend back the carpet to allow the support plate to be withdrawn.
10 Undo the bolts securing the cable entry cover plate to the bulkhead. Where applicable, release the shift lock cable from the selector cable.

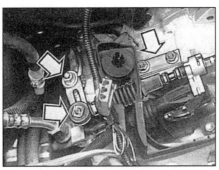

3.3 Selector inner cable locking clip (lower arrow) and outer cable bracket nuts (right arrow)

11 Note the routing of the cable under the facia, and in the engine compartment, as an aid to refitting. Release any adjacent components as necessary then pull the cable into the passenger compartment and remove it from the car.

Refitting and adjustment

12 From inside the car, carefully feed the cable through into the engine compartment ensuring correct routing.
13 Reconnect the cable to the selector lever and housing and secure with the retaining clips.
14 Refit the cable entry cover plate, carpet support plate and the trim/sound proofing panel.
15 Refit the centre console as described in Chapter 11.
16 Move the gear selector lever to position R (Reverse). Ensure that the gear lever and cable position do not move during subsequent operations.
17 Move the selector lever on the transmission as far forward as it will go to the P (Park) position. Ensure that P is selected by releasing the handbrake and trying to roll the car; the transmission should be locked. Re-apply the handbrake.

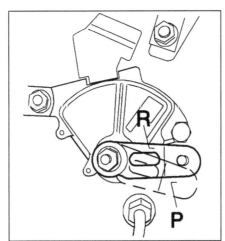

3.18 Move transmission selector lever forward to (P) then rearward one position to (R)

18 Move the transmission selector lever rearward one position to R (Reverse) **(see illustration)**.
19 Without moving the selector cable or transmission selector lever position, locate the inner cable on the selector lever and position the outer cable bracket on the transmission studs. Secure the bracket with the nuts, and where applicable the washers. and tighten the nuts to the specified torque.
20 Refit the locking clip and washer securing the cable to the transmission selector lever.
21 Check the adjustment by moving the gear selector lever inside the car to the N (neutral) position. Without touching the locking button, move the lever forward slightly then backwards slightly. Play should be felt in both directions.
22 On completion, refit the air cleaner assembly (Chapter 4A), battery tray and battery.

4 Selector housing - removal and refitting

Pre-1993 models

Removal

1 Disconnect the battery negative lead.
2 Pull the gear lever knob firmly upwards to remove it from the selector lever. Note that considerable force is necessary to release it.
3 Refer to Chapter 11 and remove the centre console.
4 Extract the retaining clip securing the selector inner cable to the gear selector lever.
5 Extract the retaining clip securing the selector outer cable to the gear selector housing.
6 Remove the selector illumination bulbholder from the base of the indicator panel.
7 Undo the bolts securing the housing to the floor and remove it from the car.

Refitting

8 Refitting is a reversal of removal. When refitting the gear lever knob, push it firmly into position ensuring that it is securely seated in the snap catches. Also ensure that the lock button locates on the catches in the gear lever push rod.

1993 models onward

Removal

9 Disconnect the battery negative lead.
10 Grasp the gear lever gaiter around the internal retaining clip, turn the gaiter and clip through 90° and pull the gaiter down. Ensure that the retaining clip returns to its original position after releasing the gaiter.
11 Pull the gear lever knob firmly upwards to remove it from the selector lever. Note that considerable force is necessary to release it.
12 Refer to Chapter 11 and remove the centre console.
13 Extract the retaining clip securing the selector inner cable to the gear selector lever.

14 Extract the retaining clip securing the selector outer cable to the gear selector housing.

15 Remove the selector illumination bulbholder from the base of the indicator panel.

16 Where applicable disconnect the shift lock solenoid wiring connector.

17 On later models, undo the two bolts and release the cross plate at the rear of the housing from the side reinforcement members on each side.

18 Undo the bolts securing the housing to the floor and remove it from the car.

Refitting

19 Refitting is a reversal of removal. When refitting the gear lever knob, push the retaining clip into the gaiter slightly then push the gaiter over the catches against the edge of the knob. Press up the retaining clip ensuring that it engages with the knob catches.

5   RPM sensor - removal and refitting

Removal

1 Refer to Chapter 5A and remove the battery.

2 Refer to Chapter 4A and remove the air cleaner assembly and inlet ducting.

3 Remove the battery tray and detach the air cleaner bracket.

4 Disconnect the transmission main wiring connector on the top of the transmission housing. Note the rubber gasket.

5 Remove the cable clamps around the cable harness and rubber grommet.

6 Insert a thin screwdriver into the end of the wiring connector housing and depress the retaining catch. Lift the cables and sockets out of the connector housing.

7 Pull the sockets apart and remove the two-pin socket containing pins 16 and 17 **(see illustration)**.

8 Wipe clean the area around the sensor, then undo the retaining bolt and remove the RPM sensor from the top of the transmission housing.

Refitting

9 Smear some petroleum jelly on the sensor O-ring seal, locate the sensor in position and secure with the retaining bolt.

10 Reconnect the wiring sockets and refit the cables and sockets into the connector housing.

11 Refit the rubber grommet and cable clamps to the cable harness then reconnect the wiring connector.

12 Refit the battery tray, battery, and air cleaner assembly with reference to Chapters 4 and 5.

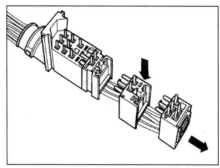

5.7 Separate the main wiring connector for access to the RPM sensor socket and pins

6   Oil temperature sensor - removal and refitting

Removal

1 Carry out the operations described in Section 5, paragraphs 1 to 6.

2 Pull the wiring connector sockets apart and remove the two-pin socket containing pins 12 and 13.

3 Depress the locking device at the base of the socket and push out the red locking lug slightly. Remove the two pins from the socket.

4 Drain the transmission fluid as described in Section 2.

5 Wipe clean the area around the sensor, then unscrew it from the front of the transmission housing **(see illustration)**. Place a container beneath the sensor as it is unscrewed as there will be fluid spillage.

6 Note the routing of the sensor wiring and carefully pull it clear. Remove the sensor from the car.

Refitting

7 Smear some petroleum jelly on the sensor O-ring seal, locate the sensor in position and tighten to the specified torque.

8 Route the sensor cables in their original positions then push the connector pins into their locations in the wiring socket. Note that pin 12 is the blue/red cable and pin 13 is the blue/black cable. Re-attach the connector sockets.

6.5 Transmission oil temperature sensor location

9 Refit the cables and sockets into the connector housing.

10 Refit the rubber grommet and cable clamps to the cable harness then reconnect the wiring connector.

11 Refit the battery tray, battery, and air cleaner assembly with reference to Chapters 4 and 5.

12 Refill the transmission with fresh fluid as described in Section 2.

7   Kickdown switch - removal and refitting

The kickdown switch is an integral part of the accelerator cable. Refer to Chapter 4A for removal and refitting procedures.

8   Electronic control unit (ECU) - removal and refitting

Note: *The automatic transmission ECU, together with the fuel and ignition ECUs, are all located in the ECU module box which is situated at the front right-hand side of the engine compartment in front of the cooling system expansion tank.*

Removal

1 Ensure that the ignition is switched off then release the two catches on the side of the module box lid. Lift off the lid and place it to one side.

2 Pull the locking lever on top of the ECU forward and withdraw the ECU from its location in slot three of the module box, nearest to the right-hand wheel arch.

Refitting

3 Locate the ECU in the module box engaging it with the connector in the base.

4 Push the locking lever down and refit the module box lid.

5 If a new ECU has been fitted it will be necessary to adapt the throttle position sensor signal as follows.

6 Chock all four wheels and apply the handbrake fully.

7 Start the engine and move the selector lever to the D (Drive) position.

8 Depress the brake pedal and hold it hard down during the following operations.

9 Depress the accelerator pedal fully, so that the kickdown switch closes, and hold it down for five seconds.

10 Release the accelerator pedal and move the selector lever to the P (Park) position. The new throttle position sensor signal will now be stored in the ECU memory

11 Switch off the engine and remove the wheel chocks.

9 Oil seals - renewal

Differential side gear oil seals

1 The procedure is the same as that described for the manual transmission in Part A, Section 4.

Input shaft/torque converter oil seal

2 Remove the transmission as described in Section 10.
3 Pull the torque converter squarely out of the transmission. Be careful, it is full of fluid.
4 Pull or lever out the old seal. Clean the seat and inspect the seal rubbing surface on the torque converter.
5 Lubricate the new seal with ATF and fit it, lips inwards. Seat it with a piece of tube.
6 Lubricate the torque converter sleeve with ATF and slide the converter into place, pushing it in as far as it will go.
7 Check that the torque converter is fully seated by measuring the distance from the edge of the transmission housing face to the retaining bolt tabs on the converter. The dimension should be approximately 14 mm.
8 Refit the transmission as described in Section 10.

All seals

9 Check the transmission fluid level as described in Chapter 1 on completion.

10 Automatic transmission - removal and refitting

Note: *Arrangements must be made to support the engine from above to allow the subframe to be detached on the left-hand side. The best way to support the engine is with a bar resting in the bonnet channels with an adjustable hook appropriately placed. Trolley jacks and the help of an assistant will also be required throughout the procedure.*

Removal

1 Set the steering wheel and roadwheels in the straight-ahead position. Release the steering column adjuster and push the steering wheel in and upwards as far as it will go. Lock it in this position.
2 Move the gear selector lever to N (neutral).
3 Refer to Chapter 5A and remove the battery, then undo the bolts and remove the battery tray.
4 Refer to Chapter 4A and remove the air cleaner assembly and all relevant inlet ducting around the left-hand side of the engine.
5 On turbo models, remove the cover over the throttle housing and disconnect the air inlet pipe to the throttle housing. Move the pipe clear and secure it with a cable-tie. Also

disconnect the upper oil cooler hose at the engine oil cooler. Additionally on later turbo models, remove the cover over the throttle housing and disconnect the accelerator cable from the control pulley and mounting bracket. Remove the inlet ducts between the turbocharger and radiator and between the air cleaner and turbocharger.
6 Disconnect the selector cable at the transmission end as described in Section 3.
7 Disconnect the main wiring harness connector on top of the transmission casing.
8 Remove the cable clamps securing the wiring harness and earth lead.
9 On early models disconnect the transmission vacuum hose from its clip. On later models, detach the cable conduit from the transmission and release the oxygen sensor connector from the transmission bracket.
10 Disconnect the transmission oil cooler inlet hose from the upper quick release connector on the side of the radiator. Disconnect the oil cooler return hose at the transmission union. Cover or seal the disconnected hoses and unions.
11 Remove the oil dipstick tube and seal the opening.
12 Refer to Chapter 5A and remove the starter motor.
13 Lift the coolant expansion tank out of its mounting and allow it to hang free.
14 Where exhaust gas recirculation is fitted, disconnect the hoses at the EGR controller above the radiator.
15 Undo the nut and remove the bolt securing the upper engine steady bar to the bracket on the engine. Note that a new nut and bolt will be required for refitting.
16 Undo the earth lead retaining bolt on the bulkhead, adjacent to the steady bar body bracket.
17 Undo all the transmission-to-engine retaining bolts that are accessible from above.
18 Referring to Chapter 8, remove the left-hand driveshaft completely, but only remove the right-hand driveshaft from the transmission, leaving it connected at the steering knuckle end.
19 Remove the splash guard under the radiator and, on early models, the large splash guard under the engine.
20 Remove the clips and release the pipe running under the front of the subframe.
21 Release the cable-ties and lift the charcoal canister from its location on the left-hand side of the subframe. Support the canister clear of the subframe using a cable-tie.
22 Release the exhaust system from its mounting at the rear of the catalytic converter.
23 Undo the steering gear fluid pipe retaining clip bolts at the front and rear of the subframe.
24 Undo the two bolts securing the lower engine steady bar bracket to the transmission.
25 On right-hand drive models, undo the two steering gear crash guard bolts at the rear of the subframe and the nut securing the crash guard base to the subframe.

26 With reference to the note at the beginning of this Section, suitably support the engine from above and adjust the support so that the load is just taken off the engine mountings.
27 Undo the bolt securing the front engine mounting to the subframe.
28 Slacken the bolt securing the rear engine mounting to the steering gear, then undo the five nuts securing the steering gear to the subframe. Note that new nuts will be required for refitting.
29 Position a sturdy trolley jack beneath, and in contact with, the left-hand side of the subframe. Ensure that the engine is securely supported from above.
30 Undo the two bolts each side securing the subframe rear mounting brackets to the body.
31 Slacken the two subframe mounting bolts on the right-hand side by approximately 15 mm. Note that new bolts will be required for refitting.
32 Undo the two subframe mounting bolts on the left-hand side. Collect the mounting bracket when the rear bolt is removed. Note that new bolts will be required for refitting.
33 Carefully lower the jack and allow the subframe to drop on the left-hand side by approximately 100 mm. Ensure that the steering gear mounting bolts clear the subframe as it is lowered.
34 On right-hand drive models, undo the bolts securing the anti-roll bar clamps on the left-hand side of the subframe, and slacken the right-hand side clamp bolts until they are only held by a few turns. Secure the left-hand side of the anti-roll bar to the steering gear using a cable-tie.
35 Lower the jack completely and allow the subframe to hang free from the right-hand side mountings.
36 Remove the earth strap from the transmission.
37 Secure the left-hand side of the steering gear to a convenient place on the underbody using strong wire.
38 Undo the nut and bolt and remove the rear engine mounting from the steering gear and the transmission bracket.
39 Disconnect the vehicle speed sensor wiring connector, and release the oxygen sensor wiring from the rear engine mounting bracket cover. Remove the cover, then remove the mounting bracket from the transmission.
40 Rotate the crankshaft, using a socket on the pulley nut, until one of the torque converter-to-driveplate retaining bolts becomes accessible through the opening on the rear facing side of the engine. Working through the opening, undo the bolt **(see illustration)**. Rotate the crankshaft as necessary and remove the remaining bolts in the same way. Note that new bolts will be required for refitting.
41 Lower the engine/transmission by means of the overhead support, until sufficient clearance exists to enable the transmission to

be withdrawn. Take care not to lower the unit too far or the exhaust downpipe will foul the steering gear. Also, make sure that the engine oil dipstick tube clears the radiator fan, and that no hoses or leads are trapped.

42 Securely and safely support the transmission from below on a trolley jack.

43 Undo the remaining bolts securing the transmission to the engine. Withdraw the transmission squarely off the engine dowels making sure that the torque converter remains in position on the transmission. Use the access hole in the transmission housing to hold the converter in place **(see illustration 10.40)**.

44 Lower the jack and remove the unit from under the car.

Refitting

45 Before refitting the transmission, flush out the oil cooler with fresh transmission fluid. To do this, attach a hose to the upper union, pour ATF through the hose and collect it in a container positioned beneath the return hose.

46 Clean the contact surfaces on the torque converter and driveplate, and the transmission and engine mating faces. Lightly lubricate the torque converter guide projection and the engine/transmission locating dowels with grease.

47 Check that the torque converter is fully seated by measuring the distance from the edge of the transmission housing face to the retaining bolt tabs on the converter. The dimension should be approximately 14 mm.

48 Manoeuvre the transmission squarely into position and engage it with the engine dowels. Refit the lower bolts securing the transmission to the engine and tighten lightly first in a diagonal sequence, then again to the specified torque.

49 Attach the torque converter to the driveplate using new bolts. Rotate the crankshaft for access to the bolts as was done for removal, then rotate the torque converter by means of the access hole in the transmission housing. Fit and tighten all the bolts hand tight first then tighten again to the specified torque.

50 Raise the engine to its approximate fitted position. Refit the rear engine mounting bracket and cover and secure with the three bolts tightened to the specified torque.

51 Refit the rear engine mounting to the transmission bracket and steering but do not fully tighten the nut and bolt at this stage.

52 Reconnect the vehicle speed sensor wiring connector and secure the oxygen sensor wiring to the mounting bracket cover.

53 On right-hand drive models, raise the subframe to within 100 mm of the body, align the steering gear and crash guard with their subframe locations then refit the anti-roll bar clamps. Tighten all the clamp bolts to the specified torque.

54 On all models raise the subframe to its fitted position ensuring that the steering gear bolts engage in their locations.

55 Fit the new subframe mounting bolts and rear mounting bracket and bolts on the left-hand side. Tighten the subframe bolts to the

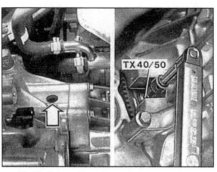

10.40 Removing the torque converter retaining bolts. Access hole in transmission housing (arrowed)

specified torque using a torque wrench, then further, through the specified angle, using an angle tightening gauge. Tighten the mounting bracket bolts to the specified torque.

56 Support the right-hand side of the subframe on the jack and remove the two previously slackened subframe bolts. Fit the new bolts and the two mounting bracket bolts and tighten them as described in the previous paragraph.

57 Secure the steering gear to the subframe using five new nuts tightened to the specified torque.

58 Refit the front engine mounting bolt then tighten both the front and rear engine mountings to the specified torque.

59 On right-hand drive models, refit the two steering gear crash guard bolts at the rear of the subframe and the nut securing the crash guard base to the subframe. Tighten to the specified torque.

60 Refit the lower engine steady bar bracket to the transmission and tighten the bolts to the specified torque using a torque wrench, then further, through the specified angle, using an angle tightening gauge.

61 Refit the steering gear fluid pipe retaining clip bolts at the front and rear of the subframe and reconnect the exhaust system mounting.

62 Reconnect the charcoal canister and the pipe clips at the front of the subframe.

63 Refit the driveshafts as described in Chapter 8.

64 Refit the splash guard under the radiator and where applicable, under the engine.

65 Refit the starter motor and all the upper transmission to engine bolts. Tighten the bolts to the specified torque.

66 On early models reconnect the transmission vacuum hose to its clip. On later models, attach the cable conduit to the transmission and secure the oxygen sensor connector to the transmission bracket.

67 Reconnect the transmission oil cooler inlet and return hoses.

68 Refit the oil dipstick tube with a new O-ring seal.

69 Refit the cable clamps securing the wiring harness and earth lead.

70 Reconnect the main wiring harness connector on top of the transmission casing.

71 Reconnect the earth lead to the bulkhead.

72 Secure the upper engine steady bar to its bracket using a new nut and bolt tightened to the specified torque using a torque wrench, then further, through the specified angle, using an angle tightening gauge.

73 Where applicable, reconnect the EGR controller hoses.

74 Refit the coolant expansion tank, the oil cooler hose and air inlet pipe (where applicable).

75 Reconnect and adjust the selector cable as described in Section 3

76 Refit the battery tray, battery, air cleaner assembly and all relevant inlet ducting.

77 Where applicable, reconnect the accelerator cable to the control pulley and mounting bracket.

78 Check, and if necessary refill or top-up the transmission oil level.

---

11 Automatic transmission - fault diagnosis

General information

1 The automatic transmission electronic control system incorporates an on-board diagnostic facility as an aid to fault finding and system testing. The diagnostic system is a feature of the electronic control unit (ECU) which continually monitors the system components and their operation. Should a fault occur, the ECU stores a series of signals (or fault codes) for subsequent read-out via the diagnostic unit located in the engine compartment.

2 If a fault occurs, indicated by the flashing of the warning light on the instrument panel, the on-board diagnostics can be used to initially pinpoint any problem areas without the use of special test equipment. Once this has been done, however, further tests may often be necessary to determine the exact nature of the fault; ie, whether it is of a mechanical or electrical nature, whether a component itself has failed, or whether it is a wiring or other inter-related problem.

Fault code read-out

Note: *On models from 1996 the diagnostic unit is located under a cover in front of the gear lever and has a 16-pin socket for connection to a fault code reader.*

3 In the event of a fault suspected in the system, or indicated by the illumination of the warning light, the first step is to check whether a fault code has been logged and if so, to interpret the meaning of the code.

4 Locate the diagnostic unit which is situated in the front right-hand side of the engine compartment, alongside the windscreen washer reservoir filler. The diagnostic unit consists of two modules mounted side by side, with a plastic cover over each. Lift off the covers and note that the two modules are marked A and B, each having six numbered sockets on their top face.

5 With the ignition switched off, unclip the flylead from the holder on the side of the unit and insert it into socket 1 of module A.

6 Have a paper and pen ready to copy down the fault codes as they are displayed. The three-digit codes will be displayed as a series of blinks of the red LED (located on the top face of module A, next to the test button) with a slight pause between each digit.

7 With the flylead inserted, switch on the ignition. Press the test button on top of module A once, for about one second, then release it and wait for the LED to flash **(see illustration)**. As the LED flashes, copy down the fault code. Now press the button again and copy down the next fault code, if there is one. Continue until the first fault code is displayed again indicating that all the stored codes have been accessed, then switch off the ignition.

8 If code 1-1-1 is obtained, this indicates that the ECU has not detected any electrical faults in the transmission circuitry or related components. In this case, if there is an obvious transmission fault, it is likely to be of a mechanical nature.

9 Given in the table below are the possible automatic transmission fault codes and their meaning.

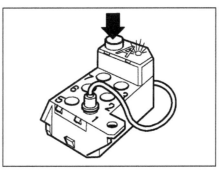

11.7 Press the button on the diagnostic module to access the fault codes

10 Once all the fault codes have been recorded they should be deleted from the ECU. Note that the fault codes cannot be deleted until all of them have been displayed at least once, and the first one is displayed again. With the flylead still inserted in position 1 of module A, switch on the ignition, press the test button and hold it down for approximately five seconds. Release the test button and after three seconds the LED will light. When the LED lights, press and hold the test button down for a further five seconds then release it - the LED will go out. Switch off the ignition and check that all the fault codes have been deleted by

switching the ignition on again and pressing the test button for one second - code 1-1-1 should appear. If a code other than 1-1-1 appears, record the code then repeat the deleting procedure. When all the codes have been deleted, switch off the ignition, locate the flylead in its holder and refit the unit covers.

11 Once the location of a fault has been established from the fault code read-out, investigations can be concentrated in that area. In many instances, the fault may be nothing more serious than a corroded, trapped or loose wiring connection, or a loose, dirty, or badly fitted component. Remember that if the fault has appeared only a short time after any part of the vehicle has been serviced or overhauled, the first place to check is where that work was carried out, however unrelated it may appear, to ensure that no carelessly-refitted components are causing the problem.

12 If the fault cannot be easily cured in this way, further detailed checking of the system components will require the use of Volvo test equipment. Therefore the only alternatives possible at this time are the substitution of a suspect component with a known good unit (where possible), or entrusting further work to a Volvo dealer.

Automatic transmission fault codes

Fault code	Meaning
1-1-1	No fault detected
1-1-2	Solenoid S1 circuit shorted to 12 volts
1-1-3	Fault in ECU
1-1-4	Break in driving mode selector circuit
1-2-1	Solenoid S1 circuit shorted to earth
1-2-2	Break in solenoid S1 circuit
1-2-3	Solenoid STH circuit shorted to 12 volts
1-2-4	Driving mode selector circuit shorted to earth
1-3-1	Break or short circuit to earth in solenoid STH circuit
1-3-2	Fault in ECU
1-3-4	Incorrect load signal
1-4-1	Oil temperature sensor circuit shorted to earth
1-4-2	Break in oil temperature sensor circuit
1-4-3	Kickdown switch circuit shorted to earth
2-1-1	Fault in ECU
2-1-2	Solenoid S2 circuit shorted to 12 volts
2-1-3	Throttle position signal too high
2-2-1	Solenoid S2 circuit shorted to earth
2-2-2	Break in solenoid S2 circuit
2-2-3	Throttle position signal too low
2-3-1	Irregular throttle position signal
2-3-2	Vehicle speed sensor signal absent
2-3-3	Incorrect speedometer signal
2-3-5	Oil temperature too high
2-4-5	Break or short circuit to earth in torque-limiting circuit
3-1-1	Transmission RPM sensor signal absent
3-1-2	Transmission RPM sensor signal faulty
3-1-3	Incorrect signal from gear position sensor
3-2-2	Incorrect gear ratio for given roadspeed
3-2-3	Lock up slips or not engaged
3-3-1	Solenoid SL circuit shorted to 12 volts
3-3-2	Break in solenoid SL circuit
3-3-3	Solenoid SL circuit shorted to earth

Notes

Chapter 8
Driveshafts

Contents

Degrees of difficulty

Easy, suitable for novice with little experience	Fairly easy, suitable for beginner with some experience	Fairly difficult, suitable for competent DIY mechanic	Difficult, suitable for experienced DIY mechanic	Very difficult, suitable for expert DIY or professional

Specifications

General

Driveshaft type	Equal length solid steel shafts, splined to inner and outer constant velocity joints. Intermediate shaft incorporated in right-hand driveshaft assembly.
Outer constant velocity joint type	Ball-and-cage
Inner constant velocity joint type:	
Manual transmission models	Ball-and-cage
Automatic transmission models	Tripod

Torque wrench settings — Nm

Driveshaft nut:*	
Stage 1	120
Stage 2	Tighten through a further 60°
Right-hand driveshaft support bearing cap bolts	25
Roadwheel bolts	110

*A new nut must be used if the original is of the staked type

1 General information

Drive is transmitted from the differential to the front wheels by means of two solid steel, equal length driveshafts equipped with constant velocity (CV) joints at their inner and outer ends. Due to the position of the transmission, an intermediate shaft and support bearing are incorporated into the right-hand driveshaft assembly.

A ball-and-cage type CV joint is fitted to the outer end of each driveshaft. The joint has an outer member, which is splined at its outer end to accept the wheel hub and is threaded so that it can be fastened to the hub by a large nut. The joint contains six balls within a cage, which engage with the inner member. The complete assembly is protected by a flexible gaiter secured to the driveshaft and joint outer member.

At the inner end, the driveshaft is splined to engage with a ball-and-cage type CV joint on manual transmission models, or a tripod type CV joint, containing needle roller bearings and cups, on automatic transmission versions. On the left-hand side, the driveshaft inner CV joint engages directly with the differential sun wheel. On the right-hand side, the inner joint is integral with the intermediate shaft, the inner end of which engages with the differential sun wheel. As on the outer joints, a flexible gaiter secured to the driveshaft and CV joint outer member protects the complete assembly.

2 Driveshafts - removal and refitting

Note: *On pre-1995 models, the driveshaft is secured by an M20 nut which is locked after tightening by staking it to the groove in the CV joint stub shaft. On later models, an M22 self-locking nut is used. The M20 staked nut must be renewed whenever it is disturbed; the M22 nut can be reused.*

Removal

1 Firmly apply the handbrake and chock the rear wheels. Remove the wheel trim on the side being worked on.
2 On early models, tap up the staking securing the driveshaft nut to the groove in the CV joint stub shaft.
3 With an assistant firmly depressing the brake pedal, slacken the driveshaft retaining nut using a socket and a long extension bar. Note that this nut is extremely tight.
4 Jack up the front of the car and support it on axle stands (see *"Jacking and vehicle support"*). Remove the appropriate front roadwheel.
5 Remove the previously slackened driveshaft retaining nut. On early models with a staked driveshaft nut, discard the nut and obtain a new one for refitting. On later models the nut is self-locking and can be re-used.
6 Remove the ABS wheel sensor from the steering knuckle and release the sensor wiring from the suspension strut bracket **(see illustration)**.

2.6 Removing the ABS wheel sensor from the steering knuckle

2.10 Releasing the control arm balljoint from the steering knuckle (arrowed)

2.11 Swivel the suspension strut and steering knuckle outwards and withdraw the driveshaft CV joint from the hub flange

7 Undo the bolt securing the brake hose and ABS wiring bracket to the inner wheel arch.
8 Free the driveshaft CV joint from the hub flange by tapping it inwards approximately 10 to 15 mm with a plastic or copper mallet.
9 If removing the right-hand driveshaft on early models, remove the splash guard under the engine.
10 Undo the nut and remove the clamp bolt securing the suspension control arm balljoint to the steering knuckle. Push down on the suspension arm using a stout bar if necessary, to release the balljoint shank from the knuckle **(see illustration)**. If the balljoint is tight, spread the slot in the steering knuckle with a chisel or large screwdriver. Take care not to damage the balljoint dust cover during and after disconnection.

2.13 Removing the intermediate shaft support bearing cap from the right-hand driveshaft

11 Swivel the suspension strut and steering knuckle assembly outwards and withdraw the driveshaft CV joint from the hub flange **(see illustration)**.
12 If removing the left-hand driveshaft, free the inner CV joint from the transmission by levering between the edge of the joint and the transmission casing with a large screwdriver or similar tool. Take care not to damage the transmission oil seal or the inner CV joint gaiter. Withdraw the driveshaft from under the wheel arch.
13 If removing the right-hand driveshaft, undo the two bolts and remove the cap from the intermediate shaft support bearing **(see illustration)**. Pull the intermediate shaft out of the transmission and remove the driveshaft assembly from under the wheel arch.

Refitting

14 Refitting is a reversal of removal, but observe the following points.
  a) Prior to refitting, remove all traces of metal adhesive, rust, oil and dirt from the splines and threads of the outer CV joint.
  b) If working on the left-hand driveshaft, ensure that the inner CV joint is pushed fully into the transmission so that the retaining circlip locks into place in the differential gear.
  c) Apply a 3 to 4 mm wide bead of metal adhesive (obtainable from Volvo dealers) to the splines of the outer CV joint before engaging the joint into the hub flange (see illustration).

  d) Lubricate the threads of the CV joint and the driveshaft retaining nut with engine oil before refitting the nut. Ensure that a new nut is used if the original was of the staked type.
  e) Tighten all nuts and bolts to the specified torque (see Chapters 9 and 10 for brake and suspension component torque settings). When tightening the driveshaft nut, tighten first using a torque wrench, then further, through the specified angle, using an angle tightening gauge (see illustrations). If the nut is of the staked type, lock the nut after tightening by tapping the nut flange into the CV joint groove using a chisel.
  f) Ensure that the ABS sensor, and sensor location in the steering knuckle, are perfectly clean before refitting.

3 Outer constant velocity joint gaiter - renewal

1 Remove the driveshaft (Section 2).
2 Cut off the gaiter retaining clips, then slide the gaiter down the shaft to expose the outer constant velocity joint.
3 Scoop out as much grease as possible from the joint then expand the joint internal circlip using a screwdriver inserted between the circlip legs **(see illustration)**. At the same time, tap the exposed face of the ball hub with a hammer and drift to separate the joint from

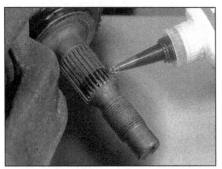

2.14a Apply a bead of metal adhesive to the CV joint splines before engaging the joint into the hub flange

2.14b Tighten the driveshaft nut using a torque wrench . . .

2.14c . . . then with an angle tightening gauge

3.3a Expand the CV joint internal circlip using a screwdriver . . .

3.3b . . . then tap off the joint using a hammer and drift

3.8 Fit a new internal circlip to the CV joint before fitting

3.11 Pack the joint and gaiter with the special grease

the driveshaft **(see illustration)**. Slide the gaiter off the driveshaft.

4 With the constant velocity joint removed from the driveshaft, clean the joint using paraffin, or a suitable solvent, and dry it thoroughly. Remove the internal retaining circlip and obtain a new one for reassembly.

5 Move the inner splined driving member from side to side, to expose each ball in turn at the top of its track. Examine the balls for cracks, flat spots or signs of surface pitting.

6 Inspect the ball tracks on the inner and outer members. If the tracks have widened, the balls will no longer be a tight fit. At the same time, check the ball cage windows for wear or cracking between the windows. Obtain a new outer joint if any wear is apparent.

7 If the joint is in satisfactory condition, obtain a repair kit from your Volvo dealer consisting of a new gaiter and retaining clips.

The correct type and quantity of the special lubricating grease will usually be supplied with the kit; if not, your dealer will be able to supply it separately.

8 Fit the new internal circlip then pack the joint with the grease supplied, working it well into the ball tracks, and into the driveshaft opening in the inner member **(see illustration)**. Use 80 grams of the grease for non-turbo models and 120 grams for turbo versions.

9 Slide the rubber gaiter onto the shaft and locate its inner end in the driveshaft groove.

10 Engage the constant velocity joint with the driveshaft splines and tap it onto the shaft until the internal circlip locates in the driveshaft groove.

11 Check that the circlip holds the joint securely on the driveshaft, then apply any remaining grease to the joint and the inside of the gaiter **(see illustration)**.

12 Locate the outer lip of the gaiter in the groove on the joint outer member then fit the two retaining clips. Remove any slack in the clips by carefully compressing the raised section using a pair of pincers **(see illustrations)**.

13 Check that the constant velocity joint moves freely in all directions, then refit the driveshaft as described in Section 2.

4 Inner constant velocity joint gaiter - renewal

Manual transmission models

1 The procedure is the same as described in Section 3 for the outer joint gaiter. If the outer CV joint has already been removed, then it will not be necessary to remove the inner joint to renew the gaiter; it can simply be withdrawn from the outer end of the driveshaft. When reassembling, note that the quantity of grease required to pack the inner CV joint is 120 grams for all models.

Automatic transmission models

Non-turbo models

2 Remove the driveshaft as described in Section 2.

3 Release the gaiter retaining clips, then slide the gaiter down the shaft to expose the joint.

4 Mark the position of the CV joint relative to the driveshaft as an aid to reassembly.

5 Using a screwdriver, carefully bend up the anti-separation plate tangs at their corners **(see illustration)**. Slide the outer member off the tripod joint.

6 Using circlip pliers, extract the circlip securing the tripod joint to the driveshaft. Mark the position of the tripod in relation to the driveshaft, using a dab of paint or a punch.

7 The tripod joint can now be removed. If it is tight, draw the joint off the driveshaft end using a puller. Ensure that the legs of the puller are located behind the joint inner member and do not contact the joint rollers. Alternatively, support the inner member of the tripod joint, and press the shaft out using a

3.12a Fit the gaiter retaining clip . . .

3.12b . . . and compress the raised section with pincers

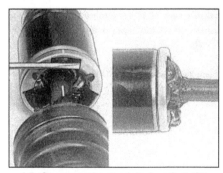

4.5 On non-turbo models, bend up the inner joint anti-separation plate tangs with a screwdriver

4.23 On turbo models, bend up the inner joint folded collar (arrowed) using pliers

hydraulic press, again ensuring that no load is applied to the joint rollers.

8 With the tripod joint removed, slide the gaiter off the end of the driveshaft.

9 Wipe clean the joint components, taking care not to remove the alignment marks made on dismantling. **Do not** use paraffin or other solvents to clean this type of joint.

10 Examine the tripod joint, rollers and outer member for any signs of scoring or wear. Check that the rollers move smoothly on the tripod stems. If wear is evident, the joint must be renewed. If the inner joint is in satisfactory condition, obtain a repair kit from your Volvo dealer consisting of a new gaiter and retaining clips. The correct type and quantity of the special lubricating grease will usually be supplied with the kit; if not, your dealer will be able to supply it separately.

11 Carefully slide the new gaiter onto the driveshaft.

12 Aligning the marks made on dismantling, engage the tripod joint with the driveshaft splines. Use a hammer and soft metal drift to tap the joint onto the shaft, taking great care not to damage the driveshaft splines or joint rollers. Alternatively, support the driveshaft, and press the joint into position using a hydraulic press and suitable tubular spacer which bears only on the joint inner member.

13 Secure the tripod joint in position with the circlip, ensuring that it is correctly located in the driveshaft groove.

14 Evenly distribute 190 grams of the special grease around the tripod joint and inside the outer member. Pack the gaiter with any excess grease.

15 Slide the outer member into position over the tripod joint ensuring that the marks made on removal are aligned.

16 Carefully tap the anti-separation plate tangs back into their original shape using a mallet.

17 Slide the gaiter up the driveshaft and locate it in the grooves on the driveshaft and joint outer member.

18 Fit the retaining clips to the gaiter. Remove any slack in the clips by carefully compressing the raised section using a pair of pincers.

19 Check that the constant velocity joint moves freely in all directions, then refit the driveshaft as described in Section 2.

Turbo models

20 Remove the driveshaft as described in Section 2.

21 Release the gaiter retaining clips, then slide the gaiter down the shaft to expose the joint.

22 Mark the position of the CV joint relative to the driveshaft as an aid to reassembly.

23 Using pliers, carefully bend up the folded collar of the joint outer member sufficiently to allow the tripod joint rollers to slide out **(see illustration)**. Withdraw the outer member off the tripod joint. Be prepared to hold the rollers in place, otherwise they may fall off the tripod ends as the outer member is withdrawn. If necessary, secure the rollers in place using tape after removal of the outer member. The rollers are matched to the tripod joint stems, and it is important that they are not interchanged.

24 Using circlip pliers, extract the circlip securing the tripod joint to the driveshaft.

25 The tripod joint can now be removed. If it is tight, draw the joint off the driveshaft end using a puller. Ensure that the legs of the puller are located behind the joint inner member and do not contact the joint rollers. Alternatively, support the inner member of the tripod joint, and press the shaft out using a hydraulic press, again ensuring that no load is applied to the joint rollers.

26 With the tripod joint removed, slide the gaiter off the end of the driveshaft.

27 Wipe clean the joint components, taking care not to remove the alignment marks made on dismantling. **Do not** use paraffin or other solvents to clean this type of joint.

28 Examine the tripod joint, rollers and outer member for any signs of scoring or wear. Check that the rollers move smoothly on the tripod stems. If wear is evident, the joint must be renewed. If the inner joint is in satisfactory condition, obtain a repair kit from your Volvo dealer consisting of a new gaiter and retaining clips. The correct type and quantity of the special lubricating grease will usually be supplied with the kit; if not, your dealer will be able to supply it separately.

29 Carefully slide the new gaiter onto the driveshaft.

30 Engage the tripod joint with the driveshaft splines. Use a hammer and soft metal drift to tap the joint onto the shaft, taking great care not to damage the driveshaft splines or joint rollers. Alternatively, support the driveshaft, and press the joint into position using a hydraulic press and suitable tubular spacer which bears only on the joint inner member.

31 Secure the tripod joint in position with the circlip, ensuring that it is correctly located in the driveshaft groove.

32 Evenly distribute 190 grams of the special grease around the tripod joint and inside the outer member. Pack the gaiter with any excess grease.

33 Slide the outer member into position over the tripod joint ensuring that the marks made on removal are aligned.

34 Carefully return the outer member folded collar back to its original shape.

35 Slide the gaiter up the driveshaft and locate it in the grooves on the driveshaft and joint outer member.

36 Fit the retaining clips to the gaiter. Remove any slack in the clips by carefully compressing the raised section using a pair of pincers.

37 Check that the constant velocity joint moves freely in all directions, then refit the driveshaft as described in Section 2.

5 Right-hand driveshaft support bearing - removal and refitting

Note: *A hydraulic press and suitable mandrels will be required for this operation.*

Removal

1 Remove the driveshaft as described in Section 2.

2 Remove the inner constant velocity joint and gaiter from the driveshaft as described in Section 4.

3 Using circlip pliers, extract the support bearing retaining circlip from the intermediate shaft.

4 Position the support bearing on a press bed with the intermediate shaft uppermost. Press the intermediate shaft out of the support bearing.

Refitting

5 Place the new support bearing on the pressbed and insert the intermediate shaft through its centre. Press the shaft and constant velocity joint into the bearing until the bearing is against the stop on the shaft.

6 Refit the circlip ensuring that it locates fully into its groove.

7 Refit the inner constant velocity joint and gaiter to the driveshaft then refit the driveshaft to the car as described in Sections 4 and 2 respectively.

6 Driveshaft overhaul - general information

1 Road test the car, and listen for a metallic clicking from the front as the car is driven slowly in a circle with the steering on full-lock. If a clicking noise is heard, this indicates wear in the outer constant velocity joints.

2 If vibration, consistent with road speed, is felt through the car when accelerating, there is a possibility of wear in the inner constant velocity joints.

3 Constant velocity joints can be dismantled and inspected for wear as described in Sections 3 and 4. If wear is apparent, the joints should be renewed.

Chapter 9
Braking system

Contents

Degrees of difficulty

| **Easy,** suitable for novice with little experience | | **Fairly easy,** suitable for beginner with some experience | | **Fairly difficult,** suitable for competent DIY mechanic | | **Difficult,** suitable for experienced DIY mechanic | | **Very difficult,** suitable for expert DIY or professional | |

Specifications

General

System type:
Footbrake . . . . Dual-circuit hydraulic with servo assistance. Anti-lock braking (ABS) on all models
Handbrake . . . . Mechanical to drums incorporated in rear brake discs

Front brakes

Type . . . . Ventilated disc, with single piston sliding calipers
Brake pad minimum lining thickness . . . . 3.0 mm
Disc diameter . . . . 280 mm
Disc thickness:
    New . . . . 26.0 mm
    Wear limit . . . . 23.0 mm
Maximum disc run out . . . . 0.04 mm
Maximum disc thickness variation . . . . 0.008 mm

Rear brakes

Type . . . . Solid disc, with twin piston fixed calipers
Brake pad minimum lining thickness . . . . 2.0 mm
Disc diameter . . . . 295 mm
Disc thickness:
    New . . . . 9.6 mm
    Wear limit . . . . 8.4 mm
Maximum disc run out . . . . 0.08 mm
Maximum disc thickness variation . . . . 0.008 mm

Handbrake

Drum diameter . . . . 178 mm
Maximum drum run-out . . . . 0.15 mm
Maximum drum out-of-round . . . . 0.15 mm

Torque wrench settings

	Nm
Front caliper bracket bolts*	100
Front caliper guide pin bolts	30
Rear caliper mounting bolts*	50
Master cylinder mounting nuts	25
Servo unit mounting nuts	25
Rigid pipe unions	14
Flexible hose unions	18
ABS wheel sensor mounting bolts	10
ABS ECU mounting bolts	5
Roadwheel bolts	110

Use new bolts every time

1 General information

The brake pedal operates disc brakes on all four wheels by means of a dual circuit hydraulic system with servo assistance. The handbrake operates separate drum brakes on the rear wheels by means of cables. An anti-lock braking system (ABS), incorporating an on-board fault diagnosis facility, is fitted to all models, and is described in further detail in Section 19.

The hydraulic system is split into two circuits, so that in the event of failure of one circuit, the other will still provide adequate braking power (although pedal travel and effort may increase). An axle-split system is employed in which one circuit serves the front brakes and the other circuit the rear brakes. A pressure reducing valve is incorporated into the brake hydraulic circuit to reduce hydraulic fluid pressure to the rear brakes under severe braking conditions.

The brake servo is of the direct-acting type, being interposed between the brake pedal and the master cylinder. The servo magnifies the effort applied by the driver. It is vacuum-operated, the vacuum being derived from the inlet manifold.

Instrument panel warning lights alert the driver to low fluid level by means of a level sensor in the master cylinder reservoir. Other warning lights remind when the handbrake is applied, and indicate the presence of a fault in the ABS system.

Note: *When servicing any part of the system, work carefully and methodically; also observe scrupulous cleanliness when overhauling any part of the hydraulic system. Always renew components (in axle sets, where applicable) if in doubt about their condition, and use only genuine Volvo replacement parts, or at least those of known good quality. Note the warnings given in "Safety first" and at relevant points in this Chapter concerning the dangers of asbestos dust and hydraulic fluid.*

2 Hydraulic system - bleeding

⚠️ *Warning: Hydraulic fluid is poisonous; wash off immediately and thoroughly in the case of skin contact, and seek immediate medical advice if any fluid is swallowed or gets into the eyes. Certain types of hydraulic fluid are inflammable, and may ignite when allowed into contact with hot components; when servicing any hydraulic system, it is safest to assume that the fluid IS inflammable, and to take precautions against the risk of fire as though it is petrol that is being handled. Hydraulic fluid is also an effective paint stripper, and will attack plastics; if any is spilt, it should be washed off immediately, using copious quantities of clean water. Finally, it is hygroscopic (it absorbs moisture from the air). The more moisture is absorbed by the fluid, the lower its boiling point becomes, leading to a dangerous loss of braking under hard use. Old fluid may be contaminated and unfit for further use. When topping-up or renewing the fluid, always use the recommended type, and ensure that it comes from a freshly-opened sealed container.*

General

1 The correct functioning of the brake hydraulic system is only possible after removing all air from the components and circuit; this is achieved by bleeding the system.

2 During the bleeding procedure, add only clean, fresh hydraulic fluid of the specified type; never re-use fluid that has already been bled from the system. Ensure that sufficient fluid is available before starting work.

3 If there is any possibility of incorrect fluid being used in the system, the brake lines and components must be completely flushed with uncontaminated fluid and new seals fitted to the components.

4 If brake fluid has been lost from the master cylinder due to a leak in the system, ensure that the cause is traced and rectified before proceeding further.

5 Park the car on level ground, switch off the ignition and select first gear (manual transmission) or Park (automatic transmission) then chock the wheels and release the handbrake.

6 Check that all pipes and hoses are secure, unions tight, and bleed screws closed. Remove the dust caps and clean any dirt from around the bleed screws.

7 Unscrew the master cylinder reservoir cap, and top-up the reservoir to the "MAX" level line. Refit the cap loosely, and remember to maintain the fluid level at least above the "MIN" level line throughout the procedure, otherwise there is a risk of further air entering the system.

8 There are a number of one-man, do-it-yourself, brake bleeding kits currently available from motor accessory shops. It is recommended that one of these kits is used wherever possible, as they greatly simplify the bleeding operation, and also reduce the risk of expelled air and fluid being drawn back into the system. If such a kit is not available, the basic (two-man) method must be used, which is described in detail below.

9 If a kit is to be used, prepare the car as described previously, and follow the kit manufacturer's instructions, as the procedure may vary slightly according to the type being used; generally, they are as outlined below in the relevant sub-section.

10 Whichever method is used, the same sequence must be followed (paragraphs 11 and 12) to ensure the removal of all air from the system.

Bleeding sequence

11 If the hydraulic system has only been partially disconnected and suitable precautions were taken to minimise fluid loss, it should only be necessary to bleed that part of the system (ie the primary or secondary circuit).

12 If the complete system is to be bled, then it should be done in the following sequence:
 a) *Rear brakes (in either order).*
 b) *Right-hand front brake.*
 c) *Left-hand front brake.*

Bleeding - basic (two-man) method

13 Collect a clean glass jar of reasonable size and a suitable length of plastic or rubber tubing, which is a tight fit over the bleed screw, and a ring spanner to fit the screws. The help of an assistant will also be required.

14 If not already done, remove the dust cap from the bleed screw of the first wheel to be bled and fit the spanner and bleed tube to the screw. Place the other end of the tube in the jar, and pour in sufficient fluid to cover the end of the tube.

15 Ensure that the master cylinder reservoir fluid level is maintained at least above the "MIN" level line throughout the procedure.

16 Have the assistant fully depress the brake pedal several times to build up pressure, then maintain it on the final downstroke.

17 While pedal pressure is maintained, unscrew the bleed screw (approximately one turn) and allow the compressed fluid and air to flow into the jar. The assistant should maintain pedal pressure, following it down to the floor if necessary, and should not release it until instructed to do so. When the flow stops, tighten the bleed screw again have the assistant release the pedal slowly, and recheck the reservoir fluid level.

18 Repeat the steps given in paragraphs 16 and 17) until the fluid emerging from the bleed screw is free from air bubbles. If the master cylinder has been drained and refilled, and air is being bled from the first screw in the sequence, allow approximately five seconds between cycles for the master cylinder passages to refill.

19 When no more air bubbles appear, tighten the bleed screw securely, remove the tube and spanner and refit the dust cap. Do not overtighten the bleed screw.

20 Repeat these procedures on the remaining calipers in sequence until all air is removed from the system and the brake pedal feels firm again.

Bleeding - using a one-way valve kit

21 As their name implies, these kits consist of a length of tubing with a one-way valve fitted, to prevent expelled air and fluid being drawn back into the system; some kits include a translucent container, which can be positioned so that the air bubbles can be more easily seen flowing from the end of the tube.

22 The kit is connected to the bleed screw, which is then opened. The user returns to the driver's seat, depresses the brake pedal with a smooth steady stroke, and slowly releases it; this is repeated until the expelled fluid is clear of air bubbles.

23 Note that these kits simplify work so much that it is easy to forget the master cylinder fluid level; ensure that this is maintained at least above the "MIN" level line at all times.

Bleeding - using a pressure-bleeding kit

24 These kits are usually operated by the reserve of pressurised air contained in the spare tyre. However, note that it will probably be necessary to reduce the pressure to a lower level than normal; refer to the instructions supplied with the kit.

25 By connecting a pressurised, fluid-filled container to the master cylinder reservoir, bleeding is then carried out by simply opening each bleed screw in turn (in the specified sequence) and allowing the fluid to run out, until no more air bubbles can be seen in the expelled fluid.

26 This method has the advantage that the large reservoir of fluid provides an additional safeguard against air being drawn into the system during bleeding.

27 Pressure bleeding is particularly effective when bleeding "difficult" systems, or when bleeding the complete system at the time of routine fluid renewal. It is also the method recommended by Volvo if the hydraulic system has been drained either wholly or partially.

All methods

28 When bleeding is complete, and firm pedal feel is restored, wash off any spilt fluid, tighten the bleed screws securely, and refit their dust caps.

29 Check the hydraulic fluid level in the master cylinder reservoir and top-up if necessary.

30 Discard any hydraulic fluid that has been bled from the system; it will not be fit for re-use.

31 Check the feel of the brake pedal. If it feels at all spongy, air must still be present in the system, and further bleeding is required. Failure to bleed satisfactorily after a reasonable repetition of the bleeding operations may be due to worn master cylinder seals.

3 Hydraulic pipes and hoses - renewal

Note: *Before starting work, refer to the warning at the beginning of Section 2 concerning the dangers of hydraulic fluid.*

1 If any pipe or hose is to be renewed, minimise hydraulic fluid loss by removing the master cylinder reservoir cap, placing a piece of plastic film over the reservoir and sealing it with an elastic band. Alternatively, flexible hoses can be sealed, if required, using a proprietary brake hose clamp; metal brake pipe unions can be plugged (if care is taken not to allow dirt into the system) or capped immediately they are disconnected. Place a wad of rag under any union that is to be disconnected, to catch any spilt fluid.

2 If a flexible hose is to be disconnected, unscrew the brake pipe union nut before removing the spring clip which secures the hose to its mounting.

3 To unscrew the union nuts, it is preferable to obtain a brake pipe spanner of the correct size; these are available from most large motor accessory shops. Failing this, a close-fitting open-ended spanner will be required, though if the nuts are tight or corroded, their flats may be rounded-off if the spanner slips. In such a case, a self-locking wrench is often the only way to unscrew a stubborn union, but it follows that the pipe and the damaged nuts must be renewed on reassembly. Always clean a union and surrounding area before disconnecting it. If disconnecting a component with more than one union, make a careful note of the connections before disturbing any of them.

4 If a brake pipe is to be renewed, it can be obtained, cut to length and with the union nuts and end flares in place, from Volvo dealers. All that is then necessary is to bend it to shape, following the line of the original, before fitting it to the car. Alternatively, most motor accessory shops can make up brake pipes from kits, but this requires very careful measurement of the original, to ensure that the replacement is of the correct length. The safest answer is usually to take the original to the shop as a pattern.

5 Before refitting, blow through the new pipe or hose with dry compressed air. Do not overtighten the union nuts. It is not necessary to exercise brute force to obtain a sound joint.

6 If flexible rubber hoses are renewed, ensure that the pipes and hoses are correctly routed, with no kinks or twists, and that they are secured in the clips or brackets provided. Original equipment flexible hoses have white lines along their length which clearly show if the hose is twisted.

7 After fitting, bleed the hydraulic system as described in Section 2, wash off any spilt fluid, and check carefully for fluid leaks.

4 Front brake pads - renewal

⚠️ *Warning: Disc brake pads must be renewed on both front wheels at the same time - never renew the pads on only one wheel as uneven braking may result. Dust created by wear of the pads may contain asbestos, which is a health hazard. Never blow it out with compressed air and do not inhale any of it. DO NOT use petroleum based solvents to clean brake parts. Use brake cleaner or methylated spirit only. DO NOT allow any brake fluid, oil or grease to contact the brake pads or disc. Also refer to the warning at the start of Section 2 concerning the dangers of hydraulic fluid.*

1 Chock the rear wheels then jack up the front of the car and support it on axle stands (see "Jacking and vehicle support"). Remove the front roadwheels.

2 Using a screwdriver, carefully extract the brake pad retaining spring clip taking care not to deform it **(see illustration)**.

4.2 Extract the brake pad retaining spring clip

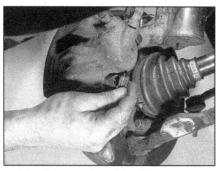

4.3a Remove the guide pin protective caps . . .

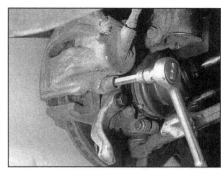

4.3b . . . then unscrew both guide pins

3 Remove the protective caps over the two caliper guide pins then unscrew both pins using a 7 mm hexagonal socket **(see illustrations)**.

4 Withdraw the caliper off the brake pads and caliper bracket taking care not to stretch the brake hose **(see illustration)**.

5 Remove the inboard pad with spring clip retainer from the caliper piston, and the outboard brake pad from the caliper bracket **(see illustrations)**. Suspend the caliper using string or wire tied to a convenient suspension component. Do not press the brake pedal whilst the caliper is removed.

6 Measure the thickness of the pad friction linings. If any one pad lining has worn down to the specified minimum, all four front pads must be renewed. Do not interchange pads in an attempt to even out wear. (Uneven pad wear may be due to the caliper sticking on the guide pins).

4.4 Withdraw the caliper off the brake pads

7 Clean the caliper and bracket with a damp rag or an old paintbrush. Inspect the caliper piston and dust boot for signs of fluid leakage. Also inspect the guide pin rubber bushes. Repair or renew as necessary (see Section 8).

8 Remove any scale or rust from the outer rim of the brake disc with a wire brush or file. Inspect the disc visually; if brake judder has been a problem, carry out a more thorough inspection (see Section 6).

9 If new pads are to be fitted, press the caliper piston back into its bore with a pair of pliers, being careful not to damage the dust boot. Remove some fluid from the master cylinder reservoir to prevent overflowing as the piston is pressed back.

 HAYNES HINT *An ideal way to remove fluid from the master cylinder reservoir is to use a clean syringe or an old poultry baster.*

10 Position the outboard pad in the caliper bracket with the friction surface towards the disc. Engage the spring clip retainer of the inboard pad with the caliper piston and push the pad fully into contact with the piston. Place the caliper over the disc and onto the caliper bracket.

11 Lubricate the guide pins with silicone grease, insert them into the caliper and tighten both to the specified torque. Refit the protective caps to the guide pins.

12 Refit the brake pad retaining spring clip.

13 Press the brake pedal several times to bring the pads up to the disc.

14 Repeat the operations on the other front brake.

15 Refit the roadwheels, lower the car and tighten the wheel bolts in a diagonal sequence to the specified torque.

16 Check the brake fluid level and top-up if necessary.

17 If new pads have been fitted, avoid hard braking as far as possible for the first few hundred miles to allow the linings to bed in.

5 Rear brake pads - renewal

⚠ *Warning: Disc brake pads must be renewed on both rear wheels at the same time - never renew the pads on only one wheel as uneven braking may result. Dust created by wear of the pads may contain asbestos, which is a health hazard. Never blow it out with compressed air and do not inhale any of it. DO NOT use petroleum-based solvents to clean brake parts. Use brake cleaner or methylated spirit only. DO NOT allow any brake fluid, oil or grease to contact the brake pads or disc. Also refer to the warning at the start of Section 2 concerning the dangers of hydraulic fluid.*

1 Chock the front wheels then jack up the rear of the car and support it on axle stands (see "Jacking and vehicle support"). Remove the rear roadwheels.

2 Drive the two retaining pins out of the caliper using a hammer and punch. Recover

4.5a Remove the inboard pad from the caliper piston . . .

4.5b . . . and the outboard pad from the caliper bracket

5.2a Tap out the two rear brake pad retaining pins . . .

5.2b ... and remove the anti-rattle spring

5.4 Withdraw the brake pads and anti-squeal shims

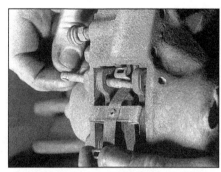

5.11a Refit the upper brake pad retaining pin and anti-rattle spring . . .

5.11b ...then refit the lower pin, passing it over the tongue of the spring

the anti-rattle spring. Obtain a new spring for reassembly **(see illustrations)**.

3 Press each pad away from the disc, using pliers. Do not lever between the pads and the disc.

4 Pull the pads out of the caliper, along with the anti-squeal shims (if fitted) **(see illustration)**. Identify their position if they are to be re-used. Do not press the brake pedal with the pads removed.

5 Measure the thickness of the pad friction linings. If any one pad lining has worn down to the specified minimum, all four rear pads must be renewed. Do not interchange pads in an attempt to even out wear.

6 Clean the caliper with a damp rag or an old paintbrush. Inspect the caliper pistons and dust boots for signs of fluid leakage. Repair or renew as necessary (see Section 9).

7 Inspect the visible surface of the brake disc. If deep scoring, cracks or grooves are evident, or if brake judder or snatch has been a problem, carry out a more thorough inspection (see Section 7). Remove the caliper if necessary for access to the inboard face of the disc.

9 If new pads are to be fitted, press the caliper pistons back into their bores using pliers. Remove some fluid from the master cylinder reservoir to prevent overflowing as the pistons are pressed back.

 HAYNES HINT *An ideal way to remove fluid from the master cylinder reservoir is to use a clean syringe or an old poultry baster.*

10 Fit the pads and shims into the jaws of the caliper with the friction surfaces towards the disc.

11 Insert the upper pad retaining pin together with the anti-rattle spring and tap the retaining pin fully home. Fit the lower pad retaining pin in the same way, making sure that the pin passes over the tongue of the spring **(see illustrations)**.

12 Pump the brake pedal several times to bring the new pads up to the discs.

13 Repeat the operations on the other rear brake.

14 Refit the roadwheels, lower the car and tighten the wheel bolts in a diagonal sequence to the specified torque.

15 Check the brake fluid level and top-up if necessary.

16 If new pads have been fitted, avoid harsh braking as far as possible for the first few hundred miles to allow the linings to bed in.

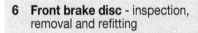

6 Front brake disc - inspection, removal and refitting

Note: *Before starting work, refer to the warning at the beginning of Section 4 concerning the dangers of asbestos dust.*

Inspection

Note: *If either disc requires renewal, BOTH should be renewed at the same time, to ensure even and consistent braking. New brake pads should also be fitted.*

1 Remove the front brake pads as described in Section 4.

2 Inspect the disc friction surfaces for cracks or deep scoring (light grooving is normal and may be ignored). A cracked disc must be renewed; a scored disc can be reclaimed by machining provided that the thickness is not reduced below the specified minimum.

3 Check the disc run-out using a dial test indicator with its probe positioned near the outer edge of the disc. If the run-out exceeds the figures given in the *Specifications*, machining may be possible, otherwise disc renewal will be necessary.

6.5 Removing the front brake caliper bracket

6.6a Undo the front disc retaining spigot pin . . .

HAYNES HINT *If a dial test indicator is not available, check the run-out by positioning a fixed pointer near the outer edge, in contact with the disc face. Rotate the disc and measure the maximum displacement of the pointer with feeler blades.*

4 Excessive disc thickness variation can also cause judder. Check this using a micrometer.

Removal

5 With the brake pads and caliper removed (Section 4), undo the two mounting bolts and remove the brake caliper bracket **(see illustration)**. Note that new bolts will be required for refitting.

6 Check whether the position of the disc in relation to the hub is marked, and if not, make

6.6b ... then remove the disc

your own mark as an aid to refitting. Remove the spigot pin which holds the disc to the hub (and also the bolt on early models) and lift off the disc **(see illustrations)**.

Refitting

7 Ensure that the hub and disc mating faces are spotlessly clean. Clean rustproofing compound off a new disc with methylated spirit and a rag.
8 Locate the disc on the hub with the orientation marks aligned and refit the retaining spigot pin (and bolt, where applicable).
9 Refit the brake caliper bracket and tighten the new bolts to the specified torque.
10 Refit the brake pads as described in Section 4.

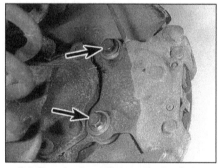

7.4 Rear brake caliper mounting bolts (arrowed)

7 Rear brake disc - inspection, removal and refitting

Note: *Before starting work, refer to the warning at the beginning of Section 5 concerning the dangers of asbestos dust.*

Inspection

Note: *If either disc requires renewal, BOTH should be renewed at the same time, to ensure even and consistent braking. New brake pads should also be fitted.*
1 With the rear brake pads removed (Section 5), the inspection procedures are the same as for the front brake disc, and reference should be made to Section 6, paragraphs 2 to 4 inclusive. Additionally, after removal, check the condition of the handbrake drums. Refinishing, run-out and out-of-round limits are given in the *Specifications*. The drums are unlikely to wear unless the handbrake is habitually used to stop the car.

Removal

2 If not already done, remove the rear brake pads as described in Section 5.
3 Release the caliper brake pipe from the retaining clip on the suspension trailing arm and, if working on the left-hand caliper, undo the brake pipe three-way connector mounting bolt.
4 Undo the two caliper mounting bolts and withdraw the caliper without straining the brake pipe **(see illustration)**. Note that new bolts will be required for refitting. Suitably support the caliper or suspend it using string or wire tied to a convenient suspension component.
5 Unscrew the wheel locating spigot pin from the disc **(see illustration)**.
6 Mark the position of the disc in relation to the hub, then pull off the disc **(see illustration)**. Tap it with a soft-faced mallet if necessary to free it. If it is not possible to remove the disc due to it binding on the handbrake shoes, proceed as follows.
7 From inside the car, lift up the centre console armrest and carefully prise out the rectangular cover panel from the base of the console.

8 Working through the cover panel aperture, and using a cranked hexagonal key, turn the adjuster bolt on the rear of the handbrake lever until there is slack in the handbrake cables.
9 Turn the rear brake disc until the handbrake adjustment hole is positioned over the handbrake shoe internal adjuster wheel. Insert a screwdriver through the hole and turn the adjuster wheel as necessary to back-off the handbrake shoes **(see illustration)**.

Refitting

10 Ensure that the hub and disc mating faces are spotlessly clean. Clean rustproofing compound off a new disc with methylated spirit and a rag.
11 Locate the disc on the hub with the orientation marks aligned, and refit the retaining spigot pin.
12 Refit the brake caliper and tighten the new bolts to the specified torque. Secure the brake pipe in the support clips or refit the three-way connector bolt as applicable.
13 Refit the brake pads as described in Section 5.
14 Adjust the handbrake as described in Section 14.

8 Front brake caliper - removal, overhaul and refitting

Note: *Before starting work, refer to the warning at the beginning of Section 2 concerning the dangers of hydraulic fluid, and to the warning at the beginning of Section 4 concerning the dangers of asbestos dust.*

Removal

1 Chock the rear wheels then jack up the front of the car and support it on axle stands (see *"Jacking and vehicle support"*). Remove the roadwheel.
2 To minimise fluid loss, unscrew the master cylinder reservoir filler cap and place a piece of polythene over the filler neck. Secure the polythene with an elastic band ensuring that an airtight seal is obtained. Alternatively, use a brake hose clamp, a G-clamp, or a similar tool with protected jaws, to clamp the front flexible hydraulic hose.

7.5 Undo the rear disc spigot pin ...

7.6 ... then remove the disc

7.9 Releasing the handbrake shoe internal adjuster wheel

3 Clean the area around the hydraulic hose-to-caliper union, then slacken the hose union half a turn. Be prepared for fluid spillage.

4 Remove the brake pads as described in Section 4.

5 Unscrew the caliper from the hydraulic hose and wipe up any spilled brake fluid immediately. Plug or cap the open unions.

6 If it is wished to remove the caliper bracket, undo the two bolts which secure it to the steering knuckle. Note that new bolts will be required for refitting.

Overhaul

7 With the brake caliper removed, clean it externally with methylated spirit and a soft brush.

8 Remove the bleed screw and empty any remaining hydraulic fluid out of the caliper.

9 Remove the piston dust boot and pull the piston out of the caliper bore. If the caliper piston is reluctant to move, refit the bleed screw and apply low air pressure (eg from a foot pump) to the fluid inlet, but note that the piston may be ejected with some force.

10 Hook out the piston seal from the bore using a blunt instrument.

11 Withdraw the two guide pin rubber bushes from their locations.

12 Clean the piston and caliper bore with a lint-free rag and some clean brake fluid or methylated spirit. Slight imperfections may be polished out with steel wool. If any pitting, scoring or wear ridges are evident, the caliper must be renewed.

13 Renew all rubber components (seal, dust boot and guide pin bushes) as a matter of course. Blow through the fluid inlet and bleed screw hole with compressed air.

14 Lubricate the new piston seal with clean brake fluid. Insert the seal into the groove in the bore, using your fingers only.

15 Fit a new dust boot to the piston ensuring that it is properly seated in the piston groove. Extend the dust boot ready for fitting.

16 Lubricate the piston and bore with clean brake fluid.

17 Offer the piston and dust boot to the caliper. Engage the dust boot with the groove in the caliper, then push the piston through the dust boot into the caliper bore.

18 Fit the new guide pin rubber bushes then refit the caliper bleed screw.

Refitting

19 If removed, refit the caliper bracket using new bolts tightened to the specified torque.

20 Refit the brake pads as described in Section 4, but screw the caliper onto the flexible hose before refitting it to the caliper bracket.

21 Tighten the flexible hose union ensuring that the hose is not kinked.

22 Remove the brake hose clamp or polythene, where fitted, and bleed the hydraulic system as described in Section 2.

23 Apply the footbrake two or three times to settle the pads then refit the roadwheel and

lower the car. Tighten the wheel bolts in a diagonal sequence to the specified torque.

9 Rear brake caliper - removal, overhaul and refitting

Note: *Before starting work, refer to the warning at the beginning of Section 2 concerning the dangers of hydraulic fluid, and to the warning at the beginning of Section 5 concerning the dangers of asbestos dust.*

Removal

1 To minimise fluid loss, unscrew the master cylinder reservoir filler cap and place a piece of polythene over the filler neck. Secure the polythene with an elastic band ensuring that an airtight seal is obtained. Alternatively, use a brake hose clamp, a G-clamp, or a similar tool with protected jaws, to clamp the rear flexible hydraulic hose.

2 Remove the rear brake pads as described in Section 5.

3 Clean around the hydraulic union on the caliper then undo the pipe union. Be prepared for fluid spillage and plug or cap the open unions.

4 Undo the two retaining bolts and remove the caliper. Note that new bolts will be required for refitting.

Overhaul

5 This is essentially the same procedure as that described for the front caliper (see Section 8), except that there are two pistons in each caliper. Do not attempt to separate the caliper halves to facilitate removal of the pistons.

Refitting

6 Fit the caliper over the disc and secure it to the stub axle bracket with two new bolts. Tighten the bolts to the specified torque.

7 Refit the brake pipe to the caliper and tighten the union securely.

8 Refit the brake pads as described in Section 5.

9 Remove the brake hose clamp or polythene, where fitted, and bleed the hydraulic system as described in Section 2.

10.4 ABS fluid hose and brake pipe attachments at the master cylinder and reservoir

10 Apply the footbrake two or three times to settle the pads then refit the roadwheel and lower the car. Tighten the wheel bolts in a diagonal sequence to the specified torque.

10 Brake master cylinder - removal and refitting

Note: *Before starting work, refer to the warning at the beginning of Section 2 concerning the dangers of hydraulic fluid.*

Note: *Overhaul of the master cylinder is not possible and internal components are not available separately. In the event of a fault in the master cylinder the unit must be renewed.*

Removal

1 Disconnect the battery negative lead.

2 Syphon as much fluid as possible from the master cylinder reservoir, using a hydrometer or old poultry baster.

Caution: Do not syphon the fluid by mouth, it is poisonous.

3 Disconnect the warning light wiring connector from the reservoir cap.

4 Disconnect the two ABS fluid hoses and, where applicable, the clutch master cylinder fluid hose from the side of the reservoir **(see illustration)**. Be prepared for fluid spillage. Plug the open end of the hoses and the reservoir orifices.

5 Disconnect the hydraulic pipe unions from the master cylinder. Be prepared for further fluid spillage. Cap the open unions to keep dirt out.

6 Remove the nuts which secure the master cylinder to the servo **(see illustration)**. Pull the master cylinder off the servo studs and remove it. Be careful not to spill hydraulic fluid on the paintwork.

Caution: On certain early models there is a possibility that the vacuum servo unit pushrod seat in the master cylinder may remain on the end of the servo pushrod when the cylinder is removed. If this happens, both the master cylinder and the vacuum servo unit must be renewed. Do not attempt to refit the seat to the master cylinder.

10.6 Master cylinder retaining nuts (arrowed)

Refitting

7 Place the master cylinder in position on the servo unit and secure with the nuts tightened to the specified torque.

8 Refit the brake pipes but do not tighten the union nuts fully at this stage.

9 Refit the ABS fluid hoses and, where applicable, the clutch fluid hose to the reservoir. Lubricate the hose ends with brake hydraulic fluid to ease fitting.

10 Reconnect the warning light connector to the reservoir cap then reconnect the battery.

11 Place absorbent rags under the brake pipe unions on the master cylinder then fill the reservoir with clean hydraulic fluid of the specified type.

12 Tighten the brake pipe unions securely when hydraulic fluid can be seen seeping out.

13 Bleed the hydraulic system as described in Section 2 on completion. On manual transmission models, bleed the clutch hydraulic system as described in Chapter 6.

14 After the system has been bled, pressure test the master cylinder by depressing the brake pedal hard and holding it down for 30 seconds. Release the pedal and check for leaks around the master cylinder pipe unions.

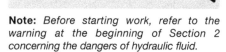

11 Pressure reducing valve - removal and refitting

Note: *Before starting work, refer to the warning at the beginning of Section 2 concerning the dangers of hydraulic fluid.*

Removal

1 To minimise fluid loss, unscrew the master cylinder reservoir filler cap and place a piece of polythene over the filler neck. Secure the polythene with an elastic band ensuring that an airtight seal is obtained.

2 Wipe clean the brake pipe unions at the pressure reducing valve and place absorbent rags beneath them to collect any spilled fluid.

3 Unscrew the brake pipe union nuts and carefully withdraw the pipes from the valve.

4 Undo the two mounting bolts and remove the valve **(see illustration)**.

11.4 Pressure reducing valve mounting bolts (arrowed)

Refitting

5 Refitting is a reversal of removal. Bleed the hydraulic system as described in Section 2 on completion.

12 Brake pedal - removal and refitting

The procedure for removal and refitting of the brake pedal is the same as for the clutch pedal. Refer to Chapter 6, Section 2.

13 Vacuum servo unit - removal and refitting

Left-hand drive models

Removal

1 Disconnect the battery negative lead then depress the brake pedal several times to destroy any vacuum in the servo unit.

2 Remove the ABS hydraulic modulator and mounting bracket assembly as described in Section 20, paragraphs 8 to 18 inclusive.

3 Remove the brake master cylinder as described in Section 10.

4 Disconnect the servo vacuum feed by levering out the non-return valve on the front of the servo unit.

5 Disconnect the wiring connector from the brake pedal position sensor.

6 Release the wiring loom and ducting around the servo as necessary, for improved access.

7 Undo the screws and remove the driver's side trim panel under the facia. Where fitted, also remove the kneeguard located behind the trim panel.

8 Disconnect the servo push rod from the brake pedal by removing the retaining clip.

9 Undo the four nuts then remove the servo from the engine compartment. Recover the O-ring seal between the servo and the bulkhead.

Refitting

10 Refitting is a reversal of removal bearing in mind the following points:
a) *Ensure that the O-ring is in position before fitting the servo.*
b) *Tighten all nuts and bolts to the specified torque.*
c) *Refit the master cylinder as described in Section 10.*
d) *Refit the ABS hydraulic modulator and bracket assembly as described in Section 20.*
e) *Bleed the hydraulic system as described in Section 2 on completion.*

Right-hand drive models

11 Due to the location of the servo unit on right-hand drive models and the very restricted working clearances, the procedure

for removal and refitting is difficult and extensive. Amongst other complications, it is necessary to detach and lower the front subframe complete with engine and transmission assembly. As this requires the use of Volvo special holding tools to avoid damage to surrounding components and attachments, plus an extensive amount of dismantling, this operation is considered beyond the scope of this manual. It is recommended therefore that any work entailing removal and refitting of the servo unit on right-hand drive models be entrusted to a Volvo dealer.

14 Handbrake - adjustment

1 Before carrying out the adjustment, drive the car slowly on a quiet road for about 400 metres with the handbrake applied by a few notches. This will clean any rust and deposits from the handbrake shoes and drum.

2 Chock the front wheels then jack up the rear of the car and support it on axle stands (see *"Jacking and vehicle support"*). Remove the rear roadwheels.

3 With the handbrake fully released, turn one of the rear brake discs until the handbrake adjustment hole is positioned over the handbrake shoe internal adjuster wheel. Insert a screwdriver through the hole and turn the adjuster wheel as necessary until the disc is locked **(see illustration 7.9)**. Now back off the adjuster wheel by about 4 to 5 notches until the disc is again free to turn without any trace of binding. Repeat this procedure on the other rear brake.

4 From inside the car, pull up the handbrake lever and check that full braking effect is achieved on the rear wheels between 3 and 5 clicks of the handbrake lever ratchet. If this is not the case, proceed as follows.

5 Lift up the centre console armrest and carefully prise out the rectangular cover panel from the base of the console **(see illustration)**.

6 Working through the cover panel aperture and using a cranked hexagonal key, turn the

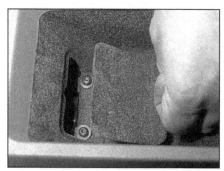

14.5 Prise up the cover panel from the base of the centre console for access to the handbrake lever adjuster bolt

14.6 Handbrake lever adjuster bolt (arrowed) as seen with the centre console removed

15.3a Unhook the handbrake shoe lower return spring . . .

adjuster bolt on the rear of the handbrake lever until the conditions described in paragraph 4 are met **(see illustration)**. Release the handbrake lever and check that the rear wheels are both free to turn without binding. Refit the centre console cover panel.

7 When adjustment is correct, refit the roadwheels and lower the car. Tighten the wheel bolts in a diagonal sequence to the specified torque.

15 Handbrake shoes - inspection and renewal

Inspection

1 Remove the rear brake disc (Section 7).

2 Inspect the shoes for wear, damage or oil contamination. Renew them if necessary and rectify the source of any contamination. As with the brake pads, the shoes must be renewed in axle sets.

Renewal

3 Unhook the handbrake shoe lower return spring, prise the shoes apart and remove them from the backplate. Unhook the upper return spring and separate the shoes. Note the correct fitted position of the adjuster mechanism as it is removed **(see illustrations)**.

4 Clean the backplate, the inside of the brake disc and the adjuster mechanism. Make sure that the adjuster wheel turns freely on its threads.

5 Apply a smear of high melting-point grease to the shoe contact areas on the brake backplate, and to the threads of the adjuster mechanism.

6 Refitting is a reversal of removal. Take care not to get grease or oil onto the brake linings or the disc friction surface.

7 Refit the brake disc as described in Section 7, then adjust the handbrake as described in Section 14.

16 Handbrake cable - removal and refitting

Removal

1 Chock the front wheels then jack up the rear of the car and support it on axle stands (see *"Jacking and vehicle support"*). Remove the rear roadwheels.

2 Refer to Chapter 11 and remove the centre console. Also remove the rear seat and carpets as necessary to gain access to the cable entry in the floorpan.

3 Ensure that the handbrake is released, then slacken the handbrake adjuster bolt at the rear of the lever until there is slack in the cables **(see illustration 14.6)**.

4 Extract the circlip and withdraw the handbrake cable operating segment from the handbrake lever shaft, then disconnect the handbrake inner cable end piece from the segment **(see illustrations)**.

15.3b . . . and upper return spring . . .

15.3c . . .then separate the shoes noting the fitted position of the adjuster

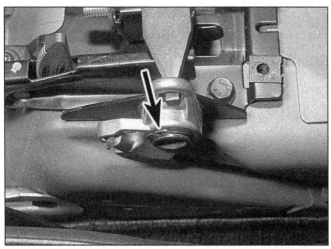

16.4a Extract the cable operating segment circlip (arrowed)

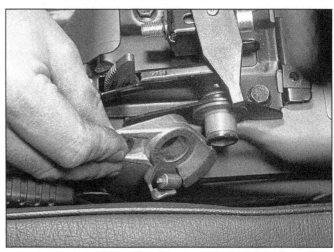

16.4b . . .then withdraw the segment and disconnect the cable

5 On early models, undo the screw securing the handbrake cable guide sleeve bracket to each brake backplate. On later models, drill out the rivet securing the handbrake cable to the suspension trailing arm on each side **(see illustration)**. On all models, undo the screw and release the cable support bracket from the trailing arm mounting just forward of the rear wheel arch **(see illustration)**.

6 On early models with a loose guide sleeve on the handbrake outer cable end, slide the guide sleeve forward away from its location

on the stub axle to reveal the handbrake inner cable. Disconnect the inner cable from the handbrake shoe expander by sliding the cable end piece out of the expander sleeve.

7 On later models with a fixed plastic guide sleeve on each handbrake outer cable end, twist the handbrake cable plastic guide sleeve back and forth to release it from the stub axle **(see illustrations)**. Disconnect the inner cable from the handbrake shoe expander by sliding the cable end piece out of the expander sleeve **(see illustration)**.

8 On all models, release any remaining cable clips and withdraw the cable out from inside the car.

Refitting

9 Attach the end of the inner cable to the handbrake shoe expander and pull it fully into place so that it locks in the expander sleeve.

10 Push the guide sleeve back into position on the stub axle.

11 Feed the cable through to the inside of the car and reconnect the inner cable end to the handbrake lever segment. Engage the segment with the handbrake lever mechanism and secure with the circlip. Ensure that the circlip locates fully into its groove.

12 Refit the cable support bracket to the trailing arm mounting.

13 On early models, refit the cable guide sleeve bracket to the brake backplate. On later models, secure the cable to the suspension trailing arm with a new pop rivet.

14 Refit any remaining cable clips then refit the centre console as described in Chapter 11. Refit the rear seat and carpets.

15 Operate the handbrake two or three times to settle the cable then adjust the handbrake as described in Section 14.

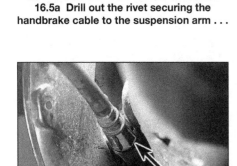

16.5a Drill out the rivet securing the handbrake cable to the suspension arm . . .

16.5b . . .and undo the support bracket screw (arrowed)

16.7a Twist the guide sleeve (arrowed) back and forth . . .

16.7b . . . to release it from the stub axle

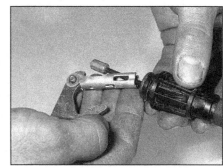

16.7c Slide the inner cable end piece out of the expander sleeve

17 Handbrake lever - removal and refitting

Removal

1 Remove the centre console as described in Chapter 11.
2 Disconnect the wiring connector from the handbrake warning light switch.
3 Undo the warning light switch mounting bolt and remove the switch.
4 Undo the three bolts securing the lever assembly to the floor.
5 Disconnect the handbrake cables and remove the lever assembly from the car.

Refitting

6 Refitting is a reversal of removal. Adjust the handbrake as described in Section 14 on completion.

18 Stop light switch - removal and refitting

Removal

Early type (manually-adjusted) switch

1 Disconnect the battery negative lead.
2 Remove the trim panel under the facia on the driver's side. On cars equipped with an airbag, remove the kneeguard (where fitted) beneath the steering column.
3 Disconnect the wiring connectors at the stop light switch which is located on the brake pedal bracket.
4 Unscrew the locknut then unscrew the switch from the bracket.

Later type (self-adjusting) switch

5 Disconnect the battery negative lead.
6 Remove the trim panel under the facia on the driver's side. On cars equipped with an airbag, remove the kneeguard (where fitted) beneath the steering column.
7 Depress the brake pedal slightly then push the stop light switch towards the pedal to release the locking sleeve.
8 Pull the locking sleeve towards the switch plunger as far as it will go.
9 Compress the switch side retaining catches and withdraw the switch from the pedal bracket. Disconnect the wiring connector and remove the switch.

Refitting

Early type (manually-adjusted) switch

10 Screw the switch into the bracket until the plunger just contacts the pedal. Depress the pedal slightly and refit the switch locknut but do not tighten the locknut at this stage.
11 Reconnect the switch wiring and the battery negative lead.

12 With the brake pedal released, unscrew the switch until the stop lights illuminate. Screw the switch back in until the stop lights just go out, then tighten the locknut.
13 Check that the wiring is not twisted, then refit the panels removed for access.

Later type (self-adjusting) switch

14 Make sure that the switch locking sleeve is fully extended toward the switch plunger.
15 Reconnect the wiring then, with the brake pedal depressed, locate the switch in the pedal bracket. Push the switch into the bracket until a click is heard as the retaining catches clip into the bracket.
16 Pull the brake pedal up as far as it will go; this will automatically adjust the switch.
17 Gently rock the switch to ensure that it is securely in place, then reconnect the battery and check the operation of the stop lights.
18 Refit the panels removed for access.

19 Anti-lock braking system (ABS) - general information

The anti-lock braking system fitted as standard equipment on all models, monitors the rotational speed of the wheels under braking. Sudden deceleration of one wheel, indicating that lock-up is occurring, causes the hydraulic pressure to that wheel's brake to be reduced or interrupted momentarily.

The main components of the system are the wheel sensors, the electronic control unit (ECU) and the hydraulic modulator assembly.

One sensor is fitted to each wheel, together with a pulse wheel carried on the wheel hub. The sensors monitor the rotational speeds of the wheels, and are able to detect when there is a risk of wheel locking (low rotational speed).

Information from the sensors is fed to the ECU which operates solenoid valves in the hydraulic modulator. The solenoid valves restrict the hydraulic fluid supply to any caliper detected to be on the verge of locking.

Should a fault develop in the system, the ECU illuminates a warning light on the instrument panel and disables the system. Normal braking will still be available but without the anti-lock function. To facilitate fault diagnosis, the system is provided with an on-board diagnostic facility. In the event of a fault, the ECU stores a series of signals (or fault codes) for subsequent read-out via the diagnostic unit located in the engine compartment. Further information on the self-diagnostic facility is given in Section 21.

On cars equipped with a traction control system (TRACS), the ABS system performs a dual role. In addition to detecting when a wheel is locking under braking, the system also detects a wheel that is spinning under acceleration. When this condition is detected, the brake on that wheel is momentarily applied to reduce, or eliminate the wheel spin.

When the rotational speed of the spinning wheel is detected to be equal to the other wheels, the brake is released.

20 Anti-lock braking system (ABS) components - removal and refitting

Removal

Front wheel sensor

1 Chock the rear wheels then jack up the front of the car and support it on axle stands (see "Jacking and vehicle support"). Remove the roadwheel.
2 Undo the bolt which secures the sensor to the steering knuckle. Withdraw the sensor and disconnect the wiring connector **(see illustration)**.

Front pulse wheel

3 The front pulse wheel is a press fit on the driveshaft constant velocity joint and special tools are required for removal. This work should be entrusted to a Volvo dealer.

Rear wheel sensor

4 Chock the front wheels then jack up the rear of the car and support it on axle stands (see "Jacking and vehicle support"). Remove the roadwheel.
5 Undo the bolt which secures the sensor to the stub axle. Withdraw the sensor and disconnect the wiring connector. On certain models it will be necessary to trace the wiring back until the connector is located and can then be disconnected. This may entail removal of the rear seats or luggage compartment trim panels (see Chapter 11).

Electronic control unit (ECU)

6 Wipe clean the area around the wiring connector on the ECU and disconnect it.
7 Undo the three retaining bolts and carefully lift the ECU from its location **(see illustration)**.

Hydraulic modulator

Note: *Before starting work, refer to the warning at the beginning of Section 2 concerning the dangers of hydraulic fluid.*
8 Disconnect the battery negative lead.

20.2 Removing the ABS front wheel sensor

20.7 ABS hydraulic modulator and ECU

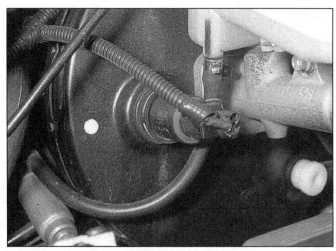

20.24 Brake pedal position sensor on the front of the servo unit

9 Drain the hydraulic fluid from the braking system. This is essentially the same operation as bleeding the system (see Section 2), but no fluid is added to the master cylinder reservoir during the procedure. Note, however that when the system is bled on completion, pressure bleeding equipment will be necessary.

10 Remove the complete air cleaner assembly as described in Chapter 4A. Additionally, on turbo models, remove the inlet duct between the air cleaner assembly and the turbocharger.

11 Wipe clean all the brake pipe unions at the pressure reducing valve and hydraulic modulator. Place absorbent rags beneath the pipe unions to catch any spilt fluid. During the following operations, label all disconnected pipe unions and wiring connectors to avoid confusion when refitting.

12 At the pressure reducing valve, undo the union nuts on the two brake pipes leading from the master cylinder. Carefully withdraw the pipes from the valve and cover the open unions and pipe ends.

13 Undo the union nuts on the three brake pipes (or four on cars with TRACS) on the side of the hydraulic modulator. Carefully withdraw the pipes and cover the open unions and pipe ends.

14 Disconnect the large wiring connector on top of the suspension strut turret and undo the two bolts securing the connector to the mounting bracket.

15 Remove the combination relay from its mounting and disconnect the connector leading from the hydraulic modulator. Move the combination relay to one side out of the way.

16 Undo the nut securing the hydraulic modulator mounting to the bracket on the suspension strut turret. Now undo the two nuts securing the bracket to the strut turret, lift up the bracket and remove the modulator mounting.

17 Disconnect the two fluid hoses at the hydraulic modulator leading from the master cylinder reservoir.

18 Carefully lift the hydraulic modulator mounting bracket complete with pressure reducing valve and ECU from its location.

19 Release the cable-tie securing the wiring harness to the mounting bracket.

20 Undo the union nuts on the two remaining brake pipes on the end of the hydraulic modulator. Carefully withdraw the pipes and cover the open unions and pipe ends.

21 Undo the four mounting bolts and remove the hydraulic modulator from the mounting bracket.

22 Note that the modulator is a sealed precision assembly and must not under any circumstances be dismantled.

Brake pedal position sensor

23 Depress the brake pedal two or three times to destroy any vacuum remaining in the servo unit.

24 Disconnect the wiring connector from the pedal sensor located on the front face of the vacuum servo unit **(see illustration)**.

25 Open the circlip and withdraw the sensor from the servo. Recover the O-ring and spacer sleeve from the sensor.

Refitting

26 In all cases, refitting is a reversal of the removal operations but note the following points:

a) *Clean off all dirt from the wheel sensors and mounting locations before refitting and also clean the pulse wheels with a stiff brush.*

b) *Bleed the hydraulic system as described in Section 2 after refitting the hydraulic modulator.*

c) *Use a new O-ring on the brake pedal position sensor and ensure that the colour coded spacer sleeve matches the colour code of the servo unit.*

21 Anti-lock braking system (ABS) - fault diagnosis

General information

1 The anti-lock braking system (together with many of the other systems on the Volvo 850) incorporates an on-board diagnostic system to facilitate fault finding and system testing. The diagnostic system is a feature of the ABS electronic control unit (ECU) which continually monitors the system components and their operation. Should a fault occur, the ECU stores a series of signals (or fault codes) for subsequent read-out via the diagnostic unit located in the engine compartment. As the ABS ECU also controls the operation of the traction control system (TRACS) the following information is relevant to cars equipped with this system as well.

2 If a fault occurs in the ABS or TRACS systems, indicated by the illumination of the relevant warning light on the instrument panel, the on-board diagnostics can be used to initially pinpoint any problem areas without the use of special test equipment. Once this has been done, however, further tests may often be necessary to determine the exact nature of the fault; ie, whether a component itself has failed, or whether it is a wiring or other inter-related problem.

Fault code read-out

Note: *On models from 1996 the diagnostic unit is located under a cover in front of the gear lever and has a 16-pin socket for connection to a fault code reader.*

3 In the event of a fault suspected in the system, or indicated by the illumination of the instrument panel warning light(s), the first step is to check whether a fault code has been logged and if so, to interpret the meaning of the code.

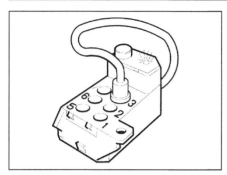

21.5 Insert the flylead into socket 3 of diagnostic module A to access the ABS fault codes

4 Locate the diagnostic unit which is situated in the front right-hand side of the engine compartment, alongside the windscreen washer reservoir filler. The diagnostic unit consists of two modules mounted side by side, with a plastic cover over each. Lift off the covers and note that the two modules are marked A and B, each having six numbered sockets on their top face.

5 With the ignition switched off, unclip the flylead from the holder on the side of the unit and insert it into socket 3 of module A **(see illustration)**.

6 Have a paper and pen ready to copy down the fault codes as they are displayed - there may be as many as ten. The three-digit codes will be displayed as a series of blinks of the red LED (located on the top face of module A, next to the test button) with a slight pause between each digit.

7 With the flylead inserted, switch on the ignition. Press the test button on top of module A once, for about one second, then release it and wait for the LED to flash. As the LED flashes, copy down the fault code. Now press the button again and copy down the next fault code, if there is one. Continue until the first fault code is displayed again indicating that all the stored codes have been accessed, then switch off the ignition.

8 If code 1-1-1 is obtained, this indicates that there are no fault codes stored in the diagnostic unit and the system is operating correctly.

9 Given in the table, shown overleaf, are the possible ABS and TRACS fault codes and their meaning.

10 Once all the fault codes have been recorded they should be deleted from the diagnostic unit. Note that the fault codes cannot be deleted until all of them have been displayed at least once, and the first one is displayed again. With the flylead still inserted in position 3 of module A, switch on the ignition, press the test button and hold it down for approximately five seconds. Release the test button and after three seconds the LED will light. When the LED lights, press and hold the test button down for a further five seconds then release it - the LED will go out. Switch off the ignition and check that all the fault codes have been deleted by switching the ignition on again and pressing the test button for one second - code 1-1-1 should appear. If a code other than 1-1-1 appears, record the code then repeat the deleting procedure. When all the codes have been deleted, switch off the ignition, locate the flylead in its holder and refit the unit covers.

11 Once the location of a fault has been established from the fault code read-out, investigations can be concentrated in that area. In many instances, the fault may be nothing more serious than a corroded or loose wiring connection, or a loose, dirty, or badly fitted component (particularly in the case of wheel sensors). Remember that if the fault has appeared only a short time after any part of the vehicle has been serviced or overhauled, the first place to check is where that work was carried out, however unrelated it may appear, to ensure that no carelessly-refitted components are causing the problem.

12 If the fault cannot be easily cured in this way, further detailed checking of the system components will require the use of Volvo test equipment. Therefore the only alternatives possible at this time are the substitution of a suspect component with a known good unit, or entrusting further work to a Volvo dealer. If a substitute unit can be obtained (or borrowed), removal and refitting procedures are given in the previous Section of this Chapter.

ABS and TRACS fault codes

Fault code	Meaning
1-1-1	No fault detected
1-2-1	LH front wheel sensor - faulty signal at speed less than 25 mph (40 km/h)
1-2-2	RH front wheel sensor - faulty signal at speed less than 25 mph (40 km/h)
1-2-3	LH rear wheel sensor - faulty signal at speed less than 25 mph (40 km/h)
1-2-4	RH rear wheel sensor - faulty signal at speed less than 25 mph (40 km/h)
1-4-1	Faulty brake pedal position sensor, shorted to earth or supply
1-4-2	Faulty stop light switch, open circuit or short circuit
1-4-3	ECU memory fault
1-4-4	Brake discs overheated (cars with TRACS only)
2-1-1	LH front wheel sensor - no signal when moving off
2-1-2	RH front wheel sensor - no signal when moving off
2-1-3	LH rear wheel sensor - no signal when moving off
2-1-4	RH rear wheel sensor - no signal when moving off
2-2-1	LH front wheel sensor - no signal from ABS system
2-2-2	RH front wheel sensor - no signal from ABS system
2-2-3	LH rear wheel sensor - no signal from ABS system
2-2-4	RH rear wheel sensor - no signal from ABS system
3-1-1	LH front wheel sensor - open circuit or short circuit
3-1-2	RH front wheel sensor - open circuit or short circuit
3-1-3	LH rear wheel sensor - open circuit or short circuit
3-1-4	RH rear wheel sensor - open circuit or short circuit
3-2-1	LH front wheel sensor - intermittent signal at speed over 25 mph (40 km/h)
3-2-2	RH front wheel sensor - intermittent signal at speed over 25 mph (40 km/h)
3-2-3	LH rear wheel sensor - intermittent signal at speed over 25 mph (40 km/h)
3-2-4	RH rear wheel sensor - intermittent signal at speed over 25 mph (40 km/h)
4-1-1	Inlet valve for LH front brake, open circuit or short circuit
4-1-2	Return valve for LH front brake, open circuit or short circuit
4-1-3	Inlet valve for RH front brake, open circuit or short circuit
4-1-4	Return valve for RH front brake, open circuit or short circuit
4-2-1	Inlet valve for rear brakes, open circuit or short circuit
4-2-2	Return valve for rear brakes, open circuit or short circuit
4-2-3	TRACS valve, open circuit or short circuit (cars with TRACS only)
4-2-4	TRACS pressure sensor, faulty or short circuit (cars with TRACS only)
4-4-1	ECU processing fault
4-4-2	Hydraulic modulator pump pressure low
4-4-3	Electrical or mechanical fault in hydraulic modulator pump motor
4-4-4	No power supply to hydraulic modulator valves

Chapter 10
Suspension and steering

Contents

Degrees of difficulty

| **Easy,** suitable for novice with little experience | | **Fairly easy,** suitable for beginner with some experience | | **Fairly difficult,** suitable for competent DIY mechanic |  | **Difficult,** suitable for experienced DIY mechanic | | **Very difficult,** suitable for expert DIY or professional | |

Specifications

Front suspension
Type . . . . Independent, with MacPherson struts incorporating coil springs and telescopic shock absorbers. Anti-roll bar fitted to all models

Rear suspension
Type . . . . Semi-independent "Delta Link", comprising two longitudinal trailing arms and integrated transverse arms. with coil springs and telescopic shock absorbers. Anti-roll bar fitted to all models

Steering
Type . . . . Power assisted rack-and-pinion
Steering fluid type . . . . See "Weekly checks"

Wheel alignment and steering angles
Front wheel:
  Camber angle . . . . $0° \pm 1.0°$
  Maximum difference between sides . . . . $1.0°$
  Castor angle . . . . $3°20' \pm 1.0°$
  Maximum difference between sides . . . . $1.0°$
  Toe setting (measured at wheel rims) . . . . $20' \pm 6'$ toe-in
Rear wheel:
  Camber angle . . . . $-1.0° \pm 30'$
  Toe setting (measured at wheel rims) . . . . $4' \pm 10'$ toe -n

Roadwheels
Type . . . . Pressed steel or aluminium alloy (depending on model)
Size . . . . 6J x 15, 6.5J x 15, 6.5J x 16, 7J x 17
Lateral run-out (maximum):
  Steel wheel . . . . 0.8 mm
  Aluminium wheel . . . . 0.6 mm
Radial run-out (maximum):
  Steel wheel . . . . 1.0 mm
  Aluminium wheel . . . . 0.6 mm

Tyres

Tyre pressures . . . . See "Weekly checks"
Tyre sizes (dependant on market and territory):
   Non-turbo models . . . . 185/65 R 15, 195/60 R 15, 205/55 R 15, T115/70 R15 (temporary spare)
   Turbo models . . . . 185/65 R 15 (winter tyres), 205/45 R 17, 205/50 R 16, 205/55 R 15,
     T115/70 R15 (temporary spare)

Torque wrench settings

Nm

Front suspension

	Nm
Driveshaft nut:*	
Stage 1	120
Stage 2	Tighten through a further 60°
Control arm balljoint clamp bolt nut	50
Hub carrier to steering knuckle:**	
Stage 1	20
Stage 2	45
Stage 3	Tighten through a further 60°
Suspension strut to steering knuckle:**	
Stage 1	65
Stage 2	Tighten through a further 90°
Suspension strut upper mounting to body	25
Anti-roll bar connecting link nuts	50
Anti-roll bar clamp bolts	50
Suspension strut to upper mounting nut	70
Shock absorber retaining nut	70
Control arm to subframe mounting nuts:**	
Stage 1	65
Stage 2	Tighten through a further 120°
Control arm balljoint to control arm nuts:**	
Stage 1	18
Stage 2	Tighten through a further 120°
Subframe rear mounting brackets to body	50
Subframe front and rear mounting bolts:**	
Stage 1	105
Stage 2	Tighten through a further 120°

Rear suspension

	Nm
Rear hub nut:	
M20 nut:**	
Stage 1	120
Stage 2	Tighten through a further 30°
M22 nut:	
Stage 1	120
Stage 2	Tighten through a further 35°
Stub axle to trailing arm:**	
Stage 1	35
Stage 2	Tighten through a further 60°
Backplate to stub axle:	
Upper bolts	25
Lower bolts	20
Shock absorber upper mounting to body	25
Shock absorber lower mounting nut	80
Shock absorber upper mounting centre nut:	
Standard shock absorber	40
Nivomat shock absorber with M12 nut	40
Nivomat shock absorber with M10 nut:**	
Stage 1	20
Stage 2	Tighten through a further 90°
Coil spring to trailing arm	40
Transverse arm to trailing arm mountings:**	
Stage 1	50
Stage 2	Tighten through a further 120°
Anti-roll bar to transverse arm mountings	50
Anti-roll bar to trailing arm mountings:**	
M10 nut:	
Stage 1	50
Stage 2	Tighten through a further 90°

Anti-roll bar to trailing arm mountings (continued):**
  M12 nut:
    Stage 1 65
    Stage 2 .... Tighten through a further 90°
Transverse arm to trailing arm mountings:**
  Stage 1 50
  Stage 2 .... Tighten through a further 120°
Trailing arm rear mounting bolt:**
  Stage 1 105
  Stage 2 .... Tighten through a further 90°
Trailing arm mounting bracket to body:**
  Stage 1 65
  Stage 2 .... Tighten through a further 60°

Steering
Steering wheel bolt 40
Air bag module to steering wheel 10
Steering column upper mounting nuts 25
Steering column lower mounting bolts 25
Steering/intermediate shaft universal joint clamp bolt 20
Steering gear crash guard bolts 80
Steering gear to subframe nuts 50
Steering gear to engine mounting 50
Steering gear centre mounting bracket 80
Steering pump guard plate 25
Steering pump mounting bolts 25
Track rod end ballpin nut 70

Roadwheels
Wheel bolts 110
*A new nut must be used if the original is of the staked type
New nuts/bolts must **always be used

1 General information

The independent front suspension is of the MacPherson strut type incorporating coil springs and integral telescopic shock absorbers. The struts are located by transverse control arms which are attached to the front subframe via rubber bushes at their inner ends and incorporate a balljoint at their outer ends. The steering knuckles which carry the hub bearings, brake calipers and the hub/disc assemblies, are bolted to the MacPherson struts, and connected to the control arms through the balljoints. A front anti-roll bar is fitted to all models and is attached to the subframe and to the MacPherson struts via link arms.

The rear suspension is of semi-independent "Delta Link" type, consisting of two longitudinal trailing arms and integrated transverse arms. The forward end of each trailing arm is attached to the underbody via rubber mountings while each transverse arm is attached to the opposite trailing arm also through a rubber mounting. A coil spring and separate telescopic shock absorber are mounted on each trailing arm. A rear anti-roll bar is fitted to all models.

Power-assisted rack and pinion steering is fitted as standard equipment. Power assistance is derived from a hydraulic pump, belt-driven from the crankshaft pulley.

Note: *Many of the components described in this Chapter are secured by nuts and bolts tightened by the angle-tightening method. These particular nuts and bolts are indicated in the "Torque wrench settings" section of the Specifications. When any of these fastenings are disturbed, it is essential that **new** nuts and/or bolts are always used when refitting. Self-locking nuts are also used in many areas and these should also be renewed, particularly if resistance cannot be felt when the locking portion passes over the bolt or stud thread.*

2 Front hub carrier and bearing - removal and refitting

Note: *The hub bearing is a sealed, pre-adjusted and pre-lubricated, double-row ball type, and is intended to last the car's entire service life without maintenance or attention. The bearing is contained within the hub carrier which is in turn bolted to the steering knuckle. The hub carrier, hub flange and bearing are serviced as a complete assembly and these components cannot be dismantled or renewed individually.*
Note: *On pre-1995 models, the driveshaft is secured by an M20 nut which is locked after tightening by staking it to the groove in the CV joint stub shaft. On later models, an M22 self-locking nut is used. The M20 staked nut must be renewed whenever it is disturbed; the M22 nut can be reused.*

Removal

1 Firmly apply the handbrake and chock the rear wheels. Remove the wheel trim on the side being worked on.
2 On early models, tap up the staking securing the driveshaft nut to the groove in the CV joint stub shaft.
3 With an assistant firmly depressing the brake pedal, slacken the driveshaft retaining nut using a socket and a long extension bar. Note that this nut is extremely tight.
4 Jack up the front of the car and support it on axle stands (see *"Jacking and vehicle support"*). Remove the appropriate front roadwheel.
5 Remove the previously slackened driveshaft retaining nut. On early models with a staked driveshaft nut, discard the nut and obtain a new one for refitting. On later models the nut is self-locking and can be re-used.
6 Remove the ABS wheel sensor from the steering knuckle and release the sensor wiring from the suspension strut bracket.
7 Undo the two bolts securing the brake caliper bracket to the steering knuckle. Note that new bolts will be required for refitting. Slide the caliper assembly, complete with brake pads off the disc and suspend it from the coil spring using string or wire.
8 Check whether the position of the brake disc in relation to the hub is marked, and if not, make your own mark as an aid to refitting. Remove the spigot pin which holds the disc to the hub (and also the bolt on early models) and lift off the disc.

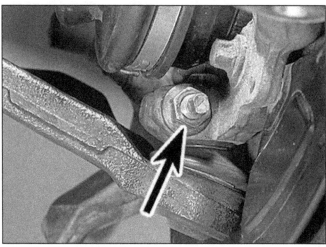

2.10 Control arm balljoint clamp bolt nut (arrowed)

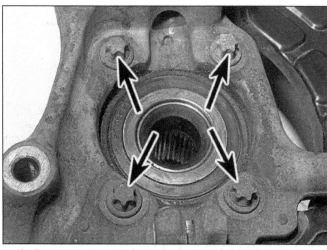

2.12 Hub carrier retaining bolts (arrowed). Steering knuckle shown removed for clarity

9 Free the driveshaft CV joint from the hub flange by tapping it inwards approximately 10 to 15 mm with a plastic or copper mallet.

10 Undo the nut and remove the clamp bolt securing the suspension control arm balljoint to the steering knuckle **(see illustration)**. Push down on the suspension arm using a stout bar if necessary, to release the balljoint shank from the knuckle. If the balljoint is tight, spread the slot in the steering knuckle with a chisel or large screwdriver. Take care not to damage the balljoint dust cover during and after disconnection.

11 Swivel the suspension strut and steering knuckle assembly outwards and withdraw the driveshaft CV joint from the hub flange.

12 Undo the four bolts and withdraw the hub carrier assembly from the steering knuckle **(see illustration)**. Note that new bolts will be required for reassembly.

Refitting

13 Prior to refitting, remove all traces of metal adhesive, rust, oil and dirt from the splines and threads of the driveshaft outer CV joint and the hub carrier mating surface on the steering knuckle.

14 Locate the hub carrier assembly on the steering knuckle. Refit the new bolts and tighten them progressively, in a diagonal sequence, first to the specified torque settings using a torque wrench, then through the specified angle using an angle tightening gauge.

15 The remainder of refitting is a reversal of removal, but observe the following points.

a) Ensure that the hub and brake disc mating faces are spotlessly clean and refit the disc with the orientation marks aligned.

b) Apply a 3 to 4 mm wide bead of metal adhesive (obtainable from Volvo dealers) to the splines of the outer CV joint before engaging the joint into the hub flange (see Chapter 8, Section 2).

c) Lubricate the threads of the CV joint and

the driveshaft retaining nut with engine oil before refitting the nut. Ensure that a new nut is used if the original was of the staked type.

d) Tighten all nuts and bolts to the specified torque (see Chapter 9 for brake component torque settings). When tightening the driveshaft nut, tighten first using a torque wrench, then further, through the specified angle, using an angle tightening gauge. If the nut is of the staked type, lock the nut after tightening by tapping the nut flange into the CV joint groove using a chisel.

e) Ensure that the ABS sensor, and sensor location in the steering knuckle, are perfectly clean before refitting.

3 Front steering knuckle - removal and refitting

Note: From the 1994 model year onwards, the diameter of the suspension strut to steering knuckle retaining bolt holes was increased from 12.1 mm to 13.0 mm to improve camber angle adjustment tolerances during manufacture. This later type steering knuckle is now the only version carried by Volvo parts stockists. If the steering knuckle is to be renewed, it will also be necessary to obtain a camber adjustment kit from your dealer consisting of spacer sleeves for the steering knuckle bolt holes. In all cases, it will be necessary to have the front camber angle checked and adjusted on completion. It is recommended that you consult your Volvo dealer concerning the availability of parts, and the implications of this modification before proceeding.

Removal

1 Carry out the operations described in Section 2, paragraphs 1 to 8.

2 Undo the retaining nut then disconnect the

steering track rod end balljoint from the steering knuckle using a balljoint separator tool.

3 Undo the two nuts and remove the bolts securing the suspension strut to the steering knuckle **(see illustration)**. Note that new nuts and bolts will be required for reassembly.

4 Undo the nut and remove the clamp bolt securing the suspension control arm balljoint to the steering knuckle. Push down on the suspension arm using a stout bar if necessary, to release the balljoint shank from the knuckle. If the balljoint is tight, spread the slot in the steering knuckle with a chisel or large screwdriver. Take care not to damage the balljoint dust cover during and after disconnection.

5 Free the steering knuckle from the suspension strut then withdraw the driveshaft CV joint from the hub flange.

6 If required, undo the four bolts and withdraw the hub carrier assembly from the steering knuckle. Note that new bolts will be required for reassembly.

Refitting

7 Prior to refitting, remove all traces of metal adhesive, rust, oil and dirt from the splines and threads of the driveshaft outer CV joint and, if removed, from the hub carrier mating surface on the steering knuckle.

3.3 Suspension strut to steering knuckle retaining bolts

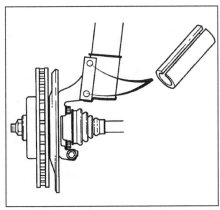

3.9 Spacer sleeves must be fitted to the steering knuckle if a new component is being fitted

8 Where applicable, locate the hub carrier assembly on the steering knuckle. Refit the new bolts and tighten them progressively, in a diagonal sequence, first to the specified torque settings using a torque wrench, then through the specified angle using an angle tightening gauge.

9 The remainder of refitting is a reversal of removal, but observe the following points:

a) *If a new steering knuckle is being fitted, ensure that the spacer sleeves supplied in the camber adjustment kit are in position in the steering knuckle bolt holes (refer to the note at the beginning of this Section)* **(see illustration)**.

b) *Thoroughly clean the hub and brake disc mating faces and refit the disc with the orientation marks aligned.*

c) *Apply a 3 to 4 mm wide bead of metal adhesive (obtainable from Volvo dealers) to the splines of the outer CV joint before engaging the joint into the hub flange (see Chapter 8, Section 2).*

d) *Lubricate the threads of the CV joint and the driveshaft retaining nut with engine oil before refitting the nut. Ensure that a new nut is used if the original was of the staked type.*

e) *Tighten all nuts and bolts to the specified torque (see Chapter 9 for brake component torque settings). When tightening the driveshaft nut and suspension strut to steering knuckle nuts and bolts, tighten first using a torque wrench, then further, through the specified angle, using an angle tightening gauge. If the driveshaft nut is of the staked type, lock the nut after tightening by tapping the nut flange into the CV joint groove using a chisel.*

f) *Ensure that the ABS sensor, and sensor location in the steering knuckle, are perfectly clean before refitting.*

g) *On completion, have the front camber angle checked and adjusted by a Volvo dealer.*

4 Front suspension strut - removal and refitting

Note: *If the strut is to be renewed on pre-1994 models, it will be necessary to obtain an ABS wheel sensor wire support bracket, available in the form of a kit from Volvo dealers. Also, from the 1994 model year onwards, the diameter of the suspension strut to steering knuckle retaining bolt holes has been increased from 12.1 mm to 13.0 mm to improve camber angle adjustment tolerances during manufacture. If a later type steering knuckle is to be fitted to an early type strut, it will be necessary to obtain a modification kit from your Volvo dealer consisting of spacer sleeves for the steering knuckle bolt holes. Note also that in all cases it will be necessary to have the front camber angle checked and adjusted on completion. It is recommended that you consult your Volvo dealer concerning the availability of parts, and the implications of this modification before proceeding.*

Removal

1 Chock the rear wheels then jack up the front of the car and support it on axle stands (see *"Jacking and vehicle support"*). Remove the appropriate front roadwheel.

2 Remove the ABS wheel sensor from the steering knuckle and release the sensor wiring from the suspension strut or steering knuckle bracket, and from the support bracket on the inner wheel arch **(see illustration)**.

3 Undo the retaining nut and separate the anti-roll bar connecting link from the bracket on the suspension strut **(see illustration)**.

4 Position a jack beneath the suspension control arm and raise the jack to just take the weight of the suspension assembly.

5 From within the engine compartment, undo the three nuts securing the strut upper mounting to the body **(see illustration)**. Note that new nuts will be required for refitting.

6 Undo the two nuts and remove the bolts securing the suspension strut to the steering knuckle. Note that new nuts and bolts will be required for refitting.

7 Free the suspension strut from the steering knuckle and manoeuvre the strut out from underneath the wheel arch.

4.2 Release the ABS wheel sensor wiring from the steering knuckle bracket

8 On 1994 onward models, check that there are two spacer sleeves located in the steering knuckle bolt holes **(see illustration 3.9)**. If there is only one sleeve, or no sleeves at all, one or two new ones (as applicable) will be required for refitting. The sleeves are used to adjust the front camber angle and, depending on the extent of adjustment necessary, one or both sleeves are then removed during the adjustment procedure. It is important, therefore, that both are in place initially.

Refitting

9 Refitting is a reversal of removal, but observe the following points:

a) *On 1994 onward models, fit new spacer sleeves to the steering knuckle bolt holes as necessary.*

b) *If a new strut is being fitted to pre-1994 models fit the new ABS wheel sensor wire support bracket to the mounting flange on the side of the strut and secure with the two bolts (see the note at the beginning of this Section).*

c) *Tighten all nuts and bolts to the specified torque using new nuts/bolts where necessary. When tightening the suspension strut to steering knuckle nuts and bolts, tighten first using a torque wrench, then further, through the specified angle, using an angle tightening gauge.*

d) *Ensure that the ABS sensor, and sensor location in the steering knuckle, are perfectly clean before refitting.*

e) *On completion, have the front camber angle checked and adjusted by a Volvo dealer.*

4.3 Anti-roll bar connecting link retaining nut (arrowed)

4.5 Suspension strut upper mounting to body retaining nuts (arrowed)

5.3a Remove the suspension strut mounting nut . . .

5.3b . . . and special washer

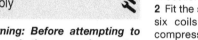

5.5a Remove the shock absorber retaining nut . . .

5 Front suspension strut - dismantling, inspection and reassembly

⚠️ **Warning: Before attempting to dismantle the suspension strut, a suitable tool to hold the coil spring in compression must be obtained.** *Adjustable coil spring compressors which can be positively secured to the spring coils are readily available, and are recommended for this operation. Any attempt to dismantle the strut without such a tool is likely to result in damage or personal injury.*
Note: *It will be necessary to obtain Volvo special tools 999 5467, 5468 and 5469 to remove and refit the strut mounting nut and the shock absorber retaining nut.*

Dismantling

1 Remove the strut from the car as described in Section 4.
2 Fit the spring compressors to catch at least six coils of the spring. Ensure that the compressors used are of a type that incorporate a method for positively locking them to the spring (usually by a small clamp bolt). Any other type may slip off or slide round the spring as they are tightened. Tighten the compressors until the load is taken off the spring seats.
3 Using Volvo tool 999 5467, unscrew the strut mounting nut while holding the protruding portion of the piston rod with tool 999 5468. Remove the nut and special washer **(see illustrations)**.
4 Using tool 999 5469, unscrew the shock absorber retaining nut while holding the

protruding portion of the piston rod with tool 999 5468.
5 Remove the shock absorber retaining nut, upper mounting and spring seat, followed by the spring, bump stop and gaiter **(see illustrations)**.
6 Remove the bump stop from the gaiter then remove the stop washer from the bump stop **(see illustration)**.

Inspection

7 With the strut assembly now completely dismantled, examine all the components for wear, damage or deformation **(see illustration)**. Renew any of the components as necessary.
8 Examine the shock absorber for signs of fluid leakage and check the strut piston for signs of pitting along its entire length. Test the operation of the shock absorber, while holding it in an upright position, by moving the piston through a full stroke and then through short strokes of 50 to 100 mm. In both cases the resistance felt should be smooth and continuous. If the resistance is jerky, or uneven, or if there is any visible sign of wear or damage, renewal is necessary.
9 If any doubt exists about the condition of the coil spring, gradually release the spring compressor, and check the spring for distortion and signs of cracking. Since no minimum free length is specified by Volvo, the only way to check the tension of the spring is to compare it to a new component. Renew the spring if it is damaged or distorted, or if there is any doubt as to its condition.

5.5b . . .upper mounting . . .

5.5c . . . spring seat . . .

5.5d . . . spring . . .

5.5e . . . and the bump stop and gaiter

5.6 Separate the bump stop from the gaiter

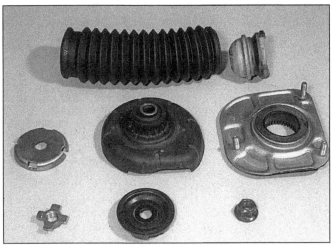

5.7 Inspect the suspension strut components for wear or damage

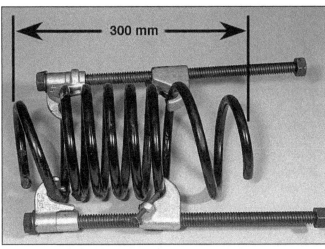

5.12 Compress the spring to the dimension shown prior to refitting

10 Inspect all other components for signs of damage or deterioration, and renew any that are suspect. On pre-1994 models, the 7.0 mm stop washer should be replaced with the later 3.0 mm version when reassembling.

11 If a new shock absorber is being fitted, hold it vertically and pump the piston a few times to prime it.

Reassembly

12 Reassembly is a reversal of dismantling, but ensure that the spring is compressed to approximately 300 mm before fitting **(see illustration)**. Make sure that the spring ends are correctly located in the upper and lower seats and tighten the shock absorber retaining nut and strut mounting nut to the specified torque.

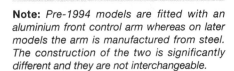

6 Front suspension control arm - removal, overhaul and refitting

Note: *Pre-1994 models are fitted with an aluminium front control arm whereas on later models the arm is manufactured from steel. The construction of the two is significantly different and they are not interchangeable.*

Removal

1 Chock the rear wheels then jack up the front of the vehicle and support it on axle stands (see *"Jacking and vehicle support"*). Remove the appropriate front roadwheel.

2 Undo the nut and remove the clamp bolt securing the suspension control arm balljoint to the steering knuckle. Push down on the suspension arm using a stout bar if necessary, to release the balljoint shank from the knuckle. If the balljoint is tight, spread the slot in the steering knuckle with a chisel or large screwdriver. Take care not to damage the balljoint dust cover during and after disconnection.

3 Undo the two inner mounting nuts,

withdraw the bolts and remove the arm from the car **(see illustrations)**. Note that new nuts and bolts will be required for refitting.

Overhaul

4 Thoroughly clean the control arm and the area around the control arm mountings. Inspect the arm for any signs of cracks damage or distortion and carefully check the inner pivot bushes for signs of swelling, cracks or deterioration of the rubber. If either bush requires renewal, the work should be entrusted to a Volvo dealer. A hydraulic press and suitable spacers are required to remove and refit the bushes and a setting gauge is needed for accurate positioning of the bushes in the arm.

5 The condition of the control arm balljoint should also be checked. On the aluminium control arm the balljoint can be renewed separately if worn (see Section 7). On the steel control arm the balljoint and arm are one assembly and if wear is detected, the complete control arm must be renewed.

Refitting

6 Locate the arm in its mountings and fit the new mounting bolts and nuts. Tighten the nuts finger tight only at this stage. Final tightening is carried out with the car lowered and on its roadwheels.

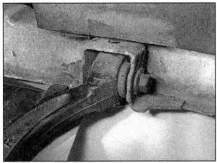

6.3a Control arm front inner mounting . . .

7 Engage the balljoint shank in the steering knuckle and align the clamp bolt slot with the steering knuckle bolt hole. Fit the clamp bolt and nut and tighten to the specified torque.

8 Refit the roadwheel, lower the car and tighten the wheel bolts in a diagonal sequence to the specified torque.

9 Tighten the control arm inner mountings to the specified torque using a torque wrench, then further, through the specified angle, using an angle tightening gauge.

7 Front suspension control arm balljoint - removal and refitting

Note: *Removal and refitting of the balljoint is only possible on pre-1994 models with aluminium control arms. On later models with steel control arms, the balljoint is an integral part of the arm.*

Removal

1 Chock the rear wheels then jack up the front of the vehicle and support it on axle stands (see *"Jacking and vehicle support"*). Remove the appropriate front roadwheel.

2 Undo the nut and remove the clamp bolt securing the suspension control arm balljoint to the steering knuckle. Push down on the

6.3b . . . and rear inner mounting

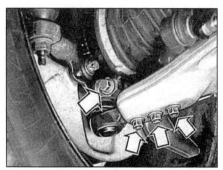

7.3 Control arm balljoint retaining nuts and steering knuckle clamp bolt (arrowed)

suspension arm using a stout bar if necessary, to release the balljoint shank from the knuckle. If the balljoint is tight, spread the slot in the steering knuckle with a chisel or large screwdriver. Take care not to damage the balljoint dust cover during and after disconnection.

3 Undo the three nuts and separate the balljoint from the control arm **(see illustration)**. Note that new nuts will be required for refitting; the bolts may be re-used.

4 Check the condition of the balljoint and renew it if there is any evidence of excessive free play, or if there is any damage to the protective dust cover.

Refitting

5 Locate the balljoint in the control arm, fit the new nuts and tighten them to the specified

8.2 Separate the connecting links from the ends of the anti-roll bar

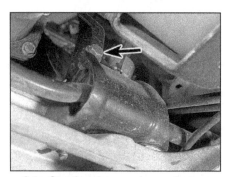

8.4a Steering gear crash guard upper retaining bolt (arrowed) . . .

torque using a torque wrench, then further, through the specified angle, using an angle tightening gauge. Tighten the inner nut first, then the centre, then the outer.

6 Engage the balljoint shank in the steering knuckle and align the clamp bolt slot with the steering knuckle bolt hole. Fit the clamp bolt and nut and tighten to the specified torque.

7 Refit the roadwheel, lower the car and tighten the wheel bolts in a diagonal sequence to the specified torque.

---

8   Front anti-roll bar - removal and refitting

Removal

1 Chock the rear wheels then jack up the front of the vehicle and support it on axle stands (see *"Jacking and vehicle support"*). Remove both front roadwheels.

2 Undo the retaining nut and separate the anti-roll bar connecting links on each side from the ends of the anti-roll bar **(see illustration)**.

3 On early models, remove the splash guard under the engine.

4 On right-hand drive models, undo the two steering gear crash guard bolts at the rear of the front subframe **(see illustrations)**.

5 Undo the five nuts securing the steering gear to the subframe and, on right-hand drive models, the nut at the base of the steering gear crash guard.

6 Undo the steering gear fluid pipe retaining clip bolts at the front and rear of the subframe.

7 Position a sturdy trolley jack beneath, and in contact with, the rear of the subframe.

Caution: Make sure that the subframe is well supported and the jack being used is capable of taking the combined weight of the engine/transmission and subframe.

8 Undo the two bolts each side securing the subframe rear mounting brackets to the body.

9 Undo the single bolt each side securing the rear mounting brackets to the subframe and recover the washers. Note that new bolts will be required for refitting.

10 Slacken the two subframe front mounting bolts by no more than 10 to 15 mm, then

carefully lower the jack and allow the subframe to drop slightly at the rear. Ensure that the steering gear mounting bolts are clear of the subframe. On right-hand drive models, check that the crash guard does not trap the steering gear fluid pipes as the subframe is lowered. Note that new subframe front mounting bolts will be required for refitting.

11 Undo the bolts securing the anti-roll bar clamps on each side of the subframe and manipulate the anti-roll bar out from under the car **(see illustration)**. On right-hand drive models, withdraw the steering gear crash guard from its location as the anti-roll bar is removed.

12 Examine the anti-roll bar for signs of damage or distortion and the connecting links and mounting bushes for signs of deterioration of the rubber. On early models the clamps and mounting bushes can be renewed separately if necessary. On later models the bushes are vulcanised to the anti-roll bar and are not available separately.

Refitting

13 Manipulate the anti-roll bar into position on the subframe together with the steering gear crash guard on right-hand drive models. Refit the clamp bolts and tighten to the specified torque.

14 Raise the subframe at the rear and engage the steering gear bolts and where applicable, the crash guard bolt.

15 Refit the rear mounting brackets to the body and tighten the bolts hand tight only at this stage.

16 Secure the rear mounting brackets to the subframe using the washers and new bolts, also tightened hand tight only.

17 Move the jack to the front of the subframe and raise it to just take the subframe weight. Unscrew the subframe front mounting bolts, fit two new bolts and tighten them hand tight only.

18 Tighten the two subframe mounting bolts on the left-hand side of the car to the specified torque using a torque wrench, then further, through the specified angle, using an angle tightening gauge. Now tighten the two mounting bolts on the right-hand side in the same way. Finally tighten the four mounting bracket-to-body bolts to the specified torque.

8.4b . . . and front mounting bolt (arrowed)

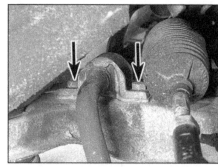

8.11 Anti-roll bar clamp retaining bolts (arrowed)

19 Secure the steering gear using new nuts tightened to the specified torque.
20 On right-hand drive models, refit the steering gear crash guard nut and the two bolts.
21 Refit the steering gear fluid pipe retaining clip bolts.
22 On early models, refit the splash guard under the engine.
23 Refit the anti-roll bar connecting links on each side to the brackets on the suspension struts.
24 Refit the roadwheels, lower the car and tighten the wheel bolts in a diagonal sequence to the specified torque.

9 Rear hub bearings - renewal

Note: *On pre-1995 models, the rear hub is secured by an M20 self-locking nut whereas on later models, an M22 nut is used. The M20 nut must be renewed whenever it is disturbed; the M22 nut can be reused. Note when refitting that there are different torque settings for the two types.*

1 The rear hub bearings cannot be renewed separately and are supplied with the rear hub as a complete assembly.
2 Remove the brake disc as described in Chapter 9, tap off the hub cap then undo the hub nut. Withdraw the hub and bearing assembly from the stub axle.
3 Fit the new assembly, lubricate the threads of the hub nut (using a new nut where applicable) and screw on the nut. Tighten the nut to the specified torque using a torque wrench, then further, through the specified angle, using an angle tightening gauge.
4 Refit the hub cap then refit the brake disc as described in Chapter 9.

10 Rear stub axle - removal and refitting

Note: *On pre-1995 models, the rear hub is secured by an M20 self-locking nut whereas on later models, an M22 nut is used. The M20 nut must be renewed whenever it is disturbed; the M22 nut can be reused. Note when refitting that there are different torque settings for the two types.*

Removal

1 Remove the rear brake disc and handbrake shoes, on the relevant side, as described in Chapter 9, Sections 7 and 15 respectively.
2 Tap off the hub cap then undo the rear hub nut. Withdraw the hub and bearing assembly from the stub axle.
3 Undo the retaining bolt and withdraw the ABS wheel sensor from the rear of the stub axle. Do not disconnect the wheel sensor connector.

10.5 Brake backplate, handbrake shoe and cable attachments at the stub axle (arrowed)

4 On early models undo the screw securing the handbrake cable guide sleeve bracket to the brake backplate.
5 Undo the four bolts and remove the brake backplate together with the two handbrake shoe retaining clips **(see illustration)**. Remove the backplate gasket and obtain a new one for refitting if the original is in any way damaged.
6 On early models with a loose guide sleeve on the handbrake outer cable end, slide the guide sleeve forward away from its location on the stub axle to reveal the handbrake inner cable. Disconnect the inner cable from the handbrake shoe expander by sliding the cable end piece out of the expander sleeve. Remove the cable and expander from the stub axle.
7 On later models with a fixed plastic guide sleeve on the handbrake outer cable end, refer to Chapter 11 and remove the centre console. From inside the car, extract the circlip and withdraw the handbrake cable operating segment from the handbrake lever shaft (refer to Chapter 9, Section 16 if necessary). Disconnect the handbrake inner cable end piece from the segment. Working at the stub axle end, pull out the inner cable slightly and disconnect it from the handbrake shoe expander by sliding the cable end piece out of the expander sleeve.
8 Undo the four bolts and remove the stub axle from the rear suspension trailing arm. Note that new bolts will be required for refitting. On later models, as the stub axle is withdrawn, twist the handbrake cable plastic guide sleeve back and forth to release it from the stub axle **(see illustration)**.

Refitting

9 Ensure that the stub axle and trailing arm mating faces are clean then locate the stub axle in position. On later models feed the handbrake cable through the stub axle as it is fitted and push the guide sleeve fully into place.
10 Secure the stub axle using new bolts tightened in a progressive diagonal sequence to the specified torque using a torque wrench, then further, through the specified angle, using an angle tightening gauge.

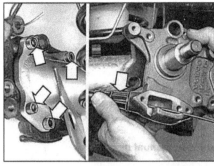

10.8 Undo the stub axle to trailing arm bolts (arrowed) and release the handbrake cable guide sleeve as the stub axle is removed

11 Attach the handbrake inner cable to the brake shoe expander. On early models push the guide sleeve back into position on the stub axle. On later models, working inside the car, reconnect the handbrake cable to the operating segment then fit the segment to the handbrake lever shaft. Secure the segment with the circlip ensuring that it locates fully into its groove.
12 On later models, refit the centre console with reference to Chapter 11.
13 Using a new gasket if necessary, locate the brake backplate on the stub axle. Fit the four bolts together with the two handbrake shoe retaining clips then tighten the bolts to the specified torque.
14 On early models refit the screw securing the handbrake cable guide sleeve bracket to the brake backplate.
15 Ensure that the ABS wheel sensor and stub axle location are perfectly clean, then refit the sensor and secure with the retaining bolt.
16 Refit the rear hub and bearing assembly, screw on the new hub nut (using a new nut where applicable) and tighten it to the specified torque using a torque wrench, then further, through the specified angle, using an angle tightening gauge. Refit the hub cap.
17 Refit the handbrake shoes and the rear brake disc as described in Chapter 9, Sections 15 and 7 respectively.

11 Rear shock absorber - removal and refitting

Removal

1 On Saloon models, fold down the rear seat backrest and release the front edge of the boot carpet. Remove the support panel under the carpet. Undo the backrest catch, release the fasteners and remove the boot side trim panel for access to the shock absorber upper mounting.
2 On Estate models, undo the retaining screws from the luggage compartment front floor panel. Pull the panel to the rear to release the front mountings and remove the panel.

11.4 Shock absorber upper mounting retaining bolts (arrowed)

11.6 Shock absorber lower mounting nut

3 On all models, chock the front wheels then jack up the rear of the vehicle and support it on axle stands (see *"Jacking and vehicle support"*).

4 From inside the luggage compartment or boot, undo the two bolts securing the shock absorber upper mounting to the body **(see illustration)**.

5 Position a jack under the rear spring pan on the suspension trailing arm and raise the jack sufficiently to take the load off the shock absorber.

6 Undo the shock absorber lower mounting nut and slide the unit off the trailing arm mounting stud **(see illustration)**.

7 Remove the shock absorber, complete with upper mounting, from inside the luggage compartment or boot.

8 To remove the upper mounting, undo the centre retaining nut while counterholding the piston rod.

9 Check the condition of the shock absorber and upper mounting and renew any components as necessary.

Refitting

10 Refitting is a reversal of removal, tightening all nuts and bolts to the specified torques and, where applicable through the specified angle.

12 Rear coil spring - removal and refitting

Removal

1 Carry out the operations described in Section 11, paragraphs 1 to 6.

2 Slowly lower the jack under the trailing arm until all tension is removed from the spring then remove the jack.

3 Undo the nut securing the spring lower mounting to the trailing arm.

4 Lift out the spring, lower mounting, bump stop and upper seat from their locations.

5 Examine all the components for wear or damage and renew as necessary.

Refitting

6 Locate the bump stop, spring and upper seat, and the lower mounting in position. Refit

the nut to the lower mounting and tighten to the specified torque.

7 Raise the trailing arm by means of the jack and engage the upper end of the spring in its recess in the body.

8 Refit the shock absorber mountings using a reversal of removal and tightening all nuts and bolts to the specified torque.

13 Rear anti-roll bar - removal and refitting

Removal

1 Chock the front wheels then jack up the rear of the vehicle and support it on axle stands (see *"Jacking and vehicle support"*).

2 Remove the exhaust silencer left-hand rubber mounting and tie up the silencer as high as possible using a cable-tie or similar.

3 Locate the right-hand transverse arm mounting nuts on the left-hand trailing arm then undo the outer nut and remove the bolt.

4 Using a punch, make a mark on the edge of the transverse arm mounting now visible, just inside the trailing arm hole **(see illustration)**. It is most important that this mark is properly made so that it can be used as an alignment datum position when refitting, otherwise the rear wheel toe-in setting will be lost.

5 With the position of the transverse arm mounting in the trailing arm marked, undo the nut and remove the other mounting bolt. Note that both the transverse arm mounting nuts and bolts must be renewed when refitting.

13.4 Right-hand transverse arm outer mounting nut (1), and alignment mark made for refitting (2)

6 Undo the two nuts and remove the mounting bolts securing the anti-roll bar to the left-hand trailing arm. Note the different bolt lengths and their locations - new nuts and bolts will be required for refitting.

7 Undo the two nuts and remove the mounting bolts at the other end of the anti-roll bar; new nuts only will be required here for refitting. Withdraw the bar from its location and remove it from under the car.

Refitting

8 Locate the anti-roll bar in position and fit the new bolts and nuts securing the bar to the left-hand trailing arm, and the bolts and new nuts securing the other end to the transverse arm. Do not tighten any of the mountings at this stage.

9 Again using new components, loosely fit the inner transverse arm mounting bolt and nut. Align the datum mark made on removal, then tighten the inner mounting just sufficiently to hold the position.

10 Fit the new outer mounting bolt and nut then tighten both nuts to the specified torque using a torque wrench, then further, through the specified angle, using an angle tightening gauge.

11 Tighten the anti-roll bar-to-transverse arm mounting nuts to the specified torque. Now tighten the anti-roll bar-to-trailing arm nuts to the specified torque using a torque wrench, then further, through the specified angle, using an angle tightening gauge. Note that there are different torque settings for these two mounting nuts.

12 Refit the silencer left-hand rubber mounting, then lower the car to the ground.

14 Rear suspension assembly - removal and refitting

Removal

1 Remove both rear brake discs as described in Chapter 9, Section 7.

2 Undo the retaining bolt and withdraw the ABS wheel sensor from the rear of the stub axle. Do not disconnect the wheel sensor connector.

3 On early models, undo the screw securing the handbrake cable guide sleeve bracket to each brake backplate. On later models, drill out the rivet securing the handbrake cable to the suspension trailing arm on each side. On all models undo the screw and release the cable support bracket from the trailing arm mounting just forward of the rear wheel arch.

4 On early models with a loose guide sleeve on each handbrake outer cable end, slide the guide sleeve forward away from its location on the stub axle to reveal the handbrake inner cable. Disconnect the inner cable from the handbrake shoe expander by sliding the cable end piece out of the expander sleeve. Repeat this procedure on the other handbrake cable.

5 On later models with a fixed plastic guide sleeve on each handbrake outer cable end, refer to Chapter 11 and remove the centre console. From inside the car, extract the circlip and withdraw the handbrake cable operating segment from the handbrake lever shaft. Disconnect the handbrake inner cable end piece from the segment (refer to Chapter 9, Section 16 if necessary). Working at the stub axle end, twist the handbrake cable plastic guide sleeve back and forth to release it from the stub axle. Disconnect the inner cable from the handbrake shoe expander by sliding the cable end piece out of the expander sleeve. Repeat this procedure on the other handbrake cable.

6 Disconnect the brake pipe from the flexible hose connection just forward of the rear suspension arm. Minimise hydraulic fluid loss by removing the master cylinder reservoir cap, place a piece of plastic film over the reservoir and seal it with an elastic band. Alternatively, clamp the flexible hose using a proprietary brake hose clamp.

7 On Saloon models, fold down the rear seat backrest and release the front edge of the boot carpet. Remove the support panel under the carpet. Undo the backrest catches, release the fasteners and remove the boot side trim panels on both sides for access to the shock absorber upper mountings.

8 On Estate models, undo the retaining screws from the luggage compartment front floor panel. Pull the panel to the rear to release the front mountings and remove the panel.

9 From inside the luggage compartment or boot, undo the two bolts securing the left-hand shock absorber upper mounting to the body **(see illustration 11.4)**.

10 Position a jack under the left-hand rear spring pan on the suspension trailing arm and raise the jack sufficiently to take the load off the shock absorber.

11 Undo the shock absorber lower mounting nut and slide the unit off the trailing arm mounting stud.

12 Slowly lower the jack under the trailing arm until all tension is removed from the spring then remove the jack.

13 Undo the nut securing the spring lower mounting to the trailing arm.

14 Lift out the spring, lower mounting, bump stop and upper seat from their locations.

15 Repeat the operations described in paragraphs 9 to 14 on the right-hand side.

16 With the spring pan still supported on the jack, undo the four bolts securing the right-hand trailing arm and the trailing arm bracket to the underbody **(see illustration)**. Note that new bolts will be required for refitting.

17 Position a second jack under and in contact with the left-hand spring pan. Undo the four bolts securing the left-hand trailing arm and the trailing arm bracket to the underbody. Note that new bolts will be required for refitting.

18 Support the rear suspension assembly and slowly lower both the jacks. When the assembly is clear of the underbody, withdraw it rearwards and out from under the car.

Refitting

19 Refitting is a reversal of removal bearing in mind the following points:
a) *Manoeuvre the suspension assembly into position using the jacks and secure with the four new mounting bolts each side, hand-tightened only.*
b) *Tighten the rear mounting bolt each side, that secures the trailing arm and mounting bracket to the underbody, first to the specified torque using a torque wrench, then further, through the specified angle, using an angle tightening gauge. Now tighten the remaining three bolts each side, which secure the mounting bracket to the underbody in the same way.*
c) *Refit the springs and shock absorbers as described in Sections 12 and 11 respectively.*
d) *With the handbrake inner cables attached to the brake shoe expanders, on early models push the guide sleeves back into position on the stub axles. On later models, working inside the car, reconnect the handbrake cables to the operating segments then fit the segments to the handbrake lever shaft. Secure each segment with the circlip ensuring that it locates fully into its groove. Use new pop rivets to secure the cables to the suspension arms.*
e) *Bleed the brake hydraulic system as described in Chapter 9.*

15 Steering wheel - removal and refitting

Models without an airbag supplemental restraint system

Removal

1 Drive the car forwards and park it with the steering wheels in the straight-ahead position.
2 Disconnect the battery negative lead.
3 Carefully prise off the steering wheel centre pad.

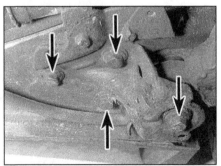

14.16 Right-hand trailing arm and trailing arm bracket bolts (arrowed)

4 Undo the steering wheel centre retaining bolt.
5 Ensure that the steering wheel is still in the straight-ahead position then pull the wheel upwards and off the column shaft.

Refitting

6 Refitting is a reversal of removal but ensure that the roadwheels and steering wheel are in the straight ahead position. Tighten the steering wheel retaining bolt to the specified torque.

Models with an airbag supplemental restraint system

 Warning: Handle the airbag unit with extreme care as a precaution against personal injury, and always hold it with the cover facing away from the body. If in doubt concerning any proposed work involving the airbag unit or its control circuitry, consult a Volvo dealer.

Removal

7 Drive the car forwards and park it with the steering wheels in the straight-ahead position.
8 Disconnect the battery negative lead.
9 Place a piece of masking tape on the top of the steering wheel hub and another piece on the top of the steering column upper shroud. Draw a pencil line across both pieces of tape to act as an alignment mark to centralise the steering wheel when refitting.
10 Turn the ignition key to position I to release the steering lock.
11 Using a suitable Torx type socket bit, undo the two airbag module retaining screws from the rear of the steering wheel **(see illustration)**. Turn the steering wheel 90° in each direction to gain access to the screws.
12 Lift the airbag module off the steering wheel, disconnect the wiring connector from the rear of the unit and remove it from the vehicle.

 Warning: Position the airbag unit in a safe place, with the mechanism facing downwards as a precaution against accidental operation. Do not attempt to open or repair the airbag unit, or apply any electrical current to it. Do not use any airbag which is visibly damaged or which has been tampered with.

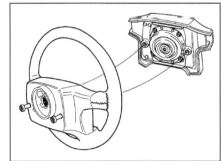

15.11 Airbag module to steering wheel attachments

13 Undo the screw securing the airbag wiring plastic retaining strip from its location in the steering wheel. Ensure that the screw remains in the plastic strip.
14 Undo the steering wheel centre retaining bolt.
15 Set the front wheels in the straight-ahead position once again by aligning the marks made on the masking tape.
16 Lift the steering wheel off the column shaft and feed the wiring and plastic strip through the hole in the wheel.

Refitting

17 Ensure that the front wheels are still in the straight ahead position.
18 Centralise the airbag contact reel by turning it clockwise as far as it will go, then turn it back anti-clockwise approximately three turns. Continue turning until the lug on the reel is at the 1 o'clock position. Lock the reel in this position by screwing in the locking screw located in the plastic retaining strip **(see illustration)**.
19 Feed the wiring through the hole in the steering wheel then engage the wheel with the steering column shaft. Ensure that the marks made on removal are aligned and that the pegs on the contact reel engage with the recesses on the steering wheel hub. Do not attempt to turn the steering wheel with the contact reel locked otherwise the reel will be damaged.
20 Refit the steering wheel retaining bolt and tighten it finger tight only.
21 Remove the contact reel locking screw and refit the screw and plastic strip to the location provided in the steering wheel.
22 Tighten the steering wheel retaining bolt to the specified torque.
23 Rest the airbag unit on the bottom edge of the steering wheel hub and reconnect the wiring connector. Swing the airbag unit up into position checking carefully that the wiring is not pinched.
24 Refit the airbag unit retaining screws and tighten to the specified torque starting with the right-hand screw first.

25 Switch on the ignition to position II then, with the ignition switched on, reconnect the battery negative lead.
Caution: Make sure that there is no one in the car when the battery is reconnected.
26 Switch off the ignition then switch it on again and check that the SRS warning light on the instrument panel is extinguished after about ten seconds.

16 Steering column - removal and refitting

Removal

1 Disconnect the battery negative lead.
2 Remove the steering wheel as described in Section 15.
3 Undo the four screws from the underside of the steering column lower shroud then lift off the upper and lower shrouds.
4 Undo the screws and remove the driver's side trim panel under the facia. Where fitted, also remove the knee bolster located behind the trim panel.
5 On cars without an airbag supplementary restraint system, undo the three screws and remove the horn slip ring from the top of the column. On cars with an airbag supplementary restraint system, release the cable clip and disconnect the wiring from the contact reel at the top of the steering column. Undo the three screws and remove the contact reel.
6 Undo the two screws each side and remove both steering column multifunction switches. Disconnect the switch wiring connectors.
7 Disconnect the ignition switch wiring connector from the side of the switch.
8 Insert the ignition key into the switch and turn the key to position I.
9 Using a 2.0 mm diameter pin punch or similar item, depress the ignition switch locking tab through the hole in the housing

above the switch, and withdraw the switch.
10 Remove the connector bracket from the top of the steering column.
11 Pull down the steering column wiring harness at its mid point.
12 Undo the column upper mounting nuts and remove the washers. On early models, it may be necessary to bend the support stays upwards slightly towards the instrument panel.
13 Withdraw the steering column from the lower mounting and intermediate shaft and remove it from the car.

Refitting

14 Refitting is a reversal of removal bearing in mind the following points:
   a) *Lubricate the intermediate shaft splines with grease before engaging the steering column.*
   b) *Centralise the column in the facia aperture before tightening the upper mounting nuts to the specified torque.*
   c) *When refitting the ignition switch, turn the key to position I, depress the locking tab, then push the switch into the barrel until the tab locates in its recess.*
   d) *Ensure that the rubber boots over the column multifunction switch stalks locate correctly in the column upper and lower shrouds.*
   e) *Refit the steering wheel as described in Section 15.*

17 Steering column intermediate shaft - removal and refitting

Removal

1 Remove the steering column as described in Section 16.
2 Undo the two bolts and remove the column lower mounting from under the facia **(see illustration)**.

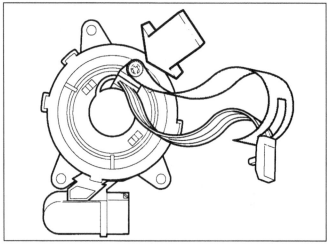

15.18 Airbag contact reel locked with the locking screw in the plastic strip

17.2 Steering column lower mounting bolts (arrowed)

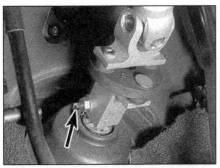

17.3 Universal joint clamp bolt and locking spring clip (arrowed)

3 Extract the locking spring clip, undo the nut and remove the clamp bolt from the intermediate shaft universal joint **(see illustration)**.

4 Pull the universal joint upwards off the steering shaft and remove the intermediate shaft from the car.

Refitting

5 Refitting is a reversal of removal. Tighten all nuts and bolts to the specified torque and secure the universal joint clamp bolt with the locking spring clip.

18 Steering shaft, gaiter and bearing - removal and refitting

Removal

1 Remove the steering column and the column intermediate shaft as described in Sections 16 and 17.

2 Fold up the top portion of the rubber boot at the base of the steering shaft.

3 Prise out the locking ring from the rubber boot lower portion and remove the rubber boot and bearing assembly.

4 Extract the locking spring clip, undo the nut and remove the clamp bolt from the steering shaft universal joint.

5 Pull the universal joint upwards off the steering gear pinion shaft and remove the steering shaft from the car.

Refitting

6 Engage the universal joint with the steering gear pinion shaft and push it fully home. On early models the slot on the universal joint must be aligned with the centre of the flat on the pinion shaft. On later models the universal joint slot must be aligned with the groove below the pinion shaft splines **(see illustration)**.

7 Refit the clamp bolt and nut, tighten the nut to the specified torque and secure with the locking spring clip.

8 Lubricate the needle bearing in the rubber boot with grease and the boot lower portion with soapy water.

9 With the top portion of the boot folded up, fit the lower portion to the collar on the bulkhead ensuring a good seal.

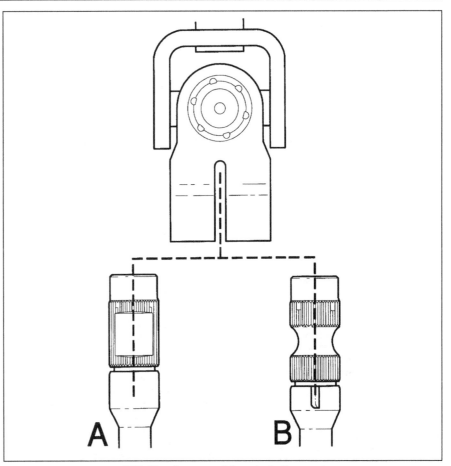

18.6 Steering gear pinion shaft alignment

A Early models   *B Later models*

10 Lubricate the locking ring with soapy water and press it into position around the boot lower portion and the bulkhead.

11 Fold down the top portion of the boot so that it seals around the locking ring flange.

12 Refit the intermediate shaft and the steering column as described in Sections 17 and 16 respectively.

19 Steering gear - removal and refitting

Removal

1 Drive the car forwards and park it with the steering wheels in the straight-ahead position. Remove the ignition key to lock the steering in this position.

2 Disconnect the battery negative lead.

3 Chock the rear wheels then jack up the front of the vehicle and support it on axle stands (see *"Jacking and vehicle support"*). Remove both front roadwheels.

4 Unscrew the left-hand track rod end ballpin nut to the end of its threads. Separate the ballpin from the steering arm with a proprietary balljoint separator, then remove

the nut and disengage the ballpin from the arm. Separate the right-hand track rod end from the steering arm in the same way.

5 On cars with an airbag supplementary restraint system, measure the length of the track rod on one side, relative to the steering gear housing and record this dimension.

6 On early models, remove the splash guard under the engine.

7 From under the car, undo the steering gear fluid pipe retaining clip bolts at the front and rear of the subframe.

8 On right-hand drive models, undo the two steering gear crash guard bolts at the rear of the front subframe and remove the crash guard. Wipe clean the area around the fluid pipe unions on the steering gear pinion housing. Place a suitable container under the steering gear, unscrew the union nuts and carefully pull the pipes clear.

9 Undo the five nuts securing the steering gear to the subframe.

10 Position a sturdy trolley jack beneath, and in contact with, the rear of the subframe.

Caution: Make sure that the subframe is well supported and the jack being used is capable of taking the combined weight of the engine/transmission and subframe.

11 Undo the two bolts each side securing the subframe rear mounting brackets to the body.

12 Undo the single bolt each side securing the rear mounting brackets to the subframe and recover the washers. Note that new bolts will be required for refitting.

13 Slacken the two subframe front mounting bolts by no more than 10 to 15 mm then carefully lower the jack and allow the subframe to drop slightly at the rear. Ensure that the steering gear mounting bolts are clear of the subframe. Note that new subframe front mounting bolts will be required for refitting.

14 On left-hand drive models, disconnect the fluid pipe unions from the steering gear as described in paragraph 8.

15 Extract the locking spring clip, undo the nut and remove the clamp bolt from the steering shaft universal joint. Push the universal joint upwards off the steering gear pinion shaft.

16 Undo the bolt securing the steering gear to the rear engine mounting. On right-hand drive models remove the heat shield then, on all models, manipulate the steering gear out from the right-hand side of the car.

17 If a new steering gear assembly is to be fitted, transfer the centre mounting bracket to the new unit but do not fully tighten the bracket bolt at this stage.

Refitting

18 On cars with an airbag supplementary restraint system, set the length of the track rod to the previously recorded dimension by turning the pinion shaft as necessary.

19 Manipulate the steering gear into position on the subframe and on right-hand drive models, refit the heat shield.

20 Support the steering gear on the rear engine mounting, position it so that it is straight relative to the subframe and tighten the engine mounting bolt to the specified torque.

21 Engage the steering shaft universal joint with the pinion shaft and push it fully home. On early models the slot on the universal joint must be aligned with the centre of the flat on the pinion shaft. On later models the universal joint slot must be aligned with the groove below the pinion shaft splines **(see illustration 18.6)**.

22 Refit the clamp bolt and nut, tighten the nut to the specified torque and secure with the locking spring clip.

23 On left-hand drive models, loosely reconnect the fluid pipe unions to the steering gear using new O-rings on the unions. Loosely refit the fluid pipe retaining clip bolts at the front, align the pipes in the clips then fully tighten the pipe unions on the steering gear.

24 Raise the subframe at the rear and engage the steering gear bolts.

25 Refit the rear mounting brackets to the body and tighten the bolts hand tight only at this stage.

26 Secure the rear mounting brackets to the

subframe using the washers and new bolts also tightened hand tight only.

27 Move the jack to the front of the subframe and raise it to just take the subframe weight. Unscrew the subframe front mounting bolts, fit two new bolts and tighten them hand tight only.

28 Tighten the two subframe mounting bolts on the left-hand side of the car to the specified torque using a torque wrench, then further, through the specified angle, using an angle tightening gauge. Now tighten the two mounting bolts on the right-hand side in the same way. Finally tighten the four mounting bracket-to-body bolts to the specified torque.

29 Secure the steering gear using new nuts tightened to the specified torque. If a new steering gear assembly is being fitted, tighten the centre mounting bracket bolt to the specified torque.

30 On right-hand drive models, reconnect the steering gear fluid pipe unions and front retaining clip bolts as described in paragraph 23.

31 On all models refit the remaining fluid pipe clips and tighten the bolts on all the clips securely.

32 On right-hand drive models, refit the steering gear crash guard.

33 Refit the track rod ends to the steering arms and secure with new nuts tightened to the specified torque.

34 On early models, refit the splash guard under the engine.

35 Reconnect the battery, refit the roadwheels then bleed the steering gear as described in Section 21.

36 With the car lowered, tighten the wheel bolts in a diagonal sequence to the specified torque.

37 Have the front wheel toe-in checked and adjusted by a Volvo dealer.

20 Steering gear gaiters - renewal

1 Remove the track rod end on the side concerned as described in Section 23.

2 Count and record the number of exposed threads on the track rod, from the end of the rod to the track rod end locknut. Unscrew the locknut from the track rod.

3 Release the two clips and peel off the gaiter.

4 Clean out any dirt and grit from the inner end of the track rod and (when accessible) the rack.

5 Pack the new gaiter with 20 grams of steering gear grease obtainable from Volvo dealers, then fit and secure the new gaiter.

6 Refit the track rod end locknut and position it so that the same number of threads counted on removal are visible.

7 Refit the track rod end as described in Section 23.

21 Steering gear - bleeding

1 The steering pump and combined fluid reservoir are mounted on the front facing side of the engine at the timing belt end.

2 The fluid level in the reservoir is checked by means of a dipstick in the filler cap. The dipstick has markings on both sides so that the fluid level can be checked with the engine cold, or hot after the car has been driven. Fluid level should not exceed the "COLD" or "HOT" mark as applicable, nor drop below the "ADD" mark.

3 If topping-up is necessary, use clean fluid of the specified type (see *"Weekly checks"*). Check for leaks if frequent topping-up is required. Do not run the engine without fluid in the reservoir.

4 After component renewal, or if the fluid level has been allowed to fall so low that air has entered the hydraulic system, bleeding must be carried out as follows.

5 Fill the reservoir to the correct level as described above.

6 Chock the rear wheels then jack up the front of the vehicle and support it on axle stands (see *"Jacking and vehicle support"*).

7 Turn the steering wheel repeatedly from full lock one way, to full lock the other way, and top-up the fluid level as necessary.

8 Lower the car to the ground then start the engine and allow it to idle.

9 Turn the steering wheel slowly to the full right lock position and hold it there for ten seconds.

10 Now turn the steering wheel slowly to the full left lock position and hold it there for ten seconds.

11 Top-up the fluid level again if necessary.

12 Repeat paragraphs 9 and 10 ten times. Move the car forward slightly to avoid excessive wear on the tyres and repeat paragraphs 9 and 10 a further ten times. Repeatedly check and if necessary top-up the fluid level during this operation.

13 On completion, stop the engine, recheck the fluid level then refit the reservoir filler cap.

22 Steering pump - removal and refitting

Removal

1 Remove the auxiliary drivebelt as described in Chapter 1.

2 Drain approximately three litres of coolant from the radiator as described in Chapter 1.

3 Disconnect the radiator top hose from the thermostat housing.

4 Remove the cold air inlet duct from the control module box and disconnect the fluid hose from the clip on the engine oil dipstick tube.

22.5 Steering pump guard plate upper mounting bolt (arrowed)

23.2 Slackening the track rod end locknut

5 Undo the guard plate upper mounting bolt and remove the spacer sleeve, then slacken the guard plate lower mounting nut **(see illustration)**.
6 Slacken the fluid pressure pipe union nut one quarter of a turn.
7 Undo the five pump mounting bolts; three are accessible through the holes in the pump pulley and two are at the rear of the pump.
8 Place absorbent rags beneath the pump then lift the pump up and out of the mounting bracket.
9 Unscrew the pressure pipe union and recover the O-ring.
10 Using a sharp knife make a small cut lengthways in the fluid return hose, just sufficiently long to enable the hose to be pulled off the pipe stub on the pump. Note that the hose must not be shortened beyond the marking stripe at the end.
11 Raise and support the front of the car so that the wheels are just clear of the ground.

12 Position a suitable container beneath the front of the car and collect the fluid from the hoses as the steering is turned from lock to lock.
13 If a new pump is to be fitted, have the pulley and reservoir transferred to it by a dealer as special tools are required.

Refitting

14 Refitting is a reversal of removal bearing in mind the following points:
a) Use a new O-ring on pressure pipe union. Trim off the cut end of the return hose before reconnecting to the pipe stub.
b) Tighten the mounting and guard plate bolts to the specified torque.
c) Refit the auxiliary drivebelt and top-up the cooling system as described in Chapter 1.
d) Refill the pump reservoir and bleed the system as described in Section 21.

23 Track rod end - removal and refitting

Removal

1 Chock the rear wheels then jack up the front of the vehicle and support it on axle stands (see "Jacking and vehicle support"). Remove the appropriate front roadwheel.
2 Counterhold the track rod and slacken the track rod end locknut by half a turn **(see illustration)**.
3 Unscrew the track rod end ballpin nut. Separate the ballpin from the steering arm with a proprietary balljoint separator, then remove the nut and disengage the ballpin from the arm **(see illustrations)**.
4 Unscrew the track rod end from the track rod, counting the number of turns needed to remove it. Record this number.

23.3a Release the track rod end ballpin using a balljoint separator . . .

23.3b . . . then remove the track rod end from the steering arm

Refitting

5 Screw the track rod end onto the track rod by the same number of turns noted during removal.

6 Engage the ballpin in the steering arm. Fit a new nut and tighten it to the specified torque.

7 Counterhold the track rod and tighten the locknut.

8 Refit the front wheel, lower the car and tighten the wheel bolts in a diagonal sequence to the specified torque.

9 Have the front wheel toe-in checked and adjusted by a Volvo dealer.

24 Wheel alignment and steering angles - general information

1 A car's steering and suspension geometry is defined in four basic settings - all angles are expressed in degrees (toe settings are also expressed as a measurement); the relevant settings are camber, castor, steering axis inclination, and toe setting. On Volvo 850 models, only the front camber and the front and rear wheel toe settings are adjustable.

2 Camber is the angle at which the front wheels are set from the vertical when viewed from the front or rear of the car. "Negative camber" is the amount (in degrees) that the wheels are tilted inward at the top from the vertical.

3 The front camber angle is adjusted by slackening the steering knuckle-to-suspension strut mounting bolts and repositioning the steering knuckle assemblies as necessary.

4 Castor is the angle between the steering axis and a vertical line when viewed from each side of the car. "Positive castor" is when the steering axis is inclined rearward at the top.

5 Steering axis inclination is the angle (when viewed from the front of the vehicle) between the vertical and an imaginary line drawn through the front suspension strut upper mounting and the control arm balljoint.

6 Toe setting is the amount by which the distance between the front inside edges of the roadwheels (measured at hub height) differs from the diametrically opposite distance measured between the rear inside edges of the roadwheels. "Toe-in" is when the roadwheels point inwards, towards each other at the front, while "toe-out" is when they splay outwards from each other at the front.

7 The front wheel toe setting is adjusted by altering the length of the steering track rods on both sides.

8 The rear wheel toe setting is adjusted by altering the position of the rear suspension transverse arm-to-trailing arm mountings.

9 With the exception of the front and rear toe settings, and front camber angles all other suspension and steering angles are set during manufacture and no adjustment is possible. It can be assumed, therefore, that unless the vehicle has suffered accident damage all the preset angles will be correct.

10 Special optical measuring equipment is necessary to accurately check and adjust the front and rear toe-settings and front camber angles and this work should be carried out by a Volvo dealer or similar expert.

Chapter 11
Bodywork and fittings

Contents

Degrees of difficulty

Easy, suitable for novice with little experience	Fairly easy, suitable for beginner with some experience	Fairly difficult, suitable for competent DIY mechanic	Difficult, suitable for experienced DIY mechanic	Very difficult, suitable for expert DIY or professional

Specifications

Torque wrench settings — Nm

	Nm
Front seat tracks to floor	40
Front seat belt inertia reels	48
Front seat belt lower anchorages to seat*	20
Rear seat belt lower anchorages	48

New bolts must be used

1 General information

The bodyshell is made of pressed-steel sections, and is available in four-door Saloon and five-door Estate versions. Most components are welded together but some use is made of structural adhesives. The doors and door pillars are reinforced against side impacts as part of the side impact protection system (SIPS).

A number of structural components and body panels are made of galvanised steel to provide a high level of protection against corrosion. Extensive use is also made of plastic materials, mainly in the interior, but also in exterior components. The front and rear bumpers are moulded from a synthetic material that is very strong and yet light.

Plastic components such as wheel arch liners are fitted to the underside of the vehicle to further improve corrosion resistance.

2 Maintenance - bodywork and underframe
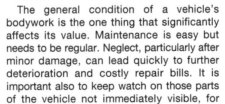

The general condition of a vehicle's bodywork is the one thing that significantly affects its value. Maintenance is easy but needs to be regular. Neglect, particularly after minor damage, can lead quickly to further deterioration and costly repair bills. It is important also to keep watch on those parts of the vehicle not immediately visible, for instance the underside, inside all the wheel arches and the lower part of the engine compartment.

The basic maintenance routine for the bodywork is washing preferably with a lot of water, from a hose. This will remove all the loose solids which may have stuck to the vehicle. It is important to flush these off in such a way as to prevent grit from scratching the finish. The wheel arches and underframe need washing in the same way to remove any accumulated mud which will retain moisture and tend to encourage rust. Oddly enough, the best time to clean the undertrame and wheel arches is in wet weather when the mud is thoroughly wet and soft. In very wet weather the underframe is usually cleaned of large accumulations automatically and this is a good time for inspection.

Periodically, except on vehicles with a wax-based underbody protective coating, it is a good idea to have the whole of the underframe of the vehicle steam cleaned, engine compartment included, so that a thorough inspection can be carried out to see what minor repairs and renovations are necessary. Steam cleaning is available at many garages and is necessary for removal of the accumulation of oily grime which sometimes is allowed to become thick in certain areas. If steam cleaning facilities are not available, there are one or two excellent grease solvents available which can be brush applied; the dirt can then be simply hosed off. Note that these methods should not be used on vehicles with wax-based underbody protective coating or the coating will be removed. Such vehicles should be inspected annually, preferably just prior to winter, when the underbody should be washed down and any damage to the wax coating repaired using underseal. Ideally, a completely fresh coat should be applied. It would also be worth considering the use of such wax-based protection for injection into door panels, sills, box sections, etc, as an additional safeguard against rust damage where such protection is not provided by the vehicle manufacturer.

After washing paintwork, wipe off with a chamois leather to give an unspotted clear finish. A coat of clear protective wax polish will give added protection against chemical pollutants in the air. If the paintwork sheen has dulled or oxidised, use a cleaner/polisher combination to restore the brilliance of the shine. This requires a little effort, but such dulling is usually caused because regular washing has been neglected. Care needs to be taken with metallic paintwork as special non-abrasive cleaner/polisher is required to avoid damage to the finish.

Always check that the door and ventilator opening drain holes and pipes are completely clear so that water can be drained out. Bright work should be treated in the same way as paint work. Windscreens and windows can be kept clear of the smeary film which often appears by the use of a proprietary glass cleaner. Never use any form of wax or other body or chromium polish on glass.

3 Maintenance - upholstery and carpets

Mats and carpets should be brushed or vacuum cleaned regularly to keep them free of grit. If they are badly stained remove them from the vehicle for scrubbing or sponging and make quite sure they are dry before refitting. Seats and interior trim panels can be kept clean by wiping with a damp cloth and a proprietary upholstery cleaner. If they do become stained (which can be more apparent on light coloured upholstery) use a little liquid detergent and a soft nail brush to scour the grime out of the grain of the material. Do not forget to keep the headlining clean in the same way as the upholstery. When using liquid cleaners inside the vehicle do not over-wet the surfaces being cleaned. Excessive damp could get into the seams and padded interior causing stains, offensive odours or even rot. If the inside of the vehicle gets wet accidentally it is worthwhile taking some trouble to dry it out properly, particularly where carpets are involved. Do not leave oil or electric heaters inside the vehicle for this purpose.

4 Minor body damage - repair

Repair of minor scratches in bodywork

If the scratch is very superficial, and does not penetrate to the metal of the bodywork, repair is very simple. Lightly rub the area of the scratch with a paintwork renovator, or a very fine cutting paste, to remove loose paint from the scratch, and to clear the surrounding bodywork of wax polish. Rinse the area with clean water.

Apply touch-up paint to the scratch using a fine paint brush; continue to apply fine layers of paint until the surface of the paint in the scratch is level with the surrounding paintwork. Allow the new paint at least two weeks to harden: then blend it into the surrounding paintwork by rubbing the scratch area with a paintwork renovator or a very fine cutting paste. Finally, apply wax polish.

Where the scratch has penetrated right through to the metal of the bodywork, causing the metal to rust, a different repair technique is required. Remove any loose rust from the bottom of the scratch with a penknife, then apply rust-inhibiting paint, to prevent the formation of rust in the future. Using a rubber or nylon applicator fill the scratch with bodystopper paste. If required, this paste can be mixed with cellulose thinners, to provide a very thin paste which is ideal for filling narrow scratches. Before the stopper-paste in the scratch hardens, wrap a piece of smooth cotton rag around the top of a finger. Dip the finger in cellulose thinners, and then quickly sweep it across the surface of the stopper-paste in the scratch; this will ensure that the surface of the stopper-paste is slightly hollowed. The scratch can now be painted over as described earlier in this Section.

Repair of dents in bodywork

When deep denting of the vehicle's bodywork has taken place, the first task is to pull the dent out, until the affected bodywork almost attains its original shape. There is little point in trying to restore the original shape completely, as the metal in the damaged area will have stretched on impact and cannot be reshaped fully to its original contour. It is better to bring the level of the dent up to a point which is about 3 mm below the level of the surrounding bodywork. In cases where the dent is very shallow anyway, it is not worth trying to pull it out at all. If the underside of the dent is accessible, it can be hammered out gently from behind, using a mallet with a wooden or plastic head. Whilst doing this, hold a suitable block of wood firmly against the outside of the panel to absorb the impact from the hammer blows and thus prevent a large area of the bodywork from being "belled-out".

Should the dent be in a section of the bodywork which has a double skin or some other factor making it inaccessible from behind, a different technique is called for. Drill several small holes through the metal inside the area - particularly in the deeper section. Then screw long self-tapping screws into the holes just sufficiently for them to gain a good purchase in the metal. Now the dent can be pulled out by pulling on the protruding heads of the screws with a pair of pliers.

The next stage of the repair is the removal of the paint from the damaged area, and from an inch or so of the surrounding "sound" bodywork. This is accomplished most easily by using a wire brush or abrasive pad on a power drill, although it can be done just as effectively by hand using sheets of abrasive paper. To complete the preparation for filling, score the surface of the bare metal with a screwdriver or the tang of a file, or alternatively, drill small holes in the affected area. This will provide a really good "key" for the filler paste.

To complete the repair see the Section on filling and re-spraying.

Repair of Rust holes or gashes in bodywork

Remove all paint from the affected area and from an inch or so of the surrounding "sound" bodywork, using an abrasive pad or a wire brush on a power drill. If these are not available a few sheets of abrasive paper will do the job just as effectively. With the paint removed you will be able to gauge the severity of the corrosion and therefore decide whether to renew the whole panel (if this is possible) or to repair the affected area. New body panels are not as expensive as most people think and it is often quicker and more satisfactory to fit a new panel than to attempt to repair large areas of corrosion.

Remove all fittings from the affected area except those which will act as a guide to the original shape of the damaged bodywork (eg headlight shells etc). Then, using tin snips or a hacksaw blade, remove all loose metal and any other metal badly affected by corrosion. Hammer the edges of the hole inwards in order to create a slight depression for the filler paste.

Wire brush the affected area to remove the powdery rust from the surface of the remaining metal. Paint the affected area with rust inhibiting paint; if the back of the rusted area is accessible treat this also.

Before filling can take place it will be necessary to block the hole in some way. This can be achieved by the use of aluminium or plastic mesh, or aluminium tape.

Aluminium or plastic mesh or glass fibre matting is probably the best material to use for a large hole. Cut a piece to the approximate size and shape of the hole to be filled, then position it in the hole so that its edges are below the level of the surrounding bodywork. It can be retained in position by several blobs of filler paste around its periphery.

Aluminium tape should be used for small or very narrow holes. Pull a piece off the roll and trim it to the approximate size and shape required, then pull off the backing paper (if used) and stick the tape over the hole; it can be overlapped if the thickness of one piece is insufficient. Burnish down the edges of the tape with the handle of a screwdriver or similar, to ensure that the tape is securely attached to the metal underneath.

Bodywork repairs - filling and re-spraying

Before using this Section, see the Sections on dent, deep scratch, rust holes and gash repairs.

Many types of bodyfiller are available, but generally speaking those proprietary kits which contain a tin of filler paste and a tube of resin hardener are best for this type of repair; some can be used directly from the tube. A wide, flexible plastic or nylon applicator will be found invaluable for imparting a smooth and well contoured finish to the surface of the filler.

Mix up a little filler on a clean piece of card or board - measure the hardener carefully (follow the maker's instructions on the pack) otherwise the filler will set too rapidly or too slowly. Using the applicator, apply the filler paste to the prepared area; draw the applicator across the surface of the filler to achieve the correct contour and to level the filler surface. As soon as a contour that approximates to the correct one is achieved, stop working the paste - if you carry on too long the paste will become sticky and begin to "pick up" on the applicator. Continue to add thin layers of filler paste at twenty-minute intervals until the level of the filler is just proud of the surrounding bodywork.

Once the filler has hardened, excess can be removed using a metal plane or file. From then on, progressively finer grades of abrasive paper should be used, starting with a 40 grade production paper and finishing with 400 grade wet-and-dry paper. Always wrap the abrasive paper around a flat rubber, cork, or wooden block - otherwise the surface of the filler will not be completely flat. During the smoothing of the filler surface the wet-and-dry paper should be periodically rinsed in water. This will ensure that a very smooth finish is imparted to the filler at the final stage.

At this stage the "dent" should be surrounded by a ring of bare metal, which in turn should be encircled by the finely "feathered" edge of the good paintwork. Rinse the repair area with clean water, until all of the dust produced by the rubbing-down operation has gone.

Spray the whole repair area with a light coat of primer - this will show up any imperfections in the surface of the filler. Repair these imperfections with fresh filler paste or bodystopper, and once more smooth the surface with abrasive paper. If bodystopper is used, it can be mixed with cellulose thinners to form a really thin paste which is ideal for filling small holes. Repeat this spray and repair procedure until you are satisfied that the surface of the filler, and the feathered edge of the paintwork are perfect. Clean the repair area with clean water and allow to dry fully.

The repair area is now ready for final spraying. Paint spraying must be carried out in a warm, dry, windless and dust free atmosphere. This condition can be created artificially if you have access to a large indoor working area, but if you are forced to work in the open, you will have to pick your day very carefully. If you are working indoors, dousing the floor in the work area with water will help to settle the dust which would otherwise be in the atmosphere. If the repair area is confined to one body panel, mask off the surrounding panels; this will help to minimise the effects of a slight mis-match in paint colours. Bodywork fittings (eg chrome strips, door handles etc) will also need to be masked off. Use genuine masking tape and several thicknesses of newspaper for the masking operations.

Before commencing to spray, agitate the aerosol can thoroughly, then spray a test area (an old tin, or similar) until the technique is mastered. Cover the repair area with a thick coat of primer; the thickness should be built up using several thin layers of paint rather than one thick one. Using 400 grade wet-and-dry paper, rub down the surface of the primer until it is really smooth. While doing this, the work area should be thoroughly doused with water, and the wet-and-dry paper periodically rinsed in water. Allow to dry before spraying on more paint.

Spray on the top coat, again building up the thickness by using several thin layers of paint. Start spraying in the centre of the repair area and then, with a single side-to-side motion, work outwards until the whole repair area and about 50 mm of the surrounding original paintwork is covered. Remove all masking material 10 to 15 minutes after spraying on the final coat of paint.

Allow the new paint at least two weeks to harden, then, using a paintwork renovator or a very fine cutting paste, blend the edges of the paint into the existing paintwork. Finally, apply wax polish.

Plastic components

With the use of more and more plastic body components by the vehicle manufacturers (eg bumpers, spoilers, and in some cases major body panels), rectification of more serious damage to such items has become a matter of either entrusting repair work to a specialist in this field, or renewing complete components. Repair of such damage by the DIY owner is not really feasible owing to the cost of the equipment and materials required for effecting such repairs. The basic technique involves making a groove along the line of the crack in the plastic using a rotary burr in a power drill. The damaged part is then welded back together by using a hot air gun to heat up and fuse a plastic filler rod into the groove. Any excess plastic is then removed and the area rubbed down to a smooth finish. It is important that a filler rod of the correct plastic is used, as body components can be made of a variety of different types (eg polycarbonate, ABS, polypropylene).

Damage of a less serious nature (abrasions, minor cracks etc) can be repaired by the DIY owner using a two-part epoxy filler repair material. Once mixed in equal proportions, this is used in similar fashion to the bodywork filler used on metal panels. The filler is usually cured in twenty to thirty minutes, ready for sanding and painting.

If the owner is renewing a complete component himself, or if he has repaired it with epoxy filler, he will be left with the problem of finding a suitable paint for finishing which is compatible with the type of plastic used. At one time the use of a universal paint was not possible owing to the complex range of plastics encountered in body component applications. Standard paints, generally speaking, will not bond to plastic or rubber satisfactorily. However, it is now possible to obtain a plastic body parts finishing kit which consists of a pre-primer treatment, a primer and coloured top coat. Full instructions are normally supplied with a kit, but basically the method of use is to first apply the pre-primer to the component concerned and allow it to dry for up to 30 minutes. Then the primer is applied and left to dry for about an hour before finally applying the special coloured top coat. The result is a correctly coloured component where the paint will flex with the plastic or rubber, a property that standard paint does not normally possess.

5   Major body damage - repair

Where serious damage has occurred or large areas need renewal due to neglect, completely new sections or panels will need welding in - this is best left to professionals. If the damage is due to impact, it will also be necessary to check completely the alignment of the body shell structure. Due to the principle of construction, the strength and shape of the whole can be affected by damage to a part. In such instances, the services of a Volvo agent with specialist checking jigs are essential. If a body is left misaligned, it is first of all dangerous as the car will not handle properly and secondly uneven stresses will be imposed on the steering, engine and transmission, causing abnormal wear or complete failure. Tyre wear may also be excessive.

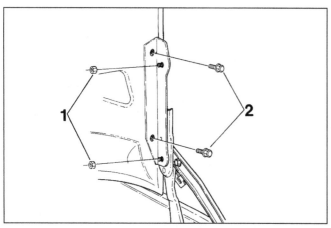

6.8a Bonnet adjustment details

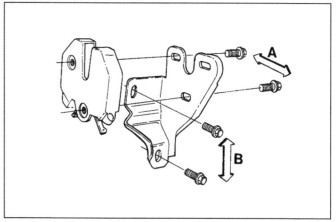

6.8b Bonnet lock adjustment points

1   Hinge nuts - vertical adjustment
2   Hinge bolts - fore and aft adjustment

A   Lateral adjustment   B   Vertical adjustment

6   Bonnet - removal, refitting and adjustment

Removal

1 Open the bonnet, release the stud fasteners and remove the inner soundproofing panel.
2 Disconnect the washer tube from the bonnet at the T-piece. Unclip the tube and move it aside.
3 Mark around the bonnet-to-hinge retaining bolts with a felt tip pen for reference when refitting.
4 With the aid of an assistant, support the bonnet and remove the hinge bolts. Lift off the bonnet and store it in a safe place.

Refitting and adjustment

5 Before refitting, place pads of rags under the corners of the bonnet near the hinges to protect the paintwork from damage.
6 Fit the bonnet and insert the hinge bolts. Just nip the bolts up in their previously marked positions.
7 Reconnect the washer tube and refit the soundproofing panel.
8 Shut the bonnet and check its fit. The two hinge bolts each side control the fore and aft adjustment; the two hinge nuts each side control the height of the bonnet at the rear. Front height is adjusted by altering the position of the bonnet lock mounting brackets on each side **(see illustrations)**.
9 Tighten the hinge nuts and bolts securely when adjustment is correct.

7   Bonnet release cable - removal, refitting and adjustment

Removal

1 The release cable assembly is in two sections - one section runs from the release handle in the passenger compartment to the left-hand, or right-hand bonnet lock, as applicable, and the other section runs between the two bonnet locks.
2 Open the bonnet then from inside the car, disconnect the inner cable end from the release handle and remove the outer cable and adjuster from the support bracket **(see illustration)**.
3 Pull the cable through the bulkhead grommet and disconnect the other end from the left-hand, or right-hand bonnet lock. Release the cable-ties and remove the cable.
4 Slacken the bonnet lock bolts and move the two locks toward each other to introduce some slack in the interconnecting cable.
5 Disconnect the cable ends from the lock levers, release the cable-ties and remove the cable.

Refitting and adjustment

6 Refit by reversing the removal operations. Adjust the threaded section of the cable at the release lever end, to take most of the slack out of the inner in the resting position. Adjust the interconnecting cable to remove the slack by moving the bonnet locks laterally. Tighten all the bolts securely on completion.

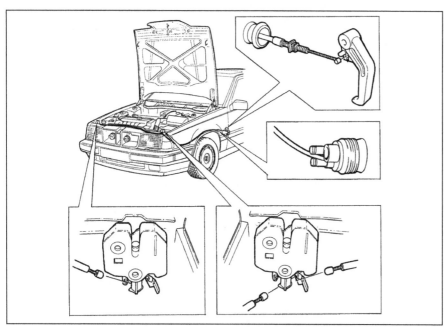

7.2 Bonnet release cable components and attachments

9.3 Turn the door wiring connector (arrowed) anti-clockwise to disconnect

9.5 Door hinge pin retaining grub screw (arrowed)

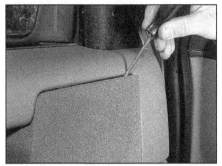

10.2 Carefully prise off the speaker grille

8 Bonnet lock - removal and refitting

Removal

1 Open the bonnet and mark the position of the bonnet lock and lock mounting bracket on the side concerned, using a felt tip pen.
2 Undo the two bolts securing the relevant bonnet lock to the mounting bracket.
3 Lift off the lock, disconnect the inter-connecting release cable and, depending to the side being worked on, the release cable leading from the release handle. Remove the lock.

Refitting

4 Refitting is a reversal of removal. Take up the slack in the interconnecting release cable by moving the lock(s) laterally in the mounting bracket. Adjust the height of the lock for correct fit and closure of the bonnet, by moving the mounting bracket up or down as necessary (see illustration 6.8b).

9 Doors - removal, refitting and adjustment

Removal

1 Disconnect the battery negative lead.
2 Open the door and support it with a jack or axle stand, using rags to protect the paintwork.

3 Disconnect the front door electrical wiring by turning the connector anti-clockwise and pulling it out of the socket on the pillar (see illustration). If removing a rear door, release the convoluted sleeve from the door pillar and disconnect the connector located inside the sleeve.
4 Release the door check strap by undoing the bolt securing it to the pillar bracket.
5 Undo the grub screw that locks the hinge pin to the hinge bracket on the pillar (see illustration).
6 With the help of an assistant, lift the door upwards to disengage the hinge pins, then remove the door.

Refitting and adjustment

7 Refit the door by reversing the removal operations then adjust as follows.
8 Close the door and check the alignment with the surrounding body panels. The gap should be equal all round and the door must be flush with the outside of the car. The rear edge of the front door should be 0 to 1.5 mm outside the front edge of the rear door.
9 Fore and aft adjustment of the door at the top and bottom is by shims inserted between the hinges and the door. Shims are available in thicknesses of 0.3 and 0.5 mm and can be slid into place after slackening the hinge retaining bolts.
10 Vertical and lateral adjustment is made by slackening the hinge retaining bolts slightly and moving the door as necessary.
11 Once the correct door fit is obtained, adjust the striker plate so that the door opens

and closes easily but firmly. With the door handle pulled out, shut the door and check that the lock slides over the striker plate without scraping.

10 Door interior trim panel - removal and refitting

Removal

1 On models with manually operated windows, lift the catch on the back of the handle and slide the handle cover plate away from the knob. Insert a 6.0 mm diameter punch into the hole in the centre of the handle, and at the same time pull the handle off the regulator shaft.
2 Remove the speaker grille by inserting a screwdriver behind one corner and carefully prising off (see illustration).
3 Undo the four speaker retaining screws, remove the speaker and disconnect the wiring connectors (see illustration).
4 Remove the inner door handle by pulling it firmly upward off the handle lever (see illustration).
5 Remove the padded panel above the door handle by levering it upward at the bottom to release it from the three internal stud fasteners. Note that some force is necessary, and it is quite likely that the fasteners will break off during this operation. Be prepared to obtain new ones for refitting.
6 Undo the two screws now exposed behind the padded panel (see illustration).

10.3 Undo the four screws and withdraw the speaker

10.4 Pull the door interior handle off the lever

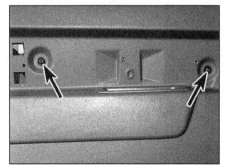

10.6 Undo the two screws (arrowed) located behind the padded panel

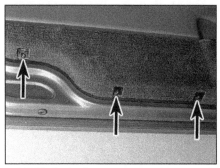

10.7 Undo the four screws at the base of the trim panel (three shown arrowed)

10.8 On the front door trim panel, release the plastic stud screw

10.9 Lift the trim panel upwards and off the door

7 Undo the four screws (or three on the rear door) securing the lower edge of the trim panel to the door **(see illustration)**.
8 On the front door, release the plastic stud screw from the front edge of the panel by undoing the screw and pulling out the sleeve **(see illustration)**.
9 Lift the trim panel upwards and off the door **(see illustration)**. If working on the rear door, disconnect the door warning light wiring at the connector.

Refitting

10 Refitting is a reversal of removal but obtain new stud fasteners for the padded panel if any were broken during removal. Transfer the original fasteners (or fit the new ones) to the padded panel then, to refit, push the panel into place so that the three fasteners engage in their holes in the main panel **(see illustrations)**.

11 Door handle and lock components - removal and refitting

Removal

Front door lock cylinder

1 Remove the door interior trim panel as described in Section 10.
2 From the edge of the door, prise out the cover plate over the outer handle retaining screws **(see illustration)**.
3 Insert the key into the lock cylinder and insert a small screwdriver into the hole in the door next to the two outer handle retaining screws. Push the screwdriver in, to depress the spring plate, and pull the lock cylinder out of the handle **(see illustration)**.

Front door outer handle

4 Remove the lock cylinder as described previously.
5 Slacken the two door lock retaining screws **(see illustration)**.
6 Undo the two outer handle retaining screws from the edge of the door **(see illustration)**.
7 Withdraw the handle from the lock assembly, then disengage the other end from the forward pivot **(see illustrations)**.

Front door lock assembly

8 Remove the window regulator cassette as described in Section 12.
9 Remove the front door lock cylinder and outer handle as described previously.
10 Undo the window guide channel lower retaining screw and remove the guide channel **(see illustration)**.
11 Disconnect the lock assembly wiring loom at the connector and release the cable clip

10.10a Fit the stud fasteners to the padded panel

10.10b Then engage the stud fasteners in the main panel holes to refit

11.2 Prise out the cover plate over the outer handle retaining screws

11.3 Pull out the cylinder while depressing the spring plate with a screwdriver

11.5 Slacken the two door lock retaining screws

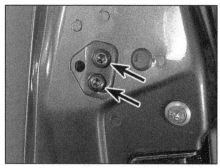

11.6 Undo the two outer handle retaining screws from the edge of the door

11.7a Withdraw the handle from the lock
assembly . . .

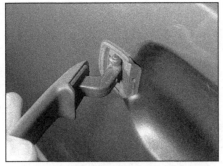

11.7b . . . then disengage the other end
from the forward pivot

11.10 Undo the window guide channel
lower retaining screw

11.11a Disconnect the lock assembly
wiring loom at the connector . . .

11.11b . . . then push the cable grommet
into the door and feed the loom through

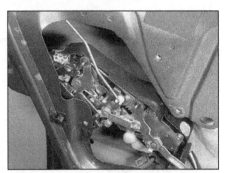

11.12 Removing the lock assembly from
the door

from the door. Push the cable grommet into
the door and feed the loom through with it
(see illustrations).
12 Undo the two lock retaining screws from
the edge of the door and manipulate the
assembly out through the door aperture **(see
illustration)**.

Rear door outer handle

13 Remove the door interior trim panel as
described in Section 10.
14 From the edge of the door, prise out the
cover plate over the outer handle retaining
screws.
15 Slacken the two door lock retaining
screws.
16 Undo the two outer handle retaining
screws from the edge of the door.
17 Withdraw the handle from the lock
assembly then disengage the other end from
the forward pivot.

Rear door lock assembly

18 Remove the window regulator cassette as
described in Section 12.
19 Remove the outer handle as described
previously.
20 Remove the weatherstrip at the rear of the
window.
21 Lower the window glass fully.
22 Remove the wiring clamp at the bottom of
the window rear guide channel, undo the two
screws and pull the channel up and out.
23 Disconnect the lock assembly wiring loom
at the connector, and release the cable clip
from the door. Push the cable grommet into

the door and feed the loom through with it.
24 Undo the two lock retaining screws from
the edge of the door, and manipulate the
assembly out through the door aperture.

Refitting

25 Refitting is a reversal of the relevant
removal procedure. Check for correct
operation before refitting the door trim.

**12 Door window regulator and
glass** - removal and refitting

Removal

Window regulator motors

1 Remove the door interior trim panel as
described in Section 10.

12.4 Removing the window regulator
motor

2 Raise the window and secure it in the raised
position with adhesive tape over the top of the
door frame.
3 Disconnect the motor wiring at the
connector.
4 Undo the three bolts and withdraw the
motor from the regulator cassette **(see
illustration)**.

Window regulator cassette

5 Remove the window regulator motor as
described previously.
6 Remove the plastic cover over the access
panel at the rear of the door **(see illustration)**.
7 Using pliers, slip the inner door handle
return spring off the handle lever **(see
illustration)**.
8 Undo the pivot bolt at the handle lever base
and collect the return spring.
9 Undo the three bolts and remove the
handle lever frame **(see illustration)**.

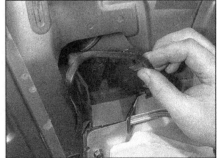

12.6 Remove the plastic cover over the
access panel at the rear of the door

12.7 Release the inner door handle return spring from the handle lever

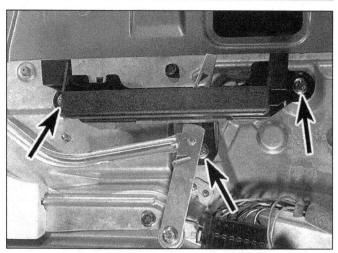

12.9 Undo the three handle lever frame retaining bolts (arrowed)

10 Lower the window glass until the lift rail slides are accessible through the apertures in the door.

11 Extract the locking clips from the lift rail slides and release the lift arms from the slides **(see illustration)**.

12 Undo the eight bolts securing the cassette to the door. Support the window glass then withdraw the cassette from the door **(see illustration)**.

Front door window glass

13 Remove the window regulator cassette as described previously.

14 Carefully prise up the inner weatherstrip and remove it from the top edge of the door panel **(see illustration)**.

15 Move the glass down as far as it will go, tip it up at the rear and lift it out of the door **(see illustration)**.

Rear door window glass

16 Remove the window regulator cassette as described previously.

17 Carefully prise up the inner weatherstrip and remove it from the top edge of the door panel.

18 Remove the wiring clamp at the bottom of the window rear guide channel, undo the two screws and pull the channel up and out.

19 Move the glass down as far as it will go, tip it up at the rear and lift it out of the door.

Refitting

20 Refitting is a reversal of the relevant removal procedure. Check for correct operation before refitting the door trim.

13 Tailgate interior trim panel - removal and refitting

Removal

1 Open the tailgate and remove the cover around the inner handle by inserting a spatula under the upper edge and forcing it down **(see illustration)**.

2 Remove the cover over the high level stop light by grasping it on each side and pulling down. Take care not to break the fragile inner retaining catches **(see illustration)**.

3 Insert a strip of cardboard about 180 x 100 mm between the upper and lower panels on each side. The edges of the lower panel are quite sharp and will easily scratch the upper panel if not protected.

4 Grip between the tailgate weatherstrip and the trim panel along the lower edge and pull

12.11 Extract the locking clips from the lift rail slides

12.12 Removing the window regulator cassette from the door

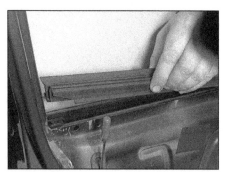

12.14 Prise up the door inner weatherstrip

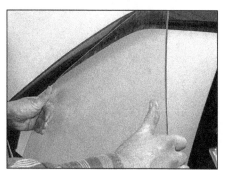

12.15 Lifting out the door window glass

13.1 Remove the tailgate inner handle cover with a spatula

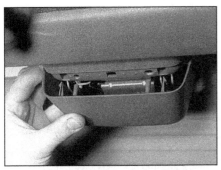

13.2 Pull off the high level stop light cover

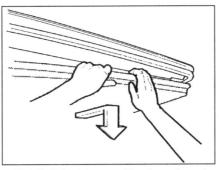

13.4 Pull the trim panel backwards and downwards to free the inner retainers

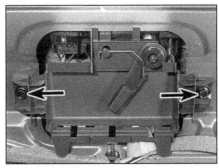

16.2 Undo the two bolts (arrowed) securing the inner handle to the tailgate

the panel backwards and downwards to free the inner retainers **(see illustration)**.
5 Bend the lower edge of the panel down to clear the tailgate then push it forwards by striking it sharply on each side. Catch the panel as the upper retainers come free.
6 Remove the small upper trim panel by pulling both edges inward and the upper edge backwards.

Refitting

7 Refitting is a reversal of removal. Ensure that the cardboard strips are used to protect the upper panel when refitting the lower panel.

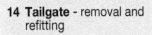
14 Tailgate - removal and refitting

Removal

1 Disconnect the battery negative lead.
2 Using a small screwdriver, carefully prise out the courtesy light in the centre of the rear roof section trim. Disconnect the wiring and remove the light.
3 Prise out the plastic caps over the two rear roof section trim retaining screws. Undo the screws and remove the trim.
4 Prise out the caps over the combined roof sill and D-pillar trim panel and undo the screws on both sides. Release the panels by pulling them free of their retaining clips.
5 Remove the tailgate interior trim panel as described in Section 13.

6 Lift up the removable floor panel at the right-hand rear of the load space area.
7 Disconnect the tailgate washer hose downstream of the in-line filter now exposed. Pull the hose from its location.
8 Disconnect the wiring connector on the left-hand side and push it through the hinge hole.
9 Undo the screws and remove the tailgate side trim rails on each side.
10 With the help of an assistant, undo the two screws each side and lift away the tailgate.

Refitting

11 Refitting is a reversal of removal.

15 Tailgate support struts - removal and refitting

Removal

1 Using a small screwdriver, carefully prise out the courtesy light in the centre of the rear roof section trim. Disconnect the wiring and remove the light.
2 Prise out the plastic caps over the two rear roof section trim retaining screws. Undo the screws and remove the trim.
3 Prise out the caps over the combined roof sill and D-pillar trim panel and undo the screws on both sides. Release the panels by pulling them free of their retaining clips.
4 Support the tailgate in the open position using a suitable prop.
5 Disconnect the bracket securing the strut to the body.

6 Release the strut balljoints and remove the strut from the car.

Refitting

7 Refitting is a reversal of removal.

16 Tailgate lock components - removal and refitting

Removal

Lock assembly

1 Remove the tailgate interior trim panel as described in Section 13.
2 Undo the two bolts securing the inner handle to the tailgate **(see illustration)**.
3 Disconnect the central locking wiring connector.
4 Disconnect the link rods to the exterior handle and lock cylinder.
5 Undo the three bolts securing the lock and manipulate the assembly out of the tailgate aperture **(see illustration)**.

Exterior handle

6 Remove the tailgate wiper motor (Chapter 12).
7 Disconnect the link rods at the lock cylinder and exterior handle lever.
8 Disconnect the number plate light wiring connector and release the cable clips.
9 Undo the four nuts, two near the centre and two at the edges and carefully withdraw the exterior handle from the tailgate **(see illustrations)**. Feed the number plate light wiring out through the tailgate with the handle.

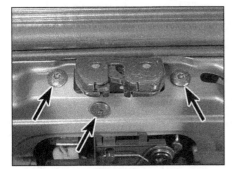

16.5 Undo the three lock retaining bolts (arrowed) and manipulate the assembly out of the tailgate

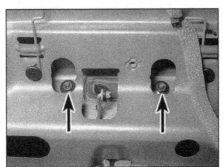

16.9a Undo the tailgate exterior handle retaining bolts (two centre bolts arrowed) . . .

16.9b . . . and withdraw the handle from the tailgate

16.11 Tailgate lock cylinder retaining circlip (arrowed)

Lock cylinder

10 Remove the exterior handle as described previously.

11 Extract the circlip at the rear of the cylinder and pull the cylinder out of the exterior handle assembly **(see illustration)**.

Refitting

12 Refitting is a reversal of the relevant removal procedure.

17 Boot lid - removal and refitting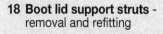

Removal

1 Open the boot and remove the soundproofing panel.

2 Disconnect the central locking system and number plate light wiring so that the boot lid is free to be removed.

3 Mark around the hinge bolts. With the aid of an assistant, undo the hinge bolts and lift away the lid.

Refitting

4 Refit by reversing the removal operations. If adjustment is necessary, first remove the rear parcel shelf as described in Section 27. Vertical and fore and aft adjustment of the front edge of the boot lid is carried out by turning the eccentric nut in the hinge below the parcel shelf. Vertical and lateral adjustment of the rear edge is carried out by repositioning the striker plate within the movement offered by the elongated bolt holes. Check the fit and closure of the boot lid, then refit the parcel shelf.

18 Boot lid support struts - removal and refitting

Removal

1 Remove the B-pillar trim panel and the rear parcel shelf as described in Section 27.

2 Release the support strut front balljoint from the mounting stud.

---

3 Extract the retaining clip securing the strut to the boot lid hinge and remove the strut.

Refitting

4 Refitting is a reversal of removal.

19 Boot lid lock components - removal and refitting

Removal

Lock assembly

1 Open the boot and remove the soundproofing panel.

2 Undo the three bolts and remove the cover plate.

3 Disconnect the link rod from the outer handle lever **(see illustration)**.

4 Disconnect the central locking motor wiring connector.

5 Open the plastic adjuster sleeve, disconnect the lock cylinder link rod, then manipulate the lock assembly out of the boot lid aperture.

Lock cylinder

6 Open the boot and remove the soundproofing panel.

7 Open the plastic adjuster sleeve and disconnect the lock cylinder link rod.

---

8 Remove the reinforcement bracket and withdraw the lock cylinder. Undo the screw in the reinforcement bracket, then insert the key and remove the cylinder.

Refitting

9 Refitting is a reversal of removal but adjust the link rod connecting the lock assembly to the lock cylinder as follows.

10 Insert the key into the lock cylinder and turn it to position 0.

11 With the link rod plastic adjuster sleeve opened and the link rods disconnected, pull the two rods toward each other and lay them in the adjuster.

12 Close the adjuster sleeve and check the operation of the lock assembly and cylinder.

13 Refit the soundproofing panel on completion.

20 Windscreen and other fixed glass - removal and refitting

Special equipment and techniques are needed for successful removal and refitting of the windscreen, rear window and side windows. Have the work carried out by a Volvo dealer or a windscreen specialist.

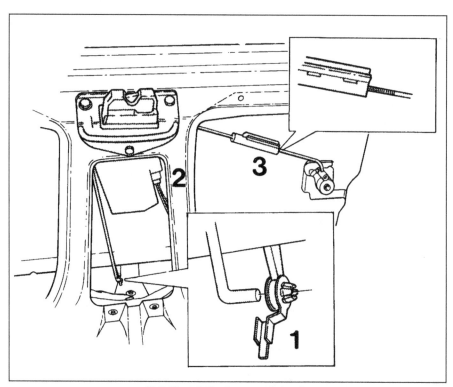

19.3 Boot lid lock removal details

1   *Disconnect the exterior handle link rod*
2   *Disconnect the wiring connector*
3   *Disconnect the lock cylinder link rod at the adjuster sleeve*

21.1 Remove the exterior mirror glass and disconnect the wiring connectors

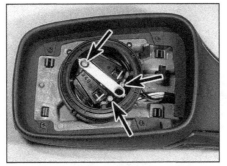

21.3 Mirror motor retaining screws (arrowed)

21.13 Prise off the trim panel from the mirror and door

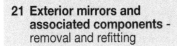

21 Exterior mirrors and associated components - removal and refitting

Removal

Mirror glass

1 Place your fingers behind the mirror glass edge nearest the door, and pull the glass straight out. Where applicable disconnect the heating element wiring **(see illustration)**.

Electrically operated mirror motor

2 Remove the mirror glass as described previously
3 Undo the three retaining screws and remove the motor, disconnecting the wiring connector as it becomes accessible **(see illustration)**.

Edge cover

4 Remove the mirror glass as described previously
5 Squeeze the four plastic retaining clips together and withdraw the front cover.
6 Undo the four screws and remove the edge cover.

Manually operated mirror (complete unit)

7 Remove the door interior trim panel as described in Section 10.

21.15a Undo the three mirror mounting bolts . . .

8 Carefully prise off the trim panel from the mirror and door and pull off the adjustment stalk rubber cover.
9 Extract the retaining clip and release the adjustment stalk from the support bracket.
10 Disconnect the wiring connector for the heating element (where applicable).
11 Undo the three retaining bolts, lift off the adjustment stalk support bracket and withdraw the mirror from the door. Release the rubber grommet from the door as the mirror is withdrawn.

Electrically operated mirror (complete unit)

12 Remove the door interior trim panel as described in Section 10.

21.15b . . . and withdraw the mirror from the door

13 Carefully prise off the trim panel from the mirror and door **(see illustration)**.
14 Disconnect the motor wiring at the connector inside the door.
15 Undo the three mounting bolts and withdraw the mirror from the door. Release the rubber grommet from the door as the mirror is withdrawn **(see illustrations)**.

Refitting

16 Refitting is a reversal of the relevant removal procedure. Where applicable, ensure that the rubber grommet is correctly located in its hole in the door.

22 Bumpers - removal and refitting

Note: *The bumpers consist of three sections; an outer plastic overrider, an energy absorbing plastic foam insert, and an aluminium inner rail. A spoiler is fitted under the front bumper on most models. Removal and refitting procedures are essentially the same for both front and rear bumpers.*

Removal

1 Undo the retaining bolt each side, release the front edge clips and remove the splash guard under the radiator.
2 If working on the front bumper, undo the screws, release the clips and remove the spoiler **(see illustrations)**.
3 Remove the rivets securing the plastic wheel arch liner to the edge of the bumper, either by drilling them out or cutting them free.

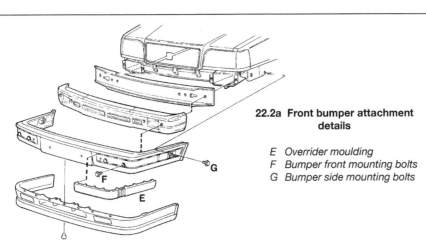

22.2a Front bumper attachment details

E *Overrider moulding*
F *Bumper front mounting bolts*
G *Bumper side mounting bolts*

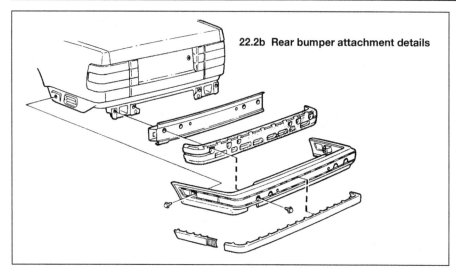

22.2b Rear bumper attachment details

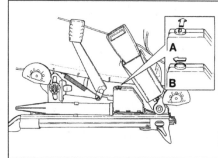

24.1 Mechanical seat belt tensioner safety locking button positions

A *Arrow on red button points across the car - tensioner is locked and safe*
B *Arrow on red button points forward - tensioner is unlocked and armed*

4 Remove the overrider moulding from the centre of the bumper by prising it free then pulling off.

5 Undo the four bolts now exposed, and the single bolt each side securing the bumper to the body. Withdraw the bumper from the car.

Refitting

6 Refit by reversing the removal operations.

23 Front grille panel - removal and refitting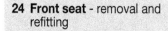

Removal

1 Open the bonnet and remove the six plastic clips at the rear of the grille by sliding them sideways.

2 Remove the grille and recover the rubber seal.

Refitting

3 Refit by reversing the removal operations.

24 Front seat - removal and refitting

Caution: Vehicles for certain markets may be equipped with a SIPS bag as part of the Side Impact Protection System. This is an air bag unit fitted into the side of the front seat backrest. Various labels around the car will advise whether the vehicle is so equipped. Identify the type of seat fitted, then proceed as follows under the appropriate sub-heading. Refer to Chapter 12 for further information on the SRS and SIPS systems.

Front seat without SIPS bag

Removal

1 If the seat is fitted with a mechanical seat belt tensioner, turn the red button in front of the seat belt stalk so that the arrow points across the belt tensioner (ie towards the side of the car) **(see illustration)**. The tensioner is now locked and the seat is safe.

⚠ *Warning: Do not carry out any work on the seat unless the seat belt tensioner is locked.*

2 If electrically operated seats are fitted,

disconnect the battery negative lead.

3 Remove the seat side compartment by releasing the forward edge and pushing backwards.

4 Undo the bolt and remove the seat belt lower anchorage from the side of the seat. Note that a new bolt will be required for refitting.

5 Move the seat forwards. Remove the single bolt from the rear of each track - these may be concealed by trim covers **(see illustrations)**.

6 Move the seat rearwards. Remove any trim covers, then remove the single bolt from the front of each track **(see illustration)**.

7 Disconnect the seat heater, seat belt switch and control unit wiring connectors (as applicable) from under the seat cushion.

8 Lift the seat upwards to release the front and rear guide pins then remove the seat from the car.

Refitting

9 Locate the seat over the guide pins, reconnect the wiring, and insert the retaining bolts. Tighten the bolts to the specified torque in the following sequence - rear inner, front outer, front inner, rear outer. Refit the bolt covers.

10 Secure the seat belt lower anchorage using a new bolt tightened to the specified torque.

24.5a **Where fitted, remove the trim cover for access to the inner seat track mounting bolt . . .**

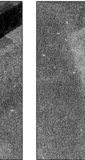

24.5b **. . . and outer mounting bolt**

24.6 **Remove the trim covers and remove the seat track front mounting bolts**

11 Refit the side compartment.
12 If the seat is fitted with a mechanical seat belt tensioner, turn the red button so that the arrow points forward to unlock the tensioner.

Front seat with SIPS bag

 Warning: There is a risk of injury if the SIPS bag is triggered inadvertently when working on the front seat. Ensure that the safety device described in the following paragraphs is installed, and never apply external force to the side of the seat. It is strongly recommended that any work involving the front seat is entrusted to a Volvo dealer. Refer to Chapter 12 for further information on the SRS system.

Removal

13 Remove the seat side compartment by releasing the forward edge and pushing backwards.
14 Remove the safety device from its holder in the side compartment and fit the safety device to the SIPS bag sensor unit on the side of the seat **(see illustration)**.
15 Ensure that the ignition is switched off then disconnect the battery negative lead.
16 Remove the seat as described previously in paragraphs 4 to 8. Do not attempt to dismantle the seat or remove any of the SIPS bag components. This work must be entrusted to a Volvo dealer.

Refitting

17 Refit the seat as described previously in paragraphs 9 and 10.
18 Remove the safety device from the SIPS bag sensor unit and return it to its holder in the side compartment. Refit the side compartment to the seat.
19 Reconnect the battery negative lead.

25 Electrically operated front seat - general information and component renewal

General information

1 An electrically operated front seat with programmable memory is optionally available for both the driver and passenger. The seat incorporates four electric motors, three under the seat and one in the backrest. The three motors under the seat control the height of the front and rear edges of the seat cushion, and the fore-and-aft position of the complete seat. The fourth motor controls the backrest vertical position.
2 A control panel on the side of the seat contains the motor control switches and the memory buttons which are used to store and adjust the various settings.
3 The operation of the seat is controlled by an electronic control unit (ECU) which also incorporates a diagnostic function. In the event of a fault in the seat components or control circuitry, a fault code will be stored in

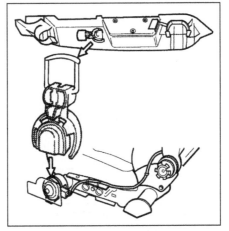

24.14 If a SIPS bag is fitted, fit the safety device to the SIPS bag sensor unit on the side of the seat before carrying out any work

the ECU memory for subsequent read-out via the diagnostic unit in the engine compartment.

Component renewal

 Warning: Do not carry out any of the following operations on cars equipped with a SIPS bag in the front seat. Some of the work in this Section entails removal of the SIPS bag sensor unit and firing circuitry which is a potentially hazardous operation. Entrust the work to a Volvo dealer on vehicles so equipped. Refer to Chapter 12 for further information on the SRS system.

Note: *Removal and refitting of any of the following components except the control panel will entail re-calibration of the seat ECU by a Volvo dealer. Until this is done the new components will not operate correctly and a fault code will be logged in the ECU memory.*

Control panel

4 Disconnect the battery negative lead.
5 Disconnect the wiring connector (yellow connector) from the ECU under the front edge of the seat cushion.
6 Remove the seat side compartment by releasing the forward edge and pushing backwards.
7 Undo the three screws on the rear of the side compartment and remove the control panel.
8 Refitting is a reversal of removal.

ECU

9 Remove the seat as described in Section 24.
10 Undo the two screws securing the ECU to the mounting bracket under the seat cushion.
11 Disconnect the wiring connectors and remove the unit.
12 Refitting is a reversal of removal. Have the ECU re-calibrated by a Volvo dealer on completion.

Fore and aft seat control motor (motor 1)

13 Remove the seat as described in Section 24.
14 Disconnect the black wiring connector for the seat motors from the ECU.
15 Undo the two bolts securing the motor to the drive gear unit. The fore and aft seat control motor is the centre of the three.
16 Trace the motor wiring back to the connector and mark the position of the contact pins in the connector. Press the pins out of the connector using a suitable tool then remove the motor from the drive gear unit.
17 Engage the wiring contact pins of the new motor into the connector.
18 Refit the motor and secure with the two bolts.
19 Refit the connector to the ECU then refit the seat as described in Section 24.
20 Have the ECU re-calibrated by a Volvo dealer on completion.

Seat cushion front height control motor (motor 4)

21 Remove the seat as described in Section 24.
22 Undo the two screws securing the ECU to the mounting bracket under the seat cushion.
23 Disconnect the wiring connectors and remove the ECU.
24 Undo the bolt securing the motor to the ECU bracket and the two bolts securing the motor to the drive gear unit.
25 Trace the motor wiring back to the connector and mark the position of the contact pins in the connector. Press the pins out of the connector using a suitable tool then remove the motor from the drive gear unit.
26 Engage the wiring contact pins of the new motor into the connector.
27 Refit the motor and secure with the three bolts.
28 Refit the ECU, then refit the seat as described in Section 24.
29 Have the ECU re-calibrated by a Volvo dealer on completion.

Seat cushion rear height control motor (motor 3)

30 The procedure is the same as described previously for the fore and aft seat control motor. The rear height control motor is the unit nearest the rear of the seat.

Drive gear unit

31 Remove the three motors from the drive gear unit as described previously, but note that it is not necessary to remove the wiring contact pins from the connector. Mark the motor locations before removal so they can be refitted in their original positions.
32 Undo the two nuts securing the height adjuster rods to the inside of the seat side.
33 Undo the two outer bolts securing the outer slide rail to the seat frame. Withdraw the slide rail and remove the drive shaft between the drive gear unit and the slide rail.
34 Undo the three bolts and two nuts

securing the drive gear unit to the inner slide rail and remove the unit.

35 Refit all the components using a reversal of removal but bearing in mind the following points:

a) *When locating the drive gear unit on the slide rail, ensure that the drive gear toothed shaft engages with the hole in the sliding block on the slide rail.*

b) *Ensure that the position of both slide rails relative to the seat tracks is the same both sides before engaging the driveshaft. If one track protrudes more than the other, the seat mounting bolts will not align when the seat is refitted.*

c) *Have the ECU re-calibrated by a Volvo dealer on completion.*

Backrest motor (motor 2)

36 Access to the backrest motor entails the removal of the seat upholstery. This is a complex operation requiring special tools and should be entrusted to a Volvo dealer.

Fault diagnosis and fault code read-out

Note: *On models from 1996 the diagnostic unit is located under a cover in front of the gear lever and has a 16-pin socket for connection to a fault code reader.*

37 As mentioned at the beginning of this Section, the electrically operated seat incorporates an on-board diagnostic system to facilitate fault finding and system testing. The diagnostic system is a feature of the seat ECU which continually monitors the system components and their operation. Should a fault occur, the ECU stores a series of signals (or fault codes) for subsequent read-out via the diagnostic unit located in the engine compartment.

38 The on-board diagnostic facility is used in many of the electronic systems on the Volvo

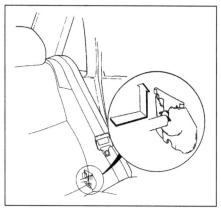

26.3 Rear seat removal on Saloon models

850 and reference should be made to Chapter 3, Section 12, for an overview of the operation of a similar system, and a full description of the use of the diagnostic unit. When using the diagnostic unit for fault diagnosis on the electrically operated seat, access the diagnostic mode of the ECU as follows.

39 Insert the flylead of the diagnostic module into socket 6 of module B.

40 Press any button on the seat control panel, keep it pressed and at the same time switch on the ignition. Keep the button pressed down for about another second then, from within the engine compartment, press the test button on the diagnostic unit once. Providing this procedure is completed within thirty seconds, the ECU will be in self-diagnostic mode ready to display any fault codes.

41 Given in the table below are the possible electrically operated seat fault codes and their meaning.

Fault code	Meaning
1-1-1	No fault detected
1-1-2	Signal position sensor, motor 1, absent or faulty
1-2-1	Signal position sensor, motor 2, absent or faulty
1-2-2	Signal position sensor, motor 3, absent or faulty
2-1-1	Signal position sensor, motor 4, absent or faulty
1-2-3	Motor 1 functions although equivalent button not activated
1-3-1	Motor 2 functions although equivalent button not activated
1-3-2	Motor 3 functions although equivalent button not activated
1-3-3	Motor 4 functions although equivalent button not activated
3-2-3	Fault in stored memory position 1
3-2-2	Fault in stored memory position 2
3-3-3	Fault in stored memory position 3
3-3-1	Lead disconnected, motor 1*
3-3-2	Lead disconnected, motor 2*
3-3-3	Lead disconnected, motor 3*
1-1-4	Lead disconnected, motor 4*
1-4-3	Motor 1 turns in wrong direction
1-4-4	Motor 2 turns in wrong direction
2-1-4	Motor 3 turns in wrong direction
2-2-4	Motor 4 turns in wrong direction
4-1-4	Faulty end position calibration

These codes may also be displayed if the motors are not allowed to reach their limit stops ie, the backrest contacting the rear seat before maximum tilt is reached.

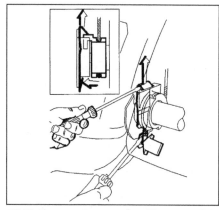

26.10 Rear seat removal on Estate models

26 Rear seat - removal and refitting

Removal

Saloon models

1 Free the seat cushion from its retaining clips by lifting the front edge, then remove the cushion.

2 Ensure that the safety locking catches in the boot, on either side of the backrest, are up, then pull the release catch forward and fold down the backrest.

3 Move one side of the backrest toward the side of the car and at the same time lift up **(see illustration)**. Remove one side of the backrest then remove the other side in the same way.

Estate models

4 If the seat is heated, disconnect the heater wiring at the connectors under the front of the cushion.

5 Fold the cushion forward and pull the red catches upward.

6 Fold the cushion back almost all the way, then lift up to remove.

7 If the backrest is heated, disconnect the wiring at the connectors.

8 Remove the side padding and undo the seat belt anchorage retaining bolts in the floor. Remove the anchorages.

9 Release the catch and fold the backrest forward very slightly.

10 Remove the clip securing the backrest mounting to the wheel arch by pressing it in at the bottom with a screwdriver and lifting it up with a second screwdriver **(see illustration)**.

11 Press the backrest out and pull it up in its outer mounting. Lift the backrest up and out of the car.

Refitting

All models

12 Refit by reversing the removal operations.

27 Interior trim - removal and refitting

Note: *Refer to earlier Sections of this Chapter for specific procedures covering door and tailgate interior trim panels.*

Interior trim panels - general

1 The interior trim panels are secured using either screws or various types of trim fasteners, usually studs or clips.
2 Check that there are no other panels overlapping the one to be removed; usually there is a sequence that has to be followed, and this will only become obvious on close inspection.
3 Remove all visible retainers such as screws, noting that these may be hidden under small plastic caps. If the panel will not come free, it is held by internal clips or fasteners. These are usually situated around the edges of the panel and can be prised up to release them; note, however that they can break quite easily so replacements should be available. The best way of releasing such clips is to use a large flat-bladed screwdriver. Note that in many cases the adjacent sealing strip must be prised back to release a panel.
4 When removing a panel **never** use excessive force or the panel may be damaged; always check carefully that all fasteners or other relevant components have been removed or released before attempting to withdraw a panel.
5 Refitting is a reversal of removal; secure the fasteners by pressing them firmly into place and ensure that all disturbed components are correctly secured to prevent rattles.

Rear parcel shelf (Saloon models)

6 If a high level brake light is fitted, remove the light cover by depressing the two catches on the side and pulling off.
7 Free the seat cushion from its retaining clips by lifting the front edge, then remove the cushion.
8 Remove the side backrest padding by pulling it out and lifting up.
9 Undo the bolt securing the centre seat belt anchorage to the floor.
10 Ensure that the safety locking catches in the boot, on either side of the backrest, are up then pull the release catch forward and fold down the backrest.
11 Release the parcel shelf from the two clips at the front edge by inserting a screwdriver and carefully prising up.
12 Pull out the shelf and thread the seat belt through the opening in the shelf.
13 If necessary lift out the soundproofing panel under the parcel shelf.
14 Refitting is a reversal of removal. Tighten the seat belt anchorage to the specified torque.

Carpets

15 The passenger compartment floor carpet is in three sections; front left, front right and rear, and is secured at the sides by the front and rear sill trim panels.
16 Carpet removal and refitting is reasonably straightforward but is very time consuming because all adjoining trim panels must be removed first, as must components such as the seats, centre console and seat belt lower anchorages.

Headlining

17 The headlining is clipped to the roof and can be withdrawn only once all fittings such as grab handles, sun visors, sunroof (if fitted), fixed window glass, and related trim panels have been removed and the relevant sealing strips have been prised clear.
18 Note that headlining removal and refitting requires considerable skill and experience if it is to be carried out without damage and is therefore best entrusted to a dealer.

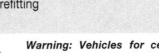

28 Seat belts - removal and refitting

⚠️ *Warning: Vehicles for certain markets may be equipped with either mechanical or pyrotechnical front seat belt tensioners as part of the Supplemental Restraint System (SRS). DO NOT attempt to remove the front seat belts on vehicles so equipped. Have any work involving front seat belt removal carried out by a Volvo dealer. Refer to Chapter 12 for further information.*

Removal

Front seat belts

1 Move the front seat forwards. Remove the seat side compartment by releasing the forward edge and pushing backwards.
2 Undo the bolt and remove the seat belt lower anchorage from the side of the seat. Note that a new bolt will be required for refitting.
3 Remove the B-pillar trim panel by pulling it off. Free the belt guide from the slot in the trim.

29.2 Undo the two screws at the front (arrowed) and lift out the cigarette lighter panel

4 Undo the two bolts securing the inertia reel unit, noting the location of any washers and spacers. Remove the belt and reel.
5 To remove the buckle, it is first necessary to remove the seat as described in Section 24.

Rear sear belts - Saloon models

6 Remove the parcel shelf as described in Section 27, then remove the side backrest padding by pulling it out and lifting up.
7 Remove the rear seat as described in Section 26.
8 Remove the soundproofing panel located under the parcel shelf.
9 Undo the retaining bolts securing the inertia reel assemblies and the lower anchorages and buckles on each side and in the centre.
10 Feed the belts through the apertures in the parcel shelf and remove them from the car.

Rear sear belts - Estate models

11 Access to the buckles and floor anchorages is gained by tipping the seat cushion forwards.
12 Access to the inertia reels, located inside the seat backrests, entails removing the seat upholstery which can easily be damaged if done carelessly or without the correct special tools. For this reason entrust this work to a Volvo dealer

Refitting

13 In all cases, refit by reversing the removal operations. Tighten the seat belt mountings to the specified torque and use a new bolt for the front belt lower anchorage on the seat.

29 Centre console - removal and refitting

Removal

1 Disconnect the battery negative lead.
2 Undo the two screws at the front and lift out the cigarette lighter panel. Disconnect the wiring at the lighter and remove the panel **(see illustration)**.
3 For improved access, undo the screws securing the ashtray compartment and withdraw the compartment **(see illustration)**.

29.3 Withdraw the ashtray compartment

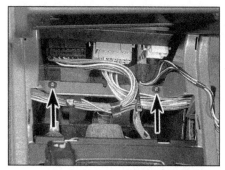

29.4 Undo the two screws (arrowed) securing the console at the front

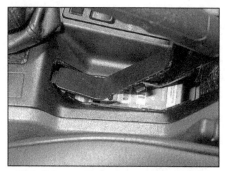

29.5 Prise up the cover panel below the handbrake lever

29.6 Release the gear lever gaiter from the console

29.7 Undo the two screws in the rear storage compartment

29.9 Move the console rearwards, and disengage it from under the facia

30 Facia - removal and refitting

Note: *For access to the instrument panel and related components it is necessary to remove the facia top cover. If the complete facia is to be removed the top cover can be left in place and removed as an assembly with the facia.*

Facia top cover

Removal

1 Disconnect the battery negative lead.
2 Open the glovebox lid. Release the lid arms by inserting a small screwdriver between the arms and the lid and carefully prising the arms free **(see illustration)**.
3 Undo the screws on the front face of the glovebox and withdraw the box from the facia.
4 On cars equipped with a passenger's side airbag, disconnect the wiring connector from the base of the airbag module. Undo the four screws securing the airbag module bracket above the glovebox **(see illustration)**.
5 Prise off the plastic caps and remove the screw adjacent to the side demister vent on each side **(see illustration)**.

Pull out the ashtray light bulbholder and remove the compartment.
4 Undo the two screws securing the console at the front **(see illustration)**.
5 Apply the handbrake fully then carefully prise up the cover panel below the handbrake lever **(see illustration)**.
6 On manual transmission models, release the gear lever gaiter from the console by first disengaging the clips at the rear. To do this insert your finger into the cover panel aperture under the handbrake lever and push the clips up. Once the rear edge is released prise up the rest of the gaiter **(see illustration)**. Twist the gaiter onto its side and push it down the

aperture in the console.
7 Open the rear storage compartment lid and prise up the cover panel in the compartment base. Undo the two screws now exposed **(see illustration)**.
8 Disconnect the switch and illumination wiring connectors at the front of the console.
9 Lift up the rear of the console and push it forward as far as possible until the handbrake lever is clear. Move the console rearwards, disengage it from under the facia at the front and remove it from the car **(see illustration)**.

Refitting

10 Refitting is a reversal of removal.

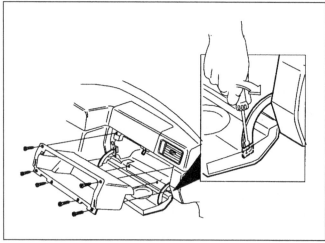

30.2 Glovebox and glovebox lid removal

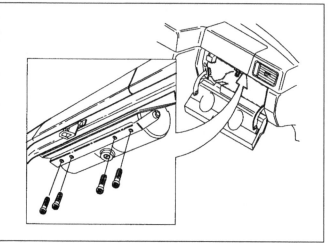

30.4 Passenger's side airbag attachments under the facia

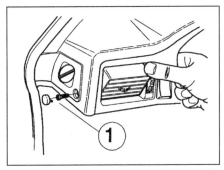

30.5 Remove the screws under the plastic caps (1) each side

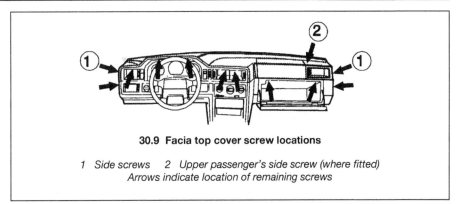

30.9 Facia top cover screw locations

1 Side screws   2 Upper passenger's side screw (where fitted)
Arrows indicate location of remaining screws

6 Remove the six air vents two in the centre of the facia and two on each side by tipping the vent downwards and pulling it out of its location. Alternatively, carefully lever out sideways using a screwdriver. On the passenger's side remove the air duct together with the side vent.

7 Carefully prise up the speaker grilles on each side of the top cover. Remove the speakers by pressing down the centre of the plastic expanding rivets and lifting the speakers up. Disconnect the wiring and remove the speakers.

8 Undo the screw (if fitted) in the speaker aperture on the passenger's side.

9 Undo the remaining screws securing the top cover as follows. Note that some models may vary slightly from the following according to specification **(see illustration)**.
  a) *Two screws above the instrument panel.*
  b) *Two (or three) screws above the glovebox.*
  c) *Two screws behind the centre air vents.*
  d) *One screw each side at the A-pillars.*
  e) *One screw behind the air vent on the driver's side.*

10 With all the screws removed, carefully lift up the top cover and remove it from the car (complete with passenger's side airbag module, where applicable).

 Warning: On cars so equipped, position the top cover and airbag module in a safe place, with the mechanism facing downwards as a precaution against accidental operation. Do not attempt to open or repair the airbag module, or apply any electrical current to it. Do not re-use any airbag which is visibly damaged or which has been tampered with.

Refitting

11 Refitting is a reversal of removal. On cars equipped with a passenger's side airbag, before re-connecting the battery, switch on the ignition to position II then, with the ignition switched on, reconnect the battery negative lead.

 Warning: Make sure that there is no one in the car when the battery is reconnected.

12 Switch off the ignition then switch it on again and check that the SRS warning light on the instrument panel is extinguished after about ten seconds.

Complete facia

Removal

13 Refer to Chapter 10 and remove the steering wheel.

14 If not already done, disconnect the battery negative lead.

15 Remove the windscreen wiper arms as described in Chapter 12.

16 Undo the five screws securing the windscreen wiper well cover to the scuttle at the front. Disconnect the two drain hoses and lift off the well cover **(see illustration)**.

17 Undo the windscreen wiper mounting bracket bolt on the passenger's side.

18 From within the windscreen wiper well, undo the four facia front retaining screws.

19 Undo the four screws from under the steering column lower shroud and lift off the upper and lower shrouds.

20 Undo the two screws each side and remove both steering column multifunction switches. Disconnect the switch wiring connectors.

21 Undo the screws and remove the driver's and passenger's side trim/soundproofing panels under the facia. Where fitted, also remove the knee bolster located behind the trim panel.

22 Prise off the plastic caps and remove the screw adjacent to the side demister vent on each side.

23 Remove the six air vents two in the centre of the facia and two on each side by tipping the vent downwards and pulling it out of its location. Alternatively, carefully lever out sideways using a screwdriver. On the passenger's side remove the air duct together with the side vent.

24 Carefully prise up the speaker grilles on each side of the top cover. Remove the speakers by pressing down the centre of the plastic expanding rivets and lifting the speakers up. Disconnect the wiring and remove the speakers.

25 Open the glovebox lid. Release the lid arms by inserting a small screwdriver between the arms and the lid and carefully prising the arms free.

26 Undo the screws on the front face of the glovebox and withdraw the box from the facia.

27 On cars equipped with a passenger's side airbag, disconnect the wiring connector from the base of the airbag module.

28 Undo the two screws each side at the extreme ends of the facia, and single screw each side under the facia in the footwell **(see illustration)**.

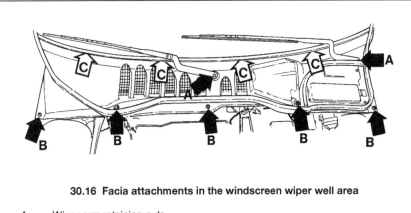

30.16 Facia attachments in the windscreen wiper well area

A   Wiper arm retaining nuts
B   Windscreen wiper well cover screws
C   Facia front mounting

29 Remove the radio as described in Chapter 12.

30 On cars with manual climate control, remove the control panel as described in Chapter 3, Section 10. On cars with electronic climate control, remove the control panel and ECU as described in Chapter 3, Section 11.

31 Undo the two screws at the front and lift out the cigarette lighter panel. Disconnect the wiring at the lighter and remove the panel.

32 Working through the facia apertures, disconnect the relevant wiring harness connectors. Note that much of the wiring is removed complete with the facia so it is only necessary to disconnect those connectors which attach to the main loom in the car.

33 With the help of an assistant, if necessary, withdraw the facia from its location, check that everything likely to impede removal is disconnected, then remove the facia from the car.

 Warning: On cars equipped with a passenger's side airbag, position the facia in a safe place, with the airbag module protected, as a precaution against accidental operation. Do not attempt to open or repair the airbag module, or apply any electrical current to it. Do not re-use any airbag which is visibly damaged or which has been tampered with.

Refitting

34 Refitting is a reversal of removal, bearing in mind the following points:

a) Ensure that all wiring is correctly routed and is not trapped as the facia is refitted.

b) Refit the control panels for the climate

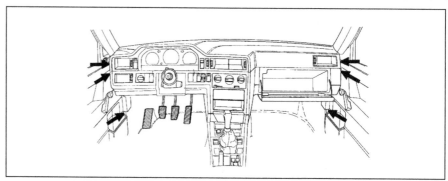

30.28 Facia internal retaining screw locations (arrowed)

control systems as described in the relevant Section of Chapter 3.

c) Refit the radio as described in Chapter 12.

d) Refit the steering wheel as described in Chapter 10, but wait until the facia is completely refitted before reconnecting the battery.

e) On cars equipped with a driver's and/or passenger's side airbag, before re-connecting the battery, switch on the ignition to position II then, with the ignition switched on, reconnect the battery negative lead. Switch off the ignition then switch it on again and check that the SRS warning light on the instrument panel is extinguished after about ten seconds.

 Warning: Make sure that there is no one in the car when the battery is reconnected.

31 Sunroof - general information

A mechanically or electrically operated sunroof is available as standard or optional equipment according to model.

The sunroof is maintenance-free, but any adjustment or removal and refitting of the component parts should be entrusted to a dealer, due to the complexity of the unit and the need to remove much of the interior trim and headlining to gain access. The latter operation is involved, and requires care and specialist knowledge to avoid damage.

Chapter 12
Body electrical system

Contents

Degrees of difficulty

| Easy, suitable for novice with little experience | | Fairly easy, suitable for beginner with some experience | | Fairly difficult, suitable for competent DIY mechanic | | Difficult, suitable for experienced DIY mechanic | | Very difficult, suitable for expert DIY or professional | |

Specifications

System type . . . . 12 volt, negative earth
Fuses . . . . See Wiring diagrams at end of Chapter and sticker on control box lid
for specific vehicle details

Torque wrench settings   Nm
Windscreen/tailgate wiper arm nuts 16
Headlight wiper arm nuts 4
Windscreen wiper motor crank arm nut 20

1 General information and precautions

General information

The electrical system is of 12-volt negative earth type. Power for the lights and all electrical accessories is supplied by a lead-acid battery which is charged by the alternator.

This Chapter covers repair and service procedures for the various electrical components and systems generally not associated with the engine. Information on the battery, ignition system, alternator, and starter motor can be found in the relevant Parts of Chapter 5.

Precautions

 Warning: Before carrying out any work on the electrical system, read through the precautions given in "Safety first!" at the beginning of this manual and in Chapter 5.
Caution: Prior to working on any component in the electrical system, the battery negative lead should first be disconnected, to prevent the possibility of electrical short-circuits and/or fires. If a radio/cassette player with anti-theft security code is fitted, refer to the information given in the reference sections of this manual before disconnecting the battery.

2 Electrical fault finding - general information

Note: Refer to the precautions given in "Safety first!" and in Section 1 of this Chapter before starting work. The following tests relate to testing of the main electrical circuits, and should not be used to test delicate electronic circuits, particularly where an electronic control unit is used.

General

1 A typical electrical circuit consists of an electrical component, any switches, relays, motors, fuses, fusible links or circuit breakers related to that component, and the wiring and

connectors which link the component to both the battery and the chassis. To help to pinpoint a problem in an electrical circuit, wiring diagrams are included at the end of this manual.

2 Before attempting to diagnose an electrical fault, first study the appropriate wiring diagram, to obtain a complete understanding of the components included in the particular circuit concerned. The possible sources of a fault can be narrowed down by noting if other components related to the circuit are operating properly. If several components or circuits fail at one time, the problem is likely to be related to a shared fuse or earth connection.

3 Electrical problems usually stem from simple causes, such as loose or corroded connections, a faulty earth connection, a blown fuse, a melted fusible link, or a faulty relay. Visually inspect the condition of all fuses, wires and connections in a problem circuit before testing the components. Use the wiring diagrams to determine which terminal connections will need to be checked in order to pinpoint the trouble-spot.

4 The basic tools required for electrical fault-finding include a circuit tester or voltmeter (a 12-volt bulb with a set of test leads can also be used for certain tests); an ohmmeter (to measure resistance and check for continuity); a battery and set of test leads; and a jumper wire, preferably with a circuit breaker or fuse incorporated, which can be used to bypass suspect wires or electrical components. Before attempting to locate a problem with test instruments, use the wiring diagram to determine where to make the connections.

⚠️ *Warning: Under no circumstances may live measuring instruments such as ohmmeters, voltmeters or a bulb and test leads be used to test any of the SRS airbag, SIPS bag, or pyrotechnical seat belt circuitry. Any testing of these components must be left to a Volvo dealer as there is a danger of activating the system if the correct procedures are not followed.*

5 To find the source of an intermittent wiring fault (usually due to a poor or dirty connection, or damaged wiring insulation), a "wiggle" test can be performed on the wiring. This involves wiggling the wiring by hand to see if the fault occurs as the wiring is moved. It should be possible to narrow down the source of the fault to a particular section of wiring. This method of testing can be used in conjunction with any of the tests described in the following sub-Sections.

6 Apart from problems due to poor connections, two basic types of fault can occur in an electrical circuit - open-circuit, or short-circuit.

7 Open-circuit faults are caused by a break somewhere in the circuit, which prevents current from flowing. An open-circuit fault will prevent a component from working.

8 Short-circuit faults are caused by a "short" somewhere in the circuit, which allows the current flowing in the circuit to "escape" along an alternative route, usually to earth. Short-circuit faults are normally caused by a breakdown in wiring insulation, which allows a feed wire to touch either another wire, or an earthed component such as the bodyshell. A short-circuit fault will normally cause the relevant circuit fuse to blow.

Finding an open-circuit

9 To check for an open-circuit, connect one lead of a circuit tester or the negative lead of a voltmeter either to the battery negative terminal or to a known good earth.

10 Connect the other lead to a connector in the circuit being tested, preferably nearest to the battery or fuse. At this point, battery voltage should be present, unless the lead from the battery or the fuse itself is faulty (bearing in mind that some circuits are live only when the ignition switch is moved to a particular position).

11 Switch on the circuit, then connect the tester lead to the connector nearest the circuit switch on the component side.

12 If voltage is present (indicated either by the tester bulb lighting or a voltmeter reading, as applicable), this means that the section of the circuit between the relevant connector and the switch is problem-free.

13 Continue to check the remainder of the circuit in the same fashion.

14 When a point is reached at which no voltage is present, the problem must lie between that point and the previous test point with voltage. Most problems can be traced to a broken, corroded or loose connection.

Finding a short-circuit

15 To check for a short-circuit, first disconnect the load(s) from the circuit (loads are the components which draw current from a circuit, such as bulbs, motors, heating elements, etc).

16 Remove the relevant fuse from the circuit, and connect a circuit tester or voltmeter to the fuse connections.

17 Switch on the circuit, bearing in mind that some circuits are live only when the ignition switch is moved to a particular position.

18 If voltage is present (indicated either by the tester bulb lighting or a voltmeter reading, as applicable), this means that there is a short-circuit.

19 If no voltage is present during this test, but the fuse still blows with the load(s) reconnected, this indicates an internal fault in the load(s).

Finding an earth fault

20 The battery negative terminal is connected to "earth" - the metal of the engine/transmission and the vehicle body - and many systems are wired so that they only receive a positive feed, the current returning via the metal of the car body. This means that

the component mounting and the body form part of that circuit. Loose or corroded mountings can therefore cause a range of electrical faults, ranging from total failure of a circuit, to a puzzling partial failure. In particular, lights may shine dimly (especially when another circuit sharing the same earth point is in operation), motors (eg wiper motors or the radiator cooling fan motor) may run slowly, and the operation of one circuit may have an apparently-unrelated effect on another. Note that on many vehicles, earth straps are used between certain components, such as the engine/transmission and the body, usually where there is no metal-to-metal contact between components, due to flexible rubber mountings, etc.

21 To check whether a component is properly earthed, disconnect the battery and connect one lead of an ohmmeter to a known good earth point. Connect the other lead to the wire or earth connection being tested. The resistance reading should be zero; if not, check the connection as follows.

22 If an earth connection is thought to be faulty, dismantle the connection, and clean both the bodyshell and the wire terminal (or the component earth connection mating surface) back to bare metal. Be careful to remove all traces of dirt and corrosion, then use a knife to trim away any paint, so that a clean metal-to-metal joint is made. On reassembly, tighten the joint fasteners securely; if a wire terminal is being refitted, use serrated washers between the terminal and the bodyshell, to ensure a clean and secure connection. When the connection is remade, prevent the onset of corrosion in the future by applying a coat of petroleum jelly or silicone-based grease, or by spraying on (at regular intervals) a proprietary ignition sealer, or a water-dispersant lubricant.

3 Fuses and relays - general information

Fuses

1 The fuses are located in the electrical control box situated in the engine compartment on the driver's side, just in front of the windscreen.

2 If a fuse blows, the electrical circuit(s) protected by that fuse will cease to operate. The fuse positions and the circuits protected depends on vehicle specification, model year and country. Refer to the wiring diagrams at the rear of this manual, and the sticker on the control box lid which gives details for the particular vehicle.

3 To remove a fuse, first switch off the ignition, then lift up the cover on the electrical control box. Using the plastic removal tool provided, pull the fuse out of its terminals **(see illustration)**. The wire within the fuse should be visible; if the fuse is blown the wire will be broken or melted.

3.3 Use the removal tool to pull the fuse from its location

3.9a Undo the four screws and lift off the control box lid . . .

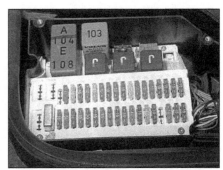

3.9b . . . for access to the control box relays

4 Always renew a fuse with one of an identical rating; never use a fuse with a different rating from the original or substitute anything else. Never renew a fuse more than once without tracing the source of the trouble. The fuse rating is stamped on top of the fuse; note that fuses are also colour-coded for easy recognition. Spare fuses are provided in the electrical control box.

5 Persistent blowing of a particular fuse indicates a fault in the circuit(s) protected. Where more than one circuit is involved, switch on one item at a time until the fuse blows, so showing in which circuit the fault lies.

6 Besides a fault in the electrical component concerned, a blown fuse can also be caused by a short-circuit in the wiring to the component. Look for trapped or frayed wires allowing a live wire to touch vehicle metal, and for loose or damaged connectors.

Relays - general

7 A relay is an electrically-operated switch, which is used for the following reasons:
  a) *A relay can switch a heavy current remotely from the circuit in which the current is flowing, allowing the use of lighter gauge wiring and switch contacts.*
  b) *A relay can receive more than one control input, unlike a mechanical switch.*
  c) *A relay can have a timer function - for example an intermittent wiper delay.*

8 If a circuit which includes a relay develops a

fault, remember that the relay itself could be faulty. Testing is by substitution of a known good relay. Do not assume that relays which look similar are necessarily identical for purposes of substitution.

9 Most relays are located in the electrical control box, alongside the fuses. For access, undo the four screws and lift off the control box lid **(see illustrations)**. Make sure that the ignition is switched off, then pull the relay from its socket. Push the new relay firmly in to refit.

10 Additional relays are located on the underside of the electrical control box, accessible from under the facia on the drivers side, after removing the soundproofing panel.

11 Depending on equipment and vehicle specification, further relays relating to the fuel, ignition, emission control, climate control, and braking systems are located in the engine compartment, or behind the facia.

---

4 Switches - removal and refitting

Steering column multi-function switches

1 Disconnect the battery negative lead.
2 Release the steering wheel/column adjuster and pull the steering wheel away from the facia as far as possible.

3 Undo the four screws from the underside of the steering column lower shroud then lift off the upper and lower shrouds.

4 Remove the switch in question. Each switch is secured by two screws. Remove the screws, pull the switch out and disconnect the wiring connector **(see illustration)**.

5 Refit the relevant switch using a reversal of removal, ensuring that the earth lead is secured by the lower retaining screw.

Ignition/starter switch

6 Remove the windscreen wiper switch as described previously.

7 Disconnect the ignition switch wiring connector.

8 Insert the ignition key into the switch and turn the key to position I.

9 Using a 2.0 mm diameter pin punch or similar item, depress the ignition switch locking tab through the hole in the housing above the switch, and withdraw the switch.

10 Refitting is a reversal of removal. Insert the ignition key into the new switch when refitting.

Facia toggle switches and headlight switch

11 Carefully prise the switch from its location using a small screwdriver or plastic lever. Take care not to mark the surrounding panel.

12 Withdraw the switch and disconnect the wiring connector at the rear **(see illustrations)**.

4.4 Steering column multi-function switch retaining screws (arrowed) - steering wheel shown removed for clarity

4.12a Prise out the headlight switch using a small screwdriver . . .

4.12b . . . then disconnect the wiring connector

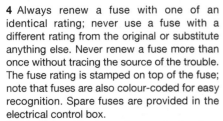

4.12c The facia toggle switches are removed in the same way

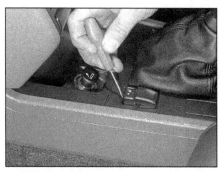

4.14 Removing a centre console seat heater switch

4.25 Handbrake warning light switch retaining screw (arrowed)

13 Refitting is a reversal of removal.

Centre console seat heater switches

14 These switches are removed and refitted in the same way as the facia toggle switches (see illustration).

Centre console window and mirror switches

15 Remove the centre console as described in Chapter 11.
16 Turn the console upside down and disconnect the switch control panel wiring connector and the connector to the window lift control module.
17 Release the cable harness retaining clips, depress the retaining tabs and push out the control panel. The switches and control panel are a unit; the switches cannot be removed from the panel.
18 Refitting is a reversal of removal.

Centre console rear ashtray panel switches

19 Push the top of the ashtray panel down to release it from the console.
20 Disconnect the switch wiring connector and push the switch out of the panel from behind.
21 Refit the switch, connect the wiring then engage the panel catch at the top and push in at the bottom.

Door courtesy light microswitch

22 The courtesy light microswitches are incorporated in the door lock assembly together with the central locking motor. Renewal entails unsoldering a number of small contacts and soldering in the new wires. As there is a risk of damage to the central locking motor and the lock itself, this work should be entrusted to a dealer.

Stop light switch

23 Refer to Chapter 9, Section 18.

Handbrake warning switch

24 Remove the centre console (Chapter 11).
25 Undo the screw securing the switch to the handbrake lever (see illustration).
26 Lift out the switch, disconnect the lead and remove it.

27 Refitting is a reversal of removal. Check for correct operation of the switch before refitting the console.

Other switches

28 Some switches will be found in the Chapter dealing with their system or equipment - for example, climate control switches in Chapter 3, and transmission-operated switches in Chapter 7.

---

5 Instrument panel - general information

Note: *On models from 1996 the diagnostic unit is located under a cover in front of the gear lever and has a 16-pin socket for connection to a fault code reader.*

Instrument panel identification

1 Two types of instrument panel are used on the Volvo 850 range, one manufactured by VDO and the other by Yazaki. The main difference between the two is that the VDO panel contains an electronic control unit (ECU) microprocessor which incorporates a diagnostic function. In the event of a fault in the instrument panel or control circuitry, a fault code will be stored in the ECU memory for subsequent read-out via the on-board diagnostic unit in the engine compartment.
2 For many of the operations relating to the instrument panel, it is necessary to be able to identify the unit fitted, to enable the correct procedures to be followed. The easiest way to do this is to observe the speedometer dial, noting the following:
 a) *VDO instrument panel: Both the mileage indicator (odometer) and trip meter are located below the speedometer needle.*
 b) *Yazaki instrument panel: The mileage indicator (odometer) is located above the speedometer needle and the trip meter is located below it.*

Instrument panel fault diagnosis

3 As mentioned at the beginning of this Section, the VDO instrument panel incorporates an on-board diagnostic system to facilitate fault finding and system testing. The diagnostic system is a feature of the

instrument panel ECU, which continually monitors the signal inputs and control circuitry. Should a fault occur, the ECU stores a series of signals (or fault codes) for subsequent read-out via the diagnostic unit located in the engine compartment.
4 The on-board diagnostic facility is used in many of the electronic systems on the Volvo 850 and reference should be made to Chapter 3, Section 12, for an overview of the operation of a similar system, and a full description of the use of the diagnostic unit. When using the unit for fault diagnosis on the instrument panel, access the diagnostic mode of the ECU as follows.
5 Switch on the ignition, insert the flylead of the diagnostic module into socket 7 of module A, and press the test button on the diagnostic unit once. The ECU will now be in self-diagnostic mode and the first of any stored fault codes will be displayed.
6 Given below are the possible instrument panel fault codes and their meaning.

Fault code	Meaning
1-1-1	No fault detected
1-1-2	Fuel gauge sender unit short circuit
1-1-3	Fuel gauge sender unit open circuit
1-2-1	Temperature signal interval too short
1-2-2	Temperature signal interval too long
1-2-3	Digital output 48 pulse short circuit to supply
1-3-1	Digital output 12 pulse short circuit to supply
1-3-2	No RPM sensor signal
1-3-3	Fuel level signal to trip computer short circuit to supply

Resetting the service reminder light

VDO instrument panel

7 Switch on the ignition, insert the flylead of the diagnostic module into socket 7 of module A, and press the test button on the diagnostic unit four times, briefly but firmly. When the LED illuminates and stays illuminated, the system is ready for manual code input.
8 It is now necessary to enter the code for resetting the service interval counter, which is

1-5-1. To do this, press the test button once and release it; wait for the LED to illuminate again, then press the test button five times. When the LED illuminates again, press the test button once. When the LED flashes several times in succession, the code has been successfully entered and the service interval counter should have been reset. Switch off the ignition to exit the manual input mode, replace the flylead in its holder and refit the diagnostic unit covers.

9 Switch on the ignition again and check that the service reminder light does not illuminate.

Yazaki instrument panel

10 On the Yazaki instrument panel the service interval counter is reset manually on the instrument panel itself.

6 Instrument panel - removal and refitting

Removal

1 Remove the facia top cover as described in Chapter 11.
2 Disconnect the wiring connectors at the rear of the instrument panel.
3 Release the two clip-locks at the top front and lift out the instrument panel.

Refitting

4 Refitting is a reversal of removal.

7 Instrument panel components - removal and refitting

The instruments within the panel are part of a sealed module and cannot be individually replaced. In the event of a fault which is directly attributable to the instrument panel itself, renewal of the complete assembly is likely to be necessary. It is advisable, therefore, to have any faults which cannot be secured by reference to the procedures in Section 5, dealt with by a dealer. The Volvo system test equipment will be able to locate the fault, and the dealer can advise on the best course of action.

8 Electrical system sensors - removal and refitting

Vehicle speed sensor

Removal

1 The vehicle speed sensor is used by a number of systems on the car for computation of road speed by means of electrical impulses. It replaces the function of the speedometer drive gear and cable used in conventional applications. The unit is located on the rear of the transmission, behind the right-hand driveshaft.
2 Chock the rear wheels then jack up the front of the car and support it on axle stands (see *"Jacking and vehicle support"*).
3 On early models, remove the splash guard under the engine.
4 Disconnect the wiring connector at the sensor unit.
5 Wipe clean the area around the sensor, undo the retaining bolt and remove the unit from the transmission **(see illustration)**.

Refitting

6 Refitting is a reversal of removal.

Brake fluid level sensor

7 The brake fluid level sensor is a float incorporated in the master cylinder reservoir filler cap. The sensor and cap are an assembly; renew the cap if the unit is faulty.

Coolant level sensor

Removal

8 Wait until the engine is cold then slowly unscrew the cooling system expansion tank filler cap to release any pressure remaining in the system.
9 Refit the cap then lift the expansion tank out of its mounting.
10 Disconnect the wiring connector at the sensor located in the tank base **(see illustration)**.
11 Turn the tank over and pull the sensor out of its sealing grommet.

Refitting

12 Refitting is a reversal of removal. Top-up the expansion tank as described in *"Weekly checks"* if any coolant was lost.

Oil pressure sensor

Removal

13 The oil pressure sensor is located on the front facing side of the cylinder block, between the dipstick and the starter motor.
14 Chock the rear wheels then jack up the front of the car and support it on axle stands (see *"Jacking and vehicle support"*).
15 On early models, remove the splash guard under the engine.
16 Release the locking tabs and disconnect the wiring connector from the sensor.
17 Unscrew the sensor and remove it from the engine.

Refitting

18 Refitting is a reversal of removal.

Outside temperature sensor

Removal

19 The sensor is located under the front bumper.
20 Undo the sensor retaining bolt, disconnect the wiring connector and remove the sensor.

Refitting

21 Refitting is a reversal of removal.

Oil level sensor

Removal

22 When fitted, the oil level sensor is located on the front facing side of the engine sump, next to the dipstick.

8.5 Vehicle speed sensor location on the transmission casing

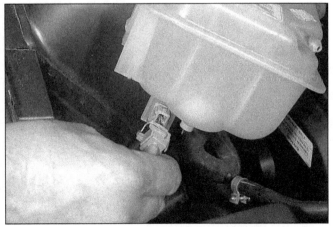

8.10 Disconnecting the wiring connector from the coolant level sensor

9.7 Remove the cover from the rear of the headlight unit

9.8 Release the retaining clip and remove the headlight bulb

23 Chock the rear wheels then jack up the front of the car and support it on axle stands (see *"Jacking and vehicle support"*).

24 On early models, remove the splash guard under the engine.

25 Release the locking tabs and disconnect the wiring connector from the sensor.

26 Undo the two retaining bolts and withdraw the sensor from the sump.

Refitting

27 Refitting is a reversal of removal but ensure that the mating faces are clean and use a new gasket.

Washer fluid level sensor

Removal

28 Remove the filler pipe from the washer fluid reservoir.

29 Prise the sensor rubber grommet from the reservoir and pull the sensor out. Disconnect the wiring connector and remove the sensor.

Refitting

30 Refitting is a reversal of removal.

9 Bulbs (exterior lights) - renewal

General

1 With all light bulbs, remember that if they have just been in use, they may be very hot. Switch off the power before renewing a bulb.

2 With quartz halogen bulbs (headlights and similar applications), use a tissue or clean cloth when handling the bulb; do not touch the bulb glass with the fingers. Even small quantities of grease from the fingers will cause blackening and premature failure. If a bulb is accidentally touched, clean it with methylated spirit and a clean rag.

3 Unless otherwise stated, fit the new bulb by reversing the removal operations.

Bulb renewal

Headlight (single bulb unit)

4 Open the bonnet. Turn the plastic cover on the rear of the light unit anti-clockwise and lift off.

5 Unplug the connector from the bulb. Press the spring-loaded retaining clip and move it aside. Remove the bulb

6 When fitting the new bulb, do not touch the

glass (paragraph 2). Make sure that the lugs on the bulb flange engage with the slots in the holder.

Headlight (twin bulb unit)

Note: *For greater access to the right-hand headlight unit, remove the ECU module box air duct behind the headlight, and lift the diagnostic unit out of its mounting and place it to one side.*

7 Open the bonnet. Turn the appropriate plastic cover on the rear of the light unit anti-clockwise and lift off **(see illustration)**.

8 Press the spring-loaded retaining clip over the bulb to be removed and move it aside. Withdraw the bulb from the light unit and unplug the connector **(see illustration)**.

9 When fitting the new bulb, do not touch the glass (paragraph 2). Make sure that the lugs on the bulb flange engage with the slots in the holder.

Front direction indicator/front side light

10 Open the bonnet and release the retaining spring which secures the light unit in position and withdraw the light unit **(see illustration)**. Disconnect the wiring connector and remove the unit complete.

11 Push up the catch at the bottom and remove the light unit from the bulbholder. Remove the appropriate bayonet fitting bulb from the bulbholder **(see illustrations)**.

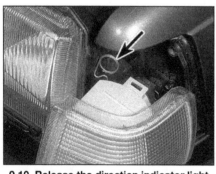

9.10 Release the direction indicator light unit retaining spring (arrowed)

9.11a Remove the direction indicator/sidelight bulbholder . . .

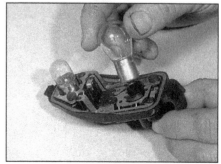

9.11b . . .and remove the relevant bulb

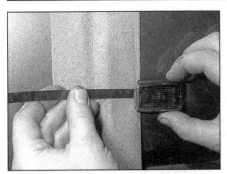

9.13 Release the front of the direction indicator side repeater lens unit

9.14 Free the lens unit from the wing and remove the bulbholder

9.15 Pull the bulb from the bulbholder

12 Ensure that the guides on the light unit engage correctly when refitting and that the spring is properly located.

Front direction indicator side repeater

13 Insert a thin feeler blade (with a piece of paper behind it to avoid scratching the paintwork) under the front edge of the lens unit and depress the internal lug **(see illustration)**.
14 When the lug releases, free the lens from the rear and withdraw it from the wing. Twist lens and remove it from the bulbholder **(see illustration)**.
15 Pull the bulb from the holder, fit a new bulb and reassemble **(see illustration)**.

Rear light cluster (Saloon models)

16 From within the boot, turn the two twist clips on the side access cover **(see illustration)**.
17 Open the cover, depress the catches and

withdraw the bulbholder.
18 Remove the relevant bayonet fitting bulb from the holder.

Upper rear light cluster (Estate models)

19 From within the luggage compartment, release the light unit access cover with the aid of a screwdriver **(see illustration)**.
20 Where fitted, withdraw the speaker for access to the bulbholder.
21 Press the retaining catch down and withdraw the bulbholder from the pillar. Withdraw the relevant bayonet fitting bulb from the holder **(see illustration)**.

Lower rear light cluster (Estate models)

22 From within the luggage compartment, lift out the outer rear floor covering on the side concerned **(see illustration)**.
23 Remove the access cover in front of the light unit by turning the locking clip through

90°, moving the cover down and lifting out **(see illustration)**.
24 Depress the two retaining catches and withdraw the bulbholder **(see illustration)**. Withdraw the relevant bayonet fitting bulb from the holder.

High level brake light (Saloon models)

25 Remove the light cover by depressing the two catches on the side and pulling off.
26 Squeeze the catches on each side of the reflector/bulbholder and withdraw it.
27 Remove the bayonet fitting bulb and fit a new one.
28 Fit the reflector and press it home until the catches engage. Check for correct operation, then refit the cover.

High level brake light (Estate models)

29 Remove the light cover by grasping it on each side and pulling down. Take care not to break the fragile inner retaining catches.

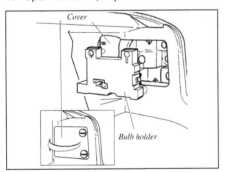

9.16 Rear light cluster details on Saloon models

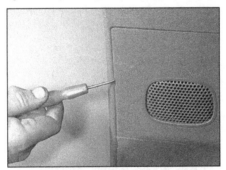

9.19 Releasing the upper light cluster access cover on Estate models

9.21 Press the retaining catch down and withdraw the bulbholder from the pillar

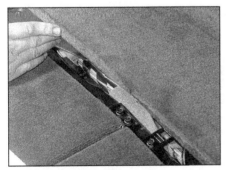

9.22 Lift out the outer rear floor covering for access to the lower light cluster

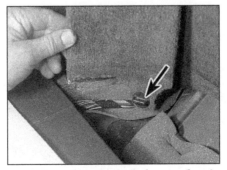

9.23 Turn the locking clip (arrowed) and lift off the cover

9.24 Withdraw the bulbholder from the pillar

9.30 Lift off the reflector for access to the high level brake light bulb

30 Lift off the reflector over the bulb, remove the bayonet fitting bulb and fit a new one **(see illustration)**.
31 Fit the reflector, check for correct operation, then refit the cover.

Spoiler brake light (Saloon models)

32 Undo the three screws on the outside of the lens.
33 Carefully prise out the lens and light unit using a screwdriver. Lift off the lens and remove the relevant push fit bulb.

Number plate light

34 Undo the two screws securing the relevant light unit or lens **(see illustration)**.
35 Carefully prise out the light unit and remove the push fit bulb **(see illustration)**.

10.3 Remove the roof mounted courtesy light lens . . .

10.4a . . . for access to the bulb inside

9.34 Remove the number plate light unit lens . . .

10 Bulbs (interior lights) - renewal

General

1 See Section 9, paragraphs 1 and 3.
2 Some switch illumination/pilot bulbs are integral with their switches and cannot be renewed separately.

Bulb renewal

Courtesy/vanity mirror lights

3 Carefully prise the light unit or lens from its location using a screwdriver **(see illustration)**.
4 Renew the bulb(s), which may be bayonet or end clip fitting **(see illustrations)**.

Glovebox light

5 Open the glovebox lid. Release the lid arms by inserting a small screwdriver between the arms and the lid and carefully prising the arms free.
6 Empty the contents of the glovebox, undo the screws on the front face and withdraw the box from the facia.
7 Pull the black dimmer sleeve off the bulbholder then remove the bayonet fitting bulb.
8 Ensure that the dimmer sleeve light aperture faces the glovebox window when refitting.

Front door edge marker lights

9 Push the light unit upward and release it at

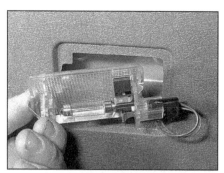

10.4b Some of the courtesy light bulbs are end clip fitting (festoon) types

9.35 . . . for access to the push-fit bulb

the bottom **(see illustration)**. Withdraw the unit from the door, twist off the bulbholder and remove the push fit bulb.

Rear door edge marker lights

10 Prise out the light unit for access to the bulb. Remove the push fit bulb from the light unit.

Automatic transmission selector light

11 Remove the centre console as described in Chapter 11.
12 Pull the bulbholder out of the selector quadrant next to the lever. Remove the contacts and remove the bulb and holder. Note that the bulb and holder are one piece and cannot be separated.

Heating/ventilation/air conditioning control panel lights

13 On cars with manual climate control, remove the control panel as described in Chapter 3. Carefully remove the clips securing the bulbholder printed circuit to the rear of the panel. The bulbs and printed circuit are an assembly and if either of the bulbs have blown, the complete printed circuit must be renewed. Attach the printed circuit and refit the control panel as described in Chapter 3.
14 On cars with electronic climate control, remove the control panel and ECU as described in Chapter 3. Undo the four screws and lift off the front panel. Remove the combined bulb and bulbholders. Fit the new bulbholder, reattach the front panel then refit the unit as described in Chapter 3.

10.9 Push the door edge marker light upwards to release it at the bottom

Switch illumination bulbs

15 When these are separable from the switch, they simply pull out after removing the switch.

Instrument panel bulbs

16 Remove the instrument panel as described in Section 6.

17 Twist the relevant bulbholder anti-clockwise and remove it from the rear of the panel.

18 All the warning and indicator bulbs are integral with their holders. Be careful to ensure that the new bulbs are of the correct rating, the same as those removed.

Front ashtray light

19 Undo the screws securing the ashtray compartment and withdraw the compartment. Pull out the ashtray light bulbholder and remove the bulb and holder from the contacts.

Rear ashtray light

20 Push the top of the ashtray panel down to release it from the centre console. Turn the panel on its side pull out the bulbholder and remove the bulb and holder from the contacts.

Cigarette lighter illumination bulb

21 Undo the two screws at the front and lift out the cigarette lighter panel. Disconnect the wiring at the bulb and remove the bulb and holder (see illustration).

---

11 Exterior light units - removal and refitting

Note: *Disconnect the battery negative lead before removing any light unit and reconnect the lead after refitting the light unit.*

Headlight

1 If working on the right-hand headlight, remove the ECU module box air duct behind the headlight. Lift the diagnostic unit out of its mounting and place it to one side. Remove the washer reservoir filler tube. If working on the left-hand headlight, remove the battery.

2 On single bulb headlight units, turn the plastic cover on the rear of the light unit anti-clockwise and lift off, then unplug the connector from the bulb. On twin bulb units, disconnect the wiring connector on the lower rear face of the light unit.

3 Where a beam height control motor is fitted, disconnect the wiring connectors on the motor.

4 Release the retaining spring securing the direction indicator/front side light unit, withdraw the light unit and let it hang by its wiring.

5 Mark the position of the bonnet lock on the side concerned using a felt tip pen, then undo the bolts and remove lock for access to the headlight.

10.21 Cigarette lighter illumination bulb at the rear of the lighter panel

6 Undo the three retaining bolts and withdraw the headlight unit from the front of the car.

7 Refitting is a reversal of removal. Have the headlight beam alignment checked on completion (see Section 12).

Front direction indicator/front side light

8 Open the bonnet and release the retaining spring which secures the light unit in position.

9 Withdraw the unit and disconnect the wiring connector at the rear

10 Refitting is a reversal of removal but ensure that the guides on the light unit engage correctly and that the spring is properly located.

Front direction indicator side repeater

11 Insert a thin feeler blade (with a piece of paper behind it to avoid scratching the paintwork) under the front edge of the lens unit and depress the internal lug.

12 When the lug releases, free the lens from the rear and withdraw it from the wing. Disconnect the wiring connector and remove the unit.

13 Refitting is a reversal of removal.

Rear light cluster (Saloon models)

14 From within the boot turn the two twist clips on the side access cover.

15 Open the cover and disconnect the wiring connectors.

16 Undo the four nuts and remove the light cluster unit from the rear of the vehicle. Recover the rubber seal and renew it if it shows signs of deterioration.

17 Refitting is a reversal of removal.

Upper rear light cluster (Estate models)

18 From within the luggage compartment, release the light unit access cover with the aid of a screwdriver.

19 Where fitted, withdraw the speaker for access to the bulbholder.

20 Press the retaining catch down and withdraw the bulbholder from the pillar. Disconnect the bulbholder wiring connector.

21 Using a long socket, undo the two nuts and remove the light cluster unit from the rear of the vehicle.

22 Refitting is a reversal of removal.

Lower rear light cluster (Estate models)

23 Remove the upper rear light cluster as described previously (the two units overlap and the upper must be removed first).

24 From within the luggage compartment, lift out the outer rear floor covering on the side concerned.

25 Remove the access cover in front of the light unit by turning the locking clip through 90°, moving the cover down and lifting out.

26 Depress the two retaining catches and withdraw the bulbholder. Disconnect the bulbholder wiring connector.

27 Fold back the luggage compartment rear floor panel, undo the screws and remove the sill guard.

28 Release the side trim panels as necessary for access to the two cluster unit retaining nuts.

29 Using a long socket, undo the nuts and remove the light cluster unit from the rear of the vehicle.

30 Refitting is a reversal of removal.

High level brake light (Saloon models)

31 Remove the light cover by depressing the two catches on the side and pulling off.

32 Depress the catch at the base of the light unit and withdraw. Disconnect the wiring connector and remove the unit.

33 Refitting is a reversal of removal.

High level brake light (Estate models)

34 Remove the light cover by grasping it on each side and pulling down. Take care not to break the fragile inner retaining catches

35 Release the wire spring retainer and lift the unit upwards (see illustration). Disconnect the wiring connectors and remove the light unit.

36 Refitting is a reversal of removal.

Spoiler brake light (Saloon models)

37 Undo the three screws on the outside of the lens.

38 Carefully prise out the lens and light unit using a screwdriver.

11.35 Release the wire spring retainer to remove the high level brake light

39 Disconnect the wiring connector and remove the light unit. Recover the rubber seal and renew it if it shows signs of deterioration.
40 Refitting is a reversal of removal.

Number plate light

41 Undo the two screws securing the relevant light unit.
42 Carefully prise out the light unit, disconnect the wiring connector and remove the unit.
43 Refitting is a reversal of removal.

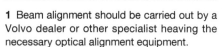

12 Headlight beam alignment - checking and adjusting

1 Beam alignment should be carried out by a Volvo dealer or other specialist heaving the necessary optical alignment equipment.
2 For reference, the headlights can be adjusted by means of the vertical and horizontal adjuster controls at the rear of the headlight unit.
3 Some models are equipped with an electrically operated headlight beam adjustment system which is controlled through the switch on the facia. On these models, ensure that the switch is set to the off position before adjusting the headlight aim.

13 Headlight beam control motor - removal and refitting

Removal

1 Disconnect the wiring connectors at the beam control motor on the rear of the headlight unit.
2 Turn the motor 90° anti-clockwise to release the motor bayonet fitting attachment.
3 Pull the motor rearwards off the light unit until the motor shaft disengages from its socket location in the headlight reflector. Remove the motor.

Refitting

4 Turn the beam height control adjuster on the motor anti-clockwise as far as it will go to extend the motor shaft fully.
5 Lightly lubricate the end of the motor shaft with medium grease then engage the shaft into the reflector socket.
6 Turn the height control adjuster clockwise to shorten the shaft until the motor can be located in the light unit. Turn the motor clockwise to lock the bayonet attachment.
7 Reconnect the wiring connectors and check the operation of the motor.
8 Have the beam adjustment basic setting checked and if necessary adjusted, by a dealer or specialist.

14.1 Horn retaining bolt and wiring connector

14 Horn - removal and refitting

Removal

1 Open the bonnet and disconnect the wires from the horn **(see illustration)**.
2 Unbolt the horn from its bracket and remove it.

Refitting

3 Refitting is a reversal of removal.

15 Washer system components - removal and refitting

Windscreen washer pump

Removal

1 From within the engine compartment, remove the washer fluid reservoir filler pipe by pulling it up and out of the tank.
2 Using long nosed pliers and a protective cloth, grip the washer pump and pull it up and out of the reservoir. Disconnect the wiring connector, detach the hose and remove the pump.

Refitting

3 Refitting is a reversal of removal.

Tailgate washer pump

Removal

4 From under the front right-hand wheel arch, carefully spread the legs of the pump mounting bracket and withdraw the pump down and out of the bracket.
5 Disconnect the wiring connector, detach the hose and remove the pump.

Refitting

6 Refitting is a reversal of removal.

Washer reservoir

Removal

7 From within the engine compartment, remove the washer fluid reservoir filler pipe by pulling it up and out of the tank.

8 Disconnect the wiring connectors from the windscreen washer pump and the fluid level sensor. Disconnect the fluid hose from the pump.
9 From under the front right-hand wheel arch, disconnect the fluid hose and wiring connector at the tailgate washer pump.
10 Undo the reservoir retaining bolts and withdraw the unit from under the car.

Refitting

11 Refitting is a reversal of removal.

Washer jets

Removal

12 Remove the relevant trim panel for access to the washer jets, then disconnect the fluid hose.
13 Release the jet from its location using a deep socket which will push the side catches together and allow removal.

Refitting

14 Push the jet into its location until the side catches spring out to lock. Reconnect the fluid hose
15 Adjust the jet nozzles using a pin so that liquid is sprayed onto the centre of the glass.

Washer fluid level sensor

16 Refer to Section 15.

16 Wiper arms - removal and refitting

Removal

1 Lift up the cover (where applicable) then remove the nut at the base of the wiper arm and pull the arm off the splines **(see illustrations)**. Use a twisting motion to most effectively release the arm.

Refitting

2 Switch the relevant wiper on, then switch it off again to ensure that the motor and linkage are parked. Position the windscreen wiper arms so that the driver's side arm is 35 mm from the top edge of the scuttle panel, and the passenger's side arm is 45 mm from the edge of the panel. Position the tailgate wiper arm so that it is horizontal.

16.1a Undo the wiper arm retaining nut . . .

16.1b ... and twist the arms free to remove

3 Fit the right-hand headlight wiper arm by positioning it with the blade just below the stop. Secure the arm, then lift the blade over the stop. Fit the left-hand headlight wiper arm with the blade resting on the stop.

17 Windscreen wiper motor and linkage - removal and refitting

Removal

1 Switch the wipers on then off again to ensure that the motor and linkage are parked.
2 Disconnect the battery negative lead.
3 Remove the windscreen wiper arms as described in Section 16.
4 Undo the five screws securing the windscreen wiper well cover to the scuttle at the front. Disconnect the two drain hoses and lift off the well cover **(see illustration)**.
5 Undo the three bolts securing the mounting frame to the wiper well **(see illustration)**.
6 Release the frame assembly from its location, disconnect the wiring connectors and remove the unit from the car.
7 Mark the position of the motor crank arm relative to the frame, undo the nut and remove

the crank arm from the motor.
8 Undo the three motor retaining bolts and remove the motor from the frame. The frame and linkage arms are an assembly and cannot be individually renewed.

Refitting

9 Refit the motor to the frame and secure with the three mounting bolts.
10 If a new motor is being fitted, temporarily reconnect the wiring connectors at the car, switch on the motor then switch it off again to ensure that it is parked.
11 Position the crank arm on the motor, with the marks made on removal aligned. Prevent the crank arm from turning by holding it with a spanner, then refit and tighten the nut.
12 Alternatively, if a new frame and linkage are being fitted, set the motor to the park position as described previously then, when connecting the crank arm to the motor, position it so that it is parallel with the linkage arm directly above.
13 The assembled components can now be refitted using a reversal of removal.

18 Tailgate wiper motor - removal and refitting

Removal

1 Switch the wiper on then off again to ensure that the motor and linkage are parked.
2 Disconnect the battery negative lead.
3 Remove the tailgate wiper arm as described in Section 16.
4 Remove the tailgate interior trim panel as described in Chapter 11.
5 Undo the three nuts securing the mounting frame to the tailgate.
6 Release the frame assembly from its location, disconnect the wiring connector and

17.4 Removing the windscreen wiper well cover

remove the unit from the car **(see illustration)**.
7 Mark the position of the motor crank arm relative to the frame, undo the nut and remove the crank arm from the motor.
8 Undo the three motor retaining bolts and remove the motor from the frame. The frame and linkage arm are an assembly and cannot be individually renewed.

Refitting

9 Refit the motor to the frame and secure with the three mounting bolts.
10 If a new motor is being fitted, temporarily reconnect the wiring connector at the car, switch on the motor then switch it off again to ensure that it is parked.
11 Position the crank arm on the motor, with the marks made on removal aligned. Prevent the crank arm from turning by holding it with a spanner, then refit and tighten the nut.
12 Alternatively, if a new frame and linkage are being fitted, set the motor to the park position as described previously then, when connecting the crank arm to the motor, position it so that it is parallel with the linkage arm directly above.
13 The assembled components can now be refitted using a reversal of removal.

17.5 Windscreen wiper mounting frame retaining bolts (arrowed)

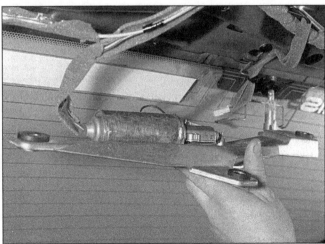

18.6 Removing the tailgate wiper motor assembly

19 Headlight wiper motor - removal and refitting

Left-hand motor

Removal

1 Disconnect the battery negative lead.
2 Remove the headlight wiper arm as described in Section 16.
3 Disconnect the wiper motor wiring connector which is located either above the headlight unit or in front of the radiator according to model.
4 Remove the trim strip under the headlight by carefully prising it out of the two retaining clips.
5 Undo the two bolts now exposed securing the motor to the body panel. Withdraw the motor from its location and remove it from the engine compartment.

Refitting

6 Refitting is a reversal of removal. Take care not to trap the washer hose when installing the motor. Before refitting the wiper arm, switch the motor on and off so that it is in the park position.

Right-hand motor (models with single bulb headlights without air conditioning)

Removal

7 Disconnect the battery negative lead.
8 Remove the ECU module box air duct behind the headlight. Remove the washer reservoir filler tube.
9 Turn the plastic cover on the rear of the light unit anti-clockwise and lift off.
10 Remove the headlight wiper arm as described in Section 16.
11 Disconnect the wiper motor wiring connector located above the headlight unit.
12 Remove the trim strip under the headlight by carefully prising it out of the two retaining clips.
13 Undo the two bolts now exposed securing the motor to the body panel. Withdraw the motor from its location and remove it from the engine compartment.

Refitting

14 Refitting is a reversal of removal. Take care not to trap the washer hose when installing the motor. Before refitting the wiper arm, switch the motor on and off so that it is in the park position.

Right-hand motor (models with twin bulb headlights and/or air conditioning)

15 Disconnect the battery negative lead.
16 Remove the headlight wiper arm as described in Section 16.
17 Disconnect the wiper motor wiring connector which is located either above the

headlight unit or in front of the radiator according to model.
18 Remove the trim strip under the headlight by carefully prising it out of the two retaining clips.
19 Undo the two bolts now exposed securing the motor to the body panel.
20 Remove the right-hand headlight unit as described in Section 11.
21 Lift the cooling system expansion tank out of its mounting bracket and place it to one side.
22 Release the two catches on the side of the ECU module box lid. Lift off the lid and place it to one side.
23 Withdraw the air duct from the rear face of the ECU module box. Release the catches and lift off the module box centre section.
24 Undo the module box lower section retaining bolt, then move the box rearward to release it from the body at the front. Lift up the module box cable duct to gain access to the wiper motor.
25 Withdraw the motor from its location, turn it on its side to clear adjacent components and remove it from the engine compartment.

Refitting

26 Refitting is a reversal of removal. Take care not to trap the washer hose or any wiring when installing the motor. Before refitting the wiper arm, switch the motor on and off so that it is in the park position.

20 Heated seat components - removal and refitting

Heating elements

On models equipped with heated seats, a heating element is fitted to both the seat back and the seat cushion. Renewal of the heating elements entails completely removing all the seat upholstery and partially dismantling the internal frame. Note that upholstery removal and refitting requires considerable skill and experience if it is to be carried out successfully and is therefore best entrusted to a Volvo dealer. In practice it will be very difficult for anyone unskilled in this work, or without the necessary tools to carry out the job without ruining the upholstery.

Seat heater switches

Refer to Section 4.

21 Radio/cassette player - removal and refitting

Note: *Radio/cassette players of various designs may be fitted, according to model, territory and optional equipment. The removal and refitting procedures for one of the common types are as follows.*

Removal

1 Disconnect the battery negative lead. If the radio/cassette player is equipped with an anti-theft security code, refer to the information given in the *Reference* sections at the end of this manual before disconnecting the battery.
2 In order to release the radio retaining clips, two U-shaped rods must be inserted into the special holes on each side of the radio. If possible, it is preferable to obtain purpose made rods from an audio specialist as these have cut-outs which snap firmly into the clips so that the radio can be pulled out. Note that on some models, it will be necessary to remove the two side bezels first, to allow access to the holes for insertion of the U-shaped removal tools. On units where no holes are visible, it will be necessary to obtain two radio removal keys from a Volvo dealer which are inserted into special slots on the side of the unit.
3 Insert the removal tools into each pair of holes at the edge of the unit, and push the tools fully home to engage the radio retaining clips.
4 Move the tools outward to depress the retaining clips, and withdraw the radio from the facia sufficiently to gain access to the wiring at the rear.
5 Note the location of the speaker wiring by recording the cable colours and their positions, then disconnect the speaker leads, aerial lead and wiring multiplug(s). Remove the unit from the car.
6 Disengage the removal tools from the retaining clips on the side of the radio, and remove the tools.

Refitting

7 Refitting is a reversal of removal.

22 Loudspeakers - removal and refitting

Facia loudspeaker

1 Carefully prise up the speaker grilles on the side of the facia top cover **(see illustration)**.
2 Remove the speaker by pressing down the centre of the plastic expanding rivets and

22.1 Carefully prise up the facia loudspeaker grille

22.2 Release the speaker by pressing the centre of the expanding rivets

22.4 Release the door loudspeaker grille

lifting the speaker up **(see illustration)**. Disconnect the wiring and remove the speaker.

3 Refitting is a reversal of removal making sure the speaker is correctly located. Pull out the centre of the expanding rivets before fitting, then press the centre to lock.

Door loudspeaker

4 Remove the speaker grille by inserting a screwdriver behind one corner and carefully prising off **(see illustration)**.
5 Undo the four speaker retaining screws, remove the speaker and disconnect the wiring connectors **(see illustration)**.
6 Refitting is a reversal of removal.

Rear loudspeaker(Estate models)

7 From within the luggage compartment, release the rear light unit access cover with the aid of a screwdriver.
8 Undo the four speaker retaining screws, remove the speaker and disconnect the wiring connectors.
9 Refitting is a reversal of removal.

23 Radio aerial - general information

On Saloon models various aerial types may be fitted as standard or optional equipment according to model and market. No specific information was available at the time of writing concerning removal and refitting procedures. In the event of aerial breakage or poor audio quality, seek the advice of a Volvo dealer or audio equipment specialist.

On Estate models, the aerial is a wire filament incorporated into the rear window glass on the left-hand side. The aerial works in conjunction with a signal booster located behind the trim panel under the rear window. Repair of small breaks in the glass filament

may be possible with special metallic repair paste but must ideally be dealt with by a specialist for satisfactory results.

24 Anti-theft alarm system - general information

Note: *This information is applicable only to the anti-theft alarm system fitted by Volvo as original equipment.*

An anti-theft alarm system may be fitted as standard or optional equipment. The alarm has switches on all the doors (including the tailgate/boot lid), the bonnet and ignition switch. If the tailgate/boot lid, bonnet or any of the doors are opened or the ignition switch is switched on whilst the alarm is set, the alarm horn will sound and the hazard warning lights will flash. The alarm also has an immobiliser function which makes the ignition inoperable whilst the alarm is triggered.

The anti-theft alarm system is available in three versions; Basic alarm, Guard alarm I and Guard alarm II. The Basic alarm is set using the standard door key or via the central locking remote control transmitter. The Guard alarm I is set using an infra-red or radio controlled remote control unit and also by the

22.5 Undo the screws and withdraw the speaker

standard door key on pre-1994 models. The Guard alarm II can only be set using a radio controlled remote control unit.

The systems are controlled by a central control centre located on the underside of the electrical control box, accessible from under the facia on the drivers side. Signals from the alarm system switches and contacts which are integral with the door, bonnet and tailgate/boot lid locks are sent to the central control centre once the system is set. The control centre monitors the signals and activates the alarm if any of the signal loops are broken or if an attempt is made to start the car (or hot wire the ignition).

The status of the system is displayed by means of a flashing LED located either in the centre of the facia, or in the status panel located on the driver's side windscreen pillar.

Should the alarm system become faulty the vehicle should be taken to a Volvo dealer for examination. They will have access to a special diagnostic tester which will quickly trace any fault present in the system.

25 Supplemental Restraint System (SRS) - general information and precautions

General information

A supplemental restraint system is available in various versions as standard or optional equipment depending on model and territory.

The system consists of a driver's airbag, which is designed to prevent serious chest and head injuries to the driver during an accident. A similar bag for the front seat passenger is also available on certain models. A crash sensor, which detects frontal impact, is located under the centre console, with a standby power unit mounted alongside. The crash sensor incorporates a deceleration sensor, and a microprocessor ECU, to monitor the severity of the impact and trigger the airbag where necessary. The airbag is inflated by a gas generator, which forces the bag out of the module cover in the centre of the steering wheel, or out of a cover on the passenger's side of the facia. A contact reel behind the steering wheel at the top of the steering column, ensures that a good electrical connection is maintained with the airbag at all times, as the steering wheel is turned in each direction.

In addition to the airbag units, the supplemental restraint system may also incorporate mechanical seat belt tensioners on the front seat belt buckles, or pyrotechnical seat belt tensioners operated by gas cartridges in the belt inertia reel assembly. The pyrotechnical units are also triggered by the crash sensor, in conjunction with the air bag, to tighten the seat belts and provide additional collision protection.

All models also incorporate a side impact protection system (SIPS) as standard

equipment. In its basic form, the SIPS system is essentially an integral part of the vehicle structure in which strengthening agents are used to distribute side impacts through the bodywork. This is done by reinforcing the lower areas of the door pillars and providing strengthening bars in the seats and centre console. In this way side impacts are absorbed by the body structure as a whole, giving exceptional impact strength.

In addition to the body reinforcement of the SIPS system, certain models may be fitted with a SIPS bag for both front passengers. The SIPS bag is an airbag located in a cushion module in the side of the front seat. The unit is triggered via its own individual sensor in the event of a severe side impact. The SIPS bag is inflated by two gas generators, which cause the bag to break open the module cover, rip open the seat upholstery seam, and inflate to its full volume toward the door.

Precautions

 Warning: The safe handling of the SRS components requires the use of Volvo special equipment. Any attempt to dismantle the airbag module, SIPS bag, crash sensors, contact reel, seat belt tensioners or any associated wiring or components without this equipment, and the specialist knowledge needed to use it correctly, could result in severe personal injury and/or malfunction of the system. For this reason the only procedures covered in this manual relating to the SRS components are those which are absolutely essential to enable access to be gained to other components or systems. It is imperative that any other work involving the SRS components is entrusted to a Volvo dealer.

Key to wiring diagrams

Wire colours

SB	Black	P	Pink
GR	Grey	BL	Blue
W	White	GN	Green
R	Red	OR	Orange
BN	Brown	VO	Violet
Y	Yellow		

Fuse no	Circuits protected	Fuse no	Circuits protected
11/1	LH 3.2 Multiport fuel injection (MFI), EZ 129 K Distributor Ignition (DI) Motronic 4.3 SFI, Automatic transmission Fenix 5.2 fuel and ignition system Main relay, Fenix 5.2 fuel system (MFI)	11/21	Low beam, left (Accessories)
		11/22	Low beam, right
		11/23	Parking lights, License plate light (Accessories)
		11/24	Parking lights
11/2	Fuel pump, Alarm	11/25	Rear fog lights, rear fog light warning
11/3	Exhaust temperature sensor (Japan), Interior lighting, Speed warning	11/26	Heated front seats, Power door mirrors
		11/27	Back-up lights, Turn signal, TRACS
		11/28	+151-rail (15/4): Heated rear window and door mirrors Seat belt reminder, Cruise control, Bulb malfunction indicator, Germany, P-shift lock automatic transmission, Heated rear seat
11/4	Spare		
11/5	Heater fan, 4th speed		
11/6	Central lock, Alarm, Relay for deadlock setting		
11/7	Radio		
11/8	Air pump	11/29	ABS, TRACS
11/9	ABS. TRACS	11/30	Cigar lighter
11/10	Heated rear seat	11/31	Heater fan speeds 1-3, Climate unit, Recirculation
11/11	Heated rear window and door mirrors		
11/12	Brake lights	11/32	Radio, Remote-controlled central locking/alarm
11/13	Turn signal/hazard lights, High beam flasher, Alarm	11/33	Data link connector (DLC) A (17/7) +X-rail (15/8) Power seat, Beam width control, Tailgate wash/wipe
11/14	ABS, TRACS		
11/15	+30-rail (15/2): Inside lighting, Glove compartment lighting, Entry lighting, Open-door warning lamps, Boot lighting, Remote-controlled central locking/alarm, Seat belt reminder, diagnostic socket OBDII (17/13)	11/34	Windshield wiper/washer, Horn, Headlight wiper/washer
		11/35	Ashtray lighting, Instrument and control lighting, Rheostat, Cigar lighter illumination, Power sunroof, (Accessories)
11/16	Power aerial, (trailer socket), (Accessories)	11/36	Spare
11/17	Key warning USA, Canada, Korea	11/37	Trip fuse for power windows and power sunroof
11/18	Front fog lights	11/38	Spare
11/19	High beam, left	11/39	Automatic fuse for power seat, left
11/20	High beam, right, High beam warning (Accessories)	11/40	Automatic fuse for power seat, right

Component list

1/1	Battery
2/1	Main headlight relay with bulb malfunction indicator
2/2	Fog light relay
2/3	Regulator, DIM-DIP
2/4	Windshield wiper intermittent relay
2/5	Seat belt reminder key/warning relay
2/7	Central lock, delayed courtesy lighting relay
2/11	Engine cooling fan relay
2/15	Relay, exhaust temperature sensor
2/16	Tailgate wiper intermittent relay
2/22	A/C relay
2/23	Fuel pump relay
2/24	Fan relay, max.
2/28	Alarm relay
2/30	Overload relay X+
2/31	Overload relay 15+
2/32	Main relay fuel system
2/42	Combination relay ABS
2/43	Heated rear seat relay
2/44	Relay, electrically heated rear window/door mirrors
2/47	Relay, deadlock setting
2/51	Speed warning
2/53	Air pump relay
2/60	Overload relay X+
3/1	Ignition switch
3/2	Light switch
3/3	Switch, turn signal/high and low beams
3/4	Controls, cruise control
3/6	Switch, hazard lights with flasher relay
3/8	Switch, electric heated rear window/door mirrors
3/9	Brake light switch
3/10	Backup (reversing) light switch
3/12	Switch, windshield wipers and washer
3/13	Switch, tailgate washer and wiper
3/25	Switch, power sunroof
3/37	Horn connectors
3/38	Contact, brake pedal
3/39	Contact, clutch pedal
3/47	Handbrake switch
3/54	REC and A/C switch
3/55	A/C panel lights
3/56	Heater fan switch
3/57	Climate control
3/58	Switch, rear fog light
3/59	Beam width control
3/61	Controls, trip computer
3/62	Alarm switch, hood
3/63	Program selector, automatic transmission
3/64	Switch for heated rear seat, left side
3/69	Switch for heated rear seat, right side
3/71	Transmission range selector indicator
3/72	Kick-down switch on throttle controls
3/74	Lock, left front
3/75	Lock, right front
3/76	Lock, left rear
3/77	Lock, right rear
3/78	Lock, tailgate
3/85	Power window switch, left rear door
3/86	Power window switch, right rear door
3/87	Switch, power door mirror, left side
3/88	Switch, power door mirror, right side
3/89	Control module, left seat
3/91	Switch, heated left seat
3/92	Switch, heated right seat
3/93	Seat belt lock, left seat
3/94	Seat belt lock, right seat
3/95	Switch, TRACS

Component list

3/97	Switch, auto-down relay, power window
3/99	Front fog light switch
4/3	Control module, cruise control
4/4	Rheostat
4/5	Safety circuit SRS
4/9	SRS sensor module
4/10	Control module EZK (DI) ignition system
4/15	DI power stage and ignition coil
4/16	ABS control module
4/19	Remote control module, central lock/anti-theft alarm
4/28	Control module, AW 50-42 automatic transmission
4/29	Control module, left seat
4/30	Control module, ECC
4/31	Power module, heater fan
4/33	Control module, power sunroof
4/34	Voltage regulator, 8 volts
4/35	Voltage regulator, 5 volts
4/36	Combined instrument microprocessor
4/37	Control module, right seat
4/41	Control module, Fenix 5.2 MFI
4/44	DI power stage and ignition coil
4/45	Control module, LH 3.2 MFI
4/46	Control module, Motronic 4.3 MFI
4/47	Ignition coil, Fenix 5.2 MFI
4/48	Ignition power stage, Fenix 5.2 MFI
5/1	Combined instrument
5/2	Clock module
5/3	Ambient temperature/clock module
5/4	Trip computer
6/1	Windshield wiper motor
6/2	Washer motor front
6/3	Right headlight wiper motor
6/4	Left headlight wiper motor
6/15	Power sunroof motor
6/24	Cruise control vacuum pump
6/25	Starter motor
6/26	Generator
6/28	Heater fan
6/29	Engine cooling fan
6/30	Tailgate washer motor
6/31	Fuel pump
6/32	Tailgate wiper motor
6/33	Fuel level sensor
6/34	Power aerial
6/35	Parking heater
6/37	Central lock motor, tank cap
6/38	Beam width control, left actuator
6/39	Beam width control, right actuator
6/45	Servo motor, temperature shutter, driver's side
6/46	Servo motor, temperature shutter, passenger's side
6/47	Servo motor, floor and defroster shutter
6/48	Servo motor, recirculation shutter
6/49	Servo motor, ventilation shutter
6/50	Motor, left seat backrest
6/51	Motor, up/down front edge of left seat
6/52	Motor, up/down rear edge of left seat
6/53	Motor, fore/aft left seat
6/54	Air pump
6/58	Power window motor, left front door
6/59	Power window motor, left rear door
6/60	Power window motor, right front door
6/61	Power window motor, right rear door
6/62	Power door mirror, left side
6/63	Power door mirror, right side
7/1	Bulb malfunction indicator, rear
7/4	Brake fluid level sensor
7/5	Washer fluid level sensor

7/6	Oil pressure sensor		10/13	Left turn signal, front
7/11	Ambient temperature sensor, ECC		10/14	Right turn signal, front
7/15	Heated oxygen sensor (HO2S) (Lambdasond), front		10/15	Left side indicator light
7/16	Engine temperature sensor		10/16	Right side indicator light
7/17	Mass air flow (MAF) sensor		10/17	Right tail light
7/21	Camshaft position sensor (CMP)		10/18	Left tail light
7/23	Knock sensor (KS), rear		10/19	High-level brake light
7/24	Knock sensor (KS), front		10/20	License plate light
7/25	Pulse sensor		10/22	Inside light, ceiling
7/31	ABS sensor, left front		10/24	Boot lighting
7/32	ABS sensor, right front		10/26	Reading light, left rear
7/33	Speedometer sensor		10/27	Reading light, right rear
7/37	Temperature sensor, EGR		10/29	Glove box lighting
7/43	Thermostat, left seat		10/30	Warning lamp, left front door
7/44	Thermostat, right seat		10/31	Warning lamp, right front door
7/47	PTC resistor, pre-heater		10/32	Warning lamp, left rear door
7/50	A/C pressure sensor		10/33	Warning lamp, right rear door
7/53	Pressostat, A/C		10/37	Cigarette lighter illumination
7/54	Throttle position, (TP) sensor		10/40	Gear selector light
7/55	Thermoelement, 3-way catalytic converter (TWC)		10/43	Rear brake light
7/56	Sensor ABS left rear		10/44	Right parking light, rear
7/57	Sensor ABS right rear		10/45	Right parking/tail light
7/58	Pedal sensor ABS		10/46	Right rear fog light
7/59	Temperature sensor, left duct		10/47	Lamp, right turn signal, rear
7/60	Temperature sensor, right duct		10/48	Right back-up light
7/64	Cabin temperature sensor, driver's side		10/50	Left brake light
7/65	Cabin temperature sensor, passenger's side		10/51	Left parking light rear
7/66	Rear seat thermostat, left side		10/52	Left parking/tail light
7/67	Rear seat thermostat, right side		10/53	Left rear fog light
7/68	Solar sensor ECC/indication LED - anti-theft alarm		10/54	Lamp, left turn signal, rear
7/69	Ambient temperature sensor, trip computer		10/55	Left back-up light
7/73	Coolant level sensor		10/64	Right high beam
7/77	Intake air temperature sensor (AT sensor)		10/66	Right low beam
7/79	Accelerometer		10/68	Left high beam
7/81	Pressure sensor, intake manifold		10/70	Left low beam
7/82	Heated oxygen sensor (HO2S) (Lambdasond), rear		10/72	Ashtray lighting, front
7/83	High-pressure sensor, A/C		10/74	Indicator lamp, exhaust gas temperature
8/3	Solenoid coupling A/C		10/77	Indicator lamp, SRS
8/5	IAC idling valve		10/79	Indicator lamp, winter programme and low gear (automatic transmission)
8/6-10	Injectors		10/82	Indicator lamp, ABS
8/15	Hydraulic unit ABS		10/83	Indicator lamp, hand brake
8/17	EGR converter		10/84	Brake warning lamp
8/18	EVAP valve		10/85	Warning light, high beam
8/28	Turbo control valve		10/86	Oil pressure warning lamp
8/30	Steering wheel module SRS		10/87	Indicator lamp, charging
8/31	SRS passenger module		10/88	Indicator light, bulb malfunction indicator
8/33	Igniter, left belt tensioner		10/89	Indicator lamp, rear fog lights
8/34	Igniter, right belt tensioner		10/90	Washer level warning lamp
8/36	Solenoid, P-shift lock		10/91	Service reminder indicator
8/43	Solenoid, auxiliary air intake		10/94	Indicator lamp, right turn signal
8/45	Solenoid, variable intake manifold		10/95	Indicator lamp, left turn signal
9/1	Cigarette lighter		10/96	Instrument lighting
9/2	Heated rear window		10/97	Entry lighting, driver's side
9/3	Backrest heater pad, left seat		10/98	Ashtray lighting, rear
9/4	Backrest heater pad, right seat		10/102	Entry lighting, passenger's side
9/5	Seat heater pad, left seat		10/105	Fuel level warning lamp
9/6	Seat heater pad, right seat		10/106	Check engine (malfunction indicator lamp) warning lamp
9/8	Seat heater pad, left rear seat		10/107	Indicator lamp, TRACS
9/9	Backrest heater pad, left rear seat		10/108	Extra brake light, spoiler
9/10	Seat heater pad, right rear seat		10/109	Indicator lamp, trailer
9/11	Backrest heater pad, right rear seat		10/110	Coolant level warning lamp
10/1	Left front light		10/113	Alarm warning LED
10/2	Right front light		10/114	Vanity mirror lighting, left side
10/5	Left front fog light assembly		10/115	Vanity mirror lighting, right side
10/6	Right front fog light assembly		11/1-40	Fuses
10/9	Left parking light and turn signal, front		15/2	30 rail in central electrical unit
10/10	Right parking light and turn signal, front		15/4	151 rail in central electrical unit
10/11	Left parking light, front		15/8	X rail in central electrical unit
10/12	Right parking light, front			

16/1	Radio
16/3	Loudspeaker right front door
16/4	Loudspeaker left front door
16/5	Loudspeaker right rear door
16/6	Loudspeaker left rear door
16/7	Loudspeaker, instrument panel, right side
16/8	Loudspeaker, instrument panel, left side
16/9	Aerial
16/10	Horn 1
16/11	Horn 2
16/16	Aerial booster
16/17	Loudspeaker, rear shelf/D-post, left side
16/18	Loudspeaker, rear shelf/D-post, right side
16/19	Alarm signal
17/1	Service socket for starter motor
17/7	OBD (Diagnostic) socket A
17/10	OBD (Diagnostic) socket B
17/13	DLC (Diagnostic) socket
18/4	Contact reel, SRS
19/1	Temperature gauge
19/2	Tachometer
19/3	Speedometer
19/5	Fuel gauge
19/6	Exciter, tachometer
19/7	Exciter, speedometer, temperature gauge, fuel gauge
20/2	Distributor
20/3-7	Spark plugs
20/11	Ballast resistor
20/18	Resistor, heater fan
23/0-601	Branching points
24/1	Connector, 14-pin Instrument panel harness - Firewall harness
24/2	Connector, 53-pin
	Engine compartment harness - Firewall harness
24/3	LHD cars, Connector, pos. 26-53 in 53-pin
	RHD cars, Connector, 53-pin
	Firewall harness - Door sill harness, left
24/4	Connector, pos. 1-37 in 53-pin
	Firewall harness - Door sill harness, right
24/5	Connector, 24-pin
	Firewall harness - Left front door harness
24/6	Connector, 24-pin
	Firewall harness - Right front door harness
24/7	Connector, 14-pin
	Firewall harness - Tunnel harness
24/9	Connector, 4-pin
	Firewall harness - Ceiling harness
24/10	Connector, 2-pin
	Firewall harness - heater fan / A/C unit
24/11	Connector, 10-pin
	Firewall harness - A/C unit
24/12	Connector, 4-pin
	Firewall harness - heater fan / A/C unit
24/13	Connector, 53-pin
	Engine compartment harness - Instrument panel harness
24/14	Connector, pos. 1-25 in 53-pin
	Engine compartment harness - Door sill harness, left
24/15	Connector, 14-pin
	Engine compartment harness - Engine harness
24/16	Connector - 26-pin
	Engine compartment harness - Front harness
24/17	Connector, 11-pin
	Rocker panel (door sill) harness, left - Left rear door harness
24/18	Connector, 11-pin
	Rocker panel (door sill) harness, right - Right rear door harness
24/19	Connector - 4-pin
	Rocker panel (door sill) harness, right - Rear wheel sensor harness
24/20	Connector - 4-pin Firewall harness - Power sunroof harness
24/21	Connector - 6-pin
	Rocker panel (door sill) harness, left - left seat

24/22	Connector - 6-pin
	Rocker panel (door sill) harness, right - right seat
24/25	Connector, 14-pin
	Rocker panel (door sill) harness, left - trunk harness
24/26	Connector, 2-pin
	Firewall harness - belt tensioner igniter harness, left side
24/27	Connector, 2-pin
	Firewall harness - belt tensioner igniter harness, right side
24/29	Connector, 2-pin at firewall
24/33	Connector, 2-pin
	Firewall harness - passenger module harness
24/34	Connector pos. 38-53 in 53-pin
	Engine compartment harness - Firewall harness
24/35A	Connector 8-pin accessories
24/35B	Connector 1-pin accessories
24/37	Connector, 6-pin
	Firewall harness - switch harness heated rear seat
24/42	Connector, 2-pin, accessories
25/9	Front fog lights, bridge
31/4	Ground point, engine
	(ground connection battery - engine)
31/7	Ground point, A-post driver's side
31/11	Ground point, trunk, left side
31/12	Ground point, trunk, right side
31/15	Ground point, A-post passenger's side
31/32	Ground point on engine (power ground)
31/33	Ground point on engine (signal ground)
31/44	Ground point, engine compartment (ground connection battery - body)
31/47	Ground point, left cross member
31/48	Ground point, right cross member
31/50	Ground point, central electrical unit (power ground)
31/51	Ground point, central electrical unit (signal ground)
31/52	Ground point, DI power state and ignition coil
31/55	Ground point, engine cooling fan
31/65	Ground point, steering column
C/BA	Connector, 2-pin, at fuel pump
C/BB	Connector, 2-pin, fuel gauge
C/BC	Connector, 4-pin, power aerial/booster
C/CE	Connector, 2-pin, heated left seat
C/CF	Connector, 2-pin, heated left seat
C/CG	Connector, 2-pin, heated right seat
C/CH	Connector, 2-pin, heated right seat
C/CJ	Connector, 6-pin, cruise control
C/CK	Connector, 14-pin, power windows
C/CL	Connector, 6-pin, tailgate wash/wipe
C/CM	Connector, 2-pin, heated rear seat, left side
C/CN	Connector, 2-pin, heated rear seat, left side
C/CP	Connector, 2-pin, heated rear seat, right side
C/CQ	Connector, 2-pin, heated rear seat, right side
C/CR	14-pin connector, audio
C/CS	10-pin connector, audio
C/EA	Connector, 1-pin, engine cooling fan
C/EB	Connector, 4-pin, high pressure sensor, A/C
C/EC	Connector, 1-pin, solenoid switch A/C
C/ED	Connector, 15-pin, ABS
C/EG	2-pin connector, engine coolant temperature sensor
C/EH	Connector, 3-pin, camshaft position sensor (CMP)
C/EJ	Connector, 2-pin, impulse sensor
C/EK	Connector, 2-pin, windshield wiper motor
C/EL	Connector, 3-pin, windshield wiper motor
C/EM	Connector, 2-pin at tunnel
C/EN	Connector, 2-pin, EGR temperature sensor
C/EP	Connector, 4-pin, heated oxygen sensor (HO2S), (Lambdasond), front
C/EQ	Connector, 4-pin, heated oxygen sensor)HO2S), (Lambdasond), rear
K/1	Relay, auto-down power window

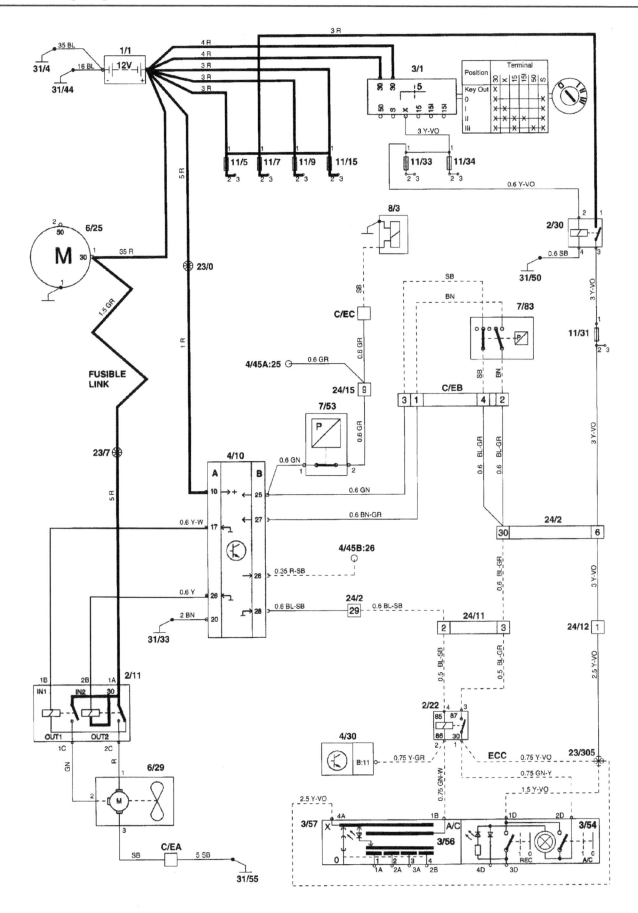

Typical engine cooling fan

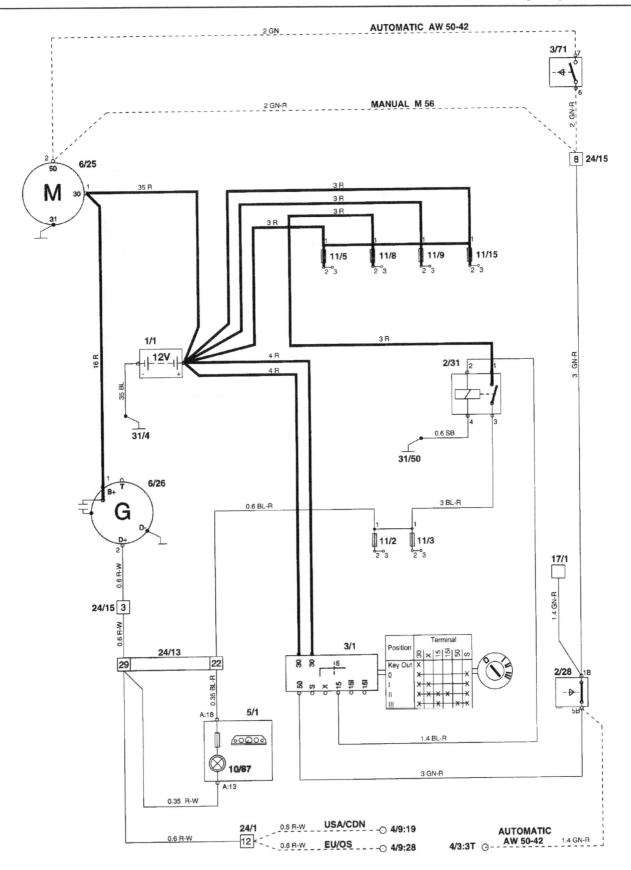

Starting and charging

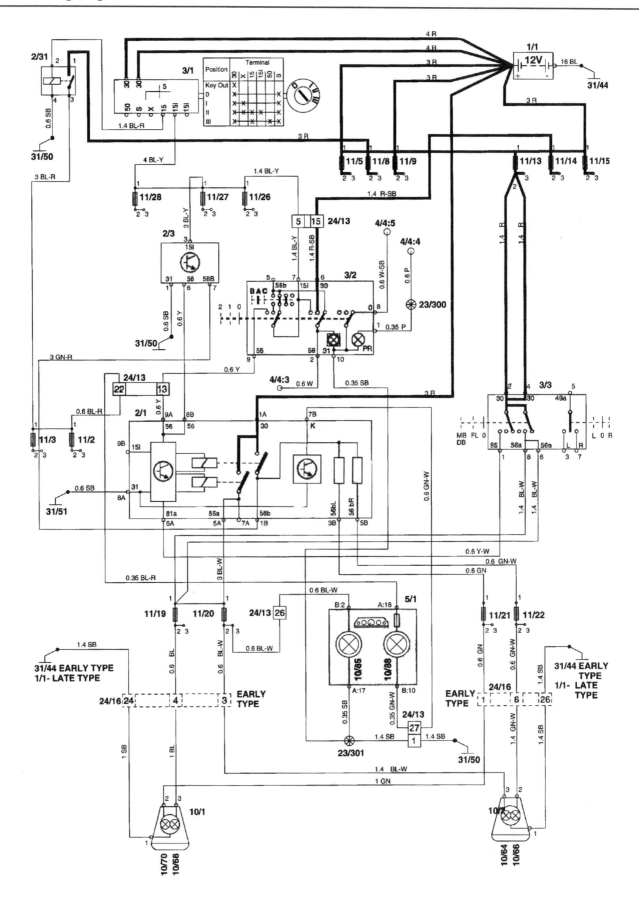

Headlights - dim/dip

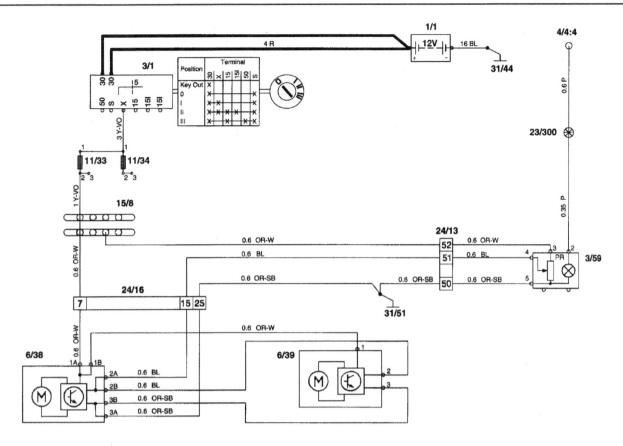

Headlight adjustment - early models

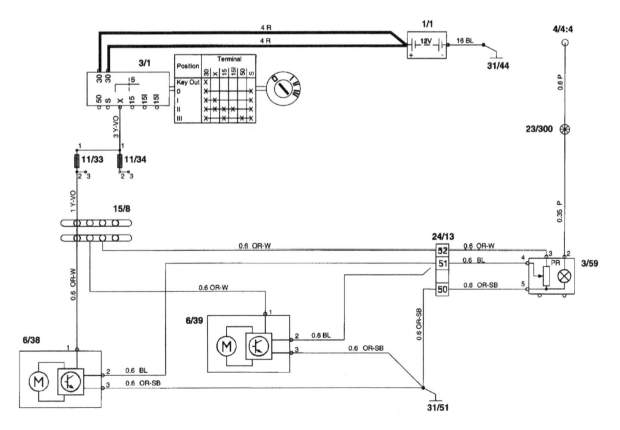

Headlight adjustment - later models

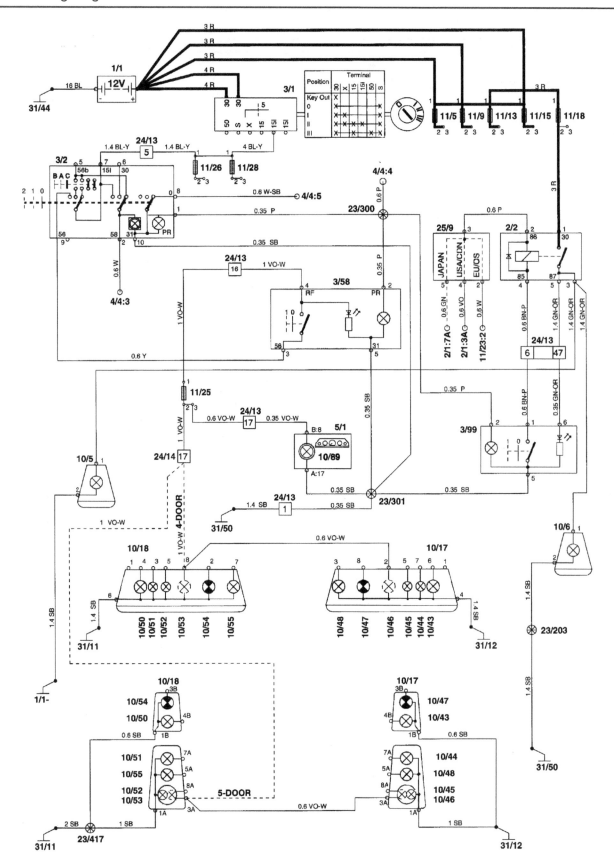

Fog lights

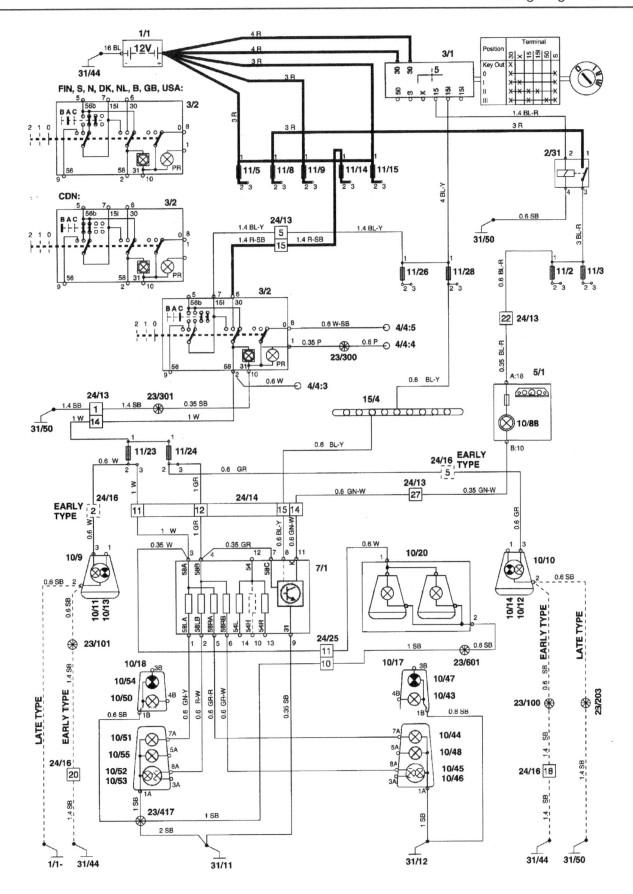

Side, tail and number plate lights

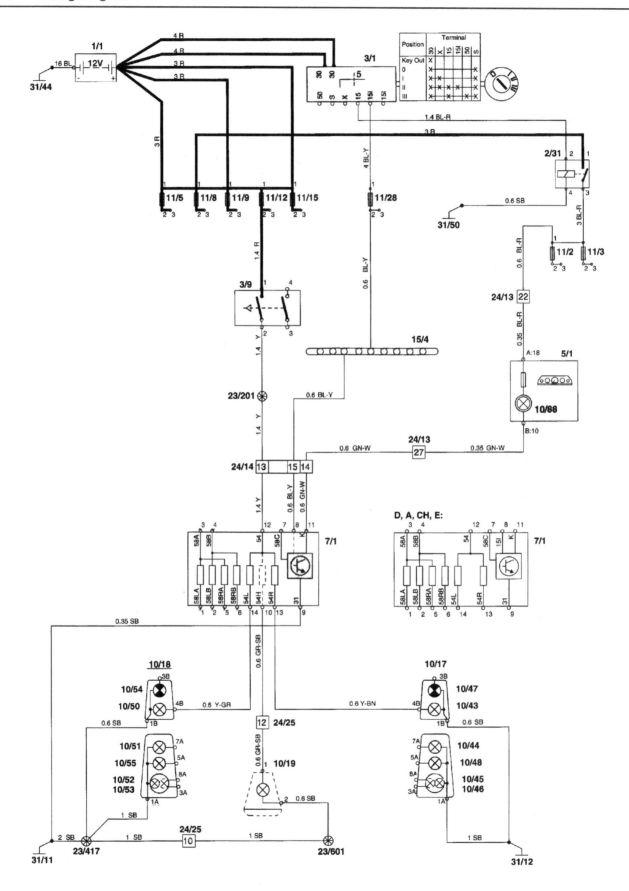

Brake lights

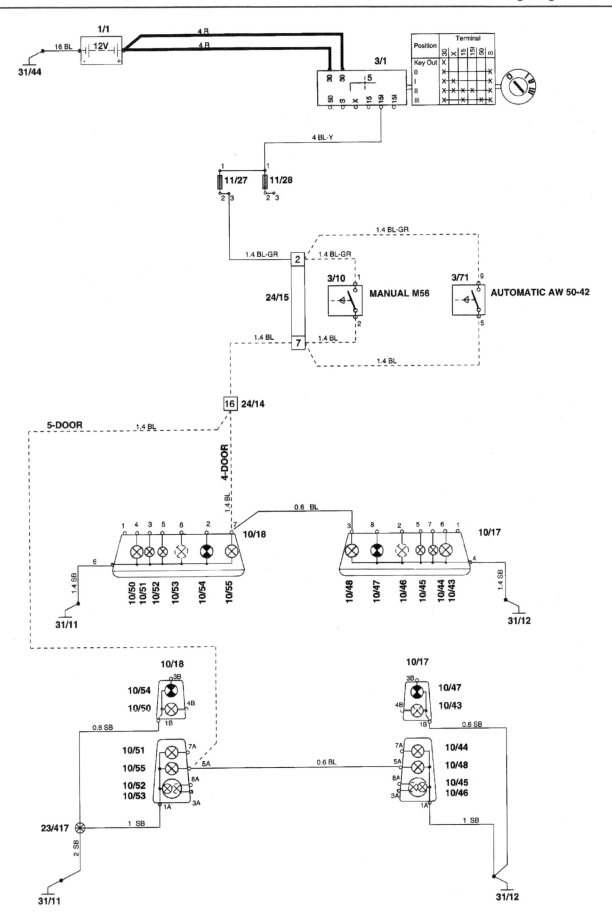

Reversing lights

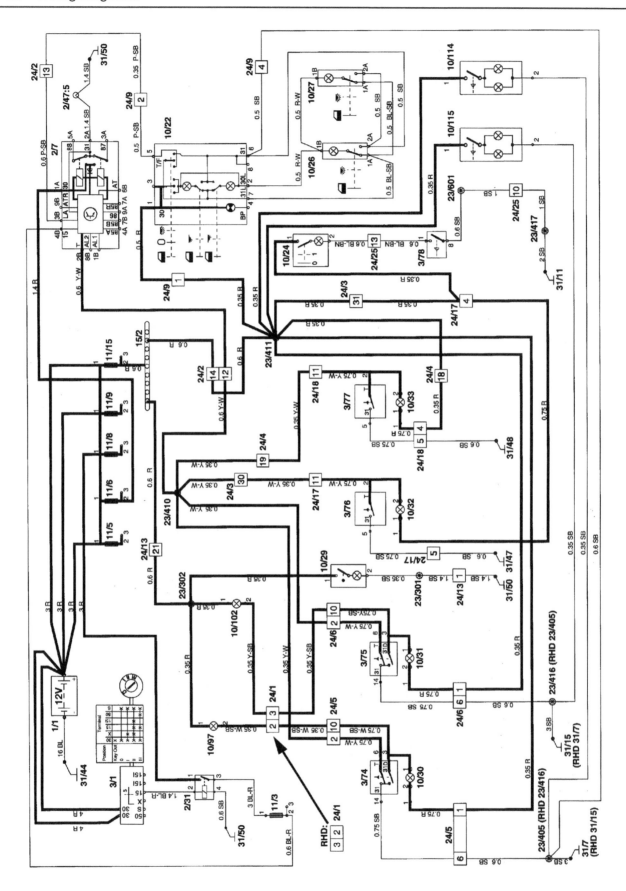

Typical interior lighting

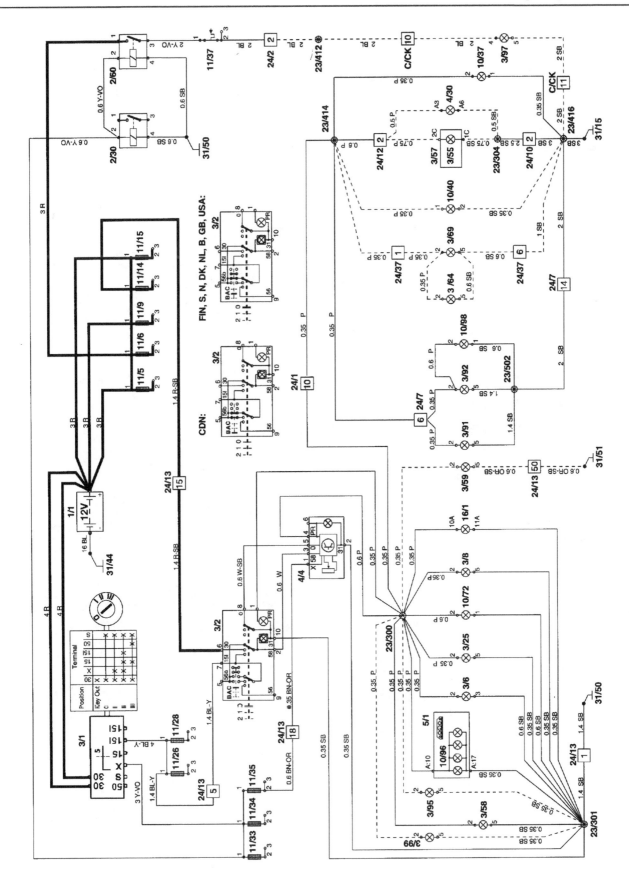

Instrument and control lighting

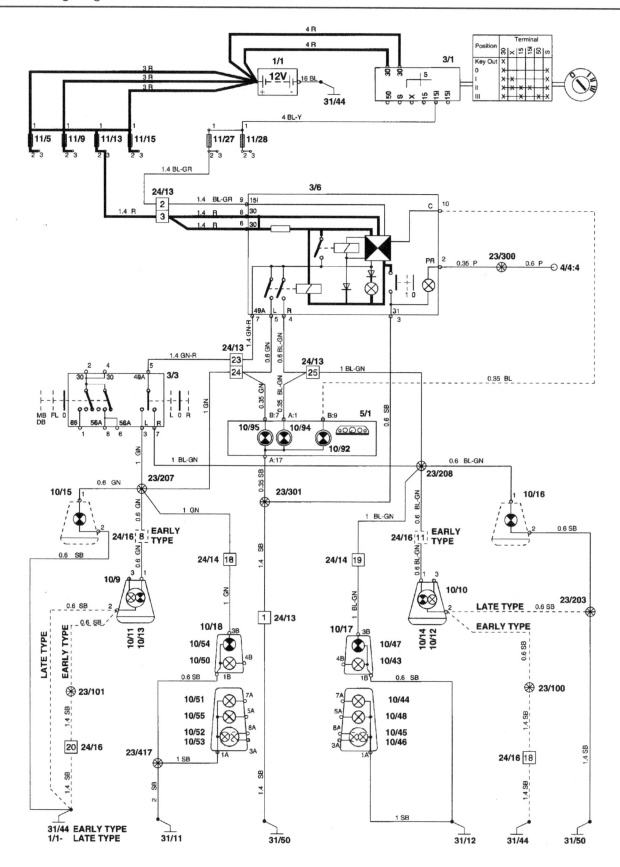

Typical direction indicators and hazard warning lights

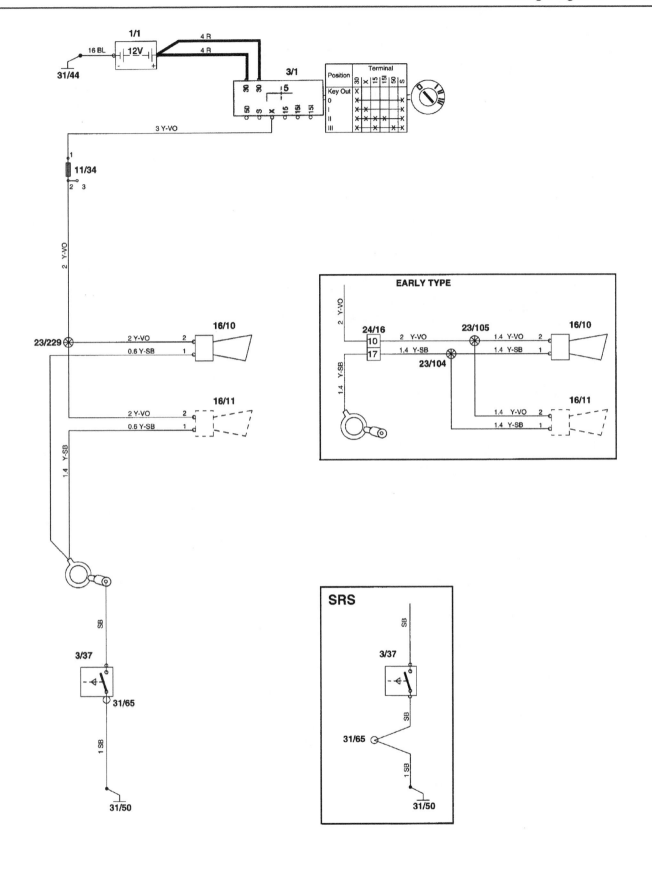

Position	Terminal						
	30	X	15	15I	50	S	
Key Out	X					X	
0	X						
I	X	X					
II	X	X	X	X			
III	X		X		X	X	

EARLY TYPE

SRS

Horn

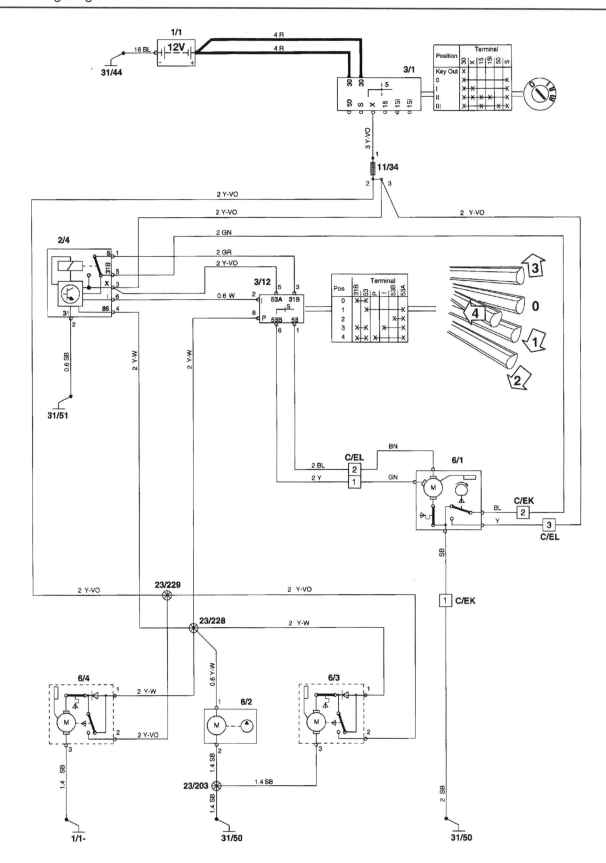

Typical windscreen and headlight wash/wipe

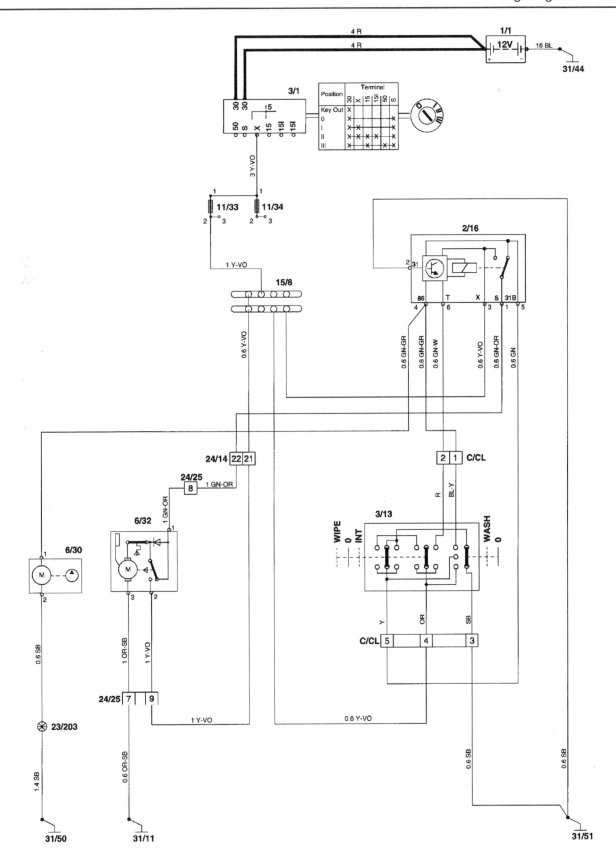

Rear wash/wipe

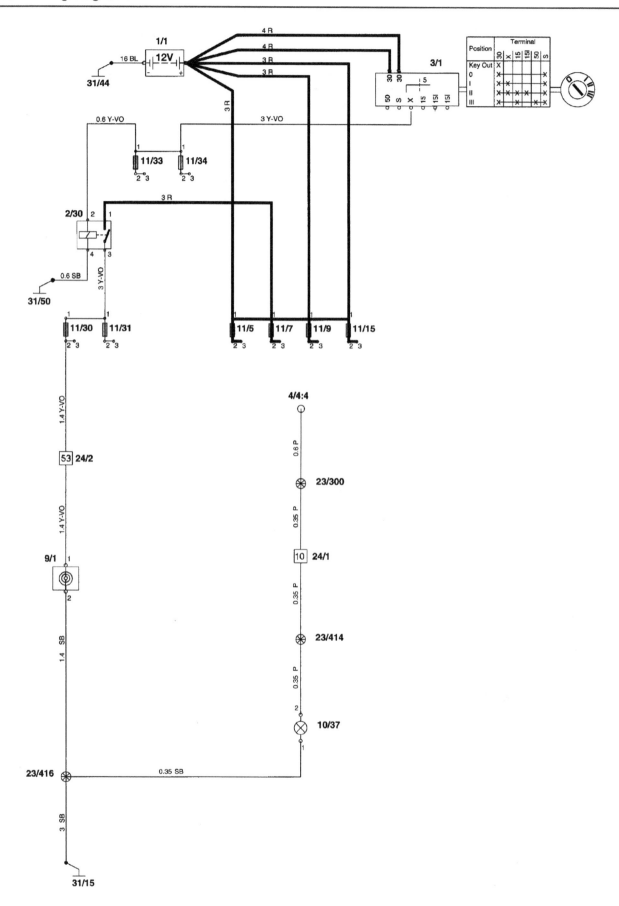

Cigar lighter

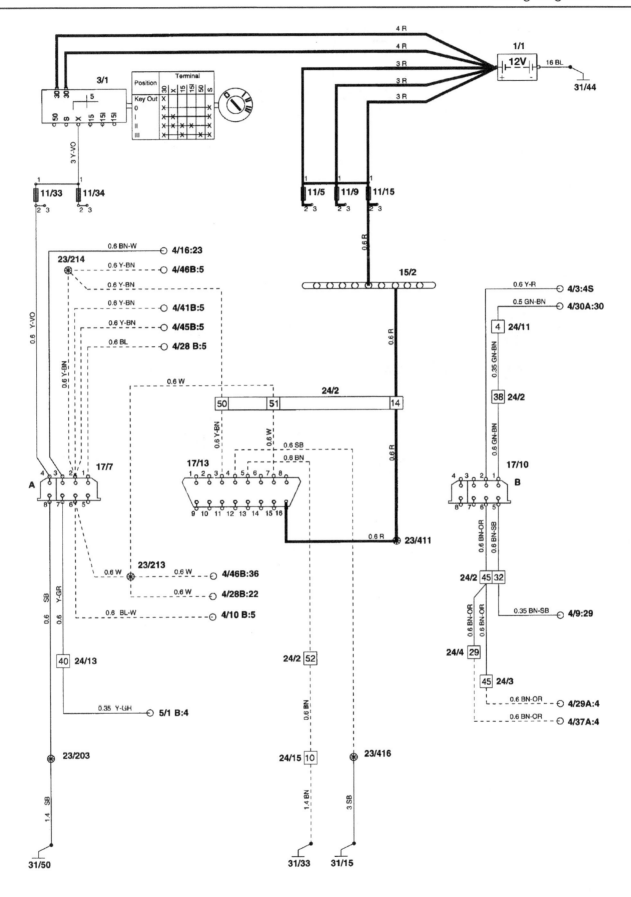

On-board diagnostic system

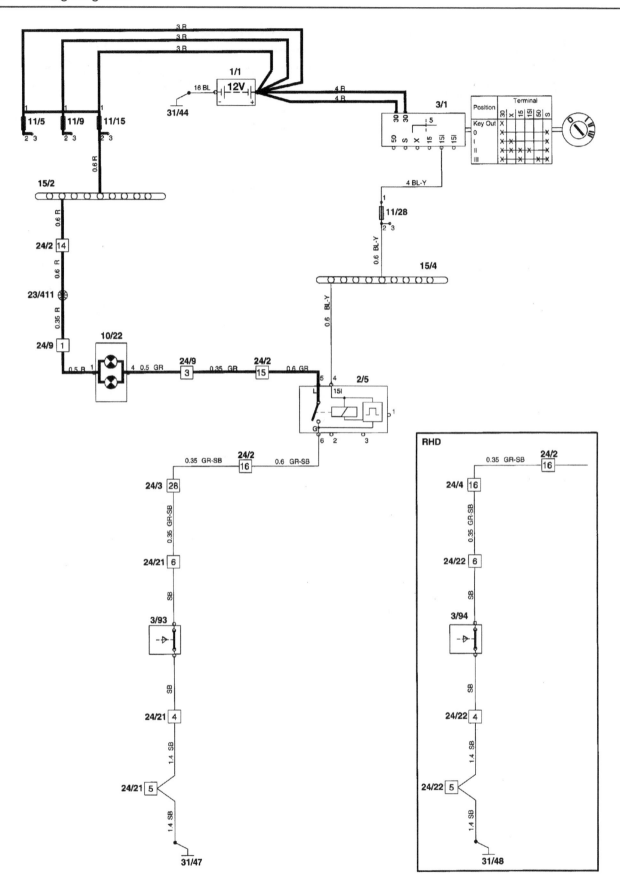

Seat belt reminder

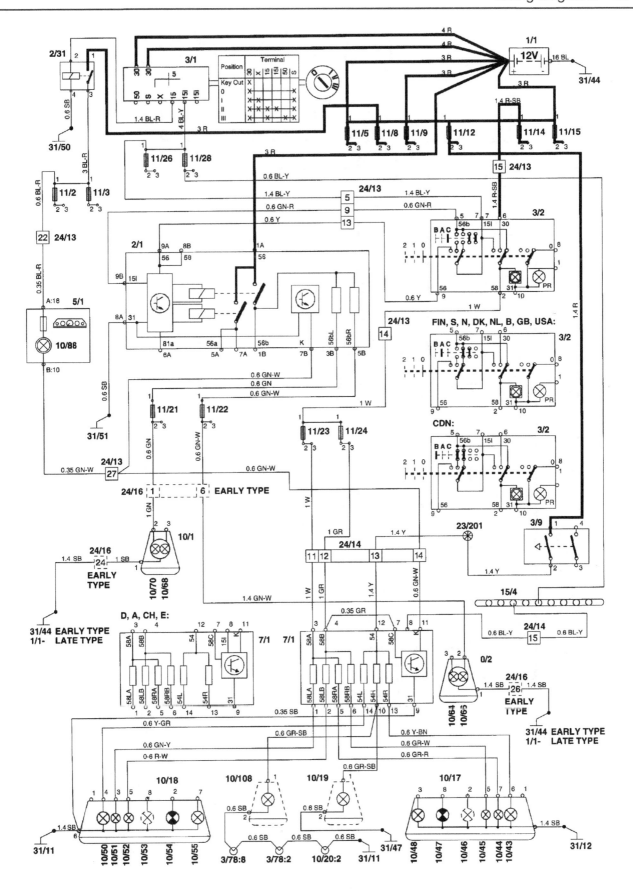

Bulb malfunction indicator

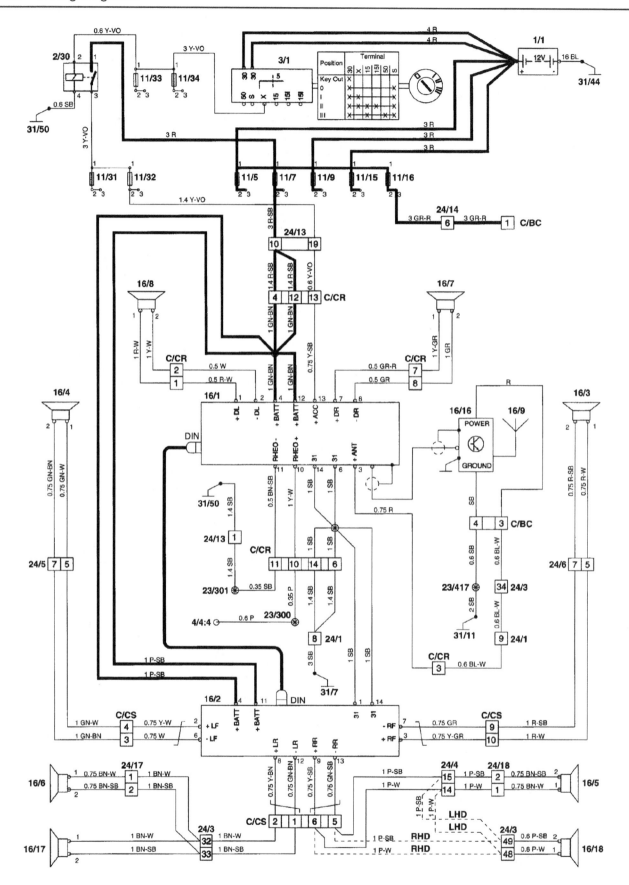

Typical radio/cassette

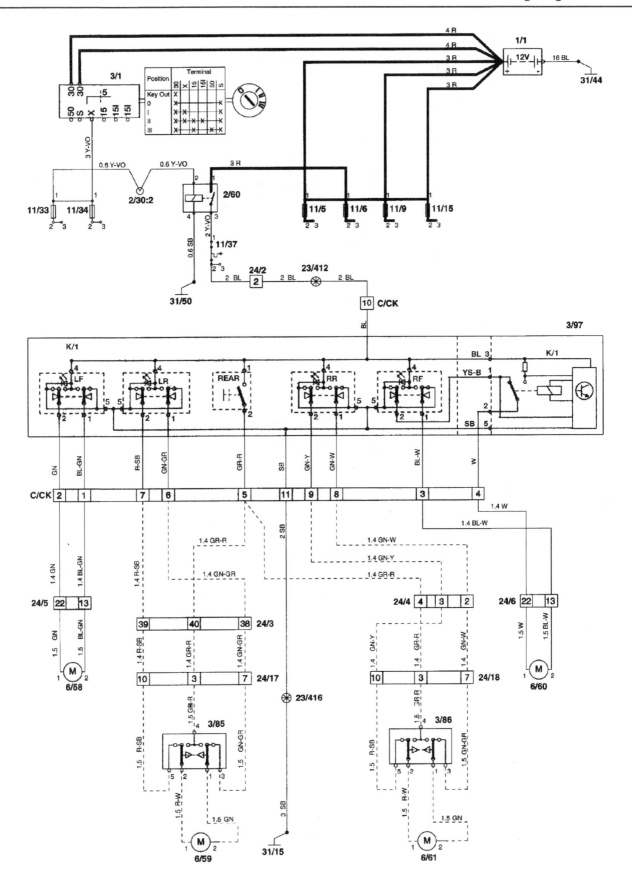

Electric windows

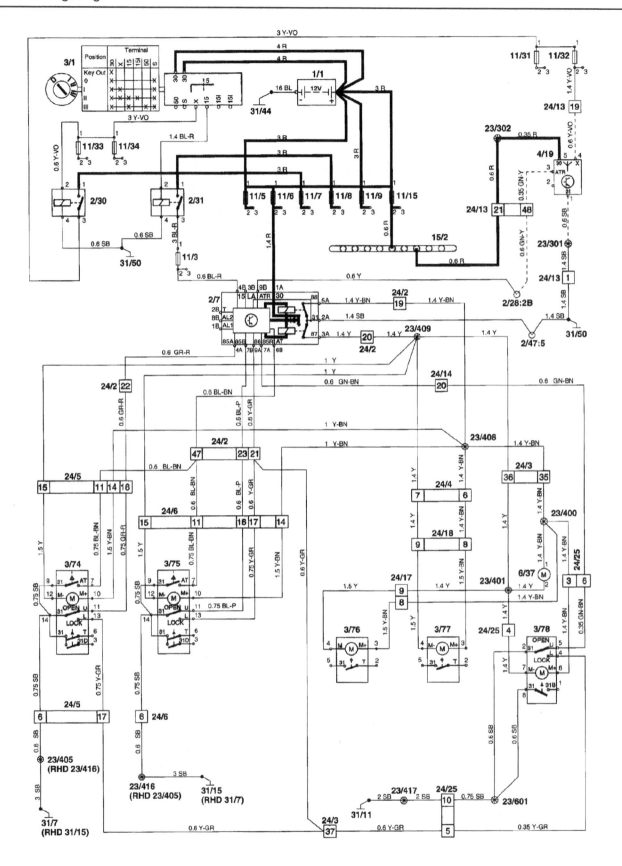

Typical central locking (without deadlocks)

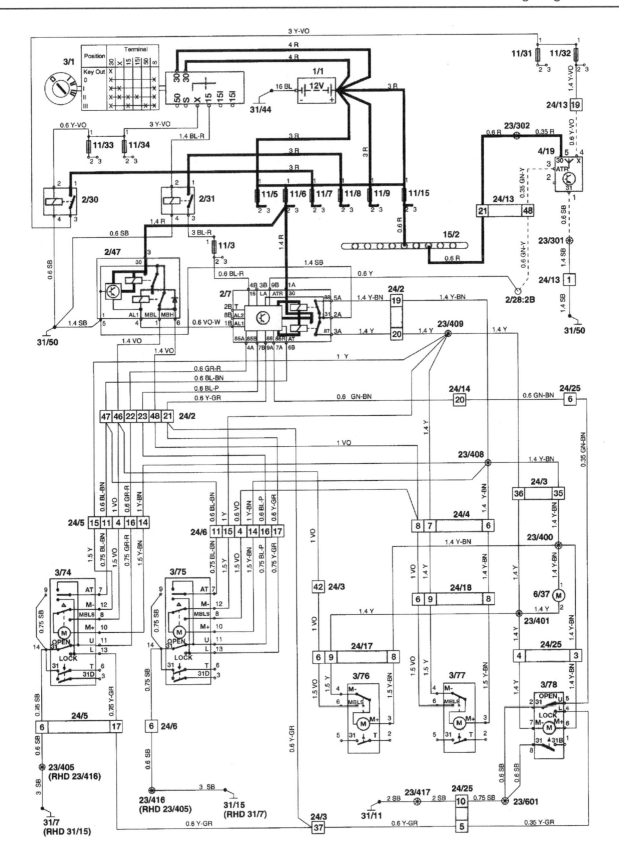

Typical central locking (with deadlocks)

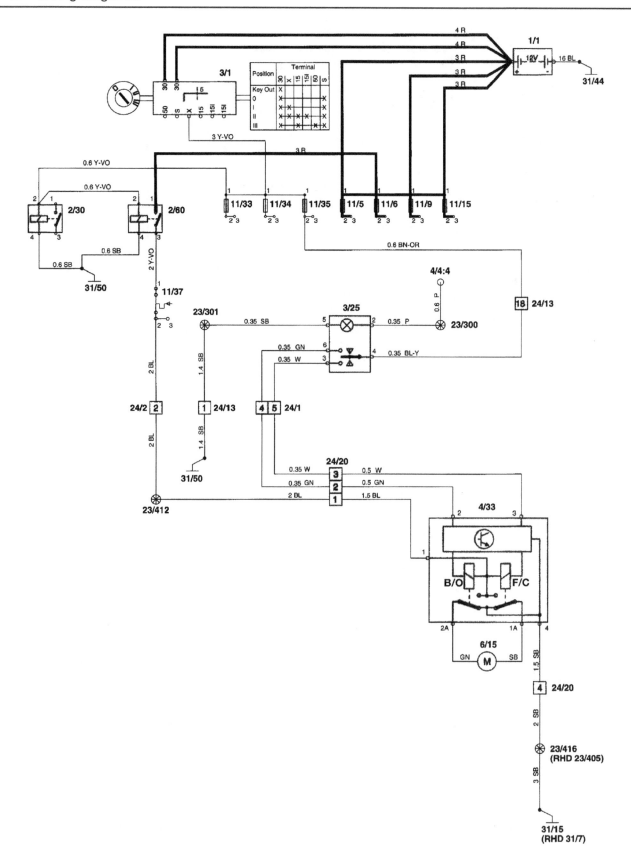

Electric sunroof

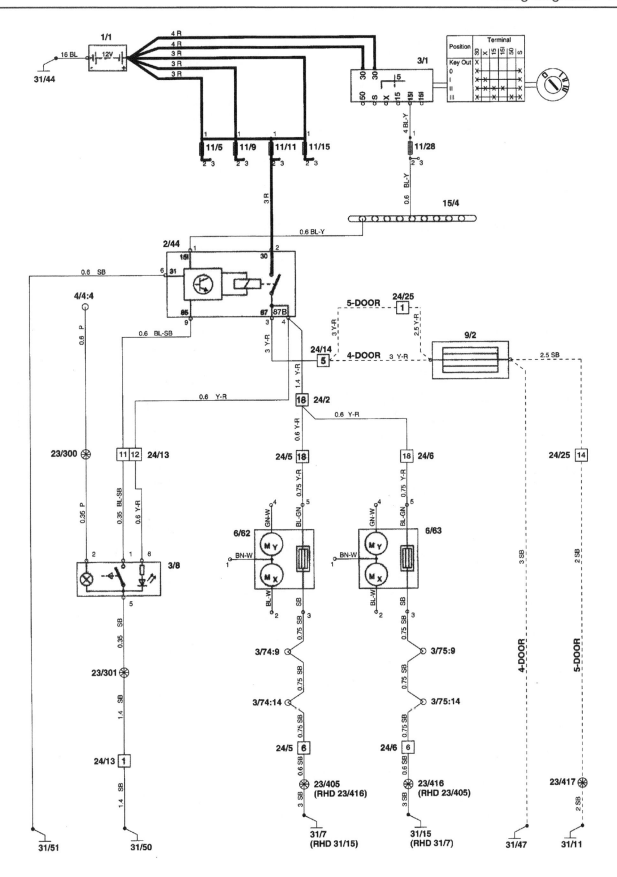

Heated rear window and door mirrors

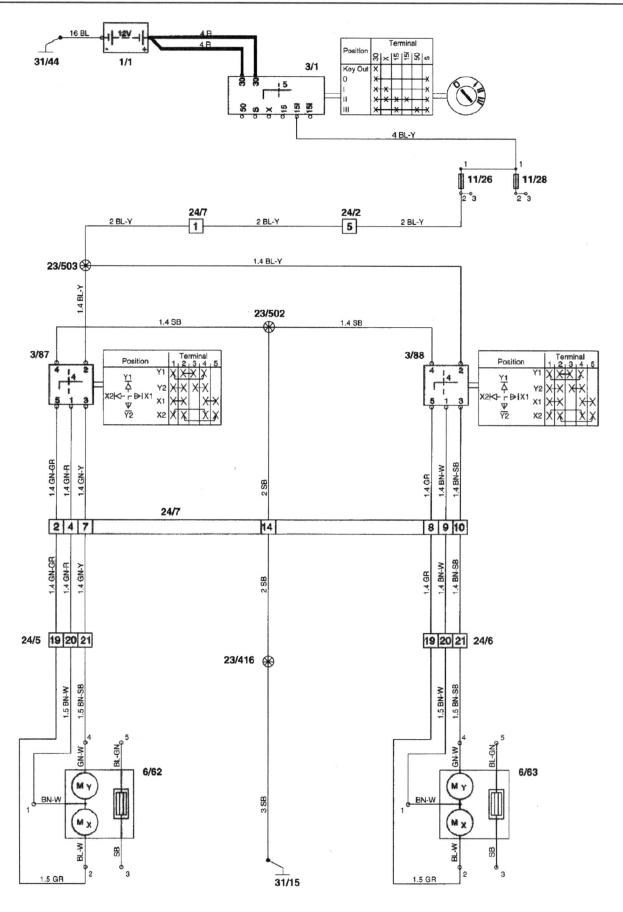

Electric door mirrors

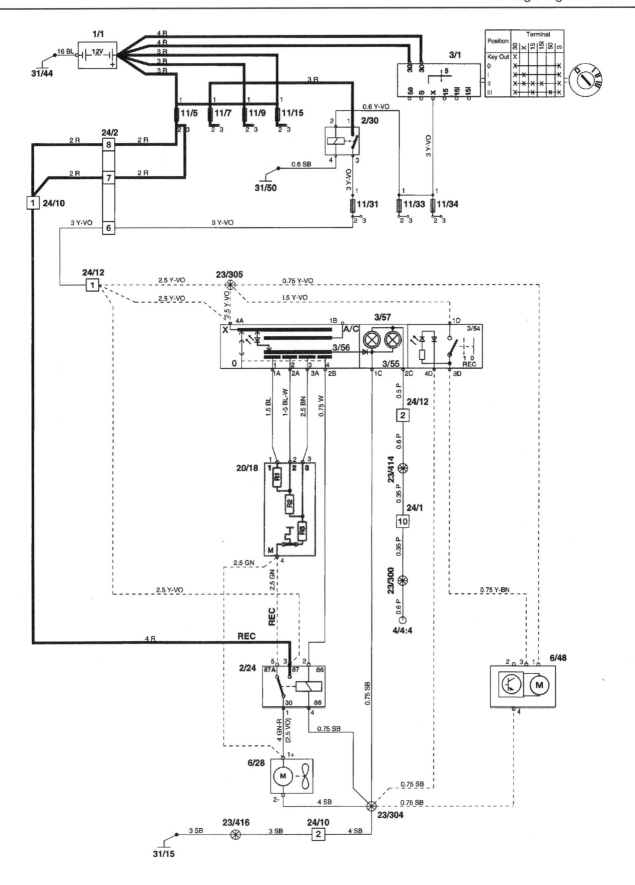

Heater blower

Dimensions and weights

Note: *All figures are approximate, and may vary according to model. Refer to manufacturer's data for exact figures.*

Dimensions

Overall length
    Saloon models . . . . 4660 mm
    Estate models . . . . 4710 mm
Overall width . . . . 1760 mm
Overall height:
    Saloon models . . . . 1420 mm
    Estate models . . . . 1440 mm
Wheelbase . . . . 2660 mm

Weights

Kerb weight . . . . Consult vehicle registration certificate
Maximum gross vehicle weight . . . . Consult type designation plate behind right-hand headlight in engine
                                                  compartment
Maximum roof rack load . . . . 100 kg

Conversion factors

Length (distance)

Inches (in)	x 25.4	= Millimetres (mm)	x 0.0394	= Inches (in)
Feet (ft)	x 0.305	= Metres (m)	x 3.281	= Feet (ft)
Miles	x 1.609	= Kilometres (km)	x 0.621	= Miles

Volume (capacity)

Cubic inches (cu in; in³)	x 16.387	= Cubic centimetres (cc; cm³)	x 0.061	= Cubic inches (cu in; in³)
Imperial pints (Imp pt)	x 0.568	= Litres (l)	x 1.76	= Imperial pints (Imp pt)
Imperial quarts (Imp qt)	x 1.137	= Litres (l)	x 0.88	= Imperial quarts (Imp qt)
Imperial quarts (Imp qt)	x 1.201	= US quarts (US qt)	x 0.833	= Imperial quarts (Imp qt)
US quarts (US qt)	x 0.946	= Litres (l)	x 1.057	= US quarts (US qt)
Imperial gallons (Imp gal)	x 4.546	= Litres (l)	x 0.22	= Imperial gallons (Imp gal)
Imperial gallons (Imp gal)	x 1.201	= US gallons (US gal)	x 0.833	= Imperial gallons (Imp gal)
US gallons (US gal)	x 3.785	= Litres (l)	x 0.264	= US gallons (US gal)

Mass (weight)

Ounces (oz)	x 28.35	= Grams (g)	x 0.035	= Ounces (oz)
Pounds (lb)	x 0.454	= Kilograms (kg)	x 2.205	= Pounds (lb)

Force

Ounces-force (ozf; oz)	x 0.278	= Newtons (N)	x 3.6	= Ounces-force (ozf; oz)
Pounds-force (lbf; lb)	x 4.448	= Newtons (N)	x 0.225	= Pounds-force (lbf; lb)
Newtons (N)	x 0.1	= Kilograms-force (kgf; kg)	x 9.81	= Newtons (N)

Pressure

Pounds-force per square inch (psi; lbf/in²; lb/in²)	x 0.070	= Kilograms-force per square centimetre (kgf/cm²; kg/cm²)	x 14.223	= Pounds-force per square inch (psi; lbf/in²; lb/in²)
Pounds-force per square inch (psi; lbf/in²; lb/in²)	x 0.068	= Atmospheres (atm)	x 14.696	= Pounds-force per square inch (psi; lbf/in²; lb/in²)
Pounds-force per square inch (psi; lbf/in²; lb/in²)	x 0.069	= Bars	x 14.5	= Pounds-force per square inch (psi; lbf/in²; lb/in²)
Pounds-force per square inch (psi; lbf/in²; lb/in²)	x 6.895	= Kilopascals (kPa)	x 0.145	= Pounds-force per square inch (psi; lbf/in²; lb/in²)
Kilopascals (kPa)	x 0.01	= Kilograms-force per square centimetre (kgf/cm²; kg/cm²)	x 98.1	= Kilopascals (kPa)
Millibar (mbar)	x 100	= Pascals (Pa)	x 0.01	= Millibar (mbar)
Millibar (mbar)	x 0.0145	= Pounds-force per square inch (psi; lbf/in²; lb/in²)	x 68.947	= Millibar (mbar)
Millibar (mbar)	x 0.75	= Millimetres of mercury (mmHg)	x 1.333	= Millibar (mbar)
Millibar (mbar)	x 0.401	= Inches of water (inH$_2$O)	x 2.491	= Millibar (mbar)
Millimetres of mercury (mmHg)	x 0.535	= Inches of water (inH$_2$O)	x 1.868	= Millimetres of mercury (mmHg)
Inches of water (inH$_2$O)	x 0.036	= Pounds-force per square inch (psi; lbf/in²; lb/in²)	x 27.68	= Inches of water (inH$_2$O)

Torque (moment of force)

Pounds-force inches (lbf in; lb in)	x 1.152	= Kilograms-force centimetre (kgf cm; kg cm)	x 0.868	= Pounds-force inches (lbf in; lb in)
Pounds-force inches (lbf in; lb in)	x 0.113	= Newton metres (Nm)	x 8.85	= Pounds-force inches (lbf in; lb in)
Pounds-force inches (lbf in; lb in)	x 0.083	= Pounds-force feet (lbf ft; lb ft)	x 12	= Pounds-force inches (lbf in; lb in)
Pounds-force feet (lbf ft; lb ft)	x 0.138	= Kilograms-force metres (kgf m; kg m)	x 7.233	= Pounds-force feet (lbf ft; lb ft)
Pounds-force feet (lbf ft; lb ft)	x 1.356	= Newton metres (Nm)	x 0.738	= Pounds-force feet (lbf ft; lb ft)
Newton metres (Nm)	x 0.102	= Kilograms-force metres (kgf m; kg m)	x 9.804	= Newton metres (Nm)

Power

Horsepower (hp)	x 745.7	= Watts (W)	x 0.0013	= Horsepower (hp)

Velocity (speed)

Miles per hour (miles/hr; mph)	x 1.609	= Kilometres per hour (km/hr; kph)	x 0.621	= Miles per hour (miles/hr; mph)

Fuel consumption*

Miles per gallon (mpg)	x 0.354	= Kilometres per litre (km/l)	x 2.825	= Miles per gallon (mpg)

Temperature

Degrees Fahrenheit = (°C x 1.8) + 32   Degrees Celsius (Degrees Centigrade; °C) = (°F - 32) x 0.56

It is common practice to convert from miles per gallon (mpg) to litres/100 kilometres (l/100km), where mpg x l/100 km = 282

Spare parts are available from many sources, including maker's appointed garages, accessory shops, and motor factors. To be sure of obtaining the correct parts, it may sometimes be necessary to quote the vehicle identification number. If possible, it can also be useful to take the old parts along for positive identification. Items such as starter motors and alternators may be available under a service exchange scheme - any parts returned should always be clean.

Our advice regarding spare part sources is as follows:

Officially-appointed garages

This is the best source of parts which are peculiar to your car, and are not otherwise generally available (eg badges, interior trim, certain body panels, etc). It is also the only place at which you should buy parts if the vehicle is still under warranty.

Accessory shops

These are very good places to buy materials and components needed for the maintenance of your car (oil, air and fuel filters, spark plugs, light bulbs, drivebelts, oils and greases, brake pads, touch-up paint, etc). Parts like this sold by a reputable shop are of the same standard as those used by the car manufacturer.

Motor factors

Good factors will stock all the more important components which wear out comparatively quickly and can sometimes supply individual components needed for the overhaul of a larger assembly. They may also handle work such as cylinder block reboring, crankshaft regrinding and balancing, etc.

Tyre and exhaust specialists

These outlets may be independent or members of a local or national chain. They frequently offer competitive prices when compared with a main dealer or local garage, but it will pay to obtain several quotes before making a decision. Also ask what 'extras' may be added to the quote - for instance, fitting a new valve and balancing the wheel are both often charged on top of the price of a new tyre.

Other sources

Beware of parts of materials obtained from market stalls, car boot sales or similar outlets. Such items are not invariably sub-standard, but there is little chance of compensation if they do prove unsatisfactory. In the case of safety-critical components such as brake pads there is the risk not only of financial loss but also of an accident causing injury or death.

Vehicle identification numbers

Modifications are a continuing and unpublicised process in vehicle manufacture, quite apart from major model changes. Spare parts manuals and lists are compiled upon a numerical basis, the individual vehicle identification numbers being essential to correct identification of the component concerned.

When ordering spare parts, always give as much information as possible. Quote the type designation, chassis number, engine number and, where applicable, the vehicle identification number as appropriate.

On models for the UK market only, the Vehicle Identification Number (VIN) is located on the top of the facia and can be viewed through the windscreen.

The type designation and chassis number are stamped in the engine compartment, below the windscreen.

Vehicle loading details and codes for colour and upholstery are located on a plate behind the right-hand headlight in the engine compartment.

Engine type designation and serial numbers are stamped on the upper side of the cylinder block beside the coolant pump. These numbers may also appear on a sticker on the upper timing belt cover.

The transmission identification numbers are located on a plate attached to the transmission casing.

The type designation and chassis number are stamped in the engine compartment

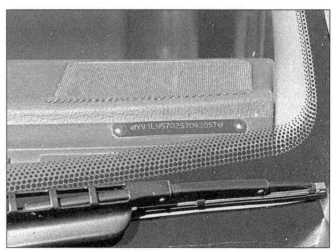

Vehicle Identification Number (VIN) location on the top of the facia

Whenever servicing, repair or overhaul work is carried out on the car or its components, observe the following procedures and instructions. This will assist in carrying out the operation efficiently and to a professional standard of workmanship.

Joint mating faces and gaskets

When separating components at their mating faces, never insert screwdrivers or similar implements into the joint between the faces in order to prise them apart. This can cause severe damage which results in oil leaks, coolant leaks, etc upon reassembly. Separation is usually achieved by tapping along the joint with a soft-faced hammer in order to break the seal. However, note that this method may not be suitable where dowels are used for component location.

Where a gasket is used between the mating faces of two components, a new one must be fitted on reassembly; fit it dry unless otherwise stated in the repair procedure. Make sure that the mating faces are clean and dry, with all traces of old gasket removed. When cleaning a joint face, use a tool which is unlikely to score or damage the face, and remove any burrs or nicks with an oilstone or fine file.

Make sure that tapped holes are cleaned with a pipe cleaner, and keep them free of jointing compound, if this is being used, unless specifically instructed otherwise.

Ensure that all orifices, channels or pipes are clear, and blow through them, preferably using compressed air.

Oil seals

Oil seals can be removed by levering them out with a wide flat-bladed screwdriver or similar implement. Alternatively, a number of self-tapping screws may be screwed into the seal, and these used as a purchase for pliers or some similar device in order to pull the seal free.

Whenever an oil seal is removed from its working location, either individually or as part of an assembly, it should be renewed.

The very fine sealing lip of the seal is easily damaged, and will not seal if the surface it contacts is not completely clean and free from scratches, nicks or grooves. If the original sealing surface of the component cannot be restored, and the manufacturer has not made provision for slight relocation of the seal relative to the sealing surface, the component should be renewed.

Protect the lips of the seal from any surface which may damage them in the course of fitting. Use tape or a conical sleeve where possible. Lubricate the seal lips with oil before fitting and, on dual-lipped seals, fill the space between the lips with grease.

Unless otherwise stated, oil seals must be fitted with their sealing lips toward the lubricant to be sealed.

Use a tubular drift or block of wood of the appropriate size to install the seal and, if the seal housing is shouldered, drive the seal down to the shoulder. If the seal housing is unshouldered, the seal should be fitted with its face flush with the housing top face (unless otherwise instructed).

Screw threads and fastenings

Seized nuts, bolts and screws are quite a common occurrence where corrosion has set in, and the use of penetrating oil or releasing fluid will often overcome this problem if the offending item is soaked for a while before attempting to release it. The use of an impact driver may also provide a means of releasing such stubborn fastening devices, when used in conjunction with the appropriate screwdriver bit or socket. If none of these methods works, it may be necessary to resort to the careful application of heat, or the use of a hacksaw or nut splitter device.

Studs are usually removed by locking two nuts together on the threaded part, and then using a spanner on the lower nut to unscrew the stud. Studs or bolts which have broken off below the surface of the component in which they are mounted can sometimes be removed using a stud extractor. Always ensure that a blind tapped hole is completely free from oil, grease, water or other fluid before installing the bolt or stud. Failure to do this could cause the housing to crack due to the hydraulic action of the bolt or stud as it is screwed in.

When tightening a castellated nut to accept a split pin, tighten the nut to the specified torque, where applicable, and then tighten further to the next split pin hole. Never slacken the nut to align the split pin hole, unless stated in the repair procedure.

When checking or retightening a nut or bolt to a specified torque setting, slacken the nut or bolt by a quarter of a turn, and then retighten to the specified setting. However, this should not be attempted where angular tightening has been used.

For some screw fastenings, notably cylinder head bolts or nuts, torque wrench settings are no longer specified for the latter stages of tightening, "angle-tightening" being called up instead. Typically, a fairly low torque wrench setting will be applied to the bolts/nuts in the correct sequence, followed by one or more stages of tightening through specified angles.

Locknuts, locktabs and washers

Any fastening which will rotate against a component or housing during tightening should always have a washer between it and the relevant component or housing.

Spring or split washers should always be renewed when they are used to lock a critical component such as a big-end bearing retaining bolt or nut. Locktabs which are folded over to retain a nut or bolt should always be renewed.

Self-locking nuts can be re-used in non-critical areas, providing resistance can be felt when the locking portion passes over the bolt or stud thread. However, it should be noted that self-locking stiffnuts tend to lose their effectiveness after long periods of use, and should then be renewed as a matter of course.

Split pins must always be replaced with new ones of the correct size for the hole.

When thread-locking compound is found on the threads of a fastener which is to be re-used, it should be cleaned off with a wire brush and solvent, and fresh compound applied on reassembly.

Special tools

Some repair procedures in this manual entail the use of special tools such as a press, two or three-legged pullers, spring compressors, etc. Wherever possible, suitable readily-available alternatives to the manufacturer's special tools are described, and are shown in use. In some instances, where no alternative is possible, it has been necessary to resort to the use of a manufacturer's tool, and this has been done for reasons of safety as well as the efficient completion of the repair operation. Unless you are highly-skilled and have a thorough understanding of the procedures described, never attempt to bypass the use of any special tool when the procedure described specifies its use. Not only is there a very great risk of personal injury, but expensive damage could be caused to the components involved.

Environmental considerations

When disposing of used engine oil, brake fluid, antifreeze, etc, give due consideration to any detrimental environmental effects. Do not, for instance, pour any of the above liquids down drains into the general sewage system, or onto the ground to soak away. Many local council refuse tips provide a facility for waste oil disposal, as do some garages. If none of these facilities are available, consult your local Environmental Health Department, or the National Rivers Authority, for further advice.

With the universal tightening-up of legislation regarding the emission of environmentally-harmful substances from motor vehicles, most vehicles have tamperproof devices fitted to the main adjustment points of the fuel system. These devices are primarily designed to prevent unqualified persons from adjusting the fuel/air mixture, with the chance of a consequent increase in toxic emissions. If such devices are found during servicing or overhaul, they should, wherever possible, be renewed or refitted in accordance with the manufacturer's requirements or current legislation.

OIL CARE
FOLLOW THE CODE

O I L   B A N K   L I N E
0800 66 33 66
www.oilbankline.org.uk

Note: It is antisocial and illegal to dump oil down the drain. To find the location of your local oil recycling bank, call this number free.

The jack supplied with the vehicle tool kit should only be used for changing the roadwheels - see *"Wheel changing"* at the front of this manual. When carrying out any other kind of work, raise the vehicle using a hydraulic (or "trolley") jack, and always supplement the jack with axle stands positioned under the vehicle jacking points.

When using a hydraulic jack or axle stands, always position the jack head or axle stand head under one of the relevant jacking points or load bearing areas.

To raise the front of the vehicle, position the jack under the engine subframe at the front centre. **Do not** jack the vehicle under the sump, or any of the steering or suspension components. With the front raised, position axle stands under the subframe on each side.

To raise the rear of the vehicle, position the jack under the reinforced plate below the spare wheel well. With the rear raised, position axle stands under the structural members just in front of the rear suspension attachments on each side.

The jack supplied with the vehicle locates in the jacking points in the reinforced area on the inside of the sills. Ensure that the jack head is correctly engaged before attempting to raise the vehicle.

Never work under, around, or near a raised vehicle, unless it is adequately supported in at least two places.

Radio/cassette unit anti-theft system - precaution

The radio/cassette unit fitted as standard equipment by Volvo is equipped with a built-in security code, to deter thieves. If the power source to the unit is cut, the anti-theft system will activate. Even if the power source is immediately reconnected, the radio/cassette unit will not function until the correct security code has been entered. Therefore, if you do not know the correct security code for the radio/cassette unit **do not** disconnect either of the battery terminals, or remove the radio/cassette unit from the vehicle.

To enter the correct security code, follow the instructions provided with the radio/cassette player or vehicle handbook.

If an incorrect code is entered, the unit will become locked, and cannot be operated.

If this happens, or if the security code is lost or forgotten, seek the advice of your Volvo dealer.

Introduction

A selection of good tools is a fundamental requirement for anyone contemplating the maintenance and repair of a motor vehicle. For the owner who does not possess any, their purchase will prove a considerable expense, offsetting some of the savings made by doing-it-yourself. However, provided that the tools purchased meet the relevant national safety standards and are of good quality, they will last for many years and prove an extremely worthwhile investment.

To help the average owner to decide which tools are needed to carry out the various tasks detailed in this manual, we have compiled three lists of tools under the following headings: *Maintenance and minor repair*, *Repair and overhaul*, and *Special*. Newcomers to practical mechanics should start off with the *Maintenance and minor repair* tool kit, and confine themselves to the simpler jobs around the vehicle. Then, as confidence and experience grow, more difficult tasks can be undertaken, with extra tools being purchased as, and when, they are needed. In this way, a *Maintenance and minor repair* tool kit can be built up into a *Repair and overhaul* tool kit over a considerable period of time, without any major cash outlays. The experienced do-it-yourselfer will have a tool kit good enough for most repair and overhaul procedures, and will add tools from the *Special* category when it is felt that the expense is justified by the amount of use to which these tools will be put.

Maintenance and minor repair tool kit

The tools given in this list should be considered as a minimum requirement if routine maintenance, servicing and minor repair operations are to be undertaken. We recommend the purchase of combination spanners (ring one end, open-ended the other); although more expensive than open-ended ones, they do give the advantages of both types of spanner.

☐ *Combination spanners:*
  Metric - 8 to 19 mm inclusive
☐ *Adjustable spanner - 35 mm jaw (approx.)*
☐ *Spark plug spanner (with rubber insert) - petrol models*
☐ *Spark plug gap adjustment tool - petrol models*
☐ *Set of feeler gauges*
☐ *Brake bleed nipple spanner*
☐ *Screwdrivers:*
  Flat blade - 100 mm long x 6 mm dia
  Cross blade - 100 mm long x 6 mm dia
  Torx - various sizes (not all vehicles)
☐ *Combination pliers*
☐ *Hacksaw (junior)*
☐ *Tyre pump*
☐ *Tyre pressure gauge*
☐ *Oil can*
☐ *Oil filter removal tool*
☐ *Fine emery cloth*
☐ *Wire brush (small)*
☐ *Funnel (medium size)*
☐ *Sump drain plug key (not all vehicles)*

Repair and overhaul tool kit

These tools are virtually essential for anyone undertaking any major repairs to a motor vehicle, and are additional to those given in the *Maintenance and minor repair* list. Included in this list is a comprehensive set of sockets. Although these are expensive, they will be found invaluable as they are so versatile - particularly if various drives are included in the set. We recommend the half-inch square-drive type, as this can be used with most proprietary torque wrenches.

The tools in this list will sometimes need to be supplemented by tools from the *Special* list:

☐ *Sockets (or box spanners) to cover range in previous list (including Torx sockets)*
☐ *Reversible ratchet drive (for use with sockets)*
☐ *Extension piece, 250 mm (for use with sockets)*
☐ *Universal joint (for use with sockets)*
☐ *Flexible handle or sliding T "breaker bar" (for use with sockets)*
☐ *Torque wrench (for use with sockets)*
☐ *Self-locking grips*
☐ *Ball pein hammer*
☐ *Soft-faced mallet (plastic or rubber)*
☐ *Screwdrivers:*
  Flat blade - long & sturdy, short (chubby), and narrow (electrician's) types
  Cross blade - long & sturdy, and short (chubby) types
☐ *Pliers:*
  Long-nosed
  Side cutters (electrician's)
  Circlip (internal and external)
☐ *Cold chisel - 25 mm*
☐ *Scriber*
☐ *Scraper*
☐ *Centre-punch*
☐ *Pin punch*
☐ *Hacksaw*
☐ *Brake hose clamp*
☐ *Brake/clutch bleeding kit*
☐ *Selection of twist drills*
☐ *Steel rule/straight-edge*
☐ *Allen keys (inc. splined/Torx type)*
☐ *Selection of files*
☐ *Wire brush*
☐ *Axle stands*
☐ *Jack (strong trolley or hydraulic type)*
☐ *Light with extension lead*
☐ *Universal electrical multi-meter*

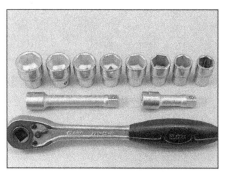

Sockets and reversible ratchet drive

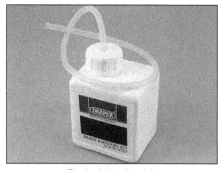

Brake bleeding kit

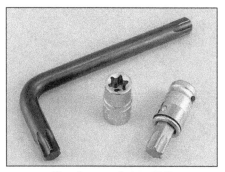

Torx key, socket and bit

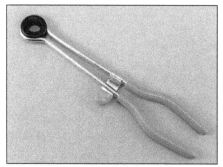

Hose clamp

Angular-tightening gauge

Special tools

The tools in this list are those which are not used regularly, are expensive to buy, or which need to be used in accordance with their manufacturers' instructions. Unless relatively difficult mechanical jobs are undertaken frequently, it will not be economic to buy many of these tools. Where this is the case, you could consider clubbing together with friends (or joining a motorists' club) to make a joint purchase, or borrowing the tools against a deposit from a local garage or tool hire specialist. It is worth noting that many of the larger DIY superstores now carry a large range of special tools for hire at modest rates.

The following list contains only those tools and instruments freely available to the public, and not those special tools produced by the vehicle manufacturer specifically for its dealer network. You will find occasional references to these manufacturers' special tools in the text of this manual. Generally, an alternative method of doing the job without the vehicle manufacturers' special tool is given. However, sometimes there is no alternative to using them. Where this is the case and the relevant tool cannot be bought or borrowed, you will have to entrust the work to a dealer.

- ☐ Angular-tightening gauge
- ☐ Valve spring compressor
- ☐ Valve grinding tool
- ☐ Piston ring compressor
- ☐ Piston ring removal/installation tool
- ☐ Cylinder bore hone
- ☐ Balljoint separator
- ☐ Coil spring compressors (where applicable)
- ☐ Two/three-legged hub and bearing puller
- ☐ Impact screwdriver
- ☐ Micrometer and/or vernier calipers
- ☐ Dial gauge
- ☐ Stroboscopic timing light
- ☐ Dwell angle meter/tachometer
- ☐ Fault code reader
- ☐ Cylinder compression gauge
- ☐ Hand-operated vacuum pump and gauge
- ☐ Clutch plate alignment set
- ☐ Brake shoe steady spring cup removal tool
- ☐ Bush and bearing removal/installation set
- ☐ Stud extractors
- ☐ Tap and die set
- ☐ Lifting tackle
- ☐ Trolley jack

Buying tools

Reputable motor accessory shops and superstores often offer excellent quality tools at discount prices, so it pays to shop around.

Remember, you don't have to buy the most expensive items on the shelf, but it is always advisable to steer clear of the very cheap tools. Beware of 'bargains' offered on market stalls or at car boot sales. There are plenty of good tools around at reasonable prices, but always aim to purchase items which meet the relevant national safety standards. If in doubt, ask the proprietor or manager of the shop for advice before making a purchase.

Care and maintenance of tools

Having purchased a reasonable tool kit, it is necessary to keep the tools in a clean and serviceable condition. After use, always wipe off any dirt, grease and metal particles using a clean, dry cloth, before putting the tools away. Never leave them lying around after they have been used. A simple tool rack on the garage or workshop wall for items such as screwdrivers and pliers is a good idea. Store all normal spanners and sockets in a metal box. Any measuring instruments, gauges, meters, etc, must be carefully stored where they cannot be damaged or become rusty.

Take a little care when tools are used. Hammer heads inevitably become marked, and screwdrivers lose the keen edge on their blades from time to time. A little timely attention with emery cloth or a file will soon restore items like this to a good finish.

Working facilities

Not to be forgotten when discussing tools is the workshop itself. If anything more than routine maintenance is to be carried out, a suitable working area becomes essential.

It is appreciated that many an owner-mechanic is forced by circumstances to remove an engine or similar item without the benefit of a garage or workshop. Having done this, any repairs should always be done under the cover of a roof.

Wherever possible, any dismantling should be done on a clean, flat workbench or table at a suitable working height.

Any workbench needs a vice; one with a jaw opening of 100 mm is suitable for most jobs. As mentioned previously, some clean dry storage space is also required for tools, as well as for any lubricants, cleaning fluids, touch-up paints etc, which become necessary.

Another item which may be required, and which has a much more general usage, is an electric drill with a chuck capacity of at least 8 mm. This, together with a good range of twist drills, is virtually essential for fitting accessories.

Last, but not least, always keep a supply of old newspapers and clean, lint-free rags available, and try to keep any working area as clean as possible.

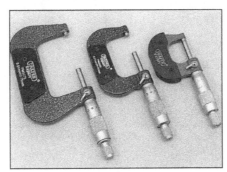

Micrometers

Dial test indicator ("dial gauge")

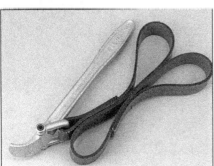

Strap wrench

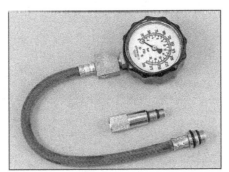

Compression tester

Fault code reader

This is a guide to getting your vehicle through the MOT test. Obviously it will not be possible to examine the vehicle to the same standard as the professional MOT tester. However, working through the following checks will enable you to identify any problem areas before submitting the vehicle for the test.

Where a testable component is in borderline condition, the tester has discretion in deciding whether to pass or fail it. The basis of such discretion is whether the tester would be happy for a close relative or friend to use the vehicle with the component in that condition. If the vehicle presented is clean and evidently well cared for, the tester may be more inclined to pass a borderline component than if the vehicle is scruffy and apparently neglected.

It has only been possible to summarise the test requirements here, based on the regulations in force at the time of printing. Test standards are becoming increasingly stringent, although there are some exemptions for older vehicles.

An assistant will be needed to help carry out some of these checks.

The checks have been sub-divided into four categories, as follows:

1 Checks carried out **FROM THE DRIVER'S SEAT**

2 Checks carried out **WITH THE VEHICLE ON THE GROUND**

3 Checks carried out **WITH THE VEHICLE RAISED AND THE WHEELS FREE TO TURN**

4 Checks carried out on **YOUR VEHICLE'S EXHAUST EMISSION SYSTEM**

---

1 Checks carried out **FROM THE DRIVER'S SEAT**

Handbrake

☐ Test the operation of the handbrake. Excessive travel (too many clicks) indicates incorrect brake or cable adjustment.
☐ Check that the handbrake cannot be released by tapping the lever sideways. Check the security of the lever mountings.

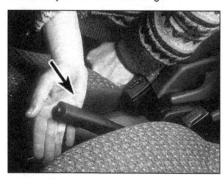

Footbrake

☐ Depress the brake pedal and check that it does not creep down to the floor, indicating a master cylinder fault. Release the pedal, wait a few seconds, then depress it again. If the pedal travels nearly to the floor before firm resistance is felt, brake adjustment or repair is necessary. If the pedal feels spongy, there is air in the hydraulic system which must be removed by bleeding.

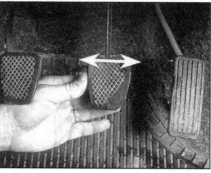

☐ Check that the brake pedal is secure and in good condition. Check also for signs of fluid leaks on the pedal, floor or carpets, which would indicate failed seals in the brake master cylinder.
☐ Check the servo unit (when applicable) by operating the brake pedal several times, then keeping the pedal depressed and starting the engine. As the engine starts, the pedal will move down slightly. If not, the vacuum hose or the servo itself may be faulty.

Steering wheel and column

☐ Examine the steering wheel for fractures or looseness of the hub, spokes or rim.
☐ Move the steering wheel from side to side and then up and down. Check that the steering wheel is not loose on the column, indicating wear or a loose retaining nut. Continue moving the steering wheel as before, but also turn it slightly from left to right.
☐ Check that the steering wheel is not loose on the column, and that there is no abnormal

movement of the steering wheel, indicating wear in the column support bearings or couplings.

Windscreen, mirrors and sunvisor

☐ The windscreen must be free of cracks or other significant damage within the driver's field of view. (Small stone chips are acceptable.) Rear view mirrors must be secure, intact, and capable of being adjusted.

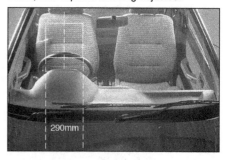

☐ The driver's sunvisor must be capable of being stored in the "up" position.

Seat belts and seats

Note: *The following checks are applicable to all seat belts, front and rear.*

☐ Examine the webbing of all the belts (including rear belts if fitted) for cuts, serious fraying or deterioration. Fasten and unfasten each belt to check the buckles. If applicable, check the retracting mechanism. Check the security of all seat belt mountings accessible from inside the vehicle.
☐ Seat belts with pre-tensioners, once activated, have a "flag" or similar showing on the seat belt stalk. This, in itself, is not a reason for test failure.
☐ The front seats themselves must be securely attached and the backrests must lock in the upright position.

Doors

☐ Both front doors must be able to be opened and closed from outside and inside, and must latch securely when closed.

2 Checks carried out WITH THE VEHICLE ON THE GROUND

Vehicle identification

☐ Number plates must be in good condition, secure and legible, with letters and numbers correctly spaced – spacing at (A) should be at least twice that at (B).

☐ The VIN plate and/or homologation plate must be legible.

Electrical equipment

☐ Switch on the ignition and check the operation of the horn.
☐ Check the windscreen washers and wipers, examining the wiper blades; renew damaged or perished blades. Also check the operation of the stop-lights.

☐ Check the operation of the sidelights and number plate lights. The lenses and reflectors must be secure, clean and undamaged.
☐ Check the operation and alignment of the headlights. The headlight reflectors must not be tarnished and the lenses must be undamaged.
☐ Switch on the ignition and check the operation of the direction indicators (including the instrument panel tell-tale) and the hazard warning lights. Operation of the sidelights and stop-lights must not affect the indicators - if it does, the cause is usually a bad earth at the rear light cluster.
☐ Check the operation of the rear foglight(s), including the warning light on the instrument panel or in the switch.
☐ The ABS warning light must illuminate in accordance with the manufacturers' design. For most vehicles, the ABS warning light should illuminate when the ignition is switched on, and (if the system is operating properly) extinguish after a few seconds. Refer to the owner's handbook.

Footbrake

☐ Examine the master cylinder, brake pipes and servo unit for leaks, loose mountings, corrosion or other damage.

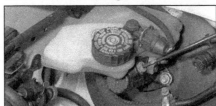

☐ The fluid reservoir must be secure and the fluid level must be between the upper (**A**) and lower (**B**) markings.

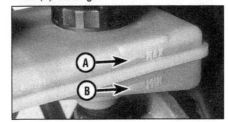

☐ Inspect both front brake flexible hoses for cracks or deterioration of the rubber. Turn the steering from lock to lock, and ensure that the hoses do not contact the wheel, tyre, or any part of the steering or suspension mechanism. With the brake pedal firmly depressed, check the hoses for bulges or leaks under pressure.

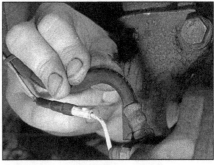

Steering and suspension

☐ Have your assistant turn the steering wheel from side to side slightly, up to the point where the steering gear just begins to transmit this movement to the roadwheels. Check for excessive free play between the steering wheel and the steering gear, indicating wear or insecurity of the steering column joints, the column-to-steering gear coupling, or the steering gear itself.
☐ Have your assistant turn the steering wheel more vigorously in each direction, so that the roadwheels just begin to turn. As this is done, examine all the steering joints, linkages, fittings and attachments. Renew any component that shows signs of wear or damage. On vehicles with power steering, check the security and condition of the steering pump, drivebelt and hoses.
☐ Check that the vehicle is standing level, and at approximately the correct ride height.

Shock absorbers

☐ Depress each corner of the vehicle in turn, then release it. The vehicle should rise and then settle in its normal position. If the vehicle continues to rise and fall, the shock absorber is defective. A shock absorber which has seized will also cause the vehicle to fail.

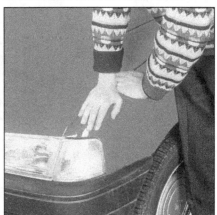

Exhaust system

☐ Start the engine. With your assistant holding a rag over the tailpipe, check the entire system for leaks. Repair or renew leaking sections.

3 Checks carried out
WITH THE VEHICLE RAISED AND THE WHEELS FREE TO TURN

Jack up the front and rear of the vehicle, and securely support it on axle stands. Position the stands clear of the suspension assemblies. Ensure that the wheels are clear of the ground and that the steering can be turned from lock to lock.

Steering mechanism

☐ Have your assistant turn the steering from lock to lock. Check that the steering turns smoothly, and that no part of the steering mechanism, including a wheel or tyre, fouls any brake hose or pipe or any part of the body structure.
☐ Examine the steering rack rubber gaiters for damage or insecurity of the retaining clips. If power steering is fitted, check for signs of damage or leakage of the fluid hoses, pipes or connections. Also check for excessive stiffness or binding of the steering, a missing split pin or locking device, or severe corrosion of the body structure within 30 cm of any steering component attachment point.

Front and rear suspension and wheel bearings

☐ Starting at the front right-hand side, grasp the roadwheel at the 3 o'clock and 9 o'clock positions and rock gently but firmly. Check for free play or insecurity at the wheel bearings, suspension balljoints, or suspension mountings, pivots and attachments.
☐ Now grasp the wheel at the 12 o'clock and 6 o'clock positions and repeat the previous inspection. Spin the wheel, and check for roughness or tightness of the front wheel bearing.

☐ If excess free play is suspected at a component pivot point, this can be confirmed by using a large screwdriver or similar tool and levering between the mounting and the component attachment. This will confirm whether the wear is in the pivot bush, its retaining bolt, or in the mounting itself (the bolt holes can often become elongated).

☐ Carry out all the above checks at the other front wheel, and then at both rear wheels.

Springs and shock absorbers

☐ Examine the suspension struts (when applicable) for serious fluid leakage, corrosion, or damage to the casing. Also check the security of the mounting points.
☐ If coil springs are fitted, check that the spring ends locate in their seats, and that the spring is not corroded, cracked or broken.
☐ If leaf springs are fitted, check that all leaves are intact, that the axle is securely attached to each spring, and that there is no deterioration of the spring eye mountings, bushes, and shackles.

☐ The same general checks apply to vehicles fitted with other suspension types, such as torsion bars, hydraulic displacer units, etc. Ensure that all mountings and attachments are secure, that there are no signs of excessive wear, corrosion or damage, and (on hydraulic types) that there are no fluid leaks or damaged pipes.
☐ Inspect the shock absorbers for signs of serious fluid leakage. Check for wear of the mounting bushes or attachments, or damage to the body of the unit.

Driveshafts (fwd vehicles only)

☐ Rotate each front wheel in turn and inspect the constant velocity joint gaiters for splits or damage. Also check that each driveshaft is straight and undamaged.

Braking system

☐ If possible without dismantling, check brake pad wear and disc condition. Ensure that the friction lining material has not worn excessively, (A) and that the discs are not fractured, pitted, scored or badly worn (B).

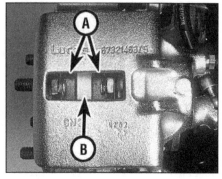

☐ Examine all the rigid brake pipes underneath the vehicle, and the flexible hose(s) at the rear. Look for corrosion, chafing or insecurity of the pipes, and for signs of bulging under pressure, chafing, splits or deterioration of the flexible hoses.
☐ Look for signs of fluid leaks at the brake calipers or on the brake backplates. Repair or renew leaking components.
☐ Slowly spin each wheel, while your assistant depresses and releases the footbrake. Ensure that each brake is operating and does not bind when the pedal is released.

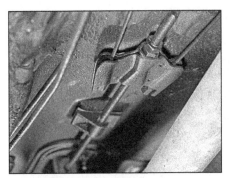

☐ Examine the handbrake mechanism, checking for frayed or broken cables, excessive corrosion, or wear or insecurity of the linkage. Check that the mechanism works on each relevant wheel, and releases fully, without binding.

☐ It is not possible to test brake efficiency without special equipment, but a road test can be carried out later to check that the vehicle pulls up in a straight line.

Fuel and exhaust systems

☐ Inspect the fuel tank (including the filler cap), fuel pipes, hoses and unions. All components must be secure and free from leaks.

☐ Examine the exhaust system over its entire length, checking for any damaged, broken or missing mountings, security of the retaining clamps and rust or corrosion.

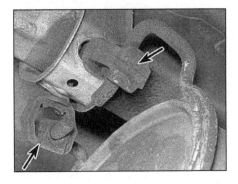

Wheels and tyres

☐ Examine the sidewalls and tread area of each tyre in turn. Check for cuts, tears, lumps, bulges, separation of the tread, and exposure of the ply or cord due to wear or damage. Check that the tyre bead is correctly seated on the wheel rim, that the valve is sound and properly seated, and that the wheel is not distorted or damaged.

☐ Check that the tyres are of the correct size for the vehicle, that they are of the same size and type on each axle, and that the pressures are correct.

☐ Check the tyre tread depth. The legal minimum at the time of writing is 1.6 mm over at least three-quarters of the tread width. Abnormal tread wear may indicate incorrect front wheel alignment.

Body corrosion

☐ Check the condition of the entire vehicle structure for signs of corrosion in load-bearing areas. (These include chassis box sections, side sills, cross-members, pillars, and all suspension, steering, braking system and seat belt mountings and anchorages.) Any corrosion which has seriously reduced the thickness of a load-bearing area is likely to cause the vehicle to fail. In this case professional repairs are likely to be needed.

☐ Damage or corrosion which causes sharp or otherwise dangerous edges to be exposed will also cause the vehicle to fail.

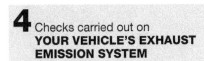

4 Checks carried out on **YOUR VEHICLE'S EXHAUST EMISSION SYSTEM**

Petrol models

☐ Have the engine at normal operating temperature, and make sure that it is in good tune (ignition system in good order, air filter element clean, etc).

☐ Before any measurements are carried out, raise the engine speed to around 2500 rpm, and hold it at this speed for 20 seconds. Allow the engine speed to return to idle, and watch for smoke emissions from the exhaust tailpipe. If the idle speed is obviously much too high, or if dense blue or clearly-visible black smoke comes from the tailpipe for more than 5 seconds, the vehicle will fail. As a rule of thumb, blue smoke signifies oil being burnt (engine wear) while black smoke signifies unburnt fuel (dirty air cleaner element, or other carburettor or fuel system fault).

☐ An exhaust gas analyser capable of measuring carbon monoxide (CO) and hydrocarbons (HC) is now needed. If such an instrument cannot be hired or borrowed, a local garage may agree to perform the check for a small fee.

CO emissions (mixture)

☐ At the time of writing, for vehicles first used between 1st August 1975 and 31st July 1986 (P to C registration), the CO level must not exceed 4.5% by volume. For vehicles first used between 1st August 1986 and 31st July 1992 (D to J registration), the CO level must not exceed 3.5% by volume. Vehicles first

used after 1st August 1992 (K registration) must conform to the manufacturer's specification. The MOT tester has access to a DOT database or emissions handbook, which lists the CO and HC limits for each make and model of vehicle. The CO level is measured with the engine at idle speed, and at "fast idle". The following limits are given as a general guide:

> *At idle speed -*
> CO level no more than 0.5%
> *At "fast idle" (2500 to 3000 rpm) -*
> CO level no more than 0.3%
> (Minimum oil temperature 60°C)

☐ If the CO level cannot be reduced far enough to pass the test (and the fuel and ignition systems are otherwise in good condition) then the carburettor is badly worn, or there is some problem in the fuel injection system or catalytic converter (as applicable).

HC emissions

☐ With the CO within limits, HC emissions for vehicles first used between 1st August 1975 and 31st July 1992 (P to J registration) must not exceed 1200 ppm. Vehicles first used after 1st August 1992 (K registration) must conform to the manufacturer's specification. The MOT tester has access to a DOT database or emissions handbook, which lists the CO and HC limits for each make and model of vehicle. The HC level is measured with the engine at "fast idle". The following is given as a general guide:

> *At "fast idle" (2500 to 3000 rpm) -*
> HC level no more than 200 ppm
> (Minimum oil temperature 60°C)

☐ Excessive HC emissions are caused by incomplete combustion, the causes of which can include oil being burnt, mechanical wear and ignition/fuel system malfunction.

Diesel models

☐ The only emission test applicable to Diesel engines is the measuring of exhaust smoke density. The test involves accelerating the engine several times to its maximum unloaded speed.

Note: *It is of the utmost importance that the engine timing belt is in good condition before the test is carried out.*

☐ The limits for Diesel engine exhaust smoke, introduced in September 1995 are:
Vehicles first used before 1st August 1979:
   Exempt from metered smoke testing, but must not emit "dense blue or clearly visible black smoke for a period of more than 5 seconds at idle" or "dense blue or clearly visible black smoke during acceleration which would obscure the view of other road users".
Non-turbocharged vehicles first used after 1st August 1979: 2.5m-1
Turbocharged vehicles first used after 1st August 1979: 3.0m-1
☐ Excessive smoke can be caused by a dirty air cleaner element. Otherwise, professional advice may be needed to find the cause.

Engine

- ☐ Engine fails to rotate when attempting to start
- ☐ Engine rotates but will not start
- ☐ Engine difficult to start when cold
- ☐ Engine difficult to start when hot
- ☐ Starter motor noisy or excessively-rough in engagement
- ☐ Engine starts but stops immediately
- ☐ Engine idles erratically
- ☐ Engine misfires at idle speed
- ☐ Engine misfires throughout the driving speed range
- ☐ Engine hesitates on acceleration
- ☐ Engine stalls
- ☐ Engine lacks power
- ☐ Engine backfires
- ☐ Oil pressure warning light illuminated with engine running
- ☐ Engine runs-on after switching off
- ☐ Engine noises

Cooling system

- ☐ Overheating
- ☐ Overcooling
- ☐ External coolant leakage
- ☐ Internal coolant leakage
- ☐ Corrosion

Fuel and exhaust system

- ☐ Excessive fuel consumption
- ☐ Fuel leakage and/or fuel odour
- ☐ Excessive noise or fumes from exhaust system

Clutch

- ☐ Pedal travels to floor - no pressure or very little resistance
- ☐ Clutch fails to disengage (unable to select gears)
- ☐ Clutch slips (engine speed increases with no increase in vehicle speed)
- ☐ Judder as clutch is engaged
- ☐ Noise when depressing or releasing clutch pedal

Manual transmission

- ☐ Noisy in neutral with engine running
- ☐ Noisy in one particular gear
- ☐ Difficulty engaging gears
- ☐ Jumps out of gear
- ☐ Vibration
- ☐ Lubricant leaks

Automatic transmission

- ☐ Fluid leakage
- ☐ Transmission fluid brown, or has burned smell
- ☐ General gear selection problems
- ☐ Transmission will not downshift (kickdown) with accelerator pedal fully depressed
- ☐ Engine will not start in any gear, or starts in gears other than Park or Neutral
- ☐ Transmission slips, is noisy, or has no drive in forward or reverse gears

Driveshafts

- ☐ Clicking or knocking noise on turns (at slow speed on full lock)
- ☐ Vibration when decelerating or accelerating

Braking system

- ☐ Vehicle pulls to one side under braking
- ☐ Noise (grinding or high-pitched squeal) when brakes applied
- ☐ Excessive brake pedal travel
- ☐ Brake pedal feels spongy when depressed
- ☐ Excessive brake pedal effort required to stop vehicle
- ☐ Judder felt through brake pedal or steering wheel when braking
- ☐ Brakes binding

Suspension and steering systems

- ☐ Vehicle pulls to one side
- ☐ Wheel wobble and vibration
- ☐ Excessive pitching and/or rolling around corners, or during braking
- ☐ Wandering or general instability
- ☐ Excessively-stiff steering
- ☐ Excessive play in steering
- ☐ Lack of power assistance
- ☐ Tyre wear excessive

Electrical system

- ☐ Battery will not hold a charge for more than a few days
- ☐ Ignition/no-charge warning light remains illuminated with engine running
- ☐ Ignition/no-charge warning light fails to come on
- ☐ Lights inoperative
- ☐ Instrument readings inaccurate or erratic
- ☐ Horn inoperative, or unsatisfactory in operation
- ☐ Windscreen/tailgate wipers inoperative or unsatisfactory in operation
- ☐ Windscreen/tailgate washers inoperative, or unsatisfactory in operation
- ☐ Electric windows inoperative, or unsatisfactory in operation
- ☐ Central locking system inoperative, or unsatisfactory in operation

Introduction

The vehicle owner who does his or her own maintenance according to the recommended service schedules should not have to use this section of the manual very often. Modern component reliability is such that, provided those items subject to wear or deterioration are inspected or renewed at the specified intervals, sudden failure is comparatively rare. Faults do not usually just happen as a result of sudden failure, but develop over a period of time. Major mechanical failures in particular are usually preceded by characteristic symptoms over hundreds or even thousands of miles. Those components which do occasionally fail without warning are often small and easily carried in the vehicle.

With any fault-finding, the first step is to decide where to begin investigations. Sometimes this is obvious, but on other occasions, a little detective work will be necessary. The owner who makes half a dozen haphazard adjustments or replacements may be successful in curing a fault (or its symptoms), but will be none the wiser if the fault recurs, and ultimately may have spent more time and money than was necessary. A calm and logical approach will be found to be more satisfactory in the long run. Always take into account any warning signs or abnormalities that may have been noticed in the period preceding the fault - power loss, high or low gauge readings, unusual smells, etc - and remember that failure of components such as fuses or spark plugs may only be pointers to some underlying fault.

These pages provide an easy reference guide to the more common problems which may occur during the operation of the vehicle. These problems and their possible causes are grouped under headings denoting various components or systems, such as Engine,

Cooling system, etc. The Chapter and/or Section which deals with the problem is also shown in brackets. Whatever the fault, certain basic principles apply. These are as follows:

Verify the fault. This is simply a matter of being sure that you know what the symptoms are before starting work. This is particularly important if you are investigating a fault for someone else, who may not have described it very accurately.

Don't overlook the obvious. For example, if the vehicle won't start, is there petrol in the tank? (Don't take anyone else's word on this particular point, and don't trust the fuel gauge either!) If an electrical fault is indicated, look for loose or broken wires before digging out the test gear.

Cure the disease, not the symptom. Substituting a flat battery with a fully-charged one will get you off the hard shoulder, but if the underlying cause is not attended to, the new battery will go the same way. Similarly, changing oil-fouled spark plugs for a new set will get you moving again, but remember that the reason for the fouling (if it wasn't simply an incorrect grade of plug) will have to be established and corrected.

Don't take anything for granted. Particularly, don't forget that a "new" component may itself be defective (especially if it's been rattling around in the boot for months), and don't leave components out of a fault diagnosis sequence just because they are new or recently fitted. When you do finally diagnose a difficult fault, you'll probably realise that all the evidence was there from the start.

Engine

Engine fails to rotate when attempting to start
- Battery terminal connections loose or corroded ("Weekly checks").
- Battery discharged or faulty (Chapter 5A).
- Broken, loose or disconnected wiring in the starting circuit (Chapter 5A).
- Defective starter solenoid or switch (Chapter 5A).
- Defective starter motor (Chapter 5A).
- Starter pinion or flywheel ring gear teeth loose or broken (Chapter 2A and 5A).
- Engine earth leads broken or disconnected (Chapter 5A).
- Automatic transmission not in Park/Neutral position, or selector cable adjustment incorrect (Chapter 7B).

Engine rotates but will not start
- Fuel tank empty.
- Battery discharged (engine rotates slowly) (Chapter 5 A).
- Battery terminal connections loose or corroded ("Weekly checks").
- Ignition components damp or damaged (Chapters 1 and 5B).
- Broken, loose or disconnected wiring in the ignition circuit (Chapters 1 and 5B).
- Worn, faulty or incorrectly-gapped spark plugs (Chapter 1).
- Low cylinder compressions (Chapter 2A) .
- Major mechanical failure (eg timing belt) (Chapter 2A).

Engine difficult to start when cold
- Battery discharged (Chapter 5A).
- Battery terminal connections loose or corroded ("Weekly checks").
- Worn, faulty or incorrectly-gapped spark plugs (Chapter 1).
- Other ignition system fault (Chapters 1 and 5B).
- Engine management system fault (Chapters 1, 4A and 5B).
- Low cylinder compressions (Chapter 2A).

Engine difficult to start when hot
- Air cleaner element dirty or clogged (Chapter 1).
- Engine management system fault (Chapters 1, 4A and 5B).
- Low cylinder compressions (Chapter 2A).

Starter motor noisy or excessively-rough in engagement
- Starter pinion or flywheel ring gear teeth loose or broken (Chapters 2A, or 5A).
- Starter motor mounting bolts loose or missing (Chapter 5A).
- Starter motor internal components worn or damaged (Chapter 5A).

Engine starts but stops immediately
- Loose or faulty electrical connections in the ignition circuit (Chapters 1 and 5B).
- Engine management system fault (Chapters 1, 4A and 5B).
- Vacuum leak at the inlet manifold or associated hoses (Chapters 1, 4A and 4B).

Engine idles erratically
- Engine management system fault (Chapters 1, 4A and 5B).
- Air cleaner element dirty or clogged (Chapter 1).
- Vacuum leak at the inlet manifold or associated hoses (Chapters 1, 4A and 4B).
- Worn, faulty or incorrectly-gapped spark plugs (Chapter 1).
- Uneven or low cylinder compressions (Chapter 2A).
- Camshaft lobes worn (Chapter 2A).

Engine misfires at idle speed
- Worn, faulty or incorrectly-gapped spark plugs (Chapter 1).
- Faulty spark plug HT leads (Chapter 1).
- Engine management system fault (Chapters 1, 4A and 5B).
- Vacuum leak at the inlet manifold or associated hoses (Chapters 1, 4A and 4B).
- Uneven or low cylinder compressions (Chapter 2A).
- Disconnected, leaking or perished crankcase ventilation hoses (Chapters 1 and 4B).

Engine misfires throughout the driving speed range
- Fuel filter choked (Chapter 1).
- Fuel pump faulty (Chapter 4A).
- Fuel tank vent blocked or fuel pipes restricted (Chapter 4A or 4B).
- Vacuum leak at the inlet manifold or associated hoses (Chapters 1, 4A and 4B).
- Worn, faulty or incorrectly-gapped spark plugs (Chapter 1).
- Faulty spark plug HT leads (Chapter 1).
- Engine management system fault (Chapters 1, 4A and 5B).
- Uneven or low cylinder compressions (Chapter 2A).

Engine hesitates on acceleration
- Worn, faulty or incorrectly-gapped spark plugs (Chapter 1).
- Engine management system fault (Chapters 1, 4A and 5B).
- Vacuum leak at the inlet manifold or associated hoses (Chapters 1, 4A and 4B).

Engine stalls
- Engine management system fault (Chapters 1, 4A and 5B).
- Vacuum leak at the inlet manifold or associated hoses (Chapters 1, 4A and 4B).
- Fuel filter choked (Chapter 1).
- Fuel pump faulty (Chapter 4A) .
- Fuel tank vent blocked or fuel pipes restricted (Chapter 4A or 4B).

Engine lacks power
- Engine management system fault (Chapters 1, 4A and 5B).
- Timing belt incorrectly fitted (Chapter 2A)
- Fuel filter choked (Chapter 1).
- Fuel pump faulty (Chapter 4A).

Engine (continued)

☐ Uneven or low cylinder compressions (Chapter 2A).
☐ Worn, faulty or incorrectly-gapped spark plugs (Chapter 1).
☐ Vacuum leak at the inlet manifold or associated hoses (Chapters 1, 4A and 4B).
☐ Brakes binding (Chapters 1 and 9).
☐ Clutch slipping (Chapter 6).
☐ Automatic transmission fluid level incorrect (Chapter 1).

Engine backfires

☐ Engine management system fault (Chapters 1, 4A and 5B).
☐ Timing belt incorrectly fitted (Chapter 2A).
☐ Vacuum leak at the inlet manifold or associated hoses (Chapters 1, 4A and 4B).
☐ Emission control system fault (Chapter 4B).

Oil pressure warning light illuminated with engine running

☐ Low oil level or incorrect oil grade (Chapter 1).
☐ Faulty oil pressure sensor (Chapter 12).
☐ Worn engine bearings and/or oil pump (Chapter 2A or 2B).
☐ High engine operating temperature (Chapter 3).
☐ Oil pressure relief valve defective (Chapter 2A).
☐ Oil pick-up pipe strainer clogged (Chapter 2B).

Engine runs-on after switching off

☐ Engine management system fault (Chapters 1, 4A and 5B).
☐ Excessive carbon build-up in engine (Chapter 2A or 2B).
☐ High engine operating temperature (Chapter 3).

Engine noises

Pre-ignition (pinking) or knocking during acceleration or under load

☐ Incorrect grade of fuel (Chapter 4A).
☐ Vacuum leak at the inlet manifold or associated hoses (Chapters 1, 4A or 4B).
☐ Excessive carbon build-up in engine (Chapter 2A or 2B).

Whistling or wheezing noises

☐ Leaking inlet manifold gasket (Chapter 4A).
☐ Leaking exhaust manifold gasket or front pipe-to-manifold joint (Chapter 4B).
☐ Leaking vacuum hose (Chapters 1, 4A, 5B and 9).
☐ Blowing cylinder head gasket (Chapter 2A).

Tapping or rattling noises

☐ Worn valve gear or camshafts (Chapter 2A or 2B).
☐ Worn or faulty hydraulic tappets (Chapters 2A or 2B).
☐ Worn timing belt, tensioner, or idler pulleys (Chapter 2A).
☐ Ancillary component fault (coolant pump, alternator, etc) (Chapters 3 and 5A).

Knocking or thumping noises

☐ Worn big-end bearings (regular heavy knocking, perhaps less under load) (Chapter 2B).
☐ Worn main bearings (rumbling and knocking, perhaps worsening under load) (Chapter 2B).
☐ Piston slap (most noticeable when cold) (Chapter 2B).
☐ Ancillary component fault (coolant pump, alternator, etc) (Chapters 3 and 5A).

Cooling system

Overheating

☐ Insufficient coolant in system (Chapter 1).
☐ Thermostat faulty (Chapter 3).
☐ Radiator core blocked or grille restricted (Chapter 3).
☐ Radiator electric cooling fan(s) or coolant temperature sensor faulty (Chapter 3).
☐ Engine management system fault (Chapters 1, 4A and 5B).
☐ Pressure cap faulty (Chapter 3).
☐ Auxiliary drivebelt worn or slipping (Chapter 1).
☐ Air-lock in cooling system (Chapter 1).

Overcooling

☐ Thermostat faulty (Chapter 3).
☐ Inaccurate coolant temperature sensor (Chapter 3).

External coolant leakage

☐ Deteriorated or damaged hoses or hose clips (Chapter 1).
☐ Radiator core or heater matrix leaking (Chapter 3).
☐ Pressure cap faulty (Chapter 3).
☐ Coolant pump seal leaking (Chapter 3).
☐ Boiling due to overheating (Chapter 3).

Internal coolant leakage

☐ Leaking cylinder head gasket (Chapter 2A).
☐ Cracked cylinder head or cylinder bore (Chapter 2B).

Corrosion

☐ Infrequent draining and flushing (Chapter 1).
☐ Incorrect antifreeze mixture, or inappropriate antifreeze type (Chapters 1 and 3).

Fuel and exhaust system

Excessive fuel consumption

☐ Unsympathetic driving style, or adverse conditions.
☐ Air cleaner filter element dirty or clogged (Chapter 1).
☐ Engine management system fault (Chapter 1, 4A and 5B).
☐ Tyres under-inflated ("Weekly checks").

Fuel leakage and/or fuel odour

☐ Damaged or corroded fuel tank, pipes or connections (Chapter 1).

Excessive noise or fumes from exhaust system

☐ Leaking exhaust system or manifold joints (Chapters 1, and 4B).
☐ Leaking, corroded or damaged silencers or pipe (Chapters 1, and 4B).
☐ Broken mountings, causing body or suspension contact (Chapters 1, and 4B).

Clutch

Pedal travels to floor - no pressure or very little resistance

- ☐ Air in clutch hydraulic system (Chapter 6).
- ☐ Faulty clutch slave cylinder (Chapter 6).
- ☐ Faulty clutch master cylinder (Chapter 6).
- ☐ Broken diaphragm spring in clutch pressure plate (Chapter 6).

Clutch fails to disengage (unable to select gears)

- ☐ Air in clutch hydraulic system (Chapter 6).
- ☐ Faulty clutch slave cylinder (Chapter 6).
- ☐ Faulty clutch master cylinder (Chapter 6).
- ☐ Clutch disc sticking on transmission mainshaft splines (Chapter 6).
- ☐ Clutch disc sticking to flywheel or pressure plate (Chapter 6).
- ☐ Faulty pressure plate assembly (Chapter 6).
- ☐ Clutch release mechanism worn or incorrectly assembled (Chapter 6).

Clutch slips (engine speed increases with no increase in vehicle speed)

- ☐ Clutch disc linings excessively worn (Chapter 6).
- ☐ Clutch disc linings contaminated with oil or grease (Chapter 6).
- ☐ Faulty pressure plate or weak diaphragm spring (Chapter 6).

Judder as clutch is engaged

- ☐ Clutch disc linings contaminated with oil or grease (Chapter 6).
- ☐ Clutch disc linings excessively worn (Chapter 6).
- ☐ Faulty or distorted pressure plate or diaphragm spring (Chapter 6).
- ☐ Worn or loose engine/transmission mountings (Chapter 2A).
- ☐ Clutch disc hub or transmission input shaft splines worn (Chapter 6).

Noise when depressing or releasing clutch pedal

- ☐ Worn clutch release bearing (Chapter 6).
- ☐ Worn or dry clutch pedal bushes (Chapter 6).
- ☐ Faulty pressure plate assembly (Chapter 6).
- ☐ Pressure plate diaphragm spring broken (Chapter 6).
- ☐ Broken clutch disc cushioning springs (Chapter 6).

Manual transmission

Noisy in neutral with engine running

- ☐ Mainshaft bearings worn (noise apparent with clutch pedal released, but not when depressed) (Chapter 7A).*
- ☐ Clutch release bearing worn (noise apparent with clutch pedal depressed, possibly less when released) (Chapter 6).

Noisy in one particular gear

- ☐ Worn, damaged or chipped gear teeth (Chapter 7A).*
- ☐ Worn bearings (Chapter 7A).*

Difficulty engaging gears

- ☐ Clutch fault (Chapter 6).
- ☐ Selector cables out of adjustment (Chapter 7A).
- ☐ Worn synchroniser assemblies (Chapter 7A).*

Jumps out of gear

- ☐ Selector cables out of adjustment (Chapter 7A).
- ☐ Worn synchroniser assemblies (Chapter 7A).*
- ☐ Worn selector forks (Chapter 7A).*

Vibration

- ☐ Lack of oil (Chapter 1).
- ☐ Worn bearings (Chapter 7A).*

Lubricant leaks

- ☐ Leaking differential side gear oil seal (Chapter 7A).
- ☐ Leaking housing joint (Chapter 7A).*
- ☐ Leaking input shaft oil seal (Chapter 7A).

Although the corrective action necessary to remedy the symptoms described is beyond the scope of the home mechanic, the above information should be helpful in isolating the cause of the condition, so that the owner can communicate clearly with a professional mechanic.

Automatic transmission

Note: *Due to the complexity of the automatic transmission, it is difficult for the home mechanic to properly diagnose and service this unit. For problems other than the following, the vehicle should be taken to a dealer service department or automatic transmission specialist.*

Fluid leakage

- ☐ Automatic transmission fluid is usually dark in colour. Fluid leaks should not be confused with engine oil, which can easily be blown onto the transmission by airflow.
- ☐ To determine the source of a leak, first remove all built-up dirt and grime from the transmission housing and surrounding areas, using a degreasing agent, or by steam-cleaning. Drive the vehicle at low speed, so airflow will not blow the leak far from its source. Raise and support the vehicle, and determine where the leak is coming from. The following are common areas of leakage:
  - a) Transmission oil sump (Chapters 1 and 7B).
  - b) Dipstick tube (Chapters 1 and 7B).
  - c) Transmission-to-fluid cooler pipes/unions (Chapter 1 and 7B).
  - d) Transmission oil seals (Chapter 7B).

Transmission fluid brown, or has burned smell

- ☐ Transmission fluid level low, or fluid in need of renewal (Chapter 1).

General gear selection problems

- ☐ Chapter 7B, deals with checking and adjusting the selector cable on automatic transmissions. The following are common problems which may be caused by a poorly-adjusted cable:
  - a) Engine starting in gears other than Park or Neutral.
  - b) Indicator on gear selector lever pointing to a gear other than the one actually being used.
  - c) Vehicle moves when in Park or Neutral.
  - d) Poor gear shift quality or erratic gear changes.
  - Refer to Chapter 7B for the selector cable adjustment procedure.

Transmission will not downshift (kickdown) with accelerator pedal fully depressed

- ☐ Low transmission fluid level (Chapter 1).
- ☐ Incorrect selector cable adjustment (Chapter 7B).
- ☐ Automatic transmission ECU or sensor fault (Chapter 7B).

Automatic transmission (continued)

Engine will not start in any gear, or starts in gears other than Park or Neutral

☐ Incorrect selector cable adjustment (Chapter 7B).
☐ Automatic transmission ECU or sensor fault (Chapter 7B).

Transmission slips, is noisy, or has no drive in forward or reverse gears

☐ There are many probable causes for the above problems, but the home mechanic should be concerned with only one possibility - fluid level. Before taking the vehicle to a dealer or transmission specialist, check the fluid level and condition of the fluid as described in Chapter 1. Correct the fluid level as necessary, or change the fluid if needed. Make reference also to the on-board fault diagnosis facility described in Chapter 7B; If the problem persists, professional help will be necessary.

Driveshafts

Clicking or knocking noise on turns (at slow speed on full lock)

☐ Lack of constant velocity joint lubricant, possibly due to damaged gaiter (Chapter 8).
☐ Worn outer constant velocity joint (Chapter 8).

Vibration when decelerating or accelerating

☐ Worn inner constant velocity joint (Chapter 8).
☐ Bent or distorted driveshaft (Chapter 8).

Braking system

Note: *Before assuming that a brake problem exists, make sure that the tyres are in good condition and correctly inflated, that the front wheel alignment is correct, and that the vehicle is not loaded with weight in an unequal manner. Apart from checking the condition of all pipe and hose connections, any faults occurring on the Anti-lock Braking System (ABS) should be investigated using the on-board diagnostic facility (see Chapter 9) then, if necessary, referred to a Volvo dealer for repair.*

Vehicle pulls to one side under braking

☐ Worn, defective, damaged or contaminated front or rear brake pads on one side (Chapter 9).
☐ Seized or partially-seized front or rear brake caliper piston (Chapter 9).
☐ A mixture of brake pad lining materials fitted between sides (Chapter 9).
☐ Brake caliper mounting bolts loose (Chapter 9).
☐ Worn or damaged steering or suspension components (Chapter 10).

Noise (grinding or high-pitched squeal) when brakes applied

☐ Brake pad friction lining material worn down to metal backing (Chapter 9).
☐ Excessive corrosion of brake disc (may be apparent after the vehicle has been standing for some time) (Chapter 9).

Excessive brake pedal travel

☐ Faulty master cylinder (Chapter 9).
☐ Air in hydraulic system (Chapter 9).

Brake pedal feels spongy when depressed

☐ Air in hydraulic system (Chapter 9).
☐ Deteriorated flexible rubber brake hoses (Chapter 9).
☐ Master cylinder mounting nuts loose (Chapter 9).
☐ Faulty master cylinder (Chapter 9).

Excessive brake pedal effort required to stop vehicle

☐ Faulty vacuum servo unit (Chapter 9).
☐ Disconnected, damaged or insecure brake servo vacuum hose (Chapter 9).
☐ Primary or secondary hydraulic circuit failure (Chapter 9).
☐ Seized brake caliper piston(s) (Chapter 9).
☐ Brake pads incorrectly fitted (Chapter 9).
☐ Incorrect grade of brake pads fitted (Chapter 9).
☐ Brake pad linings contaminated (Chapter 9).

Judder felt through brake pedal or steering wheel when braking

☐ Excessive run-out or distortion of front or rear discs (Chapter 9).
☐ Brake pad linings worn (Chapter 9).
☐ Brake caliper mounting bolts loose (Chapter 9).
☐ Wear in suspension or steering components or mountings (Chapter 10).

Brakes binding

☐ Seized brake caliper piston(s) (Chapter 9).
☐ Faulty handbrake mechanism (Chapter 9).
☐ Faulty master cylinder (Chapter 9).

Suspension and steering systems

Note: *Before diagnosing suspension or steering faults, be sure that the trouble is not due to incorrect tyre pressures, mixtures of tyre types, or binding brakes.*

Vehicle pulls to one side

- ☐ Defective tyre ("Weekly checks").
- ☐ Excessive wear in suspension or steering components (Chapter 10).
- ☐ Incorrect front or rear wheel alignment (Chapter 10).
- ☐ Accident damage to steering or suspension components (Chapter 10).

Wheel wobble and vibration

- ☐ Front roadwheels out of balance (vibration felt mainly through the steering wheel).
- ☐ Rear roadwheels out of balance (vibration felt throughout the vehicle) (Chapter 1).
- ☐ Roadwheels damaged or distorted (Chapter 1).
- ☐ Faulty or damaged tyre ("Weekly checks").
- ☐ Worn steering or suspension joints, bushes or components (Chapter 10).
- ☐ Roadwheel bolts loose (Chapter 1).

Excessive pitching and/or rolling around corners, or during braking

- ☐ Defective shock absorbers (Chapter 10).
- ☐ Broken or weak coil spring and/or suspension component (Chapter 10).
- ☐ Worn or damaged anti-roll bar or mountings (Chapter 10).

Wandering or general instability

- ☐ Incorrect wheel alignment (Chapter 10).
- ☐ Worn steering or suspension joints, bushes or components (Chapter 10).
- ☐ Roadwheels out of balance (Chapter 1).
- ☐ Faulty or damaged tyre ("Weekly checks").
- ☐ Roadwheel bolts loose (Chapter 1).
- ☐ Defective shock absorbers (Chapter 10).

Excessively-stiff steering

- ☐ Broken or slipping steering pump (auxiliary) drivebelt (Chapter 1).
- ☐ Steering pump faulty (Chapter 10).

- ☐ Seized track rod end balljoint or suspension balljoint (Chapter 10).
- ☐ Incorrect front wheel alignment (Chapter 10).
- ☐ Steering rack or column bent or damaged (Chapter 10).

Excessive play in steering

- ☐ Worn steering column universal joint(s) (Chapter 10).
- ☐ Worn steering track rod end balljoints (Chapter 10).
- ☐ Worn steering gear (Chapter 10).
- ☐ Worn steering or suspension joints, bushes or components (Chapter 10).

Lack of power assistance

- ☐ Broken or slipping steering pump (auxiliary) drivebelt (Chapter 1).
- ☐ Incorrect fluid level (Chapter 1).
- ☐ Restriction in fluid hoses (Chapter 10).
- ☐ Faulty steering pump (Chapter 10).
- ☐ Faulty steering gear (Chapter 10).

Tyre wear excessive

Tyres worn on inside or outside edges

- ☐ Tyres under-inflated ("Weekly checks").
- ☐ Incorrect camber or castor angles (wear on one edge only) (Chapter 10).
- ☐ Worn steering or suspension joints, bushes or components (Chapter 10).
- ☐ Excessively-hard cornering.
- ☐ Accident damage.

Tyre treads exhibit feathered edges

- ☐ Incorrect toe setting (Chapter 10).

Tyres worn in centre of tread

- ☐ Tyres over-inflated ("Weekly checks").

Tyres worn on inside and outside edges

- ☐ Tyres under-inflated ("Weekly checks").

Tyres worn unevenly

- ☐ Tyres out of balance ("Weekly checks").
- ☐ Excessive wheel or tyre run-out (Chapter 1).
- ☐ Worn shock absorbers (Chapter 10).
- ☐ Faulty tyre ("Weekly checks").

Electrical system

Note: *For problems associated with the starting system, refer to the faults listed under **"Engine"** earlier in this Section.*

Battery will not hold a charge for more than a few days

- ☐ Battery defective internally (Chapter 5A).
- ☐ Battery electrolyte level low (Chapter 5A).
- ☐ Battery terminal connections loose or corroded (Chapters 1 and 5A).
- ☐ Auxiliary drivebelt worn or slipping (Chapter 1).
- ☐ Alternator not charging at correct output (Chapter 5A).
- ☐ Alternator or voltage regulator faulty (Chapter 5A).
- ☐ Short-circuit causing continual battery drain (Chapters 5A and 12).

Ignition/no-charge warning light remains illuminated with engine running

- ☐ Auxiliary drivebelt worn or slipping (Chapter 1).
- ☐ Alternator brushes worn, sticking, or dirty (Chapter 5A).

- ☐ Alternator brush springs weak or broken (Chapter 5A).
- ☐ Internal fault in alternator or voltage regulator (Chapter 5A).
- ☐ Broken, disconnected, or loose wiring in charging circuit (Chapter 5A).

Ignition/no-charge warning light fails to come on

- ☐ Warning light bulb blown (Chapter 12).
- ☐ Broken, disconnected, or loose wiring in warning light circuit (Chapter 12).
- ☐ Alternator faulty (Chapter 5A).

Lights inoperative

- ☐ Bulb blown (Chapter 12).
- ☐ Corrosion of bulb or bulbholder contacts (Chapter 12).
- ☐ Blown fuse (Chapter 12).
- ☐ Faulty relay (Chapter 12).
- ☐ Broken, loose, or disconnected wiring (Chapter 12).
- ☐ Faulty switch (Chapter 12).

Electrical system (continued)

Instrument readings inaccurate or erratic

Instrument readings increase with engine speed

☐ Faulty instrument panel control components or circuitry (Chapter 12).

Fuel or temperature gauges give no reading

☐ Faulty instrument panel control components or circuitry (Chapter 12).
☐ Faulty gauge sender unit (Chapters 3, 4A or 5B).
☐ Wiring open-circuit (Chapter 12).
☐ Faulty gauge (Chapter 12).

Fuel or temperature gauges give continuous maximum reading

☐ Faulty instrument panel control components or circuitry (Chapter 12).
☐ Faulty gauge sender unit (Chapters 3, 4A or 5B).
☐ Wiring short-circuit (Chapter 12).
☐ Faulty gauge (Chapter 12).

Horn inoperative, or unsatisfactory in operation

Horn fails to operate

☐ Blown fuse (Chapter 12).
☐ Steering wheel cable connections loose, broken or disconnected (Chapter 10).
☐ Faulty horn (Chapter 12).

Horn emits intermittent or unsatisfactory sound

☐ Steering wheel cable connections loose, broken or disconnected (Chapter 10).
☐ Horn mountings loose (Chapter 12).
☐ Faulty horn (Chapter 12).

Horn operates all the time

☐ Horn push either earthed or stuck down (Chapter 10).
☐ Steering wheel cable connections earthed (Chapter 10).

Windscreen/tailgate wipers inoperative or unsatisfactory in operation

Wipers fail to operate, or operate very slowly

☐ Wiper blades stuck to screen, or linkage seized or binding (Chapter 12).
☐ Blown fuse (Chapter 12).
☐ Cable or cable connections loose, broken or disconnected (Chapter 12).
☐ Faulty relay (Chapter 12).
☐ Faulty wiper motor (Chapter 12).

Wiper blades sweep over too large or too small an area of the glass

☐ Wiper arms incorrectly-positioned on spindles (Chapter 12).
☐ Excessive wear of wiper linkage (Chapter 12).
☐ Wiper motor or linkage mountings loose or insecure (Chapter 12).

Wiper blades fail to clean the glass effectively

☐ Wiper blade rubbers worn or perished ("Weekly checks").
☐ Wiper arm tension springs broken, or arm pivots seized (Chapter 12).
☐ Insufficient windscreen washer additive to adequately remove road film ("Weekly checks").

Windscreen/tailgate washers inoperative, or unsatisfactory in operation

One or more washer jets inoperative

☐ Blocked washer jet (Chapter 12).
☐ Disconnected, kinked or restricted fluid hose (Chapter 12).
☐ Insufficient fluid in washer reservoir ("Weekly checks").

Washer pump fails to operate

☐ Broken or disconnected wiring or connections (Chapter 12).
☐ Blown fuse (Chapter 12).
☐ Faulty washer switch (Chapter 12).
☐ Faulty washer pump (Chapter 12).

Washer pump runs for some time before fluid is emitted from jets

☐ Faulty one-way valve in fluid supply hose (Chapter 12).

Electric windows inoperative, or unsatisfactory in operation

Window glass will only move in one direction

☐ Faulty switch (Chapter 12).

Window glass slow to move

☐ Incorrectly-adjusted door glass guide channels (Chapter 11).
☐ Regulator seized or damaged, or in need of lubrication (Chapter 11).
☐ Door internal components or trim fouling regulator (Chapter 11).
☐ Faulty motor (Chapter 12).

Window glass fails to move

☐ Incorrectly-adjusted door glass guide channels (Chapter 11).
☐ Blown fuse (Chapter 12).
☐ Faulty relay (Chapter 12).
☐ Broken or disconnected wiring or connections (Chapter 12).
☐ Faulty motor (Chapter 12).

Central locking system inoperative, or unsatisfactory in operation

Complete system failure

☐ Blown fuse (Chapter 12).
☐ Faulty relay (Chapter 12).
☐ Broken or disconnected wiring or connections (Chapter 12).

Latch locks but will not unlock, or unlocks but will not lock

☐ Faulty master switch (Chapter 11).
☐ Broken or disconnected latch operating rods or levers (Chapter 11).
☐ Faulty relay (Chapter 12).

One lock motor fails to operate

☐ Broken or disconnected wiring or connections (Chapter 12).
☐ Faulty lock motor (Chapter 11).
☐ Broken, binding or disconnected latch operating rods or levers (Chapter 11).
☐ Fault in door latch (Chapter 11).

A

ABS (Anti-lock brake system) A system, usually electronically controlled, that senses incipient wheel lockup during braking and relieves hydraulic pressure at wheels that are about to skid.

Air bag An inflatable bag hidden in the steering wheel (driver's side) or the dash or glovebox (passenger side). In a head-on collision, the bags inflate, preventing the driver and front passenger from being thrown forward into the steering wheel or windscreen.

Air cleaner A metal or plastic housing, containing a filter element, which removes dust and dirt from the air being drawn into the engine.

Air filter element The actual filter in an air cleaner system, usually manufactured from pleated paper and requiring renewal at regular intervals.

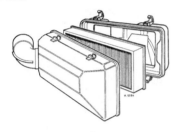

Air filter

Allen key A hexagonal wrench which fits into a recessed hexagonal hole.

Alligator clip A long-nosed spring-loaded metal clip with meshing teeth. Used to make temporary electrical connections.

Alternator A component in the electrical system which converts mechanical energy from a drivebelt into electrical energy to charge the battery and to operate the starting system, ignition system and electrical accessories.

Ampere (amp) A unit of measurement for the flow of electric current. One amp is the amount of current produced by one volt acting through a resistance of one ohm.

Anaerobic sealer A substance used to prevent bolts and screws from loosening. Anaerobic means that it does not require oxygen for activation. The Loctite brand is widely used.

Antifreeze A substance (usually ethylene glycol) mixed with water, and added to a vehicle's cooling system, to prevent freezing of the coolant in winter. Antifreeze also contains chemicals to inhibit corrosion and the formation of rust and other deposits that would tend to clog the radiator and coolant passages and reduce cooling efficiency.

Anti-seize compound A coating that reduces the risk of seizing on fasteners that are subjected to high temperatures, such as exhaust manifold bolts and nuts.

Asbestos A natural fibrous mineral with great heat resistance, commonly used in the composition of brake friction materials.

Asbestos is a health hazard and the dust created by brake systems should never be inhaled or ingested.

Axle A shaft on which a wheel revolves, or which revolves with a wheel. Also, a solid beam that connects the two wheels at one end of the vehicle. An axle which also transmits power to the wheels is known as a live axle.

Axleshaft A single rotating shaft, on either side of the differential, which delivers power from the final drive assembly to the drive wheels. Also called a driveshaft or a halfshaft.

B

Ball bearing An anti-friction bearing consisting of a hardened inner and outer race with hardened steel balls between two races.

Bearing The curved surface on a shaft or in a bore, or the part assembled into either, that permits relative motion between them with minimum wear and friction.

Bearing

Big-end bearing The bearing in the end of the connecting rod that's attached to the crankshaft.

Bleed nipple A valve on a brake wheel cylinder, caliper or other hydraulic component that is opened to purge the hydraulic system of air. Also called a bleed screw.

Brake bleeding Procedure for removing air from lines of a hydraulic brake system.

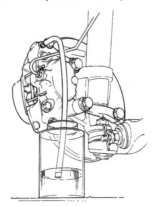

Brake bleeding

Brake disc The component of a disc brake that rotates with the wheels.

Brake drum The component of a drum brake that rotates with the wheels.

Brake linings The friction material which contacts the brake disc or drum to retard the vehicle's speed. The linings are bonded or riveted to the brake pads or shoes.

Brake pads The replaceable friction pads that pinch the brake disc when the brakes are applied. Brake pads consist of a friction material bonded or riveted to a rigid backing plate.

Brake shoe The crescent-shaped carrier to which the brake linings are mounted and which forces the lining against the rotating drum during braking.

Braking systems For more information on braking systems, consult the *Haynes Automotive Brake Manual*.

Breaker bar A long socket wrench handle providing greater leverage.

Bulkhead The insulated partition between the engine and the passenger compartment.

C

Caliper The non-rotating part of a disc-brake assembly that straddles the disc and carries the brake pads. The caliper also contains the hydraulic components that cause the pads to pinch the disc when the brakes are applied. A caliper is also a measuring tool that can be set to measure inside or outside dimensions of an object.

Camshaft A rotating shaft on which a series of cam lobes operate the valve mechanisms. The camshaft may be driven by gears, by sprockets and chain or by sprockets and a belt.

Canister A container in an evaporative emission control system; contains activated charcoal granules to trap vapours from the fuel system.

Canister

Carburettor A device which mixes fuel with air in the proper proportions to provide a desired power output from a spark ignition internal combustion engine.

Castellated Resembling the parapets along the top of a castle wall. For example, a castellated balljoint stud nut.

Castor In wheel alignment, the backward or forward tilt of the steering axis. Castor is positive when the steering axis is inclined rearward at the top.

Catalytic converter A silencer-like device in the exhaust system which converts certain pollutants in the exhaust gases into less harmful substances.

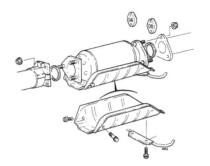

Catalytic converter

Circlip A ring-shaped clip used to prevent endwise movement of cylindrical parts and shafts. An internal circlip is installed in a groove in a housing; an external circlip fits into a groove on the outside of a cylindrical piece such as a shaft.

Clearance The amount of space between two parts. For example, between a piston and a cylinder, between a bearing and a journal, etc.

Coil spring A spiral of elastic steel found in various sizes throughout a vehicle, for example as a springing medium in the suspension and in the valve train.

Compression Reduction in volume, and increase in pressure and temperature, of a gas, caused by squeezing it into a smaller space.

Compression ratio The relationship between cylinder volume when the piston is at top dead centre and cylinder volume when the piston is at bottom dead centre.

Constant velocity (CV) joint A type of universal joint that cancels out vibrations caused by driving power being transmitted through an angle.

Core plug A disc or cup-shaped metal device inserted in a hole in a casting through which core was removed when the casting was formed. Also known as a freeze plug or expansion plug.

Crankcase The lower part of the engine block in which the crankshaft rotates.

Crankshaft The main rotating member, or shaft, running the length of the crankcase, with offset "throws" to which the connecting rods are attached.

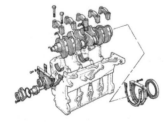

Crankshaft assembly

Crocodile clip See Alligator clip

D

Diagnostic code Code numbers obtained by accessing the diagnostic mode of an engine management computer. This code can be used to determine the area in the system where a malfunction may be located.

Disc brake A brake design incorporating a rotating disc onto which brake pads are squeezed. The resulting friction converts the energy of a moving vehicle into heat.

Double-overhead cam (DOHC) An engine that uses two overhead camshafts, usually one for the intake valves and one for the exhaust valves.

Drivebelt(s) The belt(s) used to drive accessories such as the alternator, water pump, power steering pump, air conditioning compressor, etc. off the crankshaft pulley.

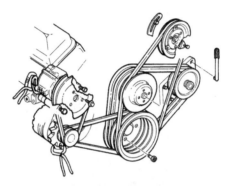

Accessory drivebelts

Driveshaft Any shaft used to transmit motion. Commonly used when referring to the axleshafts on a front wheel drive vehicle.

Drum brake A type of brake using a drum-shaped metal cylinder attached to the inner surface of the wheel. When the brake pedal is pressed, curved brake shoes with friction linings press against the inside of the drum to slow or stop the vehicle.

E

EGR valve A valve used to introduce exhaust gases into the intake air stream.

Electronic control unit (ECU) A computer which controls (for instance) ignition and fuel injection systems, or an anti-lock braking system. For more information refer to the *Haynes Automotive Electrical and Electronic Systems Manual.*

Electronic Fuel Injection (EFI) A computer controlled fuel system that distributes fuel through an injector located in each intake port of the engine.

Emergency brake A braking system, independent of the main hydraulic system, that can be used to slow or stop the vehicle if the primary brakes fail, or to hold the vehicle stationary even though the brake pedal isn't depressed. It usually consists of a hand lever that actuates either front or rear brakes mechanically through a series of cables and linkages. Also known as a handbrake or parking brake.

Endfloat The amount of lengthwise movement between two parts. As applied to a crankshaft, the distance that the crankshaft can move forward and back in the cylinder block.

Engine management system (EMS) A computer controlled system which manages the fuel injection and the ignition systems in an integrated fashion.

Exhaust manifold A part with several passages through which exhaust gases leave the engine combustion chambers and enter the exhaust pipe.

F

Fan clutch A viscous (fluid) drive coupling device which permits variable engine fan speeds in relation to engine speeds.

Feeler blade A thin strip or blade of hardened steel, ground to an exact thickness, used to check or measure clearances between parts.

Feeler blade

Firing order The order in which the engine cylinders fire, or deliver their power strokes, beginning with the number one cylinder.

Flywheel A heavy spinning wheel in which energy is absorbed and stored by means of momentum. On cars, the flywheel is attached to the crankshaft to smooth out firing impulses.

Free play The amount of travel before any action takes place. The "looseness" in a linkage, or an assembly of parts, between the initial application of force and actual movement. For example, the distance the brake pedal moves before the pistons in the master cylinder are actuated.

Fuse An electrical device which protects a circuit against accidental overload. The typical fuse contains a soft piece of metal which is calibrated to melt at a predetermined current flow (expressed as amps) and break the circuit.

Fusible link A circuit protection device consisting of a conductor surrounded by heat-resistant insulation. The conductor is smaller than the wire it protects, so it acts as the weakest link in the circuit. Unlike a blown fuse, a failed fusible link must frequently be cut from the wire for replacement.

G

Gap The distance the spark must travel in jumping from the centre electrode to the side electrode in a spark plug. Also refers to the spacing between the points in a contact breaker assembly in a conventional points-type ignition, or to the distance between the reluctor or rotor and the pickup coil in an electronic ignition.

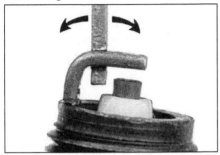

Adjusting spark plug gap

Gasket Any thin, soft material - usually cork, cardboard, asbestos or soft metal - installed between two metal surfaces to ensure a good seal. For instance, the cylinder head gasket seals the joint between the block and the cylinder head.

Gasket

Gauge An instrument panel display used to monitor engine conditions. A gauge with a movable pointer on a dial or a fixed scale is an analogue gauge. A gauge with a numerical readout is called a digital gauge.

H

Halfshaft A rotating shaft that transmits power from the final drive unit to a drive wheel, usually when referring to a live rear axle.
Harmonic balancer A device designed to reduce torsion or twisting vibration in the crankshaft. May be incorporated in the crankshaft pulley. Also known as a vibration damper.
Hone An abrasive tool for correcting small irregularities or differences in diameter in an engine cylinder, brake cylinder, etc.
Hydraulic tappet A tappet that utilises hydraulic pressure from the engine's lubrication system to maintain zero clearance (constant contact with both camshaft and valve stem). Automatically adjusts to variation in valve stem length. Hydraulic tappets also reduce valve noise.

I

Ignition timing The moment at which the spark plug fires, usually expressed in the number of crankshaft degrees before the piston reaches the top of its stroke.
Inlet manifold A tube or housing with passages through which flows the air-fuel mixture (carburettor vehicles and vehicles with throttle body injection) or air only (port fuel-injected vehicles) to the port openings in the cylinder head.

J

Jump start Starting the engine of a vehicle with a discharged or weak battery by attaching jump leads from the weak battery to a charged or helper battery.

L

Load Sensing Proportioning Valve (LSPV) A brake hydraulic system control valve that works like a proportioning valve, but also takes into consideration the amount of weight carried by the rear axle.
Locknut A nut used to lock an adjustment nut, or other threaded component, in place. For example, a locknut is employed to keep the adjusting nut on the rocker arm in position.
Lockwasher A form of washer designed to prevent an attaching nut from working loose.

M

MacPherson strut A type of front suspension system devised by Earle MacPherson at Ford of England. In its original form, a simple lateral link with the anti-roll bar creates the lower control arm. A long strut - an integral coil spring and shock absorber - is mounted between the body and the steering knuckle. Many modern so-called MacPherson strut systems use a conventional lower A-arm and don't rely on the anti-roll bar for location.
Multimeter An electrical test instrument with the capability to measure voltage, current and resistance.

N

NOx Oxides of Nitrogen. A common toxic pollutant emitted by petrol and diesel engines at higher temperatures.

O

Ohm The unit of electrical resistance. One volt applied to a resistance of one ohm will produce a current of one amp.
Ohmmeter An instrument for measuring electrical resistance.
O-ring A type of sealing ring made of a special rubber-like material; in use, the O-ring is compressed into a groove to provide the sealing action.
Overhead cam (ohc) engine An engine with the camshaft(s) located on top of the cylinder head(s).

Overhead valve (ohv) engine An engine with the valves located in the cylinder head, but with the camshaft located in the engine block.
Oxygen sensor A device installed in the engine exhaust manifold, which senses the oxygen content in the exhaust and converts this information into an electric current. Also called a Lambda sensor.

P

Phillips screw A type of screw head having a cross instead of a slot for a corresponding type of screwdriver.
Plastigage A thin strip of plastic thread, available in different sizes, used for measuring clearances. For example, a strip of Plastigage is laid across a bearing journal. The parts are assembled and dismantled; the width of the crushed strip indicates the clearance between journal and bearing.

Plastigage

Propeller shaft The long hollow tube with universal joints at both ends that carries power from the transmission to the differential on front-engined rear wheel drive vehicles.
Proportioning valve A hydraulic control valve which limits the amount of pressure to the rear brakes during panic stops to prevent wheel lock-up.

R

Rack-and-pinion steering A steering system with a pinion gear on the end of the steering shaft that mates with a rack (think of a geared wheel opened up and laid flat). When the steering wheel is turned, the pinion turns, moving the rack to the left or right. This movement is transmitted through the track rods to the steering arms at the wheels.
Radiator A liquid-to-air heat transfer device designed to reduce the temperature of the coolant in an internal combustion engine cooling system.
Refrigerant Any substance used as a heat transfer agent in an air-conditioning system. R-12 has been the principle refrigerant for many years; recently, however, manufacturers have begun using R-134a, a non-CFC substance that is considered less harmful to the ozone in the upper atmosphere.
Rocker arm A lever arm that rocks on a shaft or pivots on a stud. In an overhead valve engine, the rocker arm converts the upward movement of the pushrod into a downward movement to open a valve.

Rotor In a distributor, the rotating device inside the cap that connects the centre electrode and the outer terminals as it turns, distributing the high voltage from the coil secondary winding to the proper spark plug. Also, that part of an alternator which rotates inside the stator. Also, the rotating assembly of a turbocharger, including the compressor wheel, shaft and turbine wheel.

Runout The amount of wobble (in-and-out movement) of a gear or wheel as it's rotated. The amount a shaft rotates "out-of-true." The out-of-round condition of a rotating part.

S

Sealant A liquid or paste used to prevent leakage at a joint. Sometimes used in conjunction with a gasket.

Sealed beam lamp An older headlight design which integrates the reflector, lens and filaments into a hermetically-sealed one-piece unit. When a filament burns out or the lens cracks, the entire unit is simply replaced.

Serpentine drivebelt A single, long, wide accessory drivebelt that's used on some newer vehicles to drive all the accessories, instead of a series of smaller, shorter belts. Serpentine drivebelts are usually tensioned by an automatic tensioner.

Serpentine drivebelt

Shim Thin spacer, commonly used to adjust the clearance or relative positions between two parts. For example, shims inserted into or under bucket tappets control valve clearances. Clearance is adjusted by changing the thickness of the shim.

Slide hammer A special puller that screws into or hooks onto a component such as a shaft or bearing; a heavy sliding handle on the shaft bottoms against the end of the shaft to knock the component free.

Sprocket A tooth or projection on the periphery of a wheel, shaped to engage with a chain or drivebelt. Commonly used to refer to the sprocket wheel itself.

Starter inhibitor switch On vehicles with an automatic transmission, a switch that prevents starting if the vehicle is not in Neutral or Park.

Strut See MacPherson strut.

T

Tappet A cylindrical component which transmits motion from the cam to the valve stem, either directly or via a pushrod and rocker arm. Also called a cam follower.

Thermostat A heat-controlled valve that regulates the flow of coolant between the cylinder block and the radiator, so maintaining optimum engine operating temperature. A thermostat is also used in some air cleaners in which the temperature is regulated.

Thrust bearing The bearing in the clutch assembly that is moved in to the release levers by clutch pedal action to disengage the clutch. Also referred to as a release bearing.

Timing belt A toothed belt which drives the camshaft. Serious engine damage may result if it breaks in service.

Timing chain A chain which drives the camshaft.

Toe-in The amount the front wheels are closer together at the front than at the rear. On rear wheel drive vehicles, a slight amount of toe-in is usually specified to keep the front wheels running parallel on the road by offsetting other forces that tend to spread the wheels apart.

Toe-out The amount the front wheels are closer together at the rear than at the front. On front wheel drive vehicles, a slight amount of toe-out is usually specified.

Tools For full information on choosing and using tools, refer to the *Haynes Automotive Tools Manual*.

Tracer A stripe of a second colour applied to a wire insulator to distinguish that wire from another one with the same colour insulator.

Tune-up A process of accurate and careful adjustments and parts replacement to obtain the best possible engine performance.

Turbocharger A centrifugal device, driven by exhaust gases, that pressurises the intake air. Normally used to increase the power output from a given engine displacement, but can also be used primarily to reduce exhaust emissions (as on VW's "Umwelt" Diesel engine).

U

Universal joint or U-joint A double-pivoted connection for transmitting power from a driving to a driven shaft through an angle. A U-joint consists of two Y-shaped yokes and a cross-shaped member called the spider.

V

Valve A device through which the flow of liquid, gas, vacuum, or loose material in bulk may be started, stopped, or regulated by a movable part that opens, shuts, or partially obstructs one or more ports or passageways. A valve is also the movable part of such a device.

Valve clearance The clearance between the valve tip (the end of the valve stem) and the rocker arm or tappet. The valve clearance is measured when the valve is closed.

Vernier caliper A precision measuring instrument that measures inside and outside dimensions. Not quite as accurate as a micrometer, but more convenient.

Viscosity The thickness of a liquid or its resistance to flow.

Volt A unit for expressing electrical "pressure" in a circuit. One volt that will produce a current of one ampere through a resistance of one ohm.

W

Welding Various processes used to join metal items by heating the areas to be joined to a molten state and fusing them together. For more information refer to the *Haynes Automotive Welding Manual*.

Wiring diagram A drawing portraying the components and wires in a vehicle's electrical system, using standardised symbols. For more information refer to the *Haynes Automotive Electrical and Electronic Systems Manual*.

Note: *References throughout this index are in the form - "Chapter number" • "page number"*

Preserving Our Motoring Heritage

< The Model J Duesenberg Derham Tourster. Only eight of these magnificent cars were ever built – this is the only example to be found outside the United States of America

Almost every car you've ever loved, loathed or desired is gathered under one roof at the Haynes Motor Museum. Over 300 immaculately presented cars and motorbikes represent every aspect of our motoring heritage, from elegant reminders of bygone days, such as the superb Model J Duesenberg to curiosities like the bug-eyed BMW Isetta. There are also many old friends and flames. Perhaps you remember the 1959 Ford Popular that you did your courting in? The magnificent 'Red Collection' is a spectacle of classic sports cars including AC, Alfa Romeo, Austin Healey, Ferrari, Lamborghini, Maserati, MG, Riley, Porsche and Triumph.

A Perfect Day Out

Each and every vehicle at the Haynes Motor Museum has played its part in the history and culture of Motoring. Today, they make a wonderful spectacle and a great day out for all the family. Bring the kids, bring Mum and Dad, but above all bring your camera to capture those golden memories for ever. You will also find an impressive array of motoring memorabilia, a comfortable 70 seat video cinema and one of the most extensive transport book shops in Britain. The Pit Stop Cafe serves everything from a cup of tea to wholesome, home-made meals or, if you prefer, you can enjoy the large picnic area nestled in the beautiful rural surroundings of Somerset.

> John Haynes O.B.E., Founder and Chairman of the museum at the wheel of a Haynes Light 12.

< Graham Hill's Lola Cosworth Formula 1 car next to a 1934 Riley Sports.

The Museum is situated on the A359 Yeovil to Frome road at Sparkford, just off the A303 in Somerset. It is about 40 miles south of Bristol, and 25 minutes drive from the M5 intersection at Taunton.

Open 9.30am - 5.30pm (10.00am - 4.00pm Winter) 7 days a week, *except Christmas Day, Boxing Day and New Years Day*
Special rates available for schools, coach parties and outings Charitable Trust No. 292048